T0375108

ACTS

Verse by Verse

OSBORNE · NEW TESTAMENT COMMENTARIES

Praise for the Osborne New Testament Commentaries

"With this new series, readers will have before them what we—his students—experienced in all of Professor Osborne's classes: patient regard for every word in the text, exegetical finesse, a preference for an eclectic resolution to the options facing the interpreter, a sensitivity to theological questions, and most of all a reverence for God's word."

—**Scot McKnight**, Julius R. Mantey Chair of New Testament,
Northern Seminary

"The Osborne New Testament Commentaries draw from the deep well of a lifetime of serious study and teaching. They present significant interpretive insights in a highly accessible, spiritually nurturing format. This is a tremendous resource that will serve a new generation of Bible readers well for years to come. Highly recommended!"

—**Andreas J. Köstenberger**, founder, Biblical Foundations; senior research professor of New Testament and biblical theology,
Southeastern Baptist Theological Seminary

"Grant Osborne has spent his entire professional career teaching and writing about good principles for the interpretation of Scripture and then modeling them in his own scholarship, not least in commentaries on numerous New Testament books. The Osborne New Testament Commentaries, therefore, are a welcome new series by a veteran New Testament scholar determined to spend as much time as God gives him in his retirement years distilling the conclusions of the finest of scholarship without bogging down the reader in detailed interaction with all the various perspectives that have been suggested."

—**Craig L. Blomberg**, distinguished professor of New Testament,
Denver Seminary

"Like many others in the church and academy, I have greatly benefitted from the writings of Grant Osborne over the course of my professional career. Grant has a gift for summarizing the salient points in a passage and making clear what he thinks the text means—as well as making it relevant and applicable to believers at all levels of biblical maturity. I especially commend the usefulness of these verse-by-verse commentaries for pastors and lay leaders."

—**Stanley E. Porter**, president, dean, professor of New Testament, and
Roy A. Hope Chair in Christian Worldview, McMaster Divinity College

"For years I have found Grant Osborne's commentaries to be reliable and thoughtful guides for those wanting to better understand the New Testament. Indeed, Osborne has mastered the art of writing sound, helpful, and readable commentaries and I am confident that this new series will continue the level of excellence that we have come to expect from him. How exciting to think that pastors, students, and laity will all be able to benefit for years to come from the wise and insightful interpretation provided by Professor Osborne in this new series. The Osborne New Testament Commentaries will be a great gift for the people of God."

—**David S. Dockery**, president, Trinity International University

"One of my most valued role models, Grant Osborne is a first-tier biblical scholar who brings to the text of Scripture a rich depth of insight that is both accessible and devotional. Grant loves Christ, loves the word, and loves the church, and those loves are embodied in this wonderful new commentary series, which I cannot recommend highly enough."

—**George H. Guthrie**, Benjamin W. Perry Professor of Bible, Union University

"Grant Osborne is ideally suited to write a series of concise commentaries on the New Testament. His exegetical and hermeneutical skills are well known, and anyone who has had the privilege of being in his classes also knows his pastoral heart and wisdom."

—**Ray Van Neste**, professor of biblical studies, director of the R.C. Ryan Center for Biblical Studies, Union University

"Grant Osborne is an eminent New Testament scholar and warm-hearted professor who loves the word of God. Through decades of effective teaching at Trinity Evangelical Divinity School and church ministry around the world, he has demonstrated an ability to guide his readers in a careful understanding of the Bible. The volumes in this accessible commentary series help readers understand the text clearly and accurately. But they also draw us to consider the implications of the text, providing key insights on faithful application and preaching that reflect a lifetime of ministry experience. This unique combination of scholarship and practical experience makes this series an invaluable resource for all students of God's word, and especially those who are called to preach and teach."

—**H. Wayne Johnson**, associate academic dean and associate professor of pastoral theology, Trinity Evangelical Divinity School

ACTS

Verse by Verse

GRANT R. OSBORNE

LEXHAM PRESS

Acts: Verse by Verse
Osborne New Testament Commentaries

Copyright 2019 Grant R. Osborne

Lexham Press, 1313 Commercial St., Bellingham, WA 98225
LexhamPress.com

All rights reserved. You may use brief quotations from this resource in presentations, articles, and books. For all other uses, please write Lexham Press for permission. Email us at permissions@lexhampress.com.

Unless otherwise noted, Scripture quotations are from the Holy Bible, NEW INTERNATIONAL VERSION®. Copyright © 1973, 1978, 1984, 2011 by Biblica, Inc. Used by permission. All rights reserved worldwide.

Print ISBN: 9781683592747
Digital ISBN: 9781683592754

Lexham Editorial Team: Elliot Ritzema, Jeff Reimer, Danielle Thevenaz
Cover Design: Christine Christophersen
Typesetting: ProjectLuz.com

CONTENTS

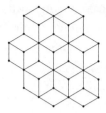

SERIES PREFACE

There are two authors of every biblical book: the human author who penned the words, and the divine Author who revealed and inspired every word. While God did not dictate the words to the biblical writers, he did guide their minds so that they wrote their own words under the influence of the Holy Spirit. If Christians really believed what they said when they called the Bible "the word of God," a lot more would be engaged in serious Bible study. As divine revelation, the Bible deserves, indeed demands, to be studied deeply.

This means that when we study the Bible, we should not be satisfied with a cursory reading in which we insert our own meanings into the text. Instead, we must always ask what God intended to say in every passage. But Bible study should not be a tedious duty we have to perform. It is a sacred privilege and a joy. The deep meaning of any text is a buried treasure; all the riches are waiting under the surface. If we learned there was gold deep under our backyard, nothing would stop us from getting the tools we needed to dig it out. Similarly, in serious Bible study all the treasures and riches of God are waiting to be dug up for our benefit.

This series of commentaries on the New Testament is intended to supply these tools and help the Christian understand more deeply the God-intended meaning of the Bible. Each volume walks the reader verse-by-verse through a book with the goal of opening up for us what God led Matthew or Paul or John to say to their readers. My goal in this series is to make sense of the historical and literary background of these ancient works, to supply the information that will enable the modern reader to understand exactly what the biblical writers were saying to their first-century audience. I want to remove the complexity of most modern commentaries and provide an easy-to-read explanation of the text.

But it is not enough to know what the books of the New Testament meant back then; we need help in determining how each text applies to our lives today. It is one thing to see what Paul was saying to his readers in Rome or Philippi, and quite another thing to see the significance of his words for us. So at key points in the commentary, I will attempt to help the reader discover areas in our modern lives that the text is addressing.

I envision three main uses for this series:

1. **Devotional Scripture reading**. Many Christians read rapidly through the Bible for devotions in a one-year program. That is extremely helpful to gain a broad overview of the Bible's story. But I strongly encourage another kind of devotional reading—namely, to study deeply a single segment of the biblical text and try to understand it. These commentaries are designed to enable that. The commentary is based on the NIV and explains the meaning of the verses, enabling the modern reader to read a few pages at a time and pray over the message.

2. **Church Bible studies.** I have written these commentaries also to serve as guides for group Bible studies. Many Bible studies today consist of people coming together and sharing what they think the text is saying. There are strengths in such an approach, but also weaknesses. The problem

is that God inspired these scriptural passages so that the church would understand and obey what he intended the text to say. Without some guidance into the meaning of the text, we are prone to commit heresy. At the very least, the leaders of the Bible study need to have a commentary so they can guide the discussion in the direction God intended. In my own church Bible studies, I have often had the class read a simple exposition of the text so they can all discuss the God-given message, and that is what I hope to provide here.

3. *Sermon aids.* These commentaries are also intended to help pastors faithfully exposit the text in a sermon. Busy pastors often have too little time to study complex thousand-page commentaries on biblical passages. As a result, it is easy to spend little time in Bible study and thereby to have a shallow sermon on Sunday. As I write this series, I am drawing on my own experience as a pastor and interim pastor, asking myself what I would want to include in a sermon.

Overall, my goal in these commentaries is simple: I would like them to be interesting and exciting adventures into New Testament texts. My hope is that readers will discover the riches of God that lie behind every passage in his divine word. I hope every reader will fall in love with God's word as I have and begin a similar lifelong fascination with these eternal truths!

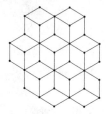

INTRODUCTION TO ACTS

The historical books of the Old Testament are important reading for us because they detail the historical development of God's people down through the centuries and help us to understand how God watched over and guided his chosen people, showing that he, not the world empires, is in control of history. That continues in the New Testament, with the Gospels paralleling the Pentateuch and Acts paralleling the historical books. God is Lord of history, and all the opposition that the world can throw at his people is ultimately inconsequential. The term "salvation history" refers to God's controlling of history in order to bring his salvation to fallen humankind. So Luke's monumental work is not built on Greco-Roman histories like those written by Thucydides or Suetonius (although he does draw on them somewhat) so much as Jewish works like the Pentateuch or Historical Books or later Jewish writings like the books of Maccabees.

Most ancient books trace the "acts" of heroes like Odysseus, Alexander the Great, or Julius Caesar. Luke's is unique because these are the "acts" of a movement. As the second part of a two-volume work, it is a historical narrative tracing how the Christ followers built on their founder and became a worldwide force.

They began as a fairly narrowly conceived Jewish "sect" and by the end of the book had expanded to "the ends of the earth" (1:8). This work tells how that came to pass in just a little over thirty years, from the ascension of Jesus (AD 30) to the imprisonment of Paul in Rome (AD 60–62).

Amazingly, all this is accomplished in the midst of incredible adversity and opposition. Virtually an entire nation turned against and sought to eradicate one small religious movement and ended up empowering a world-changing force. Thus the book should be labeled not "the Acts of the Apostles" but "the Acts of the Holy Spirit through the Apostles." It is the Triune Godhead who is the central figure in this book. The progression of these acts is both geographical (from Jerusalem, to Judea and Galilee, to Samaria, to Antioch, to Asia Minor, to Macedonia and Achaia, to "the ends of the earth," 1:8) and personal (from the Twelve to Stephen to Peter to Paul), as God orchestrates all the details.

AUTHOR

Luke and Acts are a two-part series and thus have the same author. Like the Historical Books of the Old Testament and the four Gospels, the book of Acts doesn't name its author, undoubtedly to emphasize that the true Author was God himself. Still, from the outset the church fathers unanimously claimed that its author was Luke, who also wrote the Third Gospel and was the associate of Paul. While this doesn't prove it, their unanimous witness should be taken seriously. The primary evidence is found in the "we" passages of Acts (16:10–17; 20:5–16; 21:1–18; 27:1–28:16), those parts where the author includes himself as part of the action in the scene. It is highly unlikely that these were fictive creations inserted for no particular reason. The purpose of this material is to show that Luke was not just using eyewitness testimony from others but was one of the eyewitnesses himself, having firsthand knowledge of these events.

When one considers the associates of Paul—Silas, Timothy, Aristarchus, Demas, Epaphras, John Mark, and others—Luke fits the part by far the best. His classical Greek style of writing and his hometown of Troas would indicate that he was most likely a Gentile, though the influence of the Septuagint (Greek Old Testament) on his writing and his theological nuances have led several to think of him as a Jewish Christian. I prefer the former, though he may well have been a God-fearer (a Gentile who worshipped the Jewish God) before becoming a Christ follower, as there are quite a few Jewish traits in his writing. His history writing shows both Gentile and Jewish style. He was a physician by trade (Col 4:14) and became a close friend as well as associate of Paul, staying with him during his imprisonment (2 Tim 4:11). We don't know what led him to write his two-volume masterwork, but it is likely that he did his extensive research, gathering information from eyewitnesses (Luke 1:1–4), throughout Paul's imprisonments in Caesarea and Rome.

DATE

The dating of Acts is closely aligned with the dating of Luke, so to get a fuller picture please consult the introduction to the commentary on Luke in this series. Scholars have proposed three possible dates for the writing of Acts. (1) Nineteenth- and early twentieth-century commentators often argued for an early second-century dating. A school calling itself "tendency criticism" (1850s) used the dialectical methods of Hegel to argue that there was conflict between a "thesis" (Jewish Christianity/Peter) and an "antithesis" (Gentile Christianity/Paul) that produced a "synthesis," evident in what they viewed as second-century works like John and Acts. This speculative reworking of history is no longer accepted, for it was built on false premises. Others who adopt a later date have taken a Darwinian approach and believe Christianity evolved from the melding of influences in the Jewish and **Hellenistic**[1] worlds surrounding it. In this reconstruction, the author of Acts was an editor who chronicled this lengthy process. However, if God was

---

1. Words in bold type are found in the glossary on page 489.

directing history and created the Christian movement, as the book of Acts itself attests, there is no need for a decades-long evolutionary set of changes.

The other two possibilities are far more viable. (2) Many argue that it was written before Paul's death, probably at the time where Acts ends, around AD 62. The absence of references to the results of Paul's Roman imprisonment (released or executed) or of the fall of Jerusalem in AD 70 are unlikely if the work was written later. Acts presents a positive picture of Roman justice that would have rung less true a decade later, after the persecution of Christians by Nero, the destruction of the temple, and systematic Roman persecution.

(3) The third possibility is that Luke-Acts was written around AD 75–85. This is based on the assumption that Luke built on the Gospel of Mark, which itself was written AD 65–70, and that the destruction of Jerusalem in AD 70 is presupposed in Luke 19:41–44 and 21:20. However, if we accept the possibility that Jesus was using predictive prophecy in his Olivet Discourse recorded in Luke 21 and its parallels, then Luke and Acts do not have to be written after AD 70. I find the view that Luke-Acts was written during Paul's imprisonment compelling and so prefer the early date (AD 62).

HISTORY AND THEOLOGY IN LUKE-ACTS

Even though Luke is called the primary historian of the early church, it has been almost a fad in scholarly circles to doubt the historical trustworthiness of Luke-Acts and to argue that they are largely fictional stories that were created as the early church tried to defend itself in the Greco-Roman world. This scholarly view assumes a work must be either history or theology, and that the theological core of these writings diminishes their historical worth.

Alternatively we could see Luke–Acts as both history and theology, with a blend of the two functioning equally in the production of the work. Ancient Judaism strongly stressed history, and

Christianity was more Jewish than Gentile in outlook and perspective. If God is involved in history, as Christians strongly believe he is, then it is false to separate history and theology, since theological explanations simply highlight the significance of historical events. Miracles, for example, do not happen outside history but simply explain the supernatural acting within history.

As a test case, let's consider the speeches in Acts, since nearly a third of the book (300 of the 1,000 verses) occurs in speeches. It is common for critical scholars to assume Luke created these speeches, thinking they were what would likely be said on each occasion. However, it is likely that Luke assimilated what was said in speeches and summarized material he received in notes taken during those speeches. There is quite a bit of evidence that the apostles were note-takers (especially Matthew), and Luke as a historian would have taken care to speak to people who had been present at the events. There is no evidence he made up accounts and created speeches wholesale. Furthermore, there is evidence that ancient historians like Thucydides tried to be as accurate as possible when re-creating speeches.[2] While they certainly used paraphrase and summary, they still sought accuracy. Truth had absolute priority over the fabrication of details for the sake of the narrative. In Luke 1:1–4, Luke stresses how carefully he sought eyewitness sources behind everything he wrote.

THE PURPOSE OF ACTS

Luke's purposes are closely tied to his theological emphases, but they are not identical. I find five major purposes for this work:

1. To preach the gospel. Luke wanted to proclaim the good news of Christ by relating its history in the early church. It is mainly a historical work showing how the presence of the Holy Spirit moved the people of God from a small

---

2. See Thucydides, *Peloponnesian War* 1.22.1.

Jewish sect in Jerusalem to a worldwide force bringing the gospel of salvation to a lost world.

2. To trace the Spirit's activity and show the divine impetus behind the church's mission. Here Luke is a theologian of salvation history as well as the "father of church history." The goal of this book is to forge a new movement whose mission is to bring God's truths to all the world.

3. To defend the faith. This is an apologetic work with two audiences: to defend Christianity against Jewish antipathy and the demands of the Judaizers, and to show the tolerant attitude of Roman officials, proving that Christianity was no political danger to Rome and should be tolerated.

4. To bring together the Jewish and Gentile elements of the church into one united new Israel. Both sides need to understand that God's will is for them to come together and form the new messianic community together.

5. To teach the historical beginnings of the church for the benefit of new converts and to tell those in Jerusalem about the spread of the church into Gentile lands.

OUTLINE

I. Preliminary events to the world mission (1:1–8:3)
 A. A new end and a new beginning (1:1–11)
  1. Prologue (1:1–2)
  2. The commissioning of the apostles (1:3–8)
  3. The ascension of Jesus (1:9–11)
 B. Reconstituting the Twelve (1:12–26)
  1. The ten days in the upper room (1:12–14)
  2. The end of Judas (1:15–20)
  3. The replacement of Judas (1:21–26)
 C. Pentecost and the coming of the Spirit (2:1–47)
  1. The Pentecost event (2:1–13)
   a. The setting: Pentecost in Jerusalem (2:1)
   b. The descent of the Spirit (2:2–4)

c. The reaction of the crowds (2:5–13)

2. Peter's Pentecost sermon (2:14–36)

    a. Introduction (2:14–15)

    b. The fulfillment of Joel 2:28–32 (2:16–21)

    c. The basis: the death and resurrection of Jesus (2:22–36)

        1) Introduction: Jesus of Nazareth (2:22)

        2) The death and resurrection and Jewish guilt (2:23–24)

        3) Old Testament prophecies fulfilled (2:25–35)

        4) Conclusion: Lord and Messiah (2:36)

3. Call to repentance (2:37–41)

4. Life in the Jewish Christian church (2:42–47)

    a. Four pillars of the church (2:42)

    b. Results in the life of the church (2:43–47)

D. Opening events in the new messianic community (3:1–26)

1. Healing of the lame man (3:1–10)

2. Peter's temple sermon (3:11–26)

    a. Peter responds to their astonishment (3:11–12)

    b. The true source of the power: God and Jesus (3:13–16)

    c. Call for repentance (3:17–21)

    d. The promises of Scripture (3:22–26)

E. Persecution and power: The first stage (4:1–22)

1. Peter and John arrested (4:1–4)

2. Peter's defense before the Sanhedrin (4:5–12)

    a. A hearing is called (4:5–7)

    b. Peter's defense (4:8–12)

3. Freed with a warning (4:13–22)

F. Community life of Jewish Christianity (4:23–5:16)

1. Prayer for greater boldness (4:23–31)

    a. The occasion: community prayer (4:23–24a)

    b. Plea for boldness and power (4:24b–30)

4) Further fulfillment in Christ (13:26–37)

5) Call to repentance and faith in
   Christ (13:38–41)

   c. Results: division among the people (13:42–52)

3. Mission in Iconium (14:1–7)

4. Mission in Lystra (14:8–20)

   a. Healing of the lame man (14:8–10)

   b. The reaction of the crowds (14:11–13)

   c. The response of Paul and Barnabas (14:14–18)

   d. Rejection and stoning (14:19–20)

5. Ministry in Derbe and then backtracking to
   Antioch of Syria (14:21–28)

   a. Follow-up in the three cities (14:21–23)

   b. Mission activity in Perga (14:24–25)

   c. Return to Syrian Antioch (14:26–28)

6. The Jerusalem Council (15:1–35)

   a. Delegation to Jerusalem (15:1–5)

   b. The council and Peter's speech (15:6–11)

   c. The speech by Barnabas and Paul (15:12)

   d. James settles the issue (15:13–21)

   e. Letter to the Gentile churches (15:22–29)

   f. Reception of the letter in Antioch (15:30–35)

B. Mission in Macedonia and Achaia (15:36–18:22)

1. Paul and Barnabas separate (15:36–41)

2. Revisiting Galatia: Timothy joins (16:1–5)

3. Troas and the call to Macedonia (16:6–10)

4. Mission in Philippi (16:11–40)

   a. The trip to Philippi (16:11–12)

   b. The conversion of Lydia (16:13–15)

   c. The possessed slave girl (16:16–18)

   d. The jailing of Paul and Silas (16:19–34)

   e. Freedom and departure (16:35–40)

5. Mission in Thessalonica (17:1–9)

6. Mission in Berea (17:10–15)

   c. Paul makes his defense (26:1–23)
      1) Introduction: gratitude (26:1–3)
      2) The story behind the case (26:4–18)
         a) Paul's Pharisaic background (26:4–8)
         b) Paul the persecutor (26:9–11)
         c) The Damascus road vision (26:12–18)
      3) Paul's conclusion of his defense (26:19–23)
   d. Agreement of Festus and Agrippa (26:24–32)
D. Journey to Rome (27:1–44)
   1. From Caesarea to Myra (27:1–5)
   2. From Myra to Crete (27:6–8)
   3. The debate about going or staying (27:9–12)
   4. The storm drives the ship to disaster (27:13–26)
   5. Shipwreck on Malta (27:27–44)
E. Paul in Rome (28:1–31)
   1. Paul and the viper (28:1-6)
   2. Ministry in Malta (28:7–10)
   3. The journey from Malta to Rome (28:11–15)
   4. Paul in Rome (28:16–31)
      a. Encounter with Jewish leaders (28:16–22)
      b. Further encounter with many Jews
         (28:23–28)
      c. Paul's ministry over the next two
         years (28:30–31)

MAJOR THEOLOGICAL THEMES

History does not exist without theology, for theology by definition deals with God's work within history. Since Luke-Acts is in reality a single work with two parts, the theologies of the two intertwine, and the theology of Acts studies the continuation of salvation history in the life of Jesus into the life of the church. Therefore this section must be viewed as the further development of the parallel material in the introduction to my commentary on Luke.

It should be clear that the events behind Luke-Acts have changed our world forever. It is simply the most significant (therefore the most deeply theological) period in human history, for without it there would be no future for humanity. Thus it is the greatest privilege I can imagine for me to develop this material.

SALVATION AND SALVATION HISTORY

The term "salvation" means deliverance, which we first see in Scripture at the exodus from Egypt. The deliverance of Israel from Egypt is a type of the greater deliverance achieved by Jesus on the cross, a liberation that is eternal in nature and effect. The term "salvation history," then, refers to God's performing these works in human history, orchestrating the redemption of lost, sinful humankind. In the birth, life, and death of Jesus the Christ, and then in the development and mission of the new Israel, salvation entered this world in a new way. The divine entering the world first in the incarnation of Jesus and second at the coming of the Holy Spirit transformed human history, making it a vehicle for the acts of God within it.

But history includes rejection and opposition along with redemption. In the Gospel of Luke, God's former people have turned against his Son and Messiah, Jesus, and lost their place as his chosen people, to be replaced by people selected from all humanity. Gentiles thus join Jews as the new elect. In the book of Acts, the mission of this new Israel is traced within history, as the message of the good news is taken to "the ends of the earth" (1:8). Both temporally and geographically the new salvation expands to include all of sinful humanity, from Jerusalem (Acts 1–7), to Judea (8:1–3), to Samaria (the rest of ch. 8), to Syria and especially Antioch (chs. 9–11), to Asia Minor (chs. 13–14), to Macedonia and Achaia (chs. 16–19), and then to the ends of the earth (chs. 20–28). At every level the presence of messianic salvation unites the diverse peoples of earth into a single people, the family of God.

The Proclamation of the Gospel Reality as the Center Point of the New Mission

The Triune Godhead has produced salvation in history, and the way this is communicated to fallen humanity is via the proclamation of the gospel. The good news is the message of sin and salvation, how the coming and death of Jesus as the atoning sacrifice for sin has made it possible for sinners to repent and be forgiven for their sins on the basis of the blood sacrifice of Christ on the cross. This message is the core of every chapter in Acts as the Spirit empowers and leads the saints to witness to the gospel reality and call lost humanity to repentance and belief in Jesus.

The mission of the church that energizes the action throughout this book centers on this proclamation to the lost. The disciples are commissioned to be "witnesses," empowered by the Spirit to all peoples of the earth (1:8). So Acts is a *missionary* work, continuing Jesus' work and taking it into all the world. The choice of Matthias as the twelfth apostle (1:21–26) was necessary to maintain Christ's foundation of the church in the Twelve. The number twelve establishes a typological parallel between Israel and the new Israel as those who take God's call to salvation to the earth (beginning with the Abrahamic covenant of Gen 12:3; 18:18; 22:18). The same is true of the three repetitions of Paul's call to be the missionary to the Gentiles (9:15–16; 22:15, 21; 26:17–18), which shows how central this witness is to the central purposes of Acts.

Jesus the Christ, Savior and Lord

In the Third Gospel, Jesus is the central figure, and in Acts it is not Peter or Paul but Christ who is the true actor. His human messengers are servants who carry out his will and directions. In Luke it is the incarnate Son of God who acts, and in this book it is the risen and exalted Lord who acts (3:15; 4:10; 17:3; 26:8). The powerful ministries of Peter and Paul are the result of their having been met and commissioned by this One who has risen from the dead and become Lord of all. In his suffering he becomes the Suffering

Servant of Isaiah 52–53, and with his death he becomes Savior of humankind (5:31; 13:23). He is the core of the proclaimed gospel and the only means of salvation for sinners. The Spirit is the Spirit of Jesus, sent by the risen Lord at Pentecost to guide the church and fill it with strength for mission. As the Christ he is Messiah of both Jews and Gentiles, and the church is the messianic community. Finally, he is Lord of all, who possesses the full authority of Yahweh.

The Holy Spirit

As I have said above, this book should not be labeled "the Acts of the Apostles" but "the Acts of the Holy Spirit through the Apostles." Virtually every single thing that is done properly is done through the presence and guidance of the Spirit. The Spirit permeates the book. He is promised in 1:4, 8, and arrives in 2:1–4. From that point he empowers the church and its leaders in everything they do. The Spirit's presence is proof that the messianic age of salvation has arrived. It is the Spirit who guides the witness of the church and gives saving power to the gospel as it goes forth. In fact, the unity of Jew and Gentile in the new Israel is made possible by the same Spirit bestowed on both and bringing them together (15:28). He is the Spirit of prophecy, at work in guiding the people of God into the future through Spirit-inspired prophets (11:28) and filling those brought into the church, leading them to speak in tongues as evidence of his presence (8:15–17; 10:45; 19:6).

The Gentile mission is the work of the Spirit, who separated and called Barnabas and Saul to the Gentiles (13:2) and oversaw every step as the gospel went forth (8:29, 39; 13:4; 16:6, 7). Those who surrender themselves completely are filled with the Spirit and exhibit that fullness with the joy and power of their witness (4:8, 31; 6:3; 9:17; 11:24; 13:52). In short, the Spirit is the empowering presence behind the church and makes possible all that it accomplishes for the glory of God and the salvation of sinners.

THE CHURCH

The church is the "assembly" of God's people, saved by the blood of Jesus and filled with the Spirit. It has often been thought to have originated at Pentecost, but that is not true. Pentecost was the launching of the church's mission to be "witnesses" (1:8), but not the genesis of its formation. If that can be ascertained, it would have come when Jesus chose the Twelve (Mark 3:13-19; Luke 6:12-16), but it is just as correct to see continuity between the Israel of the old covenant and the new Israel of the new covenant.

The church is anchored in teaching, fellowship, the breaking of bread, and prayer (2:42), and is the means by which God's mission to the world is conducted. Even in the midst of adversity and crisis, with the Spirit they are "filled with joy" (13:52) and rise above their circumstances. Their primary tasks are worship and evangelism as they experience all God has for them and respond by turning to the world and proclaiming the gospel as witnesses to the reality of Jesus. Their first title for themselves was "the Way" (9:2), taken from Isaiah 40:3. The church forges the "way to Yahweh," considering itself the messianic sect within Judaism. They were first called "Christians," Christ followers, in Antioch (11:26).

SOCIAL CONCERN: THE POOR AND MARGINALIZED

Building on the Third Gospel, Luke stresses the effects of the gospel not only on the spiritual life but also on the earthly life of those touched by it. In the summary paragraph describing the Jewish Christian church of Jerusalem, we are told that they were characterized by togetherness and had "everything in common," exemplified by the fact that they "sold property and possessions to give to anyone who had need" (2:44-45). A deep concern for the poor and suffering solidified their unity as God's family. This was deepened in 4:32-34, where this oneness is further characterized by complete "sharing" of possessions to such an extent that "there were no needy persons among them." One of the primary examples of this occurs in 6:1-7, where the church appoints "the

Seven" to take care of the needy Hebrew widows in the church. Congregational care was at the heart of the early church.

There has always been debate over the balance between evangelism and social concern, expressed recently in arguments about "social justice" and earlier in arguments about the "social gospel" that dominated the early twentieth-century Protestant church in North America. Luke would not have insisted that the church choose between evangelism and social concern, for both the physical and spiritual dimensions of the Christian movement are critical. It does little good if the soul is saved when the body is allowed to deteriorate through the church's neglect. Christ healed the sick and saved the lost with equal emphasis, and the early church believed in taking care of the earthly and the heavenly dimensions of life. Social concern is a core emphasis of the early church and is an essential part of the salvation of sinners.

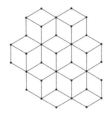

PRELIMINARY EVENTS
TO THE MISSION
(1:1–26)

Luke's two-volume masterwork on the history of Jesus and the early church is in a very real sense the core of the New Testament. Everything flows out of these two central histories. This first chapter of Acts provides a transition (ten days long) from the ascension of Jesus to the coming of the Spirit at Pentecost. We know from Acts 1:3 that he appeared to his followers over a forty-day period before being taken up to heaven in a cloud, and by definition Pentecost (meaning "fifty days") took place fifty days after Passover. Thus there was a ten-day period in which they waited to be "clothed with power from on high" (Luke 24:49). That period is described here in 1:1–26.

Jesus may be in heaven and no longer physically present, but he is every bit as central to the life of his messianic community, in fact even more so, for he is now the exalted Lord guiding the affairs of his people. The Holy Spirit is the "Spirit of Jesus," sent by him (and his Father) in the same way he had been sent by his Father. The church, if we wish to describe origins, began not with Pentecost but with Jesus' choice of the Twelve in Luke 6:12–16. The time with Jesus in Luke would constitute the training period, and graduation in a sense occurred in the breakfast scene of John 21:15–17, when

Jesus commissioned them through Peter to "feed my sheep." Now they are waiting for the full commission at Pentecost, when they will be given the Spirit to empower them for that mission.

JESUS ENDS HIS EARTHLY MINISTRY AND BEGINS THE CHURCH (1:1-11)

The ascension of Jesus in Luke 24:50-53 provides a doxological end to the earthly ministry of Jesus as he blesses his disciples then departs. Then in Acts 1:1-11 it provides an ecclesiastical beginning to the church age (and age of the Spirit) as Jesus promises the coming of the Spirit made possible by his departure. Clearly the mission of the church (indeed, its very existence) is a trinitarian act, as all three members of the Godhead undergird the events of this book. There are two main parts, the prologue (paralleling Luke 1:1-4) reminding Theophilus of the first volume (Acts 1:1-2) and the recapitulation of Jesus' ascension and the impact it had on the disciples (vv. 3-11).

PROLOGUE TO THE SECOND VOLUME (1:1-2)

These verses not only summarize the first volume but also introduce four key theological themes that will guide us through Acts: (1) The deeds and words of Jesus are essential to both volumes of Luke's works; (2) Jesus' ascension as exalted Lord is the anchor on which Acts rests; (3) the coming of the Spirit will launch and make possible everything the church does in this book; and (4) the elect apostles will lead the church in its mission to the world. He begins by defining his gospel as a compendium of what "Jesus began to do and to teach." Acts must be read and studied as a continuation of Jesus' work and his words, and the church draws its meaning from the Jesus story.

It is clear that the church was not born out of Pentecost, which provides its commissioning rather than its birth. It is actually questionable that the church was birthed at all, for there is a direct continuity between Israel and the early church as the people of

God. Israel and new Israel are intertwined in salvation history. Still, however, the origin of the church as an entity was indeed in Jesus' choice of the Twelve in Luke 6:12–16, and as indicated here, it all "began" with Jesus.

Like the Third Gospel, this book is dedicated to Theophilus, most likely the wealthy Christian patron who finances the writing of these two volumes (Luke 1:3).[1] We don't know when Luke (possibly with Paul's encouragement) conceived and began to research these works, but tracking down all the "eyewitness" sources (Luke 1:1–4) must have taken some time. I am guessing that as Luke and Paul traveled from town to town, Luke was locating participants and getting their stories. Possibly he did a lot of traveling while Paul was in prison in Caesarea and Rome as well. Here he is thanking Theophilus for making it all possible.

The deeds and teaching of Jesus lay behind everything, and Luke wants to make that clear at the outset. The teaching of the church is a critical component (2:42; 4:2; 5:21; 18:11; 20:20), which itself is thoroughly grounded in Jesus' teaching. Equally critical, this teaching did not end at the cross, for Jesus continued to teach and perform mighty deeds after his "death" on the cross. He is the *living* Word: He taught forty further days, and during this time he corrected and overturned all the misunderstandings of the disciples. His works and his words did not end at the cross but at the ascension, yet even that was continued by the Holy Spirit (John 16:12–15).

The ascension is critical because it is the basis for Jesus' exaltation at the right hand of God (Ps 110:1; see Acts 2:34–35) and his assumption of divine power as Lord of all. By being "taken up to heaven," he returned to his preexistent glory. The sending of the Spirit is an act originating in heaven. The involvement of the Trinity takes this form: the Father calls the Son to heaven, and

---

1. The name means "dear to God," and Origen, followed by some, believed it to be not a proper name but an epithet meant to describe anyone dear to the Lord. However, it was a common name and more likely refers to an actual person.

from there they send the Spirit as their Envoy in the same way that the Father had sent the Son at his incarnation. Then the Spirit commissions the apostles to lead the church on its mission. In his earthly ministry the Spirit had infused his teaching as he instructed the "apostles," a term that means they have joined the Spirit as "Sent Ones" commissioned by the Triune Godhead. The preposition "through" (*dia*) indicates that the Spirit is the means by which the disciples received and came to understand Jesus' teaching. This is in keeping with John 16:12–15, the Spirit as guide and revealer of Jesus' teaching.

THE COMMISSIONING OF THE APOSTLES (1:3–8)

The "suffering" of Jesus probably refers not just to the cross but to all of passion week as a united whole. The pent-up hatred of the leaders, the brainwashing of the crowds to demand his death, and the capitulation of Pilate and the Romans, together with the cross, defines his suffering. However, it all ends not with the grave but with the empty tomb, when he "presented himself" alive to his followers. His death was an atoning sacrifice that established a new covenant age (Luke 22:19–20). Luke here calls his resurrection appearances "convincing proofs" (*tekmēria*), decisive evidence for the reality of the event. The term "presented" places a great deal of emphasis on the apologetic value of the evidence. All of his followers were totally convinced of the physical resurrection, and our future is secure as a result of it (see 1 Cor 15). This fact was a major theme in Luke 24, as the risen Lord again and again provided proof that his resurrection was real.

It is here that we learn Jesus appeared over a forty-day period, thus ascending ten days before Pentecost. This does not mean he stayed with them that entire time. Looking at the four Gospels and 1 Corinthians 15:5–8, we see that Jesus visited them at specific times over a forty-day period. His appearances were specific and brief, and the purpose of each was to prepare them further for their future world-encompassing mission.

According to Luke here, the overall subject of Jesus' teaching was the kingdom of God. This refers both to the new era being established and to the fact of God's reign over it. Jesus inaugurated this new reign, and his followers would populate it as the messianic community, the church. The kingdom in Jesus' ministry had arrived and yet had not come to consummation. We call this "inaugurated **eschatology**," the view that the kingdom is already here yet not in a final sense. We are living in the time of tension between the ages, with the last days begun but not come to fruition. Here the emphasis is on the presence and reality of the kingdom in the mission of the disciples to the world.

Luke now (1:4) turns to Jesus' appearance to the Eleven (Luke 24:36–49) when Jesus told them to wait in Jerusalem for the Spirit to come (24:49). Luke says that Jesus "was eating with them," emphasizing that the Spirit will arrive in the midst of that Christ-centered table fellowship. As also in the Emmaus road incident of Luke 24:13–35, Jesus teaches truths and opens eyes via fellowship with him, which he emphasizes by adding "which you have heard me speak about." As we bask in the presence of the Lord and open ourselves to his words, he imparts eternal truths to us.

God could have had the Spirit come in Galilee, where the movement began, but he clearly determined that the Holy City, Jerusalem, should be the starting point, as prophesied in Joel 2:28–32: "On Mount Zion and in Jerusalem there will be deliverance." The trinitarian foundation for the arrival of God's kingdom demands that the Spirit come upon the new movement and fill it with divine power. The new messianic age is to begin in Jerusalem with the Spirit's arrival, so they must wait for God's timing.

John's baptism was an immersion in water signifying repentance and forgiveness of sin, by which he called the nation back to God (Luke 3:3, 16). Jesus uses baptism to signify that the new age of the Spirit—the new covenant that the Spirit would introduce—would be an immersion in the Spirit's power (1:5). This would constitute a baptism with the Holy Spirit, an immersion in God's salvation and in that new messianic reality identified with the Spirit's taking up residence in every believer (Rom 8:14-17). The mission of Jesus to the nations is to be completed by the church, but the church must be empowered by the Spirit to successfully accomplish that directive. So they must wait for God to fulfill his promise and send the Spirit to provide that impetus.

In Luke, the ascension entailed the doxological end of Jesus' earthly ministry, as he blessed his followers and departed. Here in Acts it entails an ecclesiastical beginning for the church's mission, as Jesus prepares for the coming of the Spirit and the launching of the universal mission to the world. Jesus came to restore not political power (vv. 6-7) but spiritual power (v. 8) to God's people.

When the disciples ask Jesus if he is now "going to restore the kingdom to Israel," they are still assuming political liberation rather than spiritual restoration. They assume the Spirit's arrival will be accompanied by heaven's armies, and that the last days will mean the defeat of the Romans and the instituting of Jewish rule over the nations. So they still have failed to learn that the victory over the nations will not come until Jesus' second coming.

Jesus' response (1:7) corrects this failure by pointing out to them that they have the wrong time in mind. The coming of the Spirit is for the mission of the church (v. 8) rather than for the restoration of Israel, and "the times or dates the Father has set by his own authority" are not for them to know. Their question is valid but not for that occasion. They should be focused on the mission God has inaugurated through the Spirit, not on the events associated with the end of the age. Jesus says this as well in Mark 13:32: "But about that day or hour no one knows, not even the angels in heaven, nor the Son, but only the Father." Jesus is building on that here.

There is an important lesson in this for today. An inordinate interest in the end-time events has often eroded the present mission of the church for us as well. Many preachers have given themselves entirely over to "prophecy preaching" and signs that this

age is to end soon. Many are like the disciples here, too focused
on eschatology and ignoring the current mission to the world
that God wants to have first place in our lives. The doctrine of the
second coming is important, but it is not meant to consume our
interests. We are to remain focused on our present walk with the
Lord and the mission to the lost he has entrusted to us.

Jesus is not denying the place of Israel's restoration and his
parousia in the life of the church. Rather, he is redirecting their
focus to what has greater importance, the coming of the Spirit
and launching of the church's mission to the nations. He refuses
to answer their question, for that issue is for a later time. However,
the exact time will never be revealed and is God's alone to determine. The important issue is not the time of the restoration but
rather her part in the witness to the world.

So in 1:8 Jesus directs them to the critical point of power for
witness. This is the true reason why the Spirit is coming. The
Spirit is the "power from on high" (Luke 24:49) and will come to
empower God's people for their calling and send them into the
world. This "coming" does not stress the continuous nature of
the Spirit's presence but announces the specific coming of the
Spirit at Pentecost. It is at that moment that Jesus' followers will
"receive power." The same divine power that was present in creation and evident throughout the Old Testament will now reside
in the church as it fulfills its destiny.

The result of the Spirit's presence will be "witness." This is
one of the central themes of Acts and fulfills Israel's task to be
witnesses and bless the world (Isa 43:10; 44:8), the one aspect of
the Abrahamic covenant (Gen 12:3; 22:18; 26:4; 28:14) she ignored.
The church as true Israel will complete that mission. Yet there
is an official cast to this "witness" as well. They have seen and
walked with the risen Lord and can provide proof that he is truly
alive. This group is at the heart of the "eyewitness" emphasis in
Luke (Luke 1:1–4). They could attest to the reality of his suffering,
death, and resurrection. When they spoke of him as Messiah and

Son of God, they knew the truth of what they were saying. There is double meaning in "my [*mou*] witnesses." They were witnesses to the truth of Jesus, and they were witnesses who belonged to Jesus and were sent by him.

The last part of this verse is virtually a table of contents describing the material in Acts and the route of the mission—to Jerusalem (1:9–8:3), Judea (8:2–3), Samaria (8:4–25), and the "ends of the earth" (the Gentile mission in the rest of Acts). This too is a fulfillment of Old Testament promises, for Isaiah 49:6 describes Israel as "a light for the Gentiles [or 'to the nations'], that my salvation may reach to the ends of the earth." There is quite an extensive debate on the meaning of "ends of the earth." Some think it refers to Ethiopia (the farthest south), Spain (the farthest west), the Gentiles (in Isaiah), or even Rome (the penultimate nation). When all is considered, Spain and Ethiopia are not really central to Acts, and most likely the reference is to the farthest reaches of planet earth, made up of Gentiles. The stress is on all the people of earth as the goal of the Christian mission.

THE ASCENSION OF JESUS (1:9–11)

These verses stress the apostles as official witnesses, for in all three verses Luke points out that they "looked intently" and watched him ascend into heaven. The ascension is not merely a symbolic way of providing a conclusion to the Jesus story. It actually happened and was witnessed by the 120 gathered together (1:15), perhaps even the "five hundred" of 1 Corinthians 15:6. This taking up is presented as a sudden, perhaps unexpected turn of events. The idea of a heaven up there and an earth down here sounds mythical, but of course God is simply accommodating the picture to human spatial perception. The heavens/sky is indeed up there, and so the picture makes sense.

As Jesus was speaking, a cloud suddenly enveloped him and took him away. The presence of the cloud echoes the **Shekinah** cloud over the tabernacle in Exodus 40:34, reenacting Sinai and drawing together the three major instances of the glory of Christ manifested—the transfiguration, ascension, and parousia (1:11). The catching up of Jesus also echoes that of Enoch (Gen 5:24), Elijah (2 Kgs 2:11), and, in Jewish tradition, Moses (Josephus, *Antiquities* 4.326).

The appearance of "two men dressed in white" (1:10) reenacts the angels in the empty tomb (Luke 24:4), who now escort Jesus back to heaven. The white robes picture the transfiguration as well as the resurrection and depict the glory the angels share with the exalted Jesus as he returns to his home in heaven. These are two heavenly witnesses (Deut 19:15) of this new reality.

There is a bit of a rebuke in their message (1:11). Jesus' followers are just standing there transfixed as they gaze upward. They are followers from Galilee standing on the Mount of Olives, where their mission to the world is to begin. God wants action, not paralysis. They should have expected Jesus to return home to heaven and been ready to begin the ministry to which he had just commissioned them. They undoubtedly want Jesus to stay there with them, but the next phase of salvation history is even now being initiated, and it is time to get to work.

They proceed to encourage these Christ followers that he will indeed return, and in fact he will do so in the same way he has just been taken from them, as the angels will accompany him and the saints will be "caught up … in the clouds" (1 Thess 4:16–17; Rev 19:14). The church age begins here and will be consummated at his second coming. The intervening time is intended for the mission to the nations, which the disciples are to commence now as they return to Jerusalem to begin their witness.

THE TWELVE ARE RECONSTITUTED (1:12–26)

The Jerusalem portion of the mission constitutes the first seven chapters of Acts, consummating in the persecution of 8:1 that drove the church into Judea and Samaria. This period began with the ten days between the ascension and Pentecost, and during that time the disciples were led to choose a twelfth member of the apostolic band to replace Judas. Thus there are three sections to this passage: the centrality of prayer (vv. 12–14), the end of Judas (vv. 15–20), and his replacement by Matthias (vv. 21–26).

THE TEN DAYS IN THE UPPER ROOM (1:12–14)

Jesus told the disciples to wait in Jerusalem, so they obey and return. Luke tells us the Mount of Olives, the site for Gethsemane as well as the ascension, was "a Sabbath day's walk from the city." The "mount" was just across the Kidron Valley from Jerusalem and was where Jesus and his disciples had stayed during passion week. A "Sabbath day's walk" was the distance a Jew was allowed to walk on the Sabbath (Exod 16:29), traditionally seen as two thousand cubits, or about three-quarters of a mile. This doesn't mean Jesus ascended on a Sabbath. It is just Luke's way of measuring the distance.

The upper "room where they were staying" (1:13) could have been the room where they shared the Last Supper (Luke 22:12), though many connect it to Mary, John Mark's mother's home (Acts 12:12). To house that many would have required a large, expensive home. Still, Luke is not saying that all 120 were sleeping there, but rather it was the common meeting area. The concept of an "upper room" refers to the flatbed roof of the home, used as a common room for groups and for hosting people. The eleven names agree with the list in Luke 6:14–16[2] (with the omission of Judas). The list contains two groups of four plus a final three, with the first four being the leading group, the three who formed the inner circle (for example, at the transfiguration) plus Andrew, Simon Peter's brother. Apart from this, the differences in order with Luke 6:14–16 are not important.

The activity that dominated those intervening ten days was prayer, and we are told they "joined together constantly" (Acts 1:14)

---

2. See the Luke commentary in this series for descriptions of the individuals.

or "devoted themselves" (2:42) to corporate prayer. The worship
that ensued from the ascension (Luke 24:52–53, "joy … praising
God") continued to dominate, and in a sense they had a ten-day
prayer meeting. The radical change initiated at the resurrection
was apparent. Before, each of them had looked out for number
one and fled, hiding themselves for Jesus' entire time on the cross
and in the grave lest they be arrested. That is no longer the case;
they are centered entirely on God, and when they are arrested
(which is often), it is simply an opportunity to let God take over.
"Together" is a weak translation for *homothymadon* here. It means
"with a single mind" or "united in heart and mind." They were
totally focused on prayer.

Luke wants us to know that it was not only the male followers
of Jesus in the upper room; it was the women (including the God-
chosen witnesses of Luke 23:49, 55; 24:10) and Jesus' family, "Mary
the mother of Jesus, and … his brothers." His brothers are named
in Mark 6:3 as "James, Joseph, Judas and Simon." They were unbelievers during Jesus' life (John 7:5) but became believers after his
resurrection (1 Cor 15:7 mentions an appearance to James). They
later became leaders in the church and traveled in mission work
with their wives (1 Cor 9:5).

The End of Judas (1:15–20)

"Those days" are the ten days between the ascension and Pentecost,
and at some point, probably early in that period, Peter "stood up"
and addressed the assembled group. It is clear that he was led
to do so by the Lord as a result of the deep prayers of the faithful. He has become Peter the rock (John 1:42; Matt 16:18), the first
leader of the church. Luke adds that the group gathered in the
upper room numbered "about a hundred and twenty," a number
thought sufficient for a town to have a council or *sanhedrin* governing it (m. Sanhedrin 1:6), but here Luke is probably showing
simply that the church leadership has grown from the Seventy of
Luke 10 to the 120 here.

The emphasis of Peter's words is on the fact that Judas' betrayal was not a shock to God and was actually planned ahead of time as part of God's elect will.[3] This is the mystery of free will and divine election. Judas freely chose to betray Jesus, and yet his decision was part of God's predetermined will. This mystery must simply stand, for both aspects are true. Peter's point is that both Judas' defection and the choice of a twelfth apostle to replace him were, as part of God's will, necessary. The exact texts from the Davidic psalms are presented in verse 20 below. The point here is that both aspects fulfilled these prophetic scriptural texts.

Peter emphasizes David's divine inspiration, as "the Holy Spirit" spoke through him, demonstrating the divine will in the process. Since Scripture is the word of God, it is completely valid to think of the Spirit "speaking" in it. This is critical for our own reading and study of Scripture. We are not simply perusing the ideas of Jeremiah or Paul but listening to God and his Spirit speaking directly to us through the words of Scripture. The subject of this divine revelation is "Judas, who served as guide for those who arrested Jesus." This goes back to Luke 22:47-48, when Judas led the mob to Jesus at Gethsemane. So Judas was not just betraying Jesus for money but was in doing so performing God's will and fulfilling Scripture by acting out what God had prophesied earlier.

The purpose of 1:17 is to explain why Judas had to be replaced. He not only was "one of our number"; he "shared in our ministry," by which he means the ministry of the Twelve. He was last on the list of members in Luke 6:14-16 but was nevertheless part of what constituted the new Israel, in direct continuity with the twelve patriarchs and twelve tribes. Peter's point is that by divine necessity the nucleus of "twelve" must be kept intact, so Judas has to be replaced. He had controlled the common purse of the group

---

3. Peter addresses the group as "men [*andres*], brothers," but the NIV properly translates "brothers and sisters" since the women of verse 14 would certainly have been included in his words.

(John 12:6; 13:29) and been an essential member. But more than that, Jesus chose them to be the "Twelve" who continued the life of Israel in the church as true Israel.

Readers would ask, "What happened to him?" so Luke proceeds to tell us. There are some major discrepancies in the account here and in Matthew 26:14-15; 27:3-10, and this is one place where harmonizing accounts actually works.

Matthew	Acts	Harmonizing
Chief priests bought the field.	Judas bought it.	They purchased it in his name.
He hanged himself.	He fell into the field and "burst open."	His body was thrown into the field after he hanged himself.

Matthew was writing to Jewish Christians and centers on his death, while Luke, writing to Gentiles used to suicide, goes into the details. Matthew also emphasizes the Jewish leadership and the bribe money they gave to Judas, Judas' repentance and throwing the bribe money back into the temple, and their using the money to purchase the "field of blood." Luke is concerned entirely with Judas' terrible end and so omits those details.

The results of his death are described in gruesome language: Judas "fell headlong" into the field and "all his intestines spilled out." The severity of his act leads to the severity of his end. Luke stresses divine justice, a life for a life. This is cause-and-effect language. Judas brought it on himself. The second result is the renaming of the field (1:19) as "Akeldama, that is, Field of Blood." The story of his suicide became very well known to the inhabitants of Jerusalem, so much so that it was given a new name befitting the bloody end of Judas. Matthew 27:7 tells us it had been a "potter's field [and] a burial place for foreigners." For Matthew that fulfilled Jeremiah 19:1-3 and 32:6-16 (see also Zech 11:12-13). Putting the two accounts together, the priests used the thirty pieces of silver as "blood money" (Matt 27:6) and purchased the field as a graveyard for non-Jews (it was unclean), but it became known for that reason as "the Field of Blood." Divine justice was served.

The actual passages fulfilled in Judas' defection and betrayal Luke lists in 1:20. Two are drawn from Psalm 69:25 and 109:8. Psalm 69 is a prayer for deliverance from David's enemies and a cry for justice. In verse 25 the psalmist calls for divine judgment on them: "May his place be deserted; let there be no one to dwell in it." Judas is seen as an enemy of the Davidic messiah, and the desolate Field of Blood is his judgment. Since he had purchased the field, it has rightfully become his "dwelling place." The switch from the plural of the psalm to the singular here applies it to Judas. Paul applies this psalm to the Jews as enemies of Jesus (Rom 11:9–10), Luke of this one specific enemy.

Psalm 109:8 is another lament psalm petitioning God for justice, this time, "May another take his place of leadership." In it David calls on God to place a list of curses on the individual within the community who had turned against him. The one applying to Judas specifically looked to him as one of the Twelve who had been appointed to judge Israel (Luke 22:30). He forfeited that right, and it is time for his share in the ministry (Acts 1:17) to pass to another.

The Replacement of Judas (1:21–26)

These verses actually contain the criteria for the apostolic office: they must have walked with Christ and actually seen the risen Lord. The idea of divine necessity (*dei*, "it is necessary") occurs twice in the larger passage, first in 1:16, with Judas' betrayal, which was necessary to fulfill Scripture, and now here in terms of finding his replacement to keep the "Twelve" intact so that the church could be anchored in a renewed and restored Israel made up of believing Jews and Gentiles. "With us the whole time" does not mean he had to have been a follower from the beginning. Only Peter and Andrew and Philip and Nathanael (John 1:35–51) could say that. Technically, "the whole time" means from the Baptist's beginning ministry to the resurrection, but it doesn't require only the longest-running followers. Rather, it means those who have experienced the full gamut of Jesus' mighty words and deeds.

In addition, it was necessary that the man also be a true witness to the resurrection, the core to the preaching in Acts (for instance, 2:24–28; 3:15, 21; 4:10–12). They must be official "witnesses" to the reality of the risen Lord. Paul had to anchor his apostolic office in the fact that he had actually "seen" the resurrected Jesus in his Damascus road vision (1 Cor 9:1), and these criteria here restrict the apostolic office to those who had personally experienced Jesus in his life and especially his resurrection. Paul did not fulfill the first requirement, and that was only overcome by the fact that Jesus had personally called Paul to that office. Yet still Paul felt he had to stress the fact that he fulfilled the second requirement.

When they had examined all the possibilities (probably from the Seventy of Luke 10:1) and done all they could, they had two nearly equal candidates. It is interesting that none of Jesus' brothers like James or Judas (both of whom wrote letters) were chosen, but they did not become believers until the resurrection appearances (John 7:5; 1 Cor 15:7) and so did not fulfill the first criterion. We know very little about either candidate. Joseph had two nicknames to distinguish him from others of the same name—the Aramaic "Barsabbas," meaning either "son of the Sabbath" (sabba) or "son of the elderly father" (abba), and also the Latin "Justus," which could be what he was called in his later ministry in Gentile lands. The other candidate, Matthias, is not mentioned elsewhere in the New Testament. Eusebius (Ecclesiastical History 1.12.3) says simply that he had been one of the Seventy.

Those in the upper room could not choose between these two and so prayed, asking God to "show us which of these two you have chosen" (1:24). The decision is too important to be made by human reasoning, and so they rely entirely on God's greater knowledge and will. God alone fully knows "everyone's heart," and so they want the choice to be based on his omniscience and not on their finite perspectives. Jesus had personally chosen the Twelve, and they wished that to continue.[4]

God's elect will concerned who will "take over this apostolic ministry" (v. 25), which in the original Greek translates "the place of his ministry and apostleship." To replace Judas and join the Twelve will effect both what he does (apostolic ministry) and the position and authority he will hold (apostolic office). It is the most serious choice imaginable and will have great effect on the messianic movement being launched here. Judas defected and "left to go where he belongs," meaning he both forfeited his office and fulfilled his eternal destiny of hellfire. "His own place" refers to the fact that he never was a believer but rather was "a devil" from the beginning (John 6:70), so he is now where he belongs, in eternal punishment.

The casting of lots (1:26) to make major decisions was a Jewish method used several times (Lev 16:8; Josh 18:6; 19:51; 23:4; 1 Sam 14:42; 1 Chr 6:65; 25:8–9; 26:13–14; Neh 10:34; 11:1; Prov 16:33; Isa 34:17; Jon 1:7) and intended to allow God to guide the actions of his people and to find his will in the situation. Casting lots consisted of writing the names on stones and then drawing one out, designating thereby God's choice for the office. Some have said this was a mistake, and that the coming of the Spirit corrected such practices. That is highly unlikely, for this was accepted throughout the Old Testament and connected with the sacred Urim and Thummim, stones or bones placed in a pouch on the high priest's breastplate for finding out God's will (Exod 28:30; Num 27:21; 1 Sam 14:41). So this was a very positive occasion and act, and God used it to make his choice known.

---

4. Most scholars debate whether it is Jesus or God being addressed here (the majority prefer God), but I doubt that this prayer is directed at one or the other but to the Godhead as a whole. Both were recipients of the prayer.

Matthias was chosen and "added to the eleven apostles." The phrase "the eleven" (Luke 24:9, 33; Acts 1:26) would have grated on the ears of the disciples, for it was never God's intention. Now "the Twelve" could finally be reconstituted and lead the church into the new age of the Spirit and of salvation.

The first chapter of Acts is in a sense the prologue of the book, showing that the ascension of Jesus was the prelude to the coming of the Spirit at Pentecost. It took place ten days before that event, and it is clear that the Spirit was sent by Jesus to continue his work on earth. Three things made the mission of the church to the world possible: the exaltation of Jesus to launch the mission of the church, the coming of the Spirit to empower the church, and the maturation of the apostles to lead the church.

The first section (vv. 1–11) covers the forty-day appearances of Jesus leading up to his ascension. The primary topics are the reality of his physical resurrection, the coming of the Spirit, and the meaning of the arrival of the kingdom. Clearly, a new age had begun, and it meant an entirely new reality that went beyond the restoration of Israel and embraced the salvation-historical new reign of God and a new messianic community that meant a new Israel. This period ended when a cloud caught Jesus up to the right hand of God ten days before the Spirit was to come.

The rest of the chapter covers what transpired during those ten days. The major event was the replacement of Judas and the reconstitution of the Twelve to lead the church. These days were dominated by prayer (vv. 14, 24). As they prayed, Peter was led first to explain the tragic end of the betrayer, Judas (vv. 15–20), which fulfilled Spirit-inspired Scripture (Pss 69:25; 109:8) regarding the necessity of Judas' death and his replacement in the apostolic band. His terrible death, with his body thrown into the very field he had purchased with his blood money, was the just penalty for his terrible act of betrayal, and he had to be replaced, as Scripture prophesied, in order for the church's mission to be launched by the Twelve, the new "patriarchs" of true Israel.

This search for the final member of the Twelve (vv. 21-26) was of divine necessity led by the Spirit. Their search led to two final candidates who were so equally qualified that the apostles could not choose between them. So they were led to use the Old Testament method of casting lots. God honored that ancient method, selecting Matthias as the twelfth apostle. The leadership of the church was now intact, and they were ready for the Spirit to descend and the mission to the world to begin.

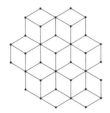

PENTECOST AND THE
COMING OF THE SPIRIT
(2:1–47)

The church's mission to the world is clearly launched in acts of supernatural power, as the twin events of the ascension and Pentecost indicate with trinitarian precision. Both in the ending of Luke (24:49) and the beginning of Acts (1:4, 8), Jesus tells his followers to remain in Jerusalem in order to receive power from heaven when the Spirit arrives. In these two passages the Spirit is seen as a gift from Jesus, and in Acts 2 that gift is unveiled. In the meantime, the people of God are prepared when the Twelve as the new Israel are reinstated to the church, and they along with the empowering presence of the Spirit are now ready to lead the messianic community into the new age. The Old Testament background to the Spirit's coming is clear, promised in Numbers 11:29; Isaiah 32:15; 44:3; Ezekiel 36:27; and Joel 2:28–32.

There are three parts to this unit: the arrival of the Spirit at Pentecost (2:1–13), Peter's sermon showing the meaning of this event (2:14–36), and the need for repentance, beginning the mission of the church (2:37–41). Everything in the book of Acts flows out of this Pentecost event, for the Spirit is behind everything the people of God accomplish in this book. Indeed, these are the Acts of the Spirit in reality, and the message is every bit as true for us today as it was then. Everything we do that is worthwhile comes as a result of the Spirit in us.

There is a significant debate as to whether there is a single outpouring of the Spirit or whether he came in two stages, first on the apostles in John 20:22, when they were in the upper room on that first day of the resurrection, and second on all believers here at Pentecost (see 2:17–18). When Jesus appeared to them that first day, he said, "Receive the Holy Spirit." The question is whether that was proleptic, promising the Spirit (thereby, "You are going to receive the Spirit"), or an actual coming of the Spirit on the Eleven. It is certainly a command and not just a promise, and so I believe the Spirit came on them for the resurrection appearances at that time, in a sense a firstfruits of what was going to come (see my John commentary for more). So we have what could be called the "Johannine Pentecost" there—a private, spiritual strengthening of the disciples, and now the full Pentecost, a public empowering of the church and the inauguration of the new era of the Spirit.

THE SPIRIT ARRIVES AT PENTECOST (2:1–13)

THE SETTING: PENTECOST IN JERUSALEM (2:1)

Finally, the promised day (Luke 24:49; Acts 1:4) arrives, and the saints (the 120 of 1:15) are still gathered in the upper room awaiting the expected event. Fifty days (the meaning of "Pentecost") have passed since the death and resurrection of Jesus, and he has appeared sporadically to his followers for forty of them. Pentecost is a harvest festival celebrating the firstfruits of the wheat crop and the second pilgrimage festival (of three after Passover, Exod 23:15–17). It was also seen as the festival celebrating the giving of the law, said to be given on Sinai fifty days after the Passover in Exodus. Thus the giving of the Spirit by Christ is seen in connection with the giving of the Torah of the Messiah as introducing the new age (Deut 30:6; Jer 31:31–34: as the law written on the heart). The new covenant period now begins, signified by the presence of the Spirit. As with Passover, several thousand pilgrims would descend on Jerusalem, and so this Pentecost outpouring would become a very public event.

The Descent of the Spirit (2:2–4)

In verses 2–4 it is clear that the coming of the Spirit is a very public event. The three signs (the audible sign—wind; the visible sign—fire; the inward sign—tongues) were observed by everyone present, and the effects were obvious to all.

1. The first sign is "a sound like the blowing of a violent wind" that "came from heaven" (to onlookers, the sky) and "filled the whole house where they were sitting." This reenacts the sound of the trumpet blast at Sinai when the law was given (Exod 19:16). The wordplay with *pneuma* (wind/spirit) is not found here, as the Greek for "violent wind" is *pnoēs biaias*, but the concept is likely present anyway. There may be an allusion to the vision of the dry bones (Ezek 37:5–6, 14), where the wind filled them with new life. The filling of the whole house signifies the coming of the Spirit on every believer, and he comes in a violent storm, a virtual hurricane of spiritual power descending on them.

2. The second sign (2:3) is "what seemed to be tongues of fire that separated and came to rest on each of them" (all the believers, see 2:17–18). The wind symbolized the coming of the Spirit, the fire of the Spirit entering each follower. This further typology relives the thunder and lightning of Sinai (Exod 19:16). It also fulfills Luke 3:16, the prophecy of the Baptist that Jesus would fill them "with the Holy Spirit and fire," referring to God's purifying fire. The "tongues" are symbolic here and become literal in verse 4, meaning that God would send his purifying Spirit to each language and people worldwide to bring them to him (God the "consuming fire" of Deut 4:24; 9:3; Heb 12:29). The picture here is of a wildfire spreading everywhere and consuming sin,

bringing spiritual revival to the nations. It is a corporate movement but also completely personal, as the fire separates and touches every single person, causing fiery conviction to embrace each one and purify them in the Lord.

3. The final symbol is the fact that as a result of the first two they "began to speak in other tongues as the Spirit enabled them" (2:4). This phenomenon describes the visible results of the Spirit's arrival. Note the progression of the signs—the coming of the Spirit from heaven (the wind), the spiritual revival as the Spirit arrived and entered the saints (the fire), and the outward movement of mission that resulted (the tongues). The Spirit entering was an invisible entity, but the results were very visible—the fire and the tongues. Every child of God there was "filled with the Holy Spirit" and could not be silent, having to speak out to all around. As a second baptism, they were immersed in the Spirit.

The "other tongues" would be the human languages from around the world, many of which were represented by the pilgrims present there for Pentecost. This phenomenon is called "glossolalia," speaking in other languages. God was telling them that the gospel was to be contextualized for every culture, and the people were to be reached in their own tongues and cultural categories. It took the church several years to fully realize this.

The ones present then are described in verses 9–11. This sign governed the rest of Acts, signifying God's will that the gospel be transmitted and proclaimed in every language and culture of planet earth. The emphasis is on Spirit-inspired preaching, often with a supernatural ability to speak the native language but mainly with a mandate to cross-culturally contextualize the gospel for every culture. These Jewish believers did not understand this and remained in Jerusalem for some time, not taking the message outward until the persecution of 8:1–3. They typically

misunderstood this command as meaning God would bring
the nations to them there in Jerusalem, as indeed is the case
on this first Pentecost. The Spirit will take over and force
them to move out via the great persecution of 8:1–3.

THE REACTION OF THE CROWDS (2:5–13)

There were often more people present at Pentecost than at
Passover, for the weather in late spring was generally better for
travel. Interestingly, though, the stress in verse 5 may be on those
"God-fearing Jews from every nation" who had permanently taken
up residence in Jerusalem. Likely both are included, pilgrims as
well as residents. There were several synagogues there just for
these **Hellenistic** Jews who had moved back to Israel. The added
"under heaven" means that the Jews in the **diaspora** were also
children of God watched over by heaven. These are the onlookers watching as the effects of the Spirit's arrival spills out into
the streets. They are not only observing but also listening, specifically as these peasant Galileans start speaking in the languages
of their homelands. These pilgrims are described as "God-fearing
Jews," literally "devout, pious" people who followed the law and
worshipped God.

Needless to say, this crowd, upon hearing the Christ followers
speaking in their own languages, were in complete "bewilder-
ment" at this miraculous phenomenon (2:6). All in the vicinity
gathered around, wondering what was taking place. It is doubtful that every one of the believers was speaking at the same time,
for the languages were discernible. Likely they spoke more or less
a few at a time. While some think this was a miracle of hearing
rather than of speaking, Luke certainly presents it as a miracle
of tongue-speaking. In one sense this could be called a reversal
of Babel (Gen 11:7), as the confusion of languages there is overturned. This wonder and perplexity dominate the next few verses.

Out of their utter amazement (2:7–8) they ask the natural question: Since all these are pilgrims from Galilee, how can they be

speaking "in our native language?" The text actually is "amazed [*existēmi*] and astonished [*thaumazō*]." Both are normally used for observance of miracles and of Jesus (amazed—Luke 2:47; 8:56; 24:22; astonished—Luke 8:25; 9:43; 11:14) and emphasize the supernatural origin of these phenomena. Actually, Galilee was more multilingual than Judea, but even there people spoke at best the languages of the region—Aramaic, Greek, and Latin (not so much the latter)—not all the languages intended here. There was likely some disparagement in this, for most Judeans considered Galileans to be backward, ignorant peasants. So there is a twofold perplexity, centered on their ethnic origins but mostly on their amazing and sudden ability to speak in other languages.

There is a lot of discussion regarding whether this tongues experience is supposed to be repeated today. Most separate the gift here from the glossolalia in 1 Corinthians 12, as this is evangelism while that is worship, but the two are clearly connected. Both are gifts of the Spirit and ecstatic utterances. There are three options.

1. To Pentecostals and charismatics, it is a normative experience and, as a sign of "baptism in the Spirit," is meant for every believer in order to have the true fullness of the Spirit.

2. To cessationists (those who believe that such gifts have ceased), it was meant entirely to authenticate the coming of the Spirit and so ceased at the end of the apostolic age. Therefore those who do so today are not led by God and his Spirit but undergo a purely human experience.

3. Growing more and more popular recently is a middle position, which could be described as "seek not, forbid not." This is my view and is built on 1 Corinthians 12:11, that the Spirit "distributes" spiritual gifts to each believer but to each individual gives only those gifts "just as he determines."

In other words, the gift of tongues is given only to those God wishes to have it. I, for instance, have been given the gift of teaching but not of tongues. I have the gift of gab but not that kind! I would love to have it but have not been blessed in that way, I would

understand, on the basis of his will. Each of us should be pleased
and thankful for the particular gifts God has for us.

There are fifteen regions named in the "roll call of the nations"
of verses 9-11, beginning with lands east of Jerusalem and then
sweeping to the south and west, with two theological emphases:
(1) the universal proclamation of the gospel, with this being a geographical list tracing the movement of the church to the world;
and (2) possibly (though quite debated) the nations brought back
to unity after Babel by the Spirit, who heals all divisions.

A brief introduction to the list might help. The first four are
east of Jerusalem: (1) The Parthians are the warlike tribes on the
other side of the Euphrates, fearsome warriors who twice defeated
Roman legions. (2) The Medes were linked to Persia, lands to which
many Jews were deported by Assyria (2 Kgs 17:6; 18:11). (3) Elam is
a region north of the Persian Gulf, again with some Jews inhabiting it. (4) Mesopotamia contained ancient Babylon and had a large
Jewish population.

The next four move south and west. (5) Judea we know.
(6) Cappadocia is part of Asia Minor, in present-day northeastern Turkey; Paul will evangelize this area in Acts 13-20. (7) Pontus
is further west in modern Turkey on the coast of the Black Sea
and also later the object of Pauline mission. (8) Asia refers to the
Roman province by that name, which was the most influential
region of Asia Minor. It was on the Aegean coast and contained the
seven cities of Revelation 2-3. (9) Phrygia was west of Galatia and
connected to Asia. (10) Pamphylia was on the east side of modern
Turkey between the provinces of Galatia and Asia.

South of this, on the continent of Africa, lay (11) Egypt and
(12) Libya, near Cyrene. Both contained large numbers of Jewish
people, in particular Alexandria. The first-century philosopher
Philo as well as Apollos in Acts came from Egypt. Carthage in
Libya produced the military commander Hannibal, and Simon of
Cyrene (Luke 23:26) was from this region. Cyrene was the source
of many believers (Acts 11:20; 13:1). Fifty to sixty thousand Jews

lived in (13) Rome, and it became central to the Christian movement. (14) Cretans lived on the Isle of Crete, and Paul wrote his
letter to Titus while the latter was serving the churches there.
With the (15) Arabs we leave geographical lines and go back to
the region of Palestine. The mention of "proselytes," Gentiles who
have converted to Judaism, is due to the fact that they play such a
prominent role in Acts. Far more proselytes than Jews respond to
the gospel, probably because they were never comfortable with
the Jewish demand for circumcision.

The content of the glossolalic messages is described in the last
part of verse 11, "the wonders of God." Most likely these "wonders"
are not just the supernatural phenomena—the wind, fire, and
tongues—but also the wonder of the gospel. The primary message for the mission of the church, the presentation of the gospel,
must have been a critical part of what the believers said in all
these languages.

In verse 7 they were "amazed and astonished" (NIV: "utterly
amazed"), and now in verse 12 they are "amazed and perplexed."
They can understand what the believers are saying, but they
are bewildered that it is Galileans who are showing this amazing linguistic dexterity. They were not ready for such a supernatural manifestation; who would be? Luke intends their question
("How is it that each of us hears them in our native language?")
to address the readers and get us to ask the same thing: "What
does this mean?" They are mystified not just about the fact of the
miraculous speech, but also about the significance or meaning of
it. This is intended to lead directly into Peter's speech, which will
answer this question.

Others in the crowd responded not with perplexity but with
mockery (2:13), echoing Jesus' teaching that his followers would
experience the same opposition he faced countless times. When
they were filled with the Spirit, the followers were undoubtedly
consumed with joy and gave expression to their exultation perhaps by dancing around and shouting. So the mockery had some

basis in fact, as the people poked fun at them: "They have had too much wine." The Greek reads "sweet wine," referring to newly fermented wine that tasted sweet and invited further drinking. They are probably also saying that the gospel content is the gibberish of a drunk and not worth paying attention to. This may lie behind Ephesians 5:18, "Do not get drunk on wine. ... Instead, be filled with the Spirit."

PETER GIVES HIS PENTECOST SERMON (2:14–36)

Luke does not supply the content of any of the ecstatic utterances but simply describes them as "wonders of God" (2:11). He probably wanted Peter's speech to supply that content. The scene has perhaps shifted to the outer court of the temple. We don't know when, perhaps between the fire and the glossolalic speech or after all three had taken place.

The speeches in Acts are widely considered to be fictional reconstructions of what the early church came to believe rather than reproductions of what Peter and the others actually said on these occasions. This is an unnecessary hypothesis, for every speech fits very closely in its context and faithfully summarizes what was likely said (they are too short to be verbatim). The eyewitnesses helped Luke reconstruct the content, and Luke would have been present for many of Paul's sermons.[1] So we can be assured that this represents the actual Pentecost sermon Peter preached. All of the speeches share certain aspects: The age of fulfillment has come; the age of salvation is here due to the death and resurrection of Jesus; the Spirit is God's gift to inaugurate this age; Christ will return and bring this age to a close; the people must repent and turn to God.

---

1. For more detail, see the section "History and Theology in Luke-Acts" in the introduction.

Introduction (2:14–15)

As spokesman for the apostles, Peter addresses the bystanders and answers the question of verse 12, "What does this mean?" He is no longer speaking in tongues but undoubtedly speaks in Aramaic, the language of Judea. He stands rather than sits because of the large crowd and because rabbis stood when preaching and sat when teaching. The opening, "Fellow Jews," is literally translated "Men of Judea" (see ESV, NRSV, NASB), but since it certainly refers to both men and women who were present, the NIV is correct. He addresses them further as "you who live in Jerusalem" not because there are no visiting pilgrims present but because the mission will be launched from Jerusalem. The inhabitants have been there from the start and were present for Jesus' death and resurrection, so they will become the official witnesses.

Peter wants them to "know" the truth about the supernatural event that has just taken place and says it two ways—literally, "Let this be known to you, and pay careful attention to my words." The first thing is an important correction to their mistaken understanding that the believers were drunk (2:13). It was only nine in the morning (the "third hour" after dawn), and much too early for strong drink. It is critical that they clear their mind of false impressions and open up to the astounding truth. The abounding joy and excitement of the believers must be understood as caused by the Spirit, not wine.

The Fulfillment of Joel 2:28–32 (2:16–21)

In explaining the scriptural background, Peter uses what was called the "pesher" style common among the writings of the Dead Sea Scrolls of **Qumran**. There were two major types of exposition in Jesus' day, the midrash of orthodox Judaism and the Talmud, used by the rabbis, and the pesher of Qumran, used by the Essenes. Midrash contains detailed exegesis and is almost atomistic at times, moving from Scripture to application and saying in essence, "This has relevance for that." Pesher takes a revelatory stance, with little exegesis and a stress on direct fulfillment, saying in essence, "This is that." Peter's passive "what was spoken" could be translated "what God had said," stressing divine inspiration. For Peter and the apostles, the Joel prophecy is directly fulfilled in the Pentecost episode. He calls the events they have witnessed "last days" events that portent the final age when God's kingdom will come. God is directly speaking to the people who will populate this messianic age and bring Joel's prophecy to fruition.

In Joel 2 this is a prophecy of the coming of the Day of Yahweh, while for Peter it is the arrival of the new age of the Spirit. Moreover, Joel does not contain the opening "in the last days." This is Peter's interpretation. The last days began with Jesus' incarnation and life, but it is the Spirit who launches the new era. In Joel's time a locust plague was sent as a warning to call the nation to repentance, and Peter also emphasizes the need for Israel to repent in his own time.

The signs characterizing the outpouring of the Spirit will affect every age group in Israel, as the children, the youth, and the elderly will all experience prophetic dreams and visions. Prophecy is the broadest category, referring to inspired declarations made directly by divine inspiration to the people. Here the prophecies came in the form of glossolalia, but Peter has in mind prophetic utterances of every type. Visions are a long-running thread throughout Acts and guide the apostles frequently: twice to Paul on the Damascus road (9:4-6, 10-12), to Peter and Cornelius (10:3-6, 10-16), and to Paul in Troas (16:9-10). The age of prophecy had ceased, but now it had been reinstated at the beginning of the last days. The interpretation of dreams was especially linked with Joseph (Gen 40:5-15; 41:1-32) and Daniel (Dan 1:17; 2:1-16, 24-45; 4:1-27).

Verse 18 extends the prophetic promise to people of all social strata, as both male and female servants will be filled with the Spirit and granted prophetic gifts. So the lowest of the groups in the first century, slaves (*douloi*) and women, will be elevated by the Spirit. People's slaves will become God's servants, and women will be given the same gifts as men. In the church equality was the name of the game.

The next part of the Joel prophecy (2:19-20) speaks directly to the Pentecost phenomena and links it with what will take place at the end of history at the **parousia** (second coming of Christ). For Peter, the "wonders in the heavens above" are the coming of the Spirit from heaven, and the "signs on the earth below" are the wind, fire, and tongues that signified the Spirit on the believers gathered there. The Pentecost phenomena are pictured as **apocalyptic** events. The last days have truly begun.

The "blood and fire and billows of smoke" are signs of judgment and fit the imagery of the darkness, earthquake, and tearing of the veil at Jesus' death. God's judgment is closely connected to the imagery of redemption, for forgiveness of sins means those who repent will not have to face the wrath of God. In Joel this refers specifically to the Day of Yahweh as the coming of divine judgment on the nations; here it describes the end of those who refuse to call on the Lord and be saved (v. 21).

This judgment theme continues with the idea that "the sun will be turned to darkness and the moon to blood." Certainly the phenomena here will not come until that final day when the Lord returns, but Peter has turned to that final period, as seen in what is called "inaugurated **eschatology**." In the life and death of Jesus and the coming of the Spirit, these last days have "already" begun, but they have "not yet" come to fulfillment and will do so only at the parousia. Still, we are living in that time of tension between the already and the not-yet. The judgment of God has been initiated and is part of gospel proclamation.

This cosmic phenomena presages "the coming of the great and glorious day of the Lord," here clearly the second coming and events of the **eschaton** (end) that will ensue from that culminating event. Then final salvation or deliverance will be experienced by the saints, and final judgment will fall on the enemies of God. This final day of human history is guaranteed, and getting ready for it is far and away the most important decision anyone will ever make, for it has eternal consequences.

Peter presents the key to everything in verse 21: "Everyone who calls on the name of the Lord will be saved." For Joel the title "the Lord" refers to Yahweh, while for Peter it refers to Christ, implying the deity of Christ, cosmic Lord of all. In both cases, the Day of Yahweh indicates salvation or deliverance, that time when the world of sinners receives its just recompense and the people of God receive their reward. For Peter it is spiritual salvation, and the reward is eternal life. To call "on the name of the Lord" means to repent and "believe in your heart that God raised him from the dead" (Rom 10:9–10). This prepares for the theology of resurrection in verses 24–35 and the call to repentance in verse 38.

The Basis: The Death and Resurrection of Jesus (2:22–36)

Introduction: Jesus of Nazareth (2:22)

They were "fellow Jews" in 2:14, and now they are "fellow Israelites" to stress the fact that the apostles belong to God's chosen people alongside them. As the chosen, they should be especially interested in the coming of their Messiah, who would be known by being "accredited by God." Now that person has appeared among them, Jesus of Nazareth. The Greek for "accredited," *apodeiknymi*, contains the idea of demonstration or proof. God provided indisputable evidence that Jesus was his chosen Messiah and Son, and he did so through "miracles, wonders and signs," utilizing all three terms used in the Gospels for the mighty works of God performed by Jesus. These could not have been done by mere mortals; they demonstrate the God who was in Jesus. They "know" the reality of this, for most of them were present for one or more of these wondrous works.

The death and resurrection of Jesus and Jewish guilt (2:23-24)

Peter skips over the life and ministry of Jesus, moving directly to his death. Peter emphasizes two things, that it was part of the divine plan and that the Jews, with the help of the "wicked" Romans, were complicit in his death. The "deliberate plan and foreknowledge" of God refers to the fact that Jesus died not just because the Jews thought him a false prophet (though that was true) but out of divine necessity (the divine "must" [*dei*] in the passion prediction of Luke 9:22). Jesus had to die as the atoning sacrifice so our sins could be forgiven. The cross was the center of God's plan of salvation, the means by which it became possible.

Wicked Romans nailed Jesus to the cross, but it was the demands of the Jews that put him there. This will be emphasized in several sermons, saying in effect, "You put Christ on the cross, but he died there for you. So repent, believe, and experience his salvation." God did not reject his covenant people because they put Christ to death but because they refused to believe in him. With repentance, that would all be turned around.

Death was Jesus' destiny (see John 3:14; 8:28; 12:32), but "it was impossible for death to keep its hold on him" (2:24). Its hold on humankind was absolute; every human being will die at some time. But it had no power over the Son of God. As part of the Triune Godhead, he was eternal, and death could only be temporary, and then only because he had taken on human flesh. Therefore God "raised him from the dead," thereby "freeing him from the agony of death." Every one of us can attest to this, for we have watched friends and loved ones as they had to undergo that dreaded "agony," a pain that is both physical and emotional. Yet it could only hold Jesus for "three days," actually thirty-six hours, from Friday at dusk until Sunday at dawn. The bonds of death holding him were broken, and from 1 Corinthians 15:20, 23, we know he did so as "firstfruits," guaranteeing our own future freedom from death.

Old Testament prophecies fulfilled (2:25-35)

Peter alludes to two further texts. This first one in verses 25–28 is taken from Psalm 16:8–11 and explains why death could not maintain its hold on Jesus. In this psalm, David expresses his joy and confidence in God, who will protect and watch over him in all situations. The idea that God is "always before me … at my right hand" looks at God's continual presence and power (right hand) available to help him overcome every obstacle. Since he knows God is always there to help, he can remain strong and serve the Lord. The result is joy and hope (2:26). There is a joyous confidence in the future uncertainties, for God is in charge. The emphasis is on the security felt across the whole body, as the various parts respond—the heart is glad, the tongue rejoices, and the body as a whole rests in hope. Peter pictures the Davidic Messiah in the midst of his suffering feeling this joy and hope in his father's presence. Since the future is secure in Yahweh, he can feel complete rest in his care.

The key verse then follows (2:27): "You will not abandon me to the realm of the dead, you will not let your holy one see decay." In the psalm itself, David was confident that the Lord would not allow him to die or his body to rot in Sheol (Greek: *hadēs*), the grave or "realm of the dead." Peter is applying this to the resurrection of Jesus from the dead as support for his statement that "it was impossible for death to keep its hold on him" (v. 24). David is the "holy one" in the psalm, and Jesus the Davidic Messiah is the focus for Peter. This means that after the three days in the tomb, Jesus' followers saw his intact body, and it had not decayed in the least. The physical resurrection is not only true but prophesied in Scripture according to Peter. The typological fulfillment follows a logic that proceeds from the lesser to the greater, from protecting David from deadly danger to raising Jesus from the dead. This conclusion would not follow from an exegesis of the psalm, but as typology it makes sense. The preservation of David from death is fulfilled in the preservation of Jesus from the grave.

Through this, Jesus the Davidic Messiah has experienced "the paths of life." He now will never die, and his eternity is certain. His triumph is complete, and he rejoices in it. Note that "paths" (*hodoi*) is plural, referring to all the benefits of eternal life as he now will spend eternity at the right hand of his Father (Ps 110:1 in v. 33). Thus the further result is "joy in your presence," with *euphrosynēs* expressing the state of joy and happiness Jesus has in his Father's presence. Again, we should note that as "firstfruits," Jesus envelopes us in his joy as we realize we too will share eternity with God.

In verses 29–32, Peter now argues that David could not have just been speaking of himself in Psalm 16 but had to have looked forward to its fulfillment in Jesus' resurrection. He calls him "the patriarch David," an unusual title because elsewhere Scripture always speaks of Abraham and his twelve sons as the patriarchs, or "fathers of Israel." Peter links David with them as another of the fathers of the nation. In reality, the emphasis is on family connections. By addressing them as "fellow Israelites," literally in the Greek "men, brothers," and emphasizing their mutual family connection with David their patriarch, Peter is implying that all believers stand with Jesus and his promise of eternal life.

Peter can "confidently" assert that this psalm is a prophecy about Christ because David "died and was buried, and his tomb is here to this day" (2:29). Since David's body is still in the grave, Psalm 16 with its assertion of resurrection could not be about him. David's burial on Mount Zion is attested in 1 Kings 2:10, and to Peter that means this prophecy is not about David but Christ. Josephus (*Antiquities* 16.179–83) tells the story of Herod's attempt to rob David's tomb for the money it contained, but fire killed two of his soldiers and stopped the attempt. Herod later built a marble memorial at the tomb site, and this story would have been well-known in Peter's day. The point is that the gravesite was pristine, and David's body was thus still resting in the grave.

In another surprising statement Peter calls David a "prophet" (2:30) because even as a hymn writer he produced several messianic psalms and here "knew that God had promised him on oath that he would place one of his descendants on his throne." As a result of these he was known in Judaism as a prophet, and Peter used this to highlight Psalm 16 as one of his messianic prophecies. Peter draws his point from Psalm 132:11, "The LORD swore an oath to David ... 'One of your own descendants I will place on your throne.' " The psalm looks to Nathan's prophetic pronouncement establishing the Davidic covenant in 2 Samuel 7:12-13, that God will "raise up your offspring ... [to] establish his kingdom." The Jews believed that it would be the Messiah who would fulfill the promise to David of an enduring throne, and Peter sees this coming to pass in the resurrection of Jesus and the coming of the Spirit. Jesus is King, and is on his throne at God's right hand in heaven. The arrival of the Spirit is the great gift and sign of the messianic kingdom.

In 2:31, Peter looks at Psalm 16:8-11 through the eyes of Psalm 132:11, once more arguing it to be a prophecy of "the resurrection of the Messiah, that he was not abandoned to the realm of the dead, nor did his body see decay." As a prophet, David foresaw "what was to come" and "spoke of the resurrection of the Messiah" in the psalm. Jesus the Davidic Messiah is reliving in even more dramatic form what David experienced in the psalm, and with him David's rule becomes an eternal throne.

Peter concludes this portion with a summary point: "God has raised this Jesus to life, and we are all witnesses of it" (2:32). Jesus could not remain dead, for Scripture demanded his resurrection to life, as made clear in verse 24. Behind this statement is the journey to faith of Luke 24. The extent of the misunderstanding and doubt of the disciples is hard to fathom, but it took all the events recorded in that chapter to overcome their spiritual blindness—from the women at the tomb to the two on the Emmaus road to Peter in his personal visit to the tomb to the Eleven in the upper room. It took several steps to produce what Peter says so simply here, "we are all witnesses of it." The risen Jesus alone could overcome the doubt, actually involving a refusal to believe, but now they along with the women could be official witnesses.

In verses 33–35, Peter argues that the resurrection and exaltation of Jesus are interdependent aspects of his glory. The primary passage teaching this in Scripture is Psalm 110:1, "The LORD says to my Lord, 'Sit at my right hand until I make your enemies a footstool for your feet.' " This is by far the most frequent Old Testament passage found in the New Testament, appearing over twenty times. To be "exalted to the right hand of God," as Peter puts it, echoes the hymn of Philippians 2:6–11, where Jesus is humiliated in his death and then exalted or lifted high when he is given the "highest place" and then "the name that is above every name." From this position of power and glory (the right hand) the risen Lord, Peter says, "received from the Father the promised Holy Spirit."

Note the progression: Jesus was given the Spirit by the Father and then in turn "poured out" this Spirit, who was promised in the Old Testament (Ezek 36:26–27; Joel 2:28–32) and by Jesus in his resurrection appearances (Luke 24:49; Acts 1:4–5, 8) to his followers. The Spirit is poured out abundantly, filling the saints (Eph 5:18) and sending them out with power from on high. "What you now see and hear" refers to the Pentecost event they have just experienced, as they saw the wind and fire and heard the tongues.

Peter uses the exact same argument for Psalm 110:1 in 2:34 as he did for Psalm 16:8–11 in verse 29. To prove that David was speaking about the coming Messiah in Psalm 110:1 and not about himself, Peter argues, "for David did not ascend to heaven." The point is that the psalm is speaking of a heavenly figure who is seated "at the right hand" of God, but since David simply "died and was buried" (verse 29) and never ascended to heaven like Enoch or Elijah, he could not be speaking of himself. Rather, it is Jesus the Christ who is seated on the throne of heaven and is the subject of Psalm 110:1.

While this is a royal psalm originally intended to affirm the throne of David, it is clear that when David wrote "The LORD said to my Lord," he was not speaking of himself but of a messianic figure behind his own role as king of Israel. So Peter's point is valid. The one behind David's authority, the royal Messiah, is placed on the heavenly throne at "the right hand of God" and promised both victory and rule over his enemies. David's authority and military prowess are given him via his own "Lord" in heaven.

Sitting at the right hand speaks of the risen Lord's present authority and throne in heaven. Making his "enemies a footstool for your feet" is his future role as conquering King when at his second coming the cosmic powers are completely defeated and all evil is assigned its eternal place in fiery punishment. Jesus is the exalted Lord, has conquered death, and is awaiting his final victory over the powers of darkness. It is this exalted Lord who has sent the Spirit to indwell and empower his people.

Conclusion: Lord and Messiah (2:36)

This verse concludes not just the last point but rather the entire section of psalms in 2:25–35 (Psalms 16:8–11; 132:11; 110:1). Peter, making his point very strongly, concludes, "Let all Israel be assured of this." This Jesus, crucified by the Jews and raised from the dead by God, has now been made "both Lord and Messiah" by the direct act of God. The movement from humiliation to exaltation and from Suffering Servant to triumphant Lord is at the heart of New Testament **Christology**. In addressing "all Israel," Peter is addressing every Jewish person ever born, for it is the single most important point that could be made since it concerns their Messiah. "Be assured" might better be translated "know with certainty"—all the data produced above proves with absolute certainty who this Jesus really is. He is not merely a peasant prophet and rabbinic wannabe who can be easily dismissed. His resurrection and ascension prove that he is Lord of all and Israel's Messiah, and there is no salvation except in him. The fact that God "made" him to be Lord and Messiah does not mean he was not such before. Rather, it means God has demonstrated who he truly had been all along through his resurrection and the pouring out of the Spirit. Truly the last days are here!

PETER ISSUES A CALL TO REPENTANCE (2:37–41)

Two things have been proved beyond a shadow of a doubt in the Pentecost event: Jesus is indeed "Lord and Messiah," and the promised Holy Spirit has come and inaugurated the new age of salvation. Having seen the Spirit descend on the believers and heard Peter's powerful message on the significance of that event, the people present were "cut to the heart," deeply convicted, with their conscience in tatters. Their earnest question is the only possible response: "Brothers [recognizing they were indeed "fellow Jews," 2:14, 22], what shall we do?" They knew they were in serious trouble with God and wanted to get right with him.

Peter's response centers on two imperatives and two promised results. Repentance entails both a turning from sin and a turning to God. John the Baptist preached "a baptism of repentance for the forgiveness of sins" (Luke 3:3), and Jesus stated it in no uncertain terms—repent or perish (Luke 13:3, 5). There can be no forgiveness and no salvation without repentance followed by belief. The place of baptism is strongly debated. In the Old Testament and Judaism, ritual immersion began with the consecration of priests and with ritual immersion in the temple, and there were six pools near the temple for these rites.

The Christians developed a new type of baptism, a one-time event similar to the proselyte baptism that initiated Gentile converts into Judaism. It was apparently first practiced by John the Baptist. Jesus did not practice it (John 4:2) but made it a requirement in his resurrection address (Matt 28:19). Contrary to what some have believed, the rite does not save but symbolizes the cleansing that repentance produces, as in 1 Peter 3:21, where it is called "the pledge of a clear conscience toward God." *Baptisma* ("baptism") means "immersion" and signifies a going under water to signify being cleansed from sin by God. This is done "in the name of Jesus Christ," not to produce salvation but to signify that salvation has been experienced. "In the name" means to be united with Jesus by faith.

The two results are immensely important. "Forgiveness of your sins" is the judicial result of repentance and the atoning sacrifice of Christ, as God then from his throne declares us forgiven and justified or right with him (Rom 3:24). Our sins are covered and canceled, and we stand reconciled before God. The second result is that we "receive the gift of the Holy Spirit," as the Spirit enters and indwells the heart of every new convert (Rom 8:14–17). Pentecost was a one-time event, but the gift of the Spirit is received every time an individual turns to Christ and is saved. When we say "Jesus lives in your heart," it is in reality the Spirit of Christ that takes up residence, with the result that we become a walking holy of holies because the Godhead dwells in us.

The promise of forgiveness and the Holy Spirit is now offered "for you and your children and for all who are far off" (2:39), meaning not just for those who happened to be present at the Pentecost event but for all Jews everywhere (and of course for us Gentiles as well). There are three stages of the promise: from the Old Testament Scriptures, to Jesus' teaching, to what Peter is saying here. Although the nation has been rejected by God for its refusal to believe in Jesus, every individual has the opportunity to repent, and the promises are still available. Wherever they live, and whatever generation they live in, the gospel is for them. The last part, "for all whom the Lord our God will call," may be a paraphrase of Joel 2:32, the promise that the Spirit would provide "deliverance … even among the survivors whom the LORD calls," which was omitted from the Joel quotation in 2:17–21. There and here every Jewish person is called by God to salvation in Christ.

Verses 40–41 summarize the rest of Peter's message ("many other words"), as he warns and pleads with them to "save yourselves from this corrupt generation." This certainly does not mean they can save themselves. They will rescue themselves by repenting and believing. It is God who justifies sinners. It is better to translate the passive command with permissive force, "Let yourselves be saved." The "corrupt generation" looks back to the wilderness generation (Deut 32:5; Ps 78:8) and sees the current nation warped by unbelief.

The last verse tells the results: an incredible revival broke out, as three thousand people became Christ followers. They are called "souls" (*psychai*) here to stress the spiritual change that came over them. This is quite the growth, from 120 (1:15) to 3,000. The conversion is seen in "accepted his message" (*logos*, "word"), meaning they accepted the gospel and became believers. They enter a period of unparalleled evangelistic success, the result of the Spirit's presence. So much flows out of this. It is commonly accepted that many churches (including Rome) may have been initiated by these Pentecost pilgrims returning home and taking the gospel with them. Only when we get to heaven will we know all that began that wondrous day in Jerusalem when the Holy Spirit came down.

LUKE DESCRIBES LIFE IN THE JEWISH CHRISTIAN CHURCH (2:42–47)

This is a very important thesis paragraph, for it summarizes the Jerusalem Christian community over the next few years until the persecution (8:1) forces many to flee Jerusalem, launching the universal mission. We learn of its internal makeup (2:42, 44–47) and its external relationship to outsiders (v. 43). This was an exciting period as they now began to realize the potential Jesus saw in the disciples when he chose them. There was no more spiritual lethargy, no more self-centeredness. They were growing spiritually by leaps and bounds, bit by bit turning into the world-changing forces God would unleash on a sinful world.

FOUR PILLARS OF THE CHURCH (2:42)

This verse tells us what constituted the most important aspects of the life and worship of the early church and provides an essential model for us to follow. Each of us should ask if these areas are as critical to our church today as they were when the church began. They should be! Are we as "devoted" to these as they were?

1. The apostles' teaching: The first Christians were enamored of truth and cared deeply about theological understanding, especially in the area of Christology, as we have seen. We can see the subject areas in the Gospel of Luke, describing the paths they themselves had taken. The movement of the disciples in their understanding (which took all the time they had with Jesus)—from rabbi to prophet to Messiah to Son of God and Lord to deity—was certainly a major focus. Old Testament fulfillment, the person and work of the Holy Spirit, the doctrine of God, would all have been carefully explained, as would ecclesiology, the people of God as Israel and then the church. Sermons would not have been shallow pep talks (as too often in our time)[2] but would center on these deep truths. Let each of us ask whether this is true in our church.

2. Fellowship: This in Greek is *koinōnia*, sharing or holding things in common. The early church began as an "assembly" (the meaning of *ekklēsia*) but became first a community and then a family. All three metaphors are correct, but the family image is primary. Paul regularly calls fellow believers "brothers and sisters," which meant both caring and sharing, the outgrowth of love between members of the body, the church. They are united with each member of the Triune Godhead and thereby with each other. The theme here is that the Holy Spirit has indwelt them and brought them together in him, and the fellowship is first of all with the Father, Son, and Spirit and thus with fellow believers,

---

2. Synagogue sermons regularly took an hour, and this was probably the case in the early church as well.

who are also one with him. Sharing and caring were the watchwords for relationships with one another.

3. The breaking of bread: These latter two flow out of the first two. Both the breaking of bread and then prayers are the result of teaching and aspects of the fellowship of the church. It is common to think of this as eucharistic worship, but it is likely broader than that, referring to table fellowship of all kinds, including fellowship at the Lord's table. Meals were viewed as sharing, first with God (they prayed at both the beginning and end of meals) and then with one another. An amazing number of scenes in the Gospel of Luke were over meals, and this continued in the early church. Meals provided the core of the theme of fellowship, then spreading to include every area of life. We should be having a lot more people over to our homes than many of us do. A friend of mine wrote a pamphlet on the family and commented that our home was all too often our castle: we build a mote around it and shut it off to outsiders. That is too often the case.

4. Prayers: This is a major emphasis in the Gospel of Luke, and a third of all the references to prayer in the New Testament are in Luke-Acts. God's people depend on him in everything they do, and they must involve and invoke him in every area of their lives. In Luke's Gospel Jesus bathed every major life occasion in prayer (Luke 3:21; 6:12; 9:18, 28; 22:41–42; 23:34, 43, 46), and this continued in the life of the church (Acts 1:14, 24–25; 3:1; 4:23–31; 6:4; 8:15; 9:11; 13:3; 14:23; 16:25). While some see these mainly as formal liturgical prayers as in the synagogue, the atmosphere of Acts favors these being personal prayers both at the corporate and individual levels.

RESULTS IN THE LIFE OF THE CHURCH (2:43–47)

As people saw "the many wonders and signs performed by the apostles," they felt *phobos*, a mixture of that fear and awe experienced also throughout the ministry of Jesus (for example, Luke 5:26; 8:37). Most think this passage describes outsiders, the people of Jerusalem primarily. Yet it seems this would be the feeling of believer and unbeliever alike. These sign-miracles authenticated Jesus, and they are doing the same for the early church. The entire city must have responded with terror at the power of God displayed in Jesus' followers and also with reverence and awe that Jesus' power had been transmitted to his followers. While many certainly felt fear, I think the primary emotion is wonder and awe, the same as found repeatedly in the Gospels of reactions to Jesus.

Luke here expands on the depth of fellowship the saints experienced as they "were together and had everything in common." Communal care was primary, and they shared the lives of fellow believers extensively (note Luke says, "*all* the believers"). This sense of a total unity that touched on every area of life is extraordinary. We all need to ask how true this is of our home church. I have heard stories of people who had been members for ten years and attended regularly who would be treated as a visitor by more than one person. The believers in Acts, however, considered themselves one and acted like it, holding "everything in common," true community. The extent to which this was true will be seen in verse 45 and in 4:32–34. Many have called this "the first communism," but it is not required here (though it was at Qumran).

The extent to which this was true is seen in 2:45: "They sold property and possessions to give to anyone who had need." These voluntary acts of love were never demanded by the apostles, which makes their behavior all the more awe-inspiring as a result. They believed that all property and goods are given to us by God and that he truly owns them. Therefore, they should be shared by all alike as he directed. Still, the giving was completely voluntary. The communal spirit is normative, but the actual giving is not. Nowhere does it say it is wrong to be wealthy, and that everyone should live menial lives. People gave as they felt led by the Spirit. Still, even land and houses were sold, with Barnabas a conspicuous positive example (4:34–37), and Ananias and Sapphira a negative contrast to Barnabas (5:1–11). Luke expresses the goal in 4:34: "there were no needy persons among them," which we see again in 6:1–7 with the Jewish and Hellenistic widows. That should be the motto of every congregational care program in every church.

As they did with Jesus, they went to the temple courts, primarily the court of the Gentiles, for worship and evangelistic activity. They participated in the morning (9:00 a.m.) and evening (3:00 p.m.) prayers (see 3:1), and the apostles would have likely taught by the colonnades in Solomon's portico there (5:12, 20), where rabbis often spoke (like Jesus did), as well as in private homes. They also regularly "broke bread [sharing meals, 2:42] in their homes" on a regular basis, not just on days of worship. We are told they "ate together with glad and sincere hearts," showing the extent of their loving relations with each other. The sense is that this was a regular practice, not just occasional. Their joy was both in Jesus and in each other. The obvious joy they felt in their community life is a model for us all. I have seen way too little community and sharing in the average church. We need to learn from this.

They worshippedworshipped as Jews in the temple, participating in the services there, and also worshipped as Christians together. We are told in verse 47 that they were "praising God and enjoying the favor of all the people," meaning the Jews in Jerusalem as well as fellow believers. Such joy and excitement is contagious and is one of the best evangelistic tools we can possess. People afraid to witness should simply get excited about the Lord and about their church life, and the witness will take care of itself. In a church like this we know we are never alone and that there are people who deeply care about everything we go through. That realization is priceless.

Luke presents the winning of converts to Christ as a "daily" result of the life of the church. Church growth is explosive when people are excited about the things of Christ. The verbs in these two verses indicate ongoing worship and ongoing conversions.

They didn't need special programs and special meetings to win the lost. A Spirit-filled, excited bunch of believers in an active church produced the results. Luke wants us to realize how simple it is to be successful for the Lord; simply let the Spirit take over and be ready to live the joyous life that results. Church growth is a divine activity: "being saved" at the end of verse 47 is a divine passive, meaning "those whom God was saving." The result is that the church began to grow exponentially in the immediate aftermath of Pentecost.

———

This is one of the truly significant chapters in the New Testament, for it is the only scriptural passage describing the coming of the Spirit upon God's people, inaugurating the church's life and mission to the world. The three stages—the ascension of Jesus, the completion of the Twelve, and Pentecost—provide the launching pad for the church age, the age of the Spirit and of salvation. In keeping with the Jewish festival itself, Pentecost celebrates the new harvest of the Spirit as he takes residence in every saint.

The Pentecost event was highly symbolic, with the wind signifying the Spirit (*pneuma*) who has come with typhoon force and blown away the believers with power, and the fire signifying the purifying force of God that consumes his people. The tongues signify the fact that the gospel must be contextually presented to every people and culture as they are, bringing them to God within their own environment. The results (vv. 5–13) were truly wondrous, as people from all over the Roman Empire (vv. 9–11) were present, fulfilling God's will by taking the gospel to the nations and establishing churches in most of the nations controlled by Rome. The evangelistic results are truly incredible, and the universal mission is present in embryo in this single event.

Peter then argues (vv. 17–21) that this has directly fulfilled the prophetic promise of the Spirit's coming in Joel 2:28–32. This means that the last days have begun, as the Spirit is now poured out on all people, producing prophecy, dreams, and visions that prove the Day of Yahweh is near. These wonders and signs have introduced the new age of salvation, open now to all who call on the Lord and believe. The key characteristic of the new age and of the book of Acts is the offer of salvation to "everyone who calls on the name of the Lord" (Acts 2:21).

Jesus was first accredited by God, then put to death by the Jews, and then raised by God (vv. 22–24) in direct fulfillment of prophetic promises (vv. 25–35). Three texts prove this point. In Psalm 16:8–11 David prophesied that the grave could not hold the Messiah (vv. 25–28); in Psalm 132:11 it is prophesied that David's descendant (Jesus the Messiah) would inherit his eternal throne (Acts 2:30); and in Psalm 110:1, David prophesied that Jesus Messiah would be exalted to the right hand of God (Acts 2:34–35). So it was foretold that Jesus would rise from the grave and assume his throne in heaven. This is just as meaningful for us today as it was for the Jews in Peter's day. Jesus is truly the exalted risen Lord, alone worthy of worship. We like Israel can be assured that Jesus is our Lord and Messiah as well as Israel's (v. 36), and we can rejoice in the privilege and joy of worshipping him.

The result of all this is the necessity of repentance and belief (vv. 37–41). We must go through the same process, and we too should be "cut to the heart" and ask, "What shall we do?" Here baptism is required along with repentance, not for salvation but as part of the salvation experience, signifying the new cleansing we have experienced. The two results are ours as well—forgiveness of sins and the coming of the Spirit to indwell us (v. 38). The incredible number who responded, three thousand, launched the church's mission in a wondrous way and set the pattern for the next few years.

The thesis paragraph of verses 42–47 is truly exciting. We have here the formula for a widely successful church in our time as well. The four pillars of verse 42 should guide us, and our churches need to center on biblical and theological truths taught in sermons and classes alike. The vertical (teaching) and the horizontal (fellowship between believers) need to become the axes of our church life. The description of church life in verses 43–47 produces a truly thrilling church I would love to be a part of: it exhibits awe, the sharing of goods, helping those around, and having the type of deep fellowship we all long to experience. This is what going to church is all about and shows to even the most rugged individualists that we all should be a part of a local body.

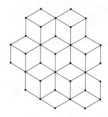

OPENING EVENTS IN THE NEW MESSIANIC COMMUNITY
(3:1–26)

The church as the new people of God, the new Israel, has now been established by the coming of the Spirit and the reconstitution of the Twelve. The first converts have been added to the church, and it has experienced a very successful beginning. It is time for it to enter into its God-given task of witness and mission. For the first few years the church remains in Jerusalem (2:1–8:3), as the leaders apparently misinterpret the mandate to take the gospel to the world (1:8; Matt 28:18–20), believing that the Abrahamic covenant (a blessing to the nations, Gen 12:3) and Isaiah 49:6 (a light to the Gentiles) meant that God would bring the nations to them in Jerusalem rather than send them out to the nations. It would take the persecution of 8:1–3 to force them out and impel them to fulfill their mission destiny.

The opening event is the miraculous healing of a lame man, anchoring the church in the power of the name of Jesus (3:6–7) and leading to Peter's second sermon (3:11–26) on the reality of Jesus' true identity and the need for the people to repent. This will become the pattern seen throughout the church's mission in Acts.

PETER HEALS A LAME MAN (3:1-10)

They had been attending the morning and evening prayers for the ten days they had waited for the coming of the Spirit, and they are still doing so as Peter and John go to the temple on one of the first afternoons at three in the afternoon (the ninth hour). The burnt offerings for the day were sacrificed in a morning (9:00 a.m.) and evening (3:00 p.m.) service, so this was the evening sacrifice, a sacred time in Jewish observance. Jewish Christians for many years continued to worship as Jews as well as Christians and would worship on Saturday as Jews and on Sunday (the Lord's Day) as Christians. So Peter and John are expressing their Jewish piety as they go for the second service of the day.

At the same time a man "lame from birth" was carried to the temple gate, and they had been passing him every time they went to the temple. He had undoubtedly been begging since he was a child, and being "over forty years old" (4:22), he had been begging for over thirty years. His would have been a sad life, for ancient people viewed such physical deformities as signs of sin and divine judgment. He would have been pitied, looked down on, and mocked at the same time.

The "gate called Beautiful" is a mystery, for no such gate is named elsewhere. It could have been the Nicanor gate on the eastern side, made of bronze and with beautiful columns, or it may have been the attractive gate on the southern side which connected the temple to the city and would have been a perfect site for a beggar. It had beautiful steps and a royal portico over it. Either would fit quite well. Almsgiving was a sacred duty to the Jews, and he probably did pretty well financially.

The exchange between the beggar and Peter (3:3-5) is classic. He asks for money, as he had done for all those years, but actually was paying little attention since Peter and his associates were just part of the crowd. He was used to people just passing by or dropping money on his pallet, and he must have been shocked when suddenly Peter and John "looked straight at him" and commanded,

"Look at us." He had hardly ever done so, and he started paying close attention, expecting a large windfall of a gift. His expectant look was about to be rewarded with a far greater windfall than he could ever have imagined.

Peter and John were as poor as the beggar was, and he must have been wondering what was going on when Peter said, "Silver or gold I do not have" (3:6). Why tell him to look at them when they had nothing to give? What follows likely shocked him to the core of his being: "What I do have I give you. In the name of Jesus Christ of Nazareth, walk." The command is in the present tense and means he will spend the rest of his life walking like a normal person. I cannot imagine how he must have felt as sudden, miraculous strength stole over his limbs and he was impelled to get up for the first time in his forty years of life (4:22).

The primary theme of this entire section is the power of Jesus' name. It is clearly not Peter and John who heal the man but Jesus, and this will be reiterated in verse 16, when in his sermon Peter states it was "by faith in the name of Jesus" that he had been healed. It is not magic but divine power behind the healing. (Compare 19:11–17, when the seven sons of Sceva are beaten up by a demon when they try to use Jesus' name this way.) It is Jesus' authority that becomes the means (*en*, "by") by which the miracle takes place. Seven times in Acts Jesus is named "of Nazareth" (2:22; 3:6; 4:10; 6:14; 22:8; 24:5; 26:9), and it stresses his earthly origins and incarnate life. It is the same Jesus who had walked among them who is now risen Lord.

The miracle immediately follows (3:7). "Taking him by the right hand," Peter "helped him up, and instantly the man's feet and ankles became strong," and the man began to walk. Since he was born with this condition, he had probably never had the muscles and bones for walking, so God probably created missing muscles and strengthened others. Luke doesn't use specific medical terms for feet and ankles, but does show real interest in the physical change.

The result (3:8) is spectacular. The whole way into the temple courts, the formerly crippled man is "walking and jumping, and praising God." Since he had been at the gate much of his life, the temple officials and many of the residents would have known him and would have been thoroughly shocked at this sight. Consider all the verbs used to describe the scene—jumped, stood (NIV: "began to walk"), walking and jumping, praising—all describing an unbelievably exciting scene. The man has instantly gone from forty years sitting or lying down to intense and frenetic, joyous action. It is hard to imagine what he was feeling as for the first time in his life he could walk, jump, and run. The temple had likely not heard that level of praise in a long, long time. While not stated directly, the praise probably indicated the man's conversion to Jesus as well.

It likely took a few minutes for onlookers to realize what had happened and for temple authorities and others to recognize him as the former beggar who had sat at the gates all those years. When it all finally hit home, they knew another miracle had taken place. Many of them undoubtedly joined the man in jumping and praising God. The news must have spread quickly, as Jerusalem was a town of about seventy thousand people (Rev 11:13), and the man was probably fairly well-known.

As always with miracles, one of the major reactions is "wonder and amazement," using two synonymous terms to designate the intense astonishment all of Jerusalem felt. The second term is the stronger one and means they were virtually out of their minds with shock at the power of Christ. (The Greek *ekstasis* has been transliterated into the English "ecstasy.") It is somewhat surprising in light of all the miracles Christ had performed, but their shock is probably due to their belief that Jesus was gone and disgraced, so such things would never happen again. This miracle is a twofold message that both justifies Jesus and shows that he has empowered his followers still. The new age of the Spirit has begun with a bang.

PETER GIVES HIS TEMPLE SERMON (3:11-26)

As in chapter 2, Peter's message explains the significance of the event for the new messianic movement: the person of Jesus stands behind everything that has taken place. The healing closely follows the coming of the Spirit at Pentecost and is part of God's work in this new movement. The two events have together launched the church and its mission with power, showing that God's kingdom has indeed arrived.

PETER RESPONDS TO THEIR ASTONISHMENT (3:11-12)

"All the people" in the temple are completely astonished and run to Peter for an explanation. We must remember that to them Jesus has been completely discredited and his movement come to naught. They hope Peter can shed some light on this astounding second event (with Pentecost). He was in that open area where Jesus had also often taught, Solomon's portico, a meeting place with columns and a roof where rabbis and others, including the early church (2:46; 5:12), often came for lectures.

Peter is surprised at their amazement. He sees the crowd rushing to him and decides as he did after Pentecost to take the opportunity to present the gospel to them. He addresses them as "fellow Israelites" (as in 1:16; 2:22) to identify with them. The believers at this stage considered themselves the messianic party within Judaism, and Peter wants his listeners to realize that. They should not be amazed, for Jesus is still at work. Moreover, they must know that neither he nor John accomplished this miracle in their own "power or godliness." They deserve no credit and have done nothing in their own strength. The term for "godliness" is *eusebeia*, "piety," and Peter means they are not Jewish sages or charismatics who can do wondrous things by their own power and walk with God. The Lord alone has the power to do such things.

THE TRUE SOURCE OF THE POWER: GOD AND JESUS (3:13–16)

The true source is "the God of our fathers," the patriarchs "Abraham, Isaac and Jacob." In essence, Peter is saying that those who labeled Jesus a false prophet were tragically wrong. The God who healed the man "in the name of Jesus Christ" (3:6) is the same God worshipped by the patriarchs, the God who is in covenant relationship with the Jewish people. At the burning bush in Exodus 3:15, "the God of your fathers—the God of Abraham, the God of Isaac and the God of Jacob" revealed himself as Yahweh. Now he is once again revealing himself as the God of the new messianic community. With Abraham and the patriarchs, the new people of God, the Israelites, were launched. Now the new Israel, the messianic community, is launched, and a new era has begun.

Moreover, he is the God who "has glorified his servant Jesus," placing him at his right hand and exalting him to his preexistent glory (2:34–35). Jesus in his passion was the Suffering Servant of Isaiah 52–53, but in his resurrection he is the exalted risen Lord. In 52:13 we read of "my servant … [who] will be raised and lifted up and highly exalted," and in 53:12 "I will give him a portion among the great." The Suffering Servant becomes great through bearing affliction in order to redeem others.

The Servant's suffering is the polar opposite of the Jewish people who are the ones who "handed him over to be killed" and who "disowned him before Pilate, though he had decided to let him go." The very people for whom the Servant suffered and died are the ones who put him to death. This theme will reverberate throughout the sermons in Acts. The point is, "you killed him, but he died for you. Repent and believe, so you can be saved."

Yet the Israelites went much further in their rejection of Jesus. In 3:14–15, they didn't realize the implications of the One they were putting to death. They didn't just hand over Jesus of Nazareth. They "disowned the Holy and Righteous One and asked that a murderer be released to you." Barabbas, an insurrectionist and brigand, a mass murderer, was released in place not just of the rabbi

Jesus, but the only "Holy and Righteous" person who ever lived on planet Earth. These are titles and not just descriptions and actually look to Jesus as the Holy and Righteous God, who is "the Holy One" (Isa 1:4; 5:19; 10:20) and "the Righteous One" (Ps 129:4; Acts 7:52; 22:14). The one they killed was not just a miracle-working prophet but "the author of life," a concept referring to Jesus as pioneer, champion, and prince (See Acts 5:31; Heb 2:10; 12:2) who has brought life to all who believe. God proved the reality of these astounding claims by raising Jesus from the dead, and the apostles are witnesses who can attest to that fact.

This mini-section concludes with an important stress on the two-sided coin of faith and the name of Jesus (3:16). Peter has already acknowledged the name of Jesus as the source of the healing power (v. 6; see also 2:38), and now he links that power with the faith of both the man and himself. (I believe both are implicit here.) Jesus' name is the cause (causal *epi*) of the miracle, which I would translate "because of faith in the name" rather than "by faith in the name." The power of that name and the presence of faith on our part are interdependent as the source of the power. The strength that flowed into the crippled man came as a result of invoking the name of Jesus, and it was the power of that name as well as the faith of Peter and the man himself that brought that power to bear on the malady.

Note also that Jesus is both the subject ("the faith that comes through him") and the object (faith in him) of our faith. There is a strong emphasis on both sides of the process. Our faith is entirely based on what Christ has done on the cross and is doing in us through the work of the Spirit. There would be no faith apart from that past and present work in us. Still, there is an objective side in that faith as well. The people "see and know" what has happened in his life, and they "saw" the miracle happen. Their faith is anchored in reality and is not irrational. The same is true of us. We haven't seen Jesus perform a miracle, but we have seen and experienced what he has done in our life and in others. We know it is real.

CALL FOR REPENTANCE (3:17–21)

Verses 17–18 provide a transition from who Jesus really is (vv. 13–16) to what their response must be (vv. 19–21). Peter recognizes that they and their leaders (the chief priests and Pharisees) "acted in ignorance," a generous statement in light of their deliberate rejection of Jesus, but Christ himself had said, "Father, forgive them, for they do not know what they are doing" (Luke 23:34). So Peter's words are based on critical precedent. They stood guilty before God because they not only had acted in unbelief but also had killed Jesus (2:23; 3:15), but God was giving them another opportunity to repent.

Moreover, the death of Jesus was not merely based on their ignorant rejection of him (3:18). God was behind it, and it "fulfilled what he had foretold through all the prophets." Jesus as the Suffering Servant had been announced beforehand in Isaiah 52–53, and "all the prophets" looked forward to the suffering of the Christ (as in the messianic psalms; Zech 12:10; Jer 11:19). So the fact that the "Messiah would suffer" was long known by the prophets and was an act of God, who inspired these prophecies. The "what" here is the suffering of the Messiah, and the "how" is the death of Christ on the cross. So the cross was God's will as the means by which sinners can repent and be saved, and it was prophesied long ago by the prophets as God's plan for the salvation of sinful humankind.

The means by which sinners can avail themselves of that salvation is to repent and believe (3:19). These covenant people are actually far from God and need a reversal in the path they have chosen. Peter stressed this also in the Pentecost sermon (2:38), and it will be at the heart of the call to salvation throughout Acts. It means to turn away from sin and, as stated here, to "turn to God." Peter states three results: (1) Their sins will be "wiped out"—their former sins will not just be in limbo but will disappear and cease to exist. Converts begin a brand-new life in Christ. (2) "Times of refreshing" will come from the Lord—this could be linked to the "rest" of Hebrews 3:7–4:13, the new rest in Christ and absence of burden that only the believer enjoys, the new "peace" we have in him. Probably it also includes the work of the Spirit in our lives. (3) He will "send the Messiah, who has been appointed for you"—of course, this has already taken place, but the promise is that we will experience more fully the results of Christ in us as we walk the Christian life. Some see this as the promise of his future return, when "all Israel will be saved" (Rom 11:25–32), indeed a real possibility as part of the meaning here.

In verse 20 Peter centers on the present results of salvation, but he now turns to the future promises (3:21): "Heaven must receive him until the time comes." The risen Lord at the right hand of God must stay there until the second coming. He will not return physically to earth until then. He of course is present here via the Spirit of Christ but will stay with his Father until that time. Peter designates this as the time when God will "restore everything," a difficult concept because it appears nowhere else in the New Testament.

The main question is whether the text is speaking of the present coming of the Spirit and inauguration of God's new kingdom or the future return of Christ. It is often connected with the phrase "times of refreshing" in 3:19 and taken in the former sense. However, the idea of Christ remaining in heaven until that time would not make a great deal of sense if that time had already arrived. So part of what Peter is describing is the restoration of Israel in a two-stage process, with Israel restored first in the church as new Israel and second in the future coming of Christ to bring all Israel to him (Rom 11:25–32).

So there is an "already and not yet" force to this restoration of all things. The time has been inaugurated in the twofold coming of Christ and the Spirit, launching the new messianic community and the new age of salvation. Then there is the consummation and eternal restoration at the return of Christ and the arrival of the "new heaven and new earth" (Rev 21:1).

THE PROMISES OF SCRIPTURE (3:22–26)

Peter anchors his call for repentance in a warning from Moses regarding hearing and heeding the prophetic imperatives, taken from the "prophet like Moses" passage, Deuteronomy 18:15, 19. As Israel entered the promised land they would encounter the false prophets of the Canaanites, and they would need to listen to the prophets of God to counter them. This was often taken as a messianic promise, and Peter is using it in exactly that way. Jesus, the prophet like Moses, has been "raised up" by God, and it is incumbent on the part of the nation to "listen to everything he tells you."

The danger of refusing to listen, which has been the reaction of the people of Israel to this point, is expressed in 3:23 in a quotation from Leviticus 23:29: "Anyone who does not listen to him will be completely cut off from their people." They had been forgiven by Christ (Luke 23:34) and are now being given a second chance, but they are being warned of the seriousness of refusing to repent. This is stated also in Romans 11:17, where Paul declares that they constitute "branches [that] have been broken off" and are no longer part of God's olive tree. The only way to remain members of the covenant people is to repent and begin to obey all Jesus the Mosaic prophet says. Complete destruction (= eternal punishment) awaits those who continue to refuse Christ.

Peter has been citing Scripture from Torah (Pentateuch) passages but wants his hearers to realize the entire Old Testament ("beginning with Samuel, all the prophets") has prophesied these final days in history (3:24). "These days" are the time of restoration discussed in verse 21, and Peter sees this fulfilled in the church age as Christ is proclaimed to the nations and the time moves forward to its culmination in Jesus' return.

The Jewish people have no excuse because they have by far the greatest pedigree of any nation in the world (3:25). It is twofold. They are "heirs of the prophets" and so have been raised with the prophetic promises and warnings. They know the truth and have to be completely aware of their obligations to God, since the prophetic voice was instilled in them by their very ancestors. So what Peter has been saying about the time of restoration could hardly be new or unknown; those truths were part of their national inheritance.

Moreover, Peter has been describing part of "the covenant God made with your fathers." There is direct continuity between the covenants of Abraham, Moses, and David and the new covenant reality of Jesus and the Spirit. To have a part in this new covenant, they must respond to the call to repentance. To anchor this, he quotes the Abrahamic covenant from Genesis 12:3; 22:18, "Through your offspring all peoples on earth will be blessed." This critical part of the covenant was never obeyed by Israel and will become the chief feature of the mission of the church in the new covenant age. This directive to bless the nations was an essential part of the covenant and is also repeated in Genesis 18:18; 26:4; 28:14, repeated to future patriarchs to make certain all Israel understood its obligation. Peter is showing another point of continuity between Israel and the church: the responsibility to evangelize the nations. "Will be blessed" is a divine passive, meaning God intends to bless all the peoples of earth through his covenant people, Israel and new Israel, united through Jesus.

The unifying presence of Jesus is seen in the fact that when "God raised up his servant, he sent him first to you" (3:26). God's true purpose was first to bring his covenant people, Israel, back to him by "turning each of you from your wicked ways." As in Romans 1:16, God intended that salvation come "first to the Jew, then to the Gentile." The entire Jesus story was meant for God's covenant people "first." He was the servant of Yahweh sent to the Jews to bring salvation to them and pour out God's blessings on them. That would have happened except for their rebellion and rejection of Jesus. So now God is giving them another chance to fulfill their destiny. That can only come when they repent, turn from their wicked ways, and place their faith in Jesus.

The new life of the messianic community, the church of Christ, begins just after Pentecost with the pious disciples heading for the evening prayers and sacrifice in the temple. By the gate into Jerusalem, they encounter a poor man who has been lame from birth and making a living by begging for alms (vv. 1-10). Jesus had promised his followers that they would inherit power and see miracles, and that is fulfilled right at the beginning as Peter is led by the Spirit to give the man not money but something far greater, the ability for the first time in his life to walk. As we will see, signs and wonders will be an authenticating gift of the Spirit that will both supplement and authenticate their ministry. The wonder and amazement of the people could be called "pre-evangelism," as many of these will join the new converts of 2:47.

Peter sees the crowd and decides to provide some perspective on the event and evangelize the astonished onlookers. He tells them that this mighty work was not the act of a mere human power but the mighty power of God (3:13-16). A new age has dawned, the age of the Spirit, and as in the time of the patriarchs the power of God is at work anchoring the new salvation-historical reality. This new movement is the work of Jesus, and it is the power of his name that has initiated the new Israel and healed the man. This is one of the deepest **christological** sections in Acts, revealing Jesus as the Holy One, the Righteous One, the Author of Life, and showing that all this comes to pass because of faith in Jesus Messiah.

The only response is to "repent" so that in the present their sins will be forgiven and in the future they will experience the times of refreshment and restoration (vv. 17-21). We now know the rest that God has prepared for us in Christ and the Spirit, and yet in eternity this will be finalized in our (eternal) lives.

In verses 22-26 Peter shows how the entire Old Testament points to Jesus. He is the prophet like Moses who must be heard, lest the people be "cut off from their people" (vv. 22-23), the fulfillment of the Abrahamic covenant, with his followers thereby being "heirs of the prophets and the covenant" (vv. 24-26). True life is found only in him.

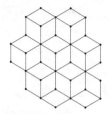

PERSECUTION AND POWER: THE FIRST STAGE
(4:1–22)

Acts 3–5 traces the struggles the church faced as they entered the "participation in his sufferings" (Phil 3:10) brought about by Jewish opposition, and the powerful experience life in Christ and sharing these troubles caused. There is an ABA pattern in chapters 4 and 5, as the persecution intensifies between the Sanhedrin warning of 4:18–22 and the beating of 5:40. The intervening section (4:23–5:16) describes the spiritual growth of the church as it faced its struggles. There are three parts to this first scene. Peter and John are arrested by the temple police by order of the Sanhedrin (vv. 1–4), Peter makes a defense speech (vv. 5–12), and resolution is made, ending in a warning (vv. 13–22). This same order will be followed in chapter 5.

PETER AND JOHN ARE ARRESTED (4:1–4)

Peter's sermon took place in Solomon's portico in the temple, and while he and John were speaking, they were approached by a delegation consisting of some priests, the captain of the temple police, and some Sadducees. The "approach" (*epestēsan*) implies negative intentions to do harm (see 17:5), and they wished to intervene and stop them from evangelizing the people. These were priests assigned to watch over the temple, and the captain of the guard is not just over the temple police (two hundred priests and mostly Levites) but the official in charge of temple affairs and keeping order in the temple. The Sadducees were aristocratic members of the upper priestly families. So they represented temple officials and the Sanhedrin itself. They considered the apostles to be not just a false religion but a threat to order in the temple.

They were especially "disturbed" by Peter's emphasis on Jesus' rising from the dead (see 2:24-36; 3:15). The idea of Jesus as the exalted risen Lord and Messiah (2:36) was repugnant to these Jewish skeptics who had long accused Jesus of blasphemy. They thought his influence would finally be over when he died on the cross, so the idea of his resurrection from the dead was scandalous to them. Then when the apostles laid the blame for it all on them, that made them especially angry. The Jewish leaders will level these same charges against the apostles in 5:28.

So they have only one recourse. They "seize" these two ringleaders and throw them in jail (4:3). Since it is already evening when they catch up with them, they have to jail them "until the next day." The Sanhedrin could not be gathered together for a formal trial that late in the day, so they had to be kept overnight. The entire incident began at three in the afternoon, so the healing miracle and the sermon took about four hours, with the arrest just at dusk. We don't really know where they were kept for the night, perhaps the Sanhedrin prison near the Western Wall.

Luke in an excursus tells us that even more came to faith with this sermon and that the converts numbered 5,000 men (4:4). It is difficult to decide whether this means 5,000 new converts on this occasion or 5,000 total believers at this time. The latter seems more realistic in terms of the likely size of such a crowd in the temple area. It is also a question whether this wording should include women (as in 1:14, 16) or just men. The language seems to reflect the latter, so that would mean many more converts. Either way the numbers in Acts keep growing, from 120 in 1:15 to 3,000 in 2:41 and now to 5,000. As in the time of Jesus, the opposition of the leaders and their persecution of the church cannot stop the new messianic movement from growing mightily.

PETER DEFENDS HIMSELF BEFORE THE SANHEDRIN (4:5-12)

A HEARING IS CALLED (4:5-7)

Three groups constituted the Sanhedrin (4:16), the ruling body of the Jews. First, the "rulers" would be the families of the high priesthood (Annas, Caiaphas, and others; see John 18:13-23): the chief priests and the aristocracy at the top of the priestly class. Many of the most influential will be named in the next verse. Second, the "elders" are the family heads, the wealthy landowners, who constituted the civic leaders of the Jews. Third, the "teachers of the law," or scribes, were the legal experts, in a sense the lawyers who interpreted the law. All of these groups were hostile toward the new messianic movement following Jesus, as they were during Jesus' lifetime. They now call a meeting to decide what to do about this movement that was gaining popularity and threatening the peace of Jerusalem.

The leading family of the priests is named to show the power of those arrayed against the believers. Annas was the patriarch of the family, the first one appointed (AD 6-15) when the Romans took over the high priesthood and turned it into a political power. He questioned Jesus at the Sanhedrin trial (John 18:13, 19-23). His family held control for several decades, for he had five sons, each of whom was named high priest at one time or another (Josephus, *Antiquities* 20.198). Caiaphas, high priest at this time, reigned from AD 18 to 36 and was Annas's son-in-law. "John" was probably Jonathan, successor of Caiaphas as high priest (AD 36-37). We do not know who "Alexander" was, but he was probably another member of Annas's extended family. Luke names them to show how the most powerful members of the Sanhedrin and leadership of the Jews were among the opponents of the Jesus movement, often called "Nazarenes" (Acts 24:5) due to the founder, Jesus of Nazareth.

According to the Talmud, the seats in the assembly hall (4:7) were arranged in a semicircle facing the center and one another (m. Sanhedrin 4:3), and so when Peter and John were brought in, they were placed at that midpoint (Greek: "stood in the middle") in order to be more easily interrogated. The first question was, "By what power or what name did you do this?" The officials undoubtedly knew the content of what Peter had said to the Jews in the temple in chapters 2 and 3, but they want to hear their explanation of the obvious power displayed in healing the lame man. They most likely continued to think that "power" came from Beelzebul, the devil (Luke 11:15), rather than from God. Ancient exorcists would cast out evil spirits by invoking a "name" like an archangel or Solomon, and so they ask for that as well. Peter already answered this in 3:16 ("Jesus' name and the faith that comes through him"), but this gives him another opportunity to testify to this reality.

Peter's Defense (4:8-12)

Jesus had encouraged his followers not to worry about how to respond to their persecutors in the midst of trials because the Spirit would tell them what to say (Luke 21:12-15). That is exactly what comes to pass here as Peter is "filled with the Holy Spirit" and speaks entirely as the Spirit guides him. While the Spirit indwelt him permanently, he is also given a burst of Spirit-filled inspiration for this one occasion. He addresses especially the rulers or leaders of the Sanhedrin as well as the elders gathered there (see 4:5), looking at the Sanhedrin officials themselves. The phrase "led by the Spirit" that we often use is quite viable in light of this.

Peter's legal defense looks first to the ethical quality of the event, the good deed or "act of kindness" (v. 9), and second to the spiritual authority behind it, the "name of Jesus Christ of Nazareth" (v. 10). The Sanhedrin is opposing an act of supreme goodness, a man born lame who can now walk. The passive voice "how he was healed" looks to the person or power that was the agent of the healing and prepares for the answer in the next verse. Peter and John did not do so by their own strength but by the power of Jesus' name. Such an act of kindness would not be done by Satan's authority (see on v. 7) but only by God. The Sanhedrin should be thanking God rather than questioning his representatives.

In light of the good deed displayed in the healing, Peter goes on to answer their question directly in 4:10, beginning with "Know this," giving the Sanhedrin important information intended to change their perspective. This information is not just for the Sanhedrin but for the nation as a whole, "all the people of Israel." Peter is praying for national revival. He prays they might realize that "it is by the name of Jesus Christ of Nazareth" that this good deed took place. The power of the name is once again declared (see 3:16), and it is linked to the one thing they cannot dispute— the former lame man now "stands" before them healed.

This indisputable truth points to the most important fact of all, that it was accomplished by the powerful name of the One "whom you crucified but whom God raised from the dead." The man himself is proof that Jesus must be alive and still retain the power to heal. I agree with those who say that "Jesus Christ" is not a proper name but a title, "Jesus the Messiah," in this situation. Peter is stating that the leaders of Israel crucified their Messiah, but God proved them wrong by raising him from the dead. It is the risen Lord who is alive and has the power to heal this man and reinstate the nation in its relationship to God. This is an indictment of the Sanhedrin itself and a call for them to repent and get right both with God and their Messiah.

In 4:11 Peter turns to the implications of what he has just said. If the resurrection is true, then Jesus is the living "stone" of Psalm 118:22 (also Isa 8:14; 28:16). This flows naturally out of the emphasis on Jesus' death and resurrection in verse 10. Psalm 118 is the last of the Hallel psalms (113–18) and centers on the king's giving "thanksgiving" to God for watching over his people. This is true of the king himself (118:22), rejected by the "builders," the surrounding nations, but reinstated and made the "cornerstone" of the entire edifice of Israel. This was a natural passage for Jesus as royal Messiah to apply to himself (Luke 20:17) and for the church to make a central passage prophesying Jesus' death and resurrection (Rom 9:33; 1 Pet 2:6–7). Here these "builders" are the very leaders who put Christ on the cross and who currently have Peter and John on trial.

The picture is of the builders of the temple rejecting a quarried stone as unsuitable, while the chief architect finds it not only suitable but turns it into the "cornerstone" or anchor of the entire edifice. Some have argued this is the "keystone" or "capstone" of an arch in the temple, but that is not nearly as likely as the cornerstone placed at the corner of the building and bearing the weight of the whole structure. Jesus is seen then as the anchor and core of the "temple of God," the church as the new messianic community. God has vindicated him through the resurrection, and he therefore is the power who healed the lame man.

Not only is Jesus the cornerstone of God's people, he is the only means of salvation that God has provided. Acts 4:12 is a justly famous passage on salvation. It is quite controversial in its claim that "there is no other name under heaven given to mankind by which we must be saved." In our age of tolerance that rejects any idea of absolute truth, the belief that Jesus is the only way is scandalous and widely rejected. Yet this makes perfect sense, for it is impossible for any sinful human being to find salvation on their own or to earn it by anything they do, for behind all human activity is sin. The reason people are offended by this claim is that they have spent their lives rationalizing their sin.

Because of sin there was only one way for God to save humanity from itself, and that was to take that sin on himself. So he sent his Son, Jesus, specifically to die on the cross as the atoning sacrifice. "Salvation is found in no one else" because he was the only perfect, sinless person who could have borne our sins and died in our place. So the declaration that it is not possible to find salvation by any other name makes perfect sense. There is no other way to have sins forgiven, for sin will taint any other attempt to be saved. No one will be able to stand before God and say, "Look, I did my best," for it will be evident that this "best" is not good enough. God provided for every person the one way that could bring salvation, and the only "best" is to accept the way through Jesus by faith. That is by necessity ("must"; Greek: *dei*) the only path to eternal life.

PETER AND JOHN ARE FREED
WITH A WARNING (4:13-22)

Peter and John[1] were now facing the very thing that had led the disciples to flee on the Mount of Olives, the threat of arrest and imprisonment. The difference is that they were now filled with the Spirit, and that gave them a "boldness" or "courage" (*parrēsia*, three times in vv. 13, 29, 31) they hadn't possessed before. This is the polar opposite of the disciples at Jesus' arrest and what followed, when they deserted Jesus entirely out of fear of arrest. This complete turnaround in so short a time "astonished" these officials, probably implying conviction via the Spirit.

As the Spirit spoke to them through the bold apostolic witness, the Sanhedrin had to find a way to reject and play down this witness, and they did so by centering on the background of these Galilean peasant preachers as "unschooled, ordinary men" and not worthy of being taken seriously. This can hardly mean they were illiterate with no education whatsoever, for they both produced letters and were gifted speakers, as Peter has already proved. Rather, they had no rabbinic or scribal training. An equivalent today would be pastors without a seminary education or a

---

1. It is "they" who were bold and spoke up, so John as well as Peter witnessed to the Sanhedrin.

teacher without a master's or PhD degree. Several translations read "untrained amateurs," a good way to put this. This enabled the leaders to dismiss everything they said. They knew "these men had been with Jesus," but that was the extent of their training (sitting at Jesus' feet), and so they could reject Peter and John in the same way they had rejected Jesus.

On the other hand, they could not ignore what they said completely, for "they could see the man who had been healed standing there with them," so "there was nothing they could say" (4:14). They could reject who the disciples were but not what they had done, for the miracle could not be denied since the healed man was standing right there. In their deliberations they were in a quandary, for they would like to have found them guilty, with Jesus as a legal precedent, but the proof of their miracle could not be denied. Ironically, at the same time that they are rendered speechless by reality, they are trying to silence the witness of the apostles. The one has nothing to say; the other can't stop speaking.

As in every trial, the accused (and probably the man who was healed) are dismissed to another room while the Sanhedrin deliberates the case. The high priest would have led the discussion, and he begins by expressing their dilemma. They want to silence the dangerous witness of the apostles, but they cannot deny the "notable sign" these men had performed, a miracle all of Jerusalem is still marveling over. The main issue is what to do with them, what kind of verdict will get these troublemakers out of their hair. During passion week, they had the same difficulty deciding how best to get rid of Jesus, but they were afraid of the crowds who revered Jesus. The same kind of problem still plagues the Sanhedrin, but now it centers on Jesus' followers.

They finally come to a decision (v. 17). They need to "stop this thing [the Jesus movement] from spreading any further." It has already grown from 120 to 3,000 to 5,000 (see on 4:4) people, and the leaders are determined not to allow this to continue. But what to do? They can only think of one thing: "warn them to speak no longer to anyone in this name" of Jesus, the source of the power exemplified in the miracle.

The Sanhedrin sees all the damage caused by the miracle and Peter's sermons after Pentecost and the healing of the lame man. The question is how to stop such things from happening. Due to the fame produced by these events, they cannot judge them guilty and either imprison or kill them. At the same time, they dare not acquit them and let them return and perform more of the same. Their only recourse is a compromise—warn or threaten them against continued witnessing in the temple and its environs. The use of "this name" is unusual but recognizes the central authority of Jesus' name in this new movement (see 3:6, 16; 4:7, 10, 12).

Armed with this resolution, the Sanhedrin delivered the verdict to Peter and John, warning them not "to speak or teach at all in the name of Jesus" (4:18). "Speaking" would refer to sermons in the temple like Peter has given in the last two chapters of Acts. "Teaching" would refer to the rabbinic style Jesus regularly used with both his followers and the crowds. Speaking (*kerygma*) would involve evangelistic presentations of the gospel, and teaching (*didachē*) would be theological expositions and explanations of divine truths to the people. None of this is allowed any longer.

Peter and John answer the Sanhedrin in unison (vv. 19–20), using a justly well-known divine logic as they refuse to obey. This has become the Christian response to ethical dilemmas: "Which is right in God's eyes: to listen to you, or to him? You be the judges!" The Sanhedrin was just as obligated as they were to do God's will in all ethical decisions, and so the challenge was just and right. The believers will repeat this again in 5:29, and it will become the dominant principle behind the persecution of these two chapters: "We must obey God rather than human beings!"

Anyone reared a Jew and cognizant of the covenant relation between God and his people would be able to "judge" the answer to that question. Note the play on words: as they "judge" Peter and John in the council chambers, they first must "judge" the priority of their relation to God and his will. If they judge rightly in the more important area, their walk with God, that will lead them to judge correctly in the lesser decision, the future of the apostles.

The decision is an easy one for the apostles: "As for us, we cannot help speaking about what we have seen" (the resurrection) "and heard" (the teaching of Jesus Christ, the risen Lord). No matter the threat, they must witness about such things, for the eternal salvation of every Jew (and Gentile) depends on their faithfulness to God's mission mandate. The double negative ("we cannot not speak") yields a powerful affirmation of the necessity of their witness ("we *must* speak").

The reaction of the Sanhedrin (4:21–22) shows that they at least are listening to the implications of what the disciples are saying to them. They have decided they cannot condemn and punish them due to their popularity with the people, so all they can do is utter "further threats" about the consequences of their continued witness in the temple and the streets of Jerusalem and then "let them go" free to return to their homes and fellow followers of Jesus. In effect, they acquit them of all charges.

The reason for this surprising reaction is that they cannot decide "how to punish them." They don't want any further ministry of these people in the temple, yet at the same time the miracle did take place, and they have no explanation for it. "All the people were praising God for what had happened," and the officials could not explain it away. To all of Jerusalem, God was behind what had happened. To punish them for performing God's work would have brought the entire city, indeed the whole nation, down on the heads of the Sanhedrin. They are afraid of the reaction of the people if they indict the apostles, and this time there is no Judas to show them a way out of their dilemma.

In 3:1 Luke told us the man had been crippled from birth, and here Luke states further that he at this time was "over forty years old." The people of Jerusalem, then, had seen him begging by the temple gates for nearly forty years and knew him well. In the

Greek the miracle is called "this sign of healing," meaning the healing was a sign-miracle signifying the power of Christ's name. Not even the Sanhedrin for all its authority in Israel dared go up against such a "sign" of God's blessing and power. So they could only release them and hope the warnings would suffice to silence them. Needless to say, they did not do so.

———

We now enter a period of growth in both number of converts and severity of opposition. The leaders more and more perceive the movement as a threat, especially since they thought they had stamped out this false sect be crucifying its founder and now realize it is bigger than ever. So they arrest the two major spokesmen, Peter and John, thinking that this might be sufficient (vv. 1–4).

Peter in his defense (vv. 5–12) claims the man was healed not by him but by "the power of the name" of Jesus the Messiah, who like the stone of Psalm 118:22 was rejected but was made by God the cornerstone of his temple, the people of God. Peter's final point is as important today as it was then, that there is "no other name under heaven … by which we *must* be saved" (4:12). Jesus the perfect God-man was the only one who in dying could bear our sins and give us eternal life. He alone, not the leaders of the Jews or faithfulness to Torah, could produce true salvation.

The Sanhedrin is in a quandary, cowed by the apostles' popularity yet wanting desperately to stifle the truths they are propounding daily in the temple (exactly the situation it earlier faced with Jesus). All they can think to do (vv. 15–18) is to warn them severely of the consequences if they don't stop witnessing in the temple and environs of Jerusalem. So they acquit Peter and John and send them home with a warning to be silent. Peter's response is another of the truly critical statements in Acts: "Which is right in God's eyes: to listen to you, or to him? You be the judges!" That means disobedience to the demands of the Sanhedrin.

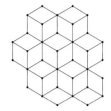

COMMUNITY LIFE OF
JEWISH CHRISTIANITY
(4:23–5:16)

There is an ABAB pattern to the structure of these chapters, moving from 2:42-47 (A = the life of the messianic community) to 3:1-4:22 (B = miracle and first persecution) to 4:23-5:16 (A = a lengthier description of community life) to 5:17-42 (B = the second great persecution). There is also intensification in the second pair, as Luke provides a great deal more detail about the life of the community in 4:23-5:16, and the persecution increases from warning in 4:17-21 to flogging in 5:40. In all of this, as the persecution increases, so does the joy, as the apostles rejoice that they have been "counted worthy of suffering disgrace for the Name" (5:41). The "participation in his sufferings" (Phil 3:10) is quite evident throughout.

There are three sections to this portrait of the Jerusalem community: (1) After the persecution of 4:1-4, 18-21, there was united prayer on the part of the believers for even greater boldness in light of the forces arrayed against them (4:23-31). (2) An even greater spirit of giving took place, exemplified especially by Barnabas (4:32-37); but in stark contrast, some like Ananias and Sapphira deceived the community and paid for their greed with their lives (5:1-11). (3) Signs and wonders characterized the church, and it continued to grow (5:12-16).

THE CHURCH PRAYS FOR GREATER
BOLDNESS (4:23-31)

The Jewish officials have reinstated their opposition to the new community as an extension of their rejection of Jesus. They have been ordered by the Jewish hierarchy to remain silent regarding Jesus, and earlier, when they fled the scene at the arrest of Jesus, they would have complied. They knew they did not possess the strength to obey God rather than the leaders (4:19), and this led them not to give in but to pray for strength.

THE OCCASION: COMMUNITY PRAYER (4:23-24A)

So after Peter and John were released from their captivity, they returned "to their own people," the saints of Jerusalem. We don't know whether this was a group gathered in a central meeting place, perhaps the upper room of Acts 1:13-15 or to Solomon's portico in the temple, where the saints often met (see 3:11). Some would restrict this group to the Twelve, but the context implies a large group of believers. The church has become a united family and here prays together in one accord. The adage is true once more that when the church faces a crisis, it responds by falling on its knees. They raise their voices "together" or in one accord (see 1:14; 2:46), recognizing that they cannot win the victory in their own strength. The early church was not like all too many churches today, where only the older believers are willing to come for corporate prayer. They longed to pray together and rejoiced at the privilege of doing so.

PLEA FOR BOLDNESS AND POWER (4:24B-30)

God alone is "Sovereign Lord" (*despota*, indicating absolute mastery) over this threat, and they begin by turning everything over to him. He is in complete charge not just of the saints but of the Jewish authorities as well. His sovereign power is proved by the fact that he "made the heavens and the earth and the sea, and everything in them." As Creator God, everyone and everything is answerable to him, an echo of Psalm 146:6, where it is part of a thanksgiving to God for his watchful care over the righteous. The God who has created every single thing and person in this world can be counted on to take care of his people in their time of need.

This all-powerful Creator can be trusted to intervene when his people are threatened. To support this they turn to Psalm 2:1–2, as spoken by David[1] but inspired by the Holy Spirit. The emphasis is on the fact that God has spoken and promised to watch over his people in spite of all the nations can do. Psalm 2 was considered a messianic psalm, and the disciples quote it here of the foolishness of the Jewish hierarchy joining the nations and turning against the messianic community, the church. When originally written, this referred to the Davidic king and then the Messiah, whom God would protect in light of the opposition of the surrounding nations. In this context, the current leadership of the Jews is part of the nations opposing God's people.

The psalmist decries the arrogant "rage" (implied in the verb) as the nations (pagan in the psalm, Jewish here) form their plots against God's anointed. Such plots are "vain," or empty and useless, because God is in charge, not them. Their meager attempts to thwart his will have no value and will in the end come to naught.

Two groups of leaders take central stage, the "kings of the earth" and its "rulers," referring in general to all the leaders of the nations and here especially of the Jews. In the context, the primary "plot" and hostile actions "against the Lord and against his anointed one" are pointed at God and his Messiah along with his messianic community, specifically in the actions of the Sanhedrin here. The "anointed one" in the psalm and here is the Messiah, as both the Hebrew and Greek (*māshiach, christos*) refer to God's "anointed one" or Messiah. Since God the Creator is in control, all attempts to thwart his will are useless and doomed to failure.

---

1. David is never named as the author of this psalm, but the psalms as a whole are often called "the psalms of David," and it is meant in this general sense here.

Continuing their prayer, the believers now explain the true purpose of quoting Psalm 2: to illustrate the opposition of Herod, Pilate, and the Jewish authorities in their opposition to Jesus and the new community, and to show it has all been part of God's predetermined plan. Herod Antipas is named here because his interrogation of Jesus is used in Luke 23:6-12 as part of the trial that led to the cross. Pilate is listed because he knew Jesus was innocent and yet for political expediency turned Jesus over to be killed (Luke 23:13-25). The Gentiles are the Romans who actually carried out the crucifixion. The "people of Israel" are the crowds who demanded that Jesus be crucified (Luke 23:18-23). All were part of the nations who raged and "conspire[d] against your holy servant Jesus, whom you anointed" (to become Messiah, Acts 4:25). "Holy servant" likely stresses that Jesus is Isaiah's Suffering Servant of Yahweh (Isa 52-53).

As was also true of the betrayal by Judas and his replacement by Matthias (1:16, 21-22), this was all part of God's predetermined plan of salvation: "What your power and will had decided beforehand should happen" (4:28). In other words, the Sanhedrin persecution was not just an act of rebellion against God and his people, it was part of God's will, set in motion by his power, first enacted in the death of Jesus and then in the opposition of the Sanhedrin here. The rejection of both Jesus and of his followers was not mere chance but "decided beforehand" by God and prophesied in his Scriptures. This is why all the efforts on the Jewish leaders are "in vain" or empty-headed (Ps 2:2 in 4:25). God is completely in charge, and all his enemies in the end are nothing, of no consequence.

A threefold prayer request concludes the corporate petition here. In light of their severe treatment by the Sanhedrin and God's sovereignty, they ask him to "consider their threats and enable your servants to speak your word with great boldness." They are "slaves" or "bond servants" (*douloi*; NIV: "servants") of God the "Sovereign Lord" (v. 24) in the here and "now." Jesus is the "holy servant" of Yahweh (*pais*, v. 27), and they form his messianic community. In light of this they first of all ask God to be aware of the "threats" made against them that very same day (vv. 17, 21) and to act on their behalf. The nefarious plots of the Gentiles and Jews against Jesus were defeated in the cross and resurrection, and now they are asking God to intervene in a similar way with his people as they are being persecuted.

When God intervenes, they ask for a great influx of Spirit-empowered boldness as they interact with their enemies. Jesus was fearless as he stood against all the world's powers—the Romans, the Sanhedrin, Herod, and Pilate—and proclaimed God's message of salvation and judgment. The believers want that same courage and power in responding as well.

Third, they beseech God to "stretch out your hand" or "act precipitously and with power" to heal as he did in 3:1–10 and in addition to "perform [other] signs and wonders" to authenticate the message of the apostles. The outstretched hand of God is always a sign of his divine power exercised on behalf of his people, often in judgment (Isa 5:25; Zeph 1:4). All mighty deeds take place as God determines, and in Acts they prove that his hand undergirds the gospel message. The miracles of Acts are to a large degree God answering this prayer. Most of Jesus' miracles are replicated in Acts, and the last part of this prayer recognizes that these wondrous works come "through the name of your holy servant Jesus" (v. 29). The power of the name (3:6, 16; 4:10, 12) is the bedrock of this section of the book, as he intervenes to reproduce his miracles in the ministry of the church.

GOD'S RESPONSE TO THE PRAYER (4:31)

God sends three powerful signs of his favor in response:

1. "The place where they were meeting was shaken": This is a reference to the giving of the law at Mount Sinai, which trembled violently when Yahweh descended on it (see Ps 18:7; Isa 2:19; 6:4). It also recalls the earthquake at the cross, which caused the temple veil to tear in two (Matt 27:51).

Here God descends on the place of prayer to confirm his acceptance of their prayers.

2. "They were all filled with the Holy Spirit": Like Peter in 4:8, they exhibit a reenactment of the Pentecost experience (2:4) to show that God indeed is filling their preaching and witness with boldness and power. This too carries through the rest of Acts as the divine truths are proclaimed with wondrous results through the empowering presence of the Spirit.

3. They "spoke the Word of God boldly": This flows out of the second sign, referring to Spirit-filled proclamation of the gospel. The leaders have warned them not to witness to Jesus, but the Spirit has reversed that and made them all the more bold to do just that. Bold preaching is every bit as needed today as it was in the early church. Too many preachers water down the message and produce pop psychology more than the deep things of God. We don't need to hear how to feel better about ourselves; we need to hear how to get right with God and experience him daily in our lives.

A SPIRIT OF GIVING IS CONTRASTED WITH A SPIRIT OF GREED (4:32–5:11)

Flowing out of the Spirit-led blessings of 4:31, Luke once again (as in 2:42–47) provides a powerful summary of life in the Jerusalem community (4:32–37), characterized by a powerful witness and incredible sacrifice in sharing with the needy.

COMMUNITY LIFE (4:32–37)

Drawn together by persecution and pressure from the Jewish leaders, the saints come together, "one in heart and mind." We must remember that this is a young church and has exploded in the number of new believers. It is remarkable that there could be this level of unity, given the diversity of new converts. This is sign of the Spirit's presence and God's pleasure in these dedicated people. The phrase "one in heart and mind" means they had a united spirit and a common way of thinking.

There are two primary descriptions of these saints in these two verses, and the rest of the paragraph builds on these descriptions as they relate to the power of their works (holding everything in common) and their words (their witness about the Risen One). Both begin with greatness (4:33), the "great power" with which they bore witness and the "great grace" (NIV: "God's grace was so powerfully at work") with which they shared their possessions.

With regard to their works, no one thought of their possessions as peculiarly their own but instead "shared everything they had." "Shared everything" is *apanta koina*, "everything in common," another term that connotes fellowship or partnership. They didn't just have a common theology or the same ethical system. Even their possessions were meant to be held in common and existed to meet the needs of others. Many have theorized that this was an early form of communism, but that is not true. Sharing possessions was not a requirement but was voluntary, and members were allowed to keep their wealth (like Zacchaeus in Luke 19). Instead, there was a sharing of possessions whenever there was a financial need, as we will see in verses 34–35 below.

The believers in their prayer meeting prayed for boldness and power (4:29–30) as they conducted their Spirit-driven mission to the lost, and here we see that they received exactly that from God, as they witnessed to the resurrection reality "with great power." They are empowered by the Spirit and guided by him as they go out in mission. This is a power in word and deed, in proclaiming Christ and in seeing that witness undergirded with signs and wonders. The new age of salvation began with the resurrection of Jesus and the coming of the Spirit, and it is typified by the powerful witness of these new converts.

The experience of God's "great grace" in their spiritual lives led to gracious sharing in their earthly lives. Persecution from the Jews affected them in multiple ways, not the least of which was economic. Many believers lost jobs or homes as they were rejected by people around them and placed under the ban of total ostracism from society (John 9:22, 34). The idea of caring for the "needy" goes back to Deuteronomy 15:4, which promises that the Israelites when they entered the promised land would have "no poor [needy] people among you," for God would bless them. This purpose to have no needy persons among them is an incredible goal and should be emphasized in all congregational care programs today.

The way this was achieved is remarkable. Many of the saints were moderately wealthy and owned homes or property. When there were serious needs in the church, they would sell their home or land and lay the proceeds "at the apostles' feet," which was then "distributed to anyone who had need." There has been a recent movement to do just this, to sell one's home for the sake of ministry and live communally together.[2] There could be no better illustration of the depth of unity and fellowship between believers than this level of caring and sharing.

The passage implies that this was a frequent practice and took place when great needs arose, with serious poverty being one of them. There will be two examples of this, first Barnabas in verses 36–37 and second the instance of the widows in 6:1–7. The apostles, already extremely busy in their preaching ministry and their general leadership over the church, took this on as well. As we will see in 6:1–7, this only lasted for a short time because of the pressure on them. Still, all the members of the community were involved in this activity, and the people of God became a family as they shared so thoroughly in each other's lives and needs.

There were undoubtedly many examples Luke could have used for this level of fellowship (see v. 32), but he chooses Barnabas

---

2. Google "Shane Claiborne" and read of his "intentional movement" and the "New Monasticism" he and others have founded.

because of his significant leadership position in the church. He
will be mentioned twenty-three times in Acts, both for his ministry in Jerusalem (9:27; 11:22, 25, 30; 12:25) and especially as the original leader of the mission team with Paul (13:2, 42–43, 46, 50). As a
Levite he was not supposed to own property (Num 18:20; Deut 10:9),
but that rule had been relaxed by the first century. He grew up in
Cyprus, and that was likely the reason the first missionary journey
was to that island off the coast of modern-day Turkey. His nick-
name, Barnabas, Luke tells us, means "son of encouragement [or
"exhortation": paraklēsis]," an apt description for one who was used
of the Spirit both to exhort and encourage others.

He becomes a model for the new community when he sells
some land and gives the profits over to the apostles to use as they
see fit. He proves that the leadership participated in the communal life and were models of the new congregational care that
was bringing the church together. Many have said this didn't last
because it wasn't practical, but there is no evidence for that conclusion. In fact, the rest of the New Testament shows that this
idea of meeting the needs of the poor was stressed throughout
the first century.

Ananias and Sapphira (5:1–11)

Not everyone was faithful and caring for others. Like Barnabas, a
couple sells a piece of property, but instead of giving the proceeds
to the apostles they hold a portion back out of greed. Then they lie,
deceiving the apostles about how much they received for the land.
Their names should have led them in a far different direction, for
Ananias means "Yahweh is gracious," and Sapphira means "beautiful." They are the polar opposite of their names.

Ananias and his wife act in concert when they deceive the
apostles and keep back some of the proceeds for themselves,
giving only a portion to them. As far as the apostles and others
knew, Ananias and Sapphira were acting faithfully in accord with
verses 34–35 and thereby keeping his promise to God. This was

not to be the case. In actual fact, they were defrauding both God and church.

We don't know how or when the deception was discovered. Peter could have received supernatural knowledge or someone discovered how much Ananias had actually received. Whichever, he is acting as a prophet and asks six questions here:

1. "How is it that Satan has so filled your heart?" This shows that it is an issue of spiritual warfare as well as ethical sin. Satan is once more trying to "sift" someone "like wheat" (Luke 22:31).

2. Why have you "lied to the Holy Spirit"? This is the reverse of 4:31, where the saints were "filled with the Holy Spirit." Their hearts are filled with Satan, and they lied to the Spirit. Some interpreters go so far as to say they were not true believers, but that is not connoted in the language here. More likely this connoted apostasy (blasphemy against the Spirit, Mark 3:29). When Ananias lied to the apostles, he lied to the Spirit, who was present in the apostles.

3. Why did you "keep for yourselves some of the money"? Their avarice led them to steal a portion of the money promised to God and his church and hide it away for their personal use.

4. "Didn't it belong to you before it was sold?" They owned it and controlled it. They didn't have to sell it if they wanted it for themselves.

5. "Wasn't the money at your disposal?" Both the act of selling it and the disposal of the profit was entirely up to them. What led them to pledge it and then keep it back? If they wanted to use a portion for themselves, all they had to do was not promise all the proceeds to the needy among them. Theirs was not only a tragic decision but a foolish one.

6. "What made you think of doing such a thing?" (Literally: "What got into your heart?") Theirs was a deliberate sin, what the Old Testament calls "sin with a high hand." This

is another reason the text hints at apostasy on their part. They committed a deliberate act of fraud against God and his people (they "have not lied just to human beings but to God"), and it would have been so easy to do it otherwise. They undoubtedly wanted to get credit and the plaudits of giving so much to the church and at the same time to keep back a large amount and spend it on themselves. Thus they committed a double sin, and they did so on purpose.

This scene is built on trial oracles of the prophets (Isa 3:13–26; Hos 4:1–19). The six questions form the indictment, and the sentence is carried out immediately. Peter, filled with supernatural power, becomes God's avenging angel. At the very moment he finishes the litany of charges against Ananias, the man "fell down and died." This is a shocking development to all of us who read it, and it is no wonder that "great fear seized all who heard what had happened" (5:5). The man's death is instantaneous, not a natural demise. Attempts to see this as a mere heart attack or a stroke are wrongheaded. God snuffed out his life, and the assembled believers are filled with absolute terror (*phobos* here means fear, not awe), probably taking this judgment as a warning to them as well.

Ananias died swiftly and suddenly, and he is buried the same way. It was expected that people would be buried the same day since Jews do not embalm their dead, but to do this so quickly is highly unusual. Ananias had mocked God via his deceit, and so neither his life nor his body was to remain on earth a second longer. The disposal of him came via "young men," probably indicating a hasty burial by means of youth who were present and acted in place of professional mourners. Its haste is indicated by four consecutive verbs. The young men "came forward, wrapped up his body" quickly in a shroud, "and carried him out and buried him." Boom, boom, boom, boom, and he is gone. If he had owned a tomb, he would have been placed there; otherwise, he was quickly placed under the ground without ceremony or grief. Family members were apparently not present, and even his wife was unaware of his death.

We don't know where Sapphira was during the trial and conviction of her husband, but she arrives back three hours later, unaware of what has transpired. She as a result falls into the same trap, trying to cover up her fraud and pretend they had given the full amount they had promised to the church. Since her lie is the same, her judgment is the same.

It only takes two questions to indict her. The first question ("Is this the price?"), designed to see whether she participated in her husband's deceit or was innocent, shows she was complicit in her husband's price gouging. Her answer shows she was well aware and as guilty as he. There were two amounts involved—the money they received for the sale and the amount they gave to the church. The discrepancy between those two was the amount they stole from God and the church.

The second question brings out divine judgment: "How could you conspire [with Ananias] to test the Spirit of the Lord?" The Holy Spirit is divine and omniscient. How could they possibly think that he would be unaware of everything they had done? Of course he would know of their conspiracy to lie and keep some of the money for themselves. In reality they were testing the Spirit in the same way the wilderness tested God with their grumbling and hardness of heart during their forty year sojourn (Exod 17:2; Deut 6:16; Ps 78:17–19). That generation lost their lives and never entered the promised land. In the same way her life is forfeit for what she has done.

Then comes the dreaded sentence, stated most gruesomely, "The feet of the men who buried your husband are at the door, and they will carry you out also." At that moment the Lord takes her life as well, and she "immediately" (not translated in the NIV) collapses and dies at Peter's feet. The very same burial detail buries her with her husband. She joined him in trying to deceive God and his followers, and now she joins him in death. They are buried in the same grave.

In verse 5 terror grips the people who were present at the death of Ananias. Now with both partners struck dead by a powerful act of divine judgment, that level of fear is magnified, and "the whole church" (ekklēsia for the first time in Acts) as well as any outsiders who hear about it tremble with abject terror at this demonstration of the wrath of God directed at sin among his people. Those people who rationalize their sin today by thinking that God majors in mercy and forgiveness need to read this episode carefully. God is a loving Father, but he is also Judge over his creation and punishes sin. He does forgive, but only when honest repentance has taken place.

This is a difficult passage. No one will ever preach this at missionary pledge time! However, it reminds God's people to take seriously their promises to God and demonstrates vividly how responsible we all are to obey the Lord in everything we do. There is great reward for those who are faithful (Barnabas) and great punishment for those who are not (Ananias and Sapphira). He expects his people to surrender all to him and follow the guidance of the Spirit. Being a Christian is not a halfway thing. He demands our all.

THE APOSTLES HEAL AND THE
CHURCH GROWS (5:12–16)

This is the third summary paragraph describing the life of the new messianic community in these early years (with 2:42–47; 4:32–37), and as before we see how God is blessing his people as they remain faithful to him. The healing of the lame man in 3:1–10 is not the only miracle they experience but instead the only one Luke has written about thus far. We learn here that there were "many signs and wonders among the people," in keeping with their prayer of 4:30. In fact, as we will see in 5:15–16, such miracles seem to have been a fairly regular experience. It is hard to know for certain whether only apostles were allowed to perform them (literally,

v. 12 says the signs and wonders were "at the hands of the apostles"), but that is likely the case. Moreover, the "among the people" probably refers to the Jewish people of Jerusalem and means they were public events meant to demonstrate God's blessing and pleasure in the new Christ followers.

As we have seen throughout these chapters, the regular public meetings of the believers took place in Solomon's portico on the east side of the temple complex (see 2:46; 3:1, 11). Again, they were Jewish Christians and considered themselves the messianic sect among the Jews, joining the Pharisees, Sadducees, and Essenes. The Zealots did not become an official movement until the late 50s and 60s. The Christians called themselves "the Way" (from Isa 40:3, "Prepare the way for the LORD"; see Acts 19:9, 23; 22:4; 24:14, 22), and so it was natural for them to go regularly to the temple not just to evangelize other Jews but also to pray and worship together as Christians.

Interestingly, Luke tells us here that "no one else dared join them" (5:13), with *loipon* ("no one else" or "the rest") referring not to other believers or the Twelve but to the Jewish people of Jerusalem. Their fear of associating with the believers was possibly due to the opposition by the Sanhedrin and Jewish officials or to the "great fear" caused by God's wrath at the death of Ananias and Sapphira. I think it could be a combination of both, but the meaning is clear. The people of Jerusalem were afraid to be with the Christians as they worshipped.

Still, the general populace of Jerusalem held the saints in high regard and refused to join their leadership in opposition, much as they did with Jesus until the trial. This was certainly due to the signs and wonders they saw regularly, but it is also the result of the preaching of Peter and others. The people recognized truth when they heard it and were greatly impressed by the saints and their gospel message.

As a result, "more and more men and women" were converted to Christ and "were added to their number" (5:14). Their fear of joining too closely to the followers of Christ did not stop them from listening to their message, and huge numbers came to faith in him. This is the fourth message detailing the church growth following Pentecost—from 120 (1:15) to 3,000 (2:41) to 5,000 (4:4) to an indistinct "more and more," indicating a stupendous evangelistic explosion of souls.

Jerusalem had never seen anything like these days, with the powerful preaching and the incredible miracles taking place one on top of the other. Note the progression of the attitudes of the Jerusalem populace (5:13-14), moving from reluctance to be seen with the Christians, to favor and high regard for them, to the conversion of many to Christ, and now to placing their sick on cots in the street, believing that even the shadow of Peter (and possibly of the other apostles) had the power to heal them.

Many have said these had to be believers, for unbelievers would never want to identify with the Christians. Yet this was not true of Jesus. Most who came to him were not followers, but they knew he had the power to heal, and so they came to him. That was the case here as well. One of the recurring themes of Acts is the church reliving and reenacting the life and ministry of Jesus. That is certainly the case here. It is the "result" of everything said in verses 12-14 regarding the growing favor the saints were having with the Jewish people and the growing numbers coming into the church. As we saw in the prayer of 4:29-30, there was a close connection between the power of the spoken word and the powerful signs and wonders that undergirded it.

The Jerusalem people had experienced both, and while many had not yet come to faith in Christ, they did come to believe in the Spirit-given power to perform miracles. They knew that Peter and the other apostles regularly came to the temple, and so they would lay their sick on mats like the beggars used and set them in the streets along the route to the temple. This was probably not because they thought Peter would refuse a direct approach. There were probably so many coming to him that they weren't sure they could get to him. They were so certain of his power that they believed they didn't need conscious attention on his part. Just his shadow as he passed by on the street to the temple, they believed, would be enough. Jesus in Luke 8:43–44 healed a woman who simply touched the tassels on his robe, and pieces of Paul's handkerchiefs or aprons heal people in Acts 19:12. So this is not as farfetched as we might think. Nor is it magic, for every healing produced this way was an act of God, not of Peter.

The fame of the apostles grew, and again as with Jesus the news quickly went to towns outside of Jerusalem. Most likely, all of Judea and possibly Galilee were enamored of the miraculous powers taking place there, and people flocked from all over. It is hard to know if they brought their sick to Jerusalem or whether they clamored for the apostles to come to them in the same way Jesus and the Twelve would go on mission trips from town to town. Probably both took place. Perhaps the mission of Acts 1:8 that was to start with Jerusalem and "all Judea" began at this point.

Both the sick and those "tormented by impure spirits" were healed. This is the first mention of unclean spirits (unclean due to their wickedness) in Acts, but we will see them often. The main thing is that again the apostles participate in Jesus' power, and thus "all" of those brought to the apostles were healed. Only God could do that.

———

This is an important section, for the vignettes assembled here describe life in the early years of the church during the Jewish Christian period. It was a time of incredible unity and caring for one another, exhibiting the new life under the Spirit. Yet it also shows the intensifying opposition they are enduring, very much a reliving of the life of Jesus under the hatred of the Jewish leaders.

When Peter and John are released, they return rejoicing to their fellow believers and participate in a prayer meeting. As they reflect

on the world-changing events of the cross and the recent persecution, they realize and rejoice in the knowledge that God is aware
of everything they have gone through and in fact planned it all
beforehand in order to use it to proclaim the good news to a lost
world. They are thrilled with his sovereign care over every detail.
As in Psalm 2, the nations' rage is part of his will, and their opposition simply furthers his plan (4:24–28). Their prayer is for greater
boldness in their proclamation of the gospel and greater power in
authenticating their witness by signs and wonders (vv. 29–30). In a
wonderful confirmation of God's pleasure, at the end of the prayer
time God shakes the very room where they are praying and pours
into them a fresh influx of the Spirit (v. 31).

Three special characteristics described this period of intense
spiritual growth: a unity that bound them together, great grace that
led them to consider everything they had to be common property,
and a bold power that gave special force to their witness (vv. 32–35).
This was exemplified well by Barnabas, who sold property and
gave the proceeds to the church to help the needy. Luke wants his
readers to realize that this age of caring and sharing is not over,
and that the people of God in our day can echo this spirit of giving.

It was wrongly exemplified in Ananias and Sapphira (5:1–11),
who committed the unbelievably foolish act of lying to God and
the church and thinking they could get away with it. How could
anyone pledge a great gift to the Lord and think God wouldn't know
when they held a large amount out to buy things for themselves?
This is a critical lesson for us all. Obeying God is the watchword for
our lives. We must know that the Lord is aware of *all* we do, and
we will answer for each and every thing by either being rewarded
or punished. This reminds us that God expects his children to be
faithful to him.

The description of life during this exciting period (vv. 12–16)
continues those of 2:42–47 and 4:32–37 and provides a valuable
model for our churches today. There were two primary aspects:
(1) the evangelistic fervor as the gospel message was proclaimed

with power, with amazing numbers becoming believers and joining the church; and (2) the numerous "signs and wonders" that
God performed through the apostles, authenticating that message with power. It is a thrilling picture, with the main streets of
Jerusalem on the way up to the temple lined with cots and sleeping mats holding the sick, with people trusting that even the shad-
ows of the apostles could heal, and actually seeing that happen.
Those were incredible times, but Luke intends that equally exciting scenes occur in every age, as the Spirit works in all of us.

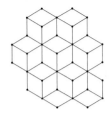

PERSECUTION: THE SECOND STAGE
(5:17–42)

The church has begun its God-sent mission to Jerusalem and
Judea, and as with Jesus the Jewish leaders have utterly opposed
it while the people have been open and receptive to the good news,
with the church growing from 3,000 just after Pentecost (2:41) to
5,000 a short time later (4:4) and now possibly a few thousand
more. As the church has grown, so has the hostility of the leaders.
The first arrest and trial led to a warning to quit witnessing in the
temple and city (4:18), and this time the persecution will be more
severe. Both periods of opposition have followed periods of success and growth, and the purpose both times has been to extin-
guish the flame of the Christian movement. The key is the same in
both instances—the courageous determination to "obey God rather
than human beings" whenever the orders of the officials conflict
with the Lord's will (4:19 = 5:29). The testimony of the church to
Jesus cannot and will not be silenced.

THE APOSTLES ARE ARRESTED
AND DELIVERED (5:17-20)

In 4:7 only Peter and John were seized, but now it is all of the
Twelve. The leadership of the followers of Jesus must be removed

so that this troublesome movement is stopped once for all. The popularity of the Jesus movement has just enjoyed an unparalleled period of growth, as we have seen in the last three chapters, and now it posed a real threat to the Jewish leadership. Here the apostles incur the wrath (and jealousy) of "the high priest and all his associates," undoubtedly the chief priests and Sadducees (see 4:1). During the period of Jesus' ministry in Galilee, it was the Pharisees who had the greater influence, but in Jerusalem the Sadducees are the party of power since they control the Sanhedrin and are wealthy aristocrats. We aren't told the focus of their envy, but probably with the ever-expanding numbers joining the church, their power base is threatened.

Their solution is the same as it was in chapter 4—arrest the apostles and put them in jail. It is called "the public jail," the basic prison used for miscreants in the dungeons of Herod's palace. This would give the apostles greater visibility as a public menace. They hope thereby to frighten the general followers by removing their leadership and labeling them criminals.

Most likely the very first night of the arrest, God intervenes and sends an angel, who "opened the doors of the jail" and brought all twelve apostles out to freedom. There is a message in this to the believers, telling them God is watching over and protecting them, and at the same time a message to the Jews, that they are acting against his will. There are three miraculous releases from prison (with 12:5–11 and 16:25–26), but James is executed by Herod while in prison (12:2), and Paul spends two years in prison in Caesarea (23:47) and two more in Rome at the end of this book.

So God is sovereign in when he frees his people as well as when he does not do so. The series of trials Paul lists in 2 Corinthians 11:23–27 is beyond belief. God decides when to intervene and when not to do so, and we must surrender to his will. The only thing we can know and trust is that "in all things God works for the good of those who love him, who have been called according to his purpose" (Rom 8:28). That must be sufficient for us as we pass through hard times.

On this occasion the angel frees the apostles and sends them out to witness for him, the very thing the authorities will not allow. They are not to flee Jerusalem because of the danger of staying there. In fact, they are to remain and "stand in the temple courts," the very place they had been ministering all this time. They would be easy to find by the authorities. They were to begin once more to preach and witness to the people, the very thing the Sanhedrin had told them not to do. They were to "tell the people all about this new life," the very subject about which the authorities did not want the people, the Jews of Jerusalem, to hear. The Lord and the apostles were hardly worried about the Sanhedrin and what they might do. The "new life" of salvation and the new age of the Spirit were to be promulgated everywhere.

THE APOSTLES WITNESS AND THE AUTHORITIES FAIL (5:21-26)

The apostles are obedient and willingly place themselves in danger, conducting another very successful time of teaching in the temple courts. They did not hesitate in the least. Freed during the night, they didn't even return to their beds for deserved rest but went immediately and began to teach at dawn, likely just a couple hours after being released.

In an ironic twist, at the very time the apostles are arriving in the temple courts, the Sanhedrin is gathering back in the courtrooms of their hall of justice (just a short distance from the jail itself) to make their judgment against the Christian leaders. To make it completely official, they have made sure "the full assembly of the elders of Israel," another name for the Sanhedrin, was present. As the officials were gathering, the very thing they wanted to prevent was taking place in the temple courts by Christian leaders they thought to be safely in jail.

When the full complement of the supreme court of the Jews was there, they sent officials from the temple police to the jail to bring the apostles for judgment. They were completely unaware that the apostles had been liberated and had escaped.

Imagine the shock when they saw the empty cells and no signs of jailbreak (5:22). We don't know why no one (guards, etc.) had noticed they were gone. From the next verse we discover that the guards were posted and the doors locked. The liberation by the angel must have been a similar scene to 12:10–11, with miracle after miracle taking place. This likely means also that their release from prison had only taken place an hour or two earlier. All the police could do was return to the council and tell them the apostles were gone.

Their report (5:23) tells us quite a lot. So far as they knew, the cell doors had been securely locked the entire night, so when the apostles left their cell, the door remained locked. Moreover, the guards were still posted and thought the prisoners safely inside the cells. We cannot know how the apostles got by them, but as in 12:10 they likely just walked by the guards, who were kept from noticing by the Lord (compare Luke 24:16). The captain of the temple police and the chief priests felt some fear, "wondering what this might lead to," either in terms of the Christian movement or their being held accountable for escaped prisoners. The latter might well be the case, for in the Roman world (and probably also in the Jewish world) there was always punishment in store for guards who allowed prisoners to get away.

At that moment another official entered from the temple precincts, reporting that the former prisoners were somehow back "standing in the temple courts teaching the people" (5:25). As we will see in verse 29, they are obeying "God rather than human beings." The angel told them to do just that, and the officials wanted to lock them away to keep them from doing just that.

All the Sanhedrin could do was send the temple police back to rearrest these Christian leaders (5:26). This time the captain accompanied his troops in order to have maximum authority present for the confrontation. It all took place with minimum fuss, and the apostles returned to the judgment hall without causing any trouble. Luke tells us they made certain that "they did not use force, because they feared that the people would stone them." Stoning was the basic method of execution in the Torah for serious offenses like blasphemy (Lev 24:14–23, the charge against Jesus) or sorcery (Lev 20:27). Obviously, that is not the connotation here, for it would be an unbelievably harsh reaction to a very unpopular action by the temple officials. Luke probably means just that the people would throw stones to show their displeasure rather than execute the leaders. This shows how extremely favorable the general populace felt regarding the Christian leaders, as already indicated in verse 13, certainly due to the many public miracles they had performed.

THE APOSTLES APPEAR BEFORE
THE SANHEDRIN (5:27–32)

Soon after the apostles are brought back, they are forced to hear the charges against them in the courtroom of the Sanhedrin. The council is led by the high priest, so he presents these charges. There are two. First, the Christians had previously been ordered "not to speak or teach at all in the name of Jesus" (4:18). They had disobeyed this order. Yet they went even further, filling "Jerusalem with [their] teaching." They not only spoke; they broadcast the good news everywhere to everyone around. The thousands of converts mentioned above (2:41; 4:4) is proof of the accuracy of this statement. This actually was a serious offense, constituting contempt for the very law of the land, since the Sanhedrin was the high court and its rulings sacrosanct.

Second, they assert that the apostles are "determined to make us guilty of this man's blood." In other words, they are accusing the believers of seeking revenge for the death of Jesus, wanting God and others to hold them accountable. It is true that at Jesus' trial the people had cried out, "His blood is on us and on our children" (Matt 27:25), and Peter's sermons stressed the Jewish guilt for the cross (2:23; 3:15; 4:10). However, the apostles' desire was for the conversion of the Jews, not divine retribution. Still, the leaders are forced to face their guilt for one of the ultimate sins, the execution of Jesus.

Peter responds exactly as he had in 4:19, "We must obey God rather than human beings." When the legal demands of officials or governments conflict with the will of God, the temporary, earthly commands must give way to God's eternal truths. God has ordered them to teach of Christ in the temple (5:20), and they "must [dei] obey God." The rules even of the high court of the Jews must give way to the high court of heaven.

The next three verses are a perfect five-stage summary of the gospel message, centering on his death, his resurrection and exaltation, the need for repentance, the eyewitness testimony of the apostles, and the gift of the Spirit to Jesus' followers. It is hard to imagine a more apt précis of all God has done in initiating the age of salvation. Its impact on the Jewish people is seen in the opening title, "the God of our ancestors": the God who inaugurated the first covenant under Abraham and Moses is the same God who brought about the new covenant age by sending his Son, Jesus. How could they remain silent about so liberating a truth?

1. The death and resurrection of Jesus is the central truth that must be proclaimed to all. "Hanging him on a tree" (NIV: "cross") is taken from Deuteronomy 21:23 and stresses that a crucified person is under God's curse and cut off from the covenant people. To the Jews his was the worst possible end, but to God it was an atoning sacrifice for sinful humanity.
2. This crucified Jesus, executed under the very ones judging the apostles at that moment, was raised from the dead by God, who "exalted him to his own right hand as Prince and Savior" (5:31). The right hand of God, as in 2:34–35, is Psalm 110:1, the primary biblical passage for the exaltation

of Christ. The word *archēgos*, referring to Jesus as the "Prince" of Israel, was also used in 3:15 of him as "the author of life," the one who "championed" God's salvation as the "pioneer" (other aspects of the term) who initiated the new age of salvation. As a result he is the "Savior" (*sōtēr*) who made eternal life possible for us.

3. The work of Christ on the cross and in his resurrection has made it both possible and mandatory for Israel to repent and be forgiven for their sins. Being the people of Torah and of the covenant is no longer sufficient, for the Messiah has come and been rejected. They have put him to death and rejected him as Messiah and Savior and so must repent and receive forgiveness, for they have lost their place as God's people and now must join the new Israel though faith in Christ.

4. The apostles themselves have been called of God as "witnesses of these things" (5:32); as eyewitnesses they can testify to the reality of these great gifts from God.

5. Not only are the apostles able to confirm these truths, but what is more, God has given the Holy Spirit "to those who obey him." He is God's gift not just to the apostles but to every believer, and he drives home these eternal realities to everyone with the eyes of faith (see 2:38). Note the trinitarian emphasis: God sends his Son to give life and the Spirit to anchor these realities in the lives of God's people. The old adage is true: God proclaims, the Son performs, and the Spirit perfects. The result is ethical and moral faithfulness as God's people "obey him."

GAMALIEL GIVES HIS ADVICE (5:33–39)

Peter's defense hits home, and the Sanhedrin is so incensed that they want to put the apostles to death. This is not just a visceral response. They understood the implications of what was proclaimed to them and undoubtedly discussed what to do, with many of them calling for the death penalty. "Wanted" in Greek is *eboulonto*, indicating deliberation to reach a decision. They were on the verge of committing once again what they did to Jesus.

Before the final decision is reached, a highly respected Pharisee named Gamaliel addresses the council. He was the grandson of Hillel and one of the best-known rabbis in the land, the first one in history to be called *rabban* ("our rabbi"). He appears again in 22:3, where Paul mentions he was trained under Gamaliel. He demands that the apostles be put outside to allow the officials to have a very private discussion. They have just caused an uproar, and he does not want any distractions. Most likely Luke learned of the contents of that talk from a believing member of the Sanhedrin like Nicodemus or Joseph of Arimathea.

Gamaliel is not so much concerned about the apostles as he is about the reputation of the Sanhedrin and warns them to "consider carefully what you intend to do to these men" (5:35). In light of their growing popularity, a hasty decision to take their lives could have serious consequences. Once more, this parallels passion week exactly.

Gamaliel then proceeds to give two illustrations where such a strong reaction regarding revolutionary movements are simply not needed. First, he mentions a Theudas who with four hundred followers revolted and was killed with his men, and "it all came to nothing." The problem is that Theudas's attempt to start a prophetic movement came in AD 44–46, too late to be this event (this is mentioned in Josephus, *Antiquities* 20.97–98). It is possible that there were two separate men, since Theudas was a much-used name. While this cannot be proved, there were many revolts in the first century, and it is quite possible. Moreover, Josephus could be the one making the mistake. We cannot know, but the example is viable however it turns out.

The second incident concerns a certain Judas the Galilean who revolted "in the days of the census," probably the one of Quirinus, governor of Syria (Luke 2:1–2) in AD 6. Likely this revolt was against the Roman taxation, which was the purpose of the census. This too is reported in Josephus, *Antiquities* 18.23–25, and his movement as well came to naught. With Judas' death, his followers "scattered" and the movement ended. The two illustrations have the same point: there is no necessity to take precipitate action against such false messiahs, for it is inevitable that they will naturally come to a swift end.

Gamaliel's advice to the Sanhedrin (5:38–39) is actually very wise: do nothing at this time and leave this Christian movement to God. If he is behind it, you cannot stop it; and if he is not, it will come to an end naturally. Jesus like Judas died, and all they have to do is wait for his followers to scatter. The key is whether the movement is of human or divine origin. If the former, it will fail like all false movements and die in and of itself. It is doomed and can be simply left to God. However, if God is behind it, nothing you can do will have any effect. You will not be able to stop it, and you will end up "fighting against God" (*theomachoi*), a term that describes an enemy of God fighting in opposition to his will. Such foolish attempts will come to nothing.

THE APOSTLES CONTINUE TO WITNESS (5:40-42)

Luke says simply that Gamaliel's logic "persuaded" the Sanhedrin. Rather than executing the apostles, they did three things: had them flogged, repeated the order from 4:17–18 to quit witnessing "in the name of Jesus," and then let them go. In Deuteronomy 25:2–3 this meant being beaten with a whip thirty-nine times or "forty lashes minus one," as it came to be called. In reality, any number could be imposed by the judge; the number of lashings was just not to exceed forty (see also Acts 16:37; 22:19, 24–25; 2 Cor 11:23–25). We know neither what kind of whip was used nor how many lashes were imposed. Most likely it was not scourging, with leather thongs tipped with pieces of metal or bone. That could kill or leave a person severely crippled. This was probably the regular with three strands and no pieces of metal. It was still a severe punishment.

The attempt to silence them and ban any witness repeats 4:17-18, a mandate the believers completely ignored (5:28), and the same happens in this second instance. The people's favorable response continues, and converts continue to join the church. To Luke this proves Gamaliel right and demonstrates to all that God is indeed behind the Christian movement.

The apostles have an amazing reaction. Their backs and chests raw and bloody from the terrible beating, instead of being bedridden and filled with sorrow, they leave "rejoicing because they had been counted worthy of suffering disgrace for the Name." Nothing could show their spiritual depth more than this. The actual goal of flogging was not pain but shame, to disgrace the person and change their behavior accordingly. It had the opposite effect here. They considered this a "participation in his sufferings" (Phil 3:10) and were thrilled at the privilege. Persecution was a great honor because they were sharing in a new level of his messianic work (Luke 6:22-23). To the unbelievers they suffered dishonor, but the opposite was actually true because God deemed them "worthy" to suffer this shame on behalf of Christ.

They not only disobeyed the command to be silent; they made witnessing virtually their full-time job (5:42). Luke says they spoke out "day after day" and went everywhere, not just in the temple environs but also "house to house." Moreover, they "never stopped teaching and proclaiming" the gospel. "Teaching and proclaiming" means both teaching other believers the tenets of the faith and proclaiming to unbelievers "that Jesus is the Messiah." Their principle remains the same—"We must obey God rather than human beings" (5:29; see also 4:19). Doing God's work has absolute priority over every human endeavor or goal. It is vastly better to work for eternal reward than for temporary possessions or plaudits.

———

God's people are called to join Christ as lights to a world of darkness. We would expect the people of this age to rejoice that we provide the path out of that darkness into light, but the fact is that they do not. Darkness hates light (John 3:18–19) and therefore has a violent reaction against all who are the light of God. They don't want what we offer them, and so they turn strongly against us. That is the case here in chapter 5. The Sanhedrin has already arrested Peter and John in 4:3 and warned them of serious consequences if they do not stop spreading the good news. They refused to do so, preferring to disobey the authorities rather than God.

The Sanhedrin does so again but now arrests all twelve disciples and throws them into prison. While they are trying to decide what to do, an angel releases them and tells them again to witness in the temple courts (vv. 17–20). In an ironic turn, the officials await the apostles to silence them at the very moment the escaped prisoners are proclaiming Christ a short distance away in the temple (vv. 21–26). All the temple police can do is rearrest the apostles, but they do so without incident. There is an important lesson here to trust the Lord in difficult times. God watches over his people, and they must place their trust in him entirely, and when the times get bad the saints must learn to "let go and let God."

The justices of the Jewish supreme court have two charges, disobedience for refusing to keep silent about Jesus and having a vendetta against the leaders, making them culpable for Jesus' blood (vv. 27–28). Peter makes a strong defense (vv. 29–32), proclaiming to these leaders that Jesus not only has died but also has been resurrected, exalted to the right hand of God, and become both Champion and Savior of the salvation he has brought to sinful humankind. The only proper response is repentance. The apostles cannot be quiet about such a salvation, and the Spirit has descended to empower them in this God-given endeavor.

Gamaliel, a very respected rabbi, enters the picture and gives the council members wise council (vv. 33-39). He tells them to do nothing and let God take over, for if these Nazarenes are not of God, they will eventually fall apart and disappear, but if they are of God nothing can stop them from succeeding. Cooler heads prevail, and the apostles are flogged then released. However, instead of cowing them, the flogging has the opposite effect, and they are filled with joy that the Lord allowed them to have a share in Christ's suffering. They become tireless in their witnessing and go everywhere sharing the gospel (vv. 41-42). What a model that is for churches today!

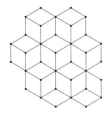

FINAL STAGES OF THE
PALESTINIAN CHURCH
(6:1–15)

The early church knew ethnic conflict similar to what we experience today. In the United States it may be black and white; there it was Hellenist and Hebrew. While in the Roman world the **Hellenistic** people completely dominated, in the Jewish world of the earliest church, it was exactly the opposite. In Jerusalem there were far more Jewish Christians than Greek believers for obvious reasons, but the church had not yet come to grips with the problems that caused. Throughout history caring for widows had always been a special problem, for inheritance always went to the sons to continue the family name, and widows were expected to be cared for by their birth families, who were often unwilling to do so. Widows were always among the most needy in any community.

In this section we get a glimpse of the cultural growth of the church. We have seen nothing of ethnic diversity heretofore, but now we realize there are Hellenists and Hebrews, and these to an extent have formed factions and created tension. These problems flow out of the recent generosity shown by members to one another. The apostles who controlled the care fund have been neglectful due to being overly busy with ministry in the temple and elsewhere. Most of the funds have inadvertently gone to

Hebrew widows rather than to Hellenistic believers. In solving this dilemma the church grows in cultural awareness and in managerial skills.

The Twelve provide inadequate leadership for a church that has become too large for such a small number of managers. So we see the church developing new leaders, Stephen and Philip, as well as new managerial groups like the seven (deacons?) in 6:3–6. The new structures the saints are developing to meet these challenges will take decades and great flexibility. In the rest of Acts we will see the church rising to meet this challenge. At the same time, the period of the Palestinian church was drawing to a close, and persecution (8:1–3) would force the church outward into a worldwide ministry of witness. The church would soon become an international movement and fulfill the prediction of the symbolic meaning of the tongues at Pentecost, that the gospel would go to every people throughout the world in their own language and culture.

THE SEVEN ARE APPOINTED (6:1–7)

The growth of the church was phenomenal in the early years after Pentecost, and the opening comment here notes how that continued growth lay behind the problems taking place here. The leaders were overwhelmed by the complex problems that began to arise, and one of the greatest was caring for the needs of the new followers, especially a poverty-stricken group of widows. The distribution of that much money to that many people was too much for their capabilities. "In those days" means that this managerial problem arose during the same period as the heavy persecution and complicated things even further. It could well be that the persecution meant that the Christian widows were denied access to Jewish sources of help for the poor, and their being Hellenistic exacerbated the problem further. Then when they were neglected by Christian care funds as well, their situation became drastic.

There were quite a number of Greek-speaking Jews in Jerusalem, enough to form several Hellenistic synagogues where they could worship God within the same cultural group. They would have included both converted Jews returning to their homeland and Gentile proselytes moving to their new sacred homeland. The widows noted here stemmed from this group. The problem was not overt racism but ignorance and neglect. They likely had their own services conducted in Greek, but there is no evidence of separate Christian congregations in conflict with each other. The first five chapters of Acts stress the unity of the church. Rather, the leaders failed to notice them in the distribution of funds rather than rejecting them.

The Twelve had been placed in charge of distributing the care funds (4:37; 5:35) and admitted their ultimate blame in the fiasco. So they called the members of the church together and called for a new chart of leadership responsibilities. The problem was that they had been trying to juggle too many balls and needed to turn several things over to others. Their priority was to be "the ministry of the word of God," and they could no longer "wait on tables" distributing food and funds to needy families in the congregation. The apostles would be in charge of preaching and teaching the word (5:21, 25, 28), and the saints would select another set of leaders for practical ministry.

"It would not be right" means that they believe it is not right in the eyes of God more than illogical or ethically incorrect. The word has first priority in the church, but practical issues remain important and should not be neglected. There were not enough hours in the day for the apostles to do both. So they needed to find new leaders to take care of the earthly needs of the congregation.

Their solution is to "choose seven men from among you" (6:3), who are to be chosen from among the people and by the people. Note that the apostles are involving all the believers in a democratic move to find their own chosen individuals. We don't know for sure why seven are chosen. Several commentators mention Josephus's note (*Antiquities* 4.214 regarding Deut 16:18) about seven judges over Israel, but that is no more than a possibility. There are three criteria: (1) They must be "of good reputation" (*martyroumenous*, "known" in the NIV), well thought of by those around them. (2) They must be "full of the Spirit" (2:4, 38; 4:8, 31), completely surrendered to and led by him in their decisions. All believers have the Spirit indwelling them, but not all are "Spirit-filled" or totally dedicated to walking in the Spirit. (3) They must also be "full of ... wisdom," the ability to make wise decisions on practical matters people face.

Theirs is a brilliant move, for the apostles were all ethnically Hebrew, and they led the people to choose all seven from the Hellenistic ranks. This will balance out the makeup of the leadership. One would think these Hellenistic leaders would simply reverse the situation, with all the money now going to the Hellenistic widows and the Hebrew widows now ignored. But that is to fail to realize the difference when they are "Spirit-filled" men, for the Spirit will guarantee absolute fairness.

Once they have been chosen, they will take over the duties to care for the needs of the congregation and thereby free the Twelve to "give our attention to prayer and the ministry of the word" (6:4). "Prayer" is undoubtedly meant in the broad sense, including the temple prayer services of nine in the morning and three in the afternoon, but especially their private prayer time and leading Christian prayer services (2:42). The ministry of the word of course is teaching the saints and preaching to the lost. The balance between these two types of ministry must continue to guide the church today. Too many are strong in one and neglect the other. Both are critical.

The solution was very pleasing to the other believers, and they chose the seven. There is no evidence that Luke was describing the origin of the diaconate here, for the term is never used. It must remain just a tantalizing possibility. The method by which they were selected is not described. The process was likely similar to the choice of Matthias in the first chapter, but without any need to cast lots because the choices were more clear-cut.

All seven have Hellenistic names and come from the Greek-speaking group. Stephen is not just named first due to his prominence in the church and in the next chapter of Acts, but he is described as "full of faith and of the Holy Spirit" to anchor him as a man of tremendous Spirit-filled power like Peter in 4:8. He was able to perform "great wonders and signs" (6:8) and was an incredibly gifted preacher and debater who functioned in Acts as the forerunner of Paul in a way similar to Elijah and Elisha and to John the Baptist and Jesus. He prepared the way for the next stage of developing leadership for the church.

The rest of the names are not developed or mentioned again except for Philip, who had the next stage in ministry after Stephen in 8:4-24 (Samaria), with the Ethiopian eunuch (8:26-39), and in many towns along the coast (8:40). In 21:8 his four prophetess daughters are mentioned. We know little about the next four (Procorus, Nicanor, Timon, and Parmenas). The final name, Nicolas, is labelled a proselyte, a convert to Judaism, from Antioch in Syria. This implies that the others are born Jews, though we don't know which were from Palestine and which from the **diasporic** lands outside Palestine.

These seven chosen are then presented to the Twelve, who commission and appoint them to their new office by praying and laying hands on them (6:6). The prayer would have been one of dedication as the apostles in turn present them to the Lord. Laying on of hands (Acts 13:3; 1 Tim 4:14; 5:22) is not a rite of ordination but a commissioning event as they are being given authority by God. This also does not mean they are being appointed successors to the Twelve like Joshua by Moses in Deuteronomy 34:9, but here there is the idea of an appointment to ministry.

Verse 7, a summary passage, is an example of how the many crises the church faces and triumphs over actually spur it on to even greater growth. After the crisis caused by the betrayal and death of Judas, the Twelve were made intact and the Spirit descended, leading to the first growth spurt of 2:41. As Peter and

John were being arrested, we are told the numbers have grown to 5,000 (4:4). After they were released, the believers had a prayer meeting, resulting in the place shaking and the Spirit filling the saints (4:31). After the death of Ananias and Sapphira, great fear fell on all and "the word of God spread," with even more converts (5:14). Now after the first ingrown crisis, a huge number joined the church, even including some priests, their arch-enemy. Crises force the people of God to their knees, creating more Spirit power, and the church always grows.

All three verbs in verse 7 are imperfects, stressing ongoing activity. The "word" is not just the gospel but an epithet for the church as the people of the word. So it means, "the church kept on growing." Moreover, it did not just grow; it "increased rapidly" (or "kept on multiplying greatly"), perhaps even more than earlier. Most astoundingly of all, "a large number of priests," who had replaced the Pharisees as the major opponents of God's people, "became obedient to the faith," another epithet for conversion. Scholars estimate there were between 18,000 and 20,000 priests and Levites all told. That a significant number became Christ followers is a major sign of God's blessing on the church. The principle is clear—every crisis is a Spirit-led opportunity to surrender further to him and discover a newfound depth of strength, resulting in an even greater growth of the church.

STEPHEN MINISTERS IN JERUSALEM (6:8–15)

In verse 8 Luke begins with further accolades for Stephen, describing his character and his works. He was "full of God's grace and power," meaning he was not only a man of God but a model of spiritual depth and strength. This defines both his gifts in mighty works (v. 8b) and mighty words (v. 9). The Spirit filled him in special ways due to the nature of his spiritual walk with God and Christ.

The "great wonders and signs," which we have seen several times already, will continue to be a primary focus throughout all of Acts. As I have noted, the Spirit used these miracles to authenticate the truth of the gospel they proclaimed. Ministering to the poor as one of the seven would lead the men to meet a great many needy people, and there would be no shortage of those needing these wondrous works. Luke probably doesn't name anyone specifically because he wants to center on their gospel preaching and debates rather than on them individually.

He next does decide to center on Stephen, and a ministry as powerful as his would naturally bring him a great deal of attention, a lot of it unwanted. He reproduces not just Jesus' miracles but his opposition as well. Being a Hellenistic Jew, his main ministry would be in their Greek-speaking synagogues. These named are four groups of diaspora Jews, some from North Africa (Cyrene and Alexandria) and others from the area of the second missionary journey (Cilicia and Asia). We have no idea how many synagogues they might represent—perhaps one or two, likely one with people from these different Roman provinces. The "Synagogue of the Freedmen" would have been attended by people who had won their freedom from slavery, and that would have included a great many in the first century, as Pompeii when he invaded in 63 BC took thousands back as slaves.

They begin to debate with Stephen but cannot "stand up" to his reasoning or the spiritual power in his speaking. "The wisdom the Spirit gave him" (6:10) refers to his Spirit-inspired ability to show that Jesus was indeed the Messiah prophesied in the Scriptures. When his opponents sought to show his understanding wrong, he had the wisdom/knowledge to prove that the Scriptures indeed did point to Jesus. Jesus in Luke 21:15 told them that when they would be put on trial, "I will give you words and wisdom that none of your adversaries will be able to resist or contradict." This certainly came to pass with Stephen, who won every debate.

These Hellenistic Jews could not overcome Stephen's Spirit-led ability to interpret Scripture correctly. Yet, instead of being persuaded, they became even more hardened in their rejection of him and the Christ he proclaimed. They could not deny the truth, so they turned to deliberate lies and "instigated" (*hypebalon*; NIV: "secretly persuaded") some men to start a rumor that they had heard Stephen blaspheming Moses and God, the very charge that carried the death penalty (Lev 24:11-16) for Christ (Matt 26:65).

These rumormongers caused quite a stir, and their charges aroused a great deal of anger among the inhabitants of Jerusalem as well as high officials—elders and scribes—referring to members of the Sanhedrin, or ruling council. Debates now flowed over Stephen more than Christ, but the opposition is much the same. The officials have him arrested and brought before the same main court of the land as in chapters 4 and 5. Since this is the third time Christian leaders have been tried in a short time, feelings are running very high.

A second group of nefarious characters enter the picture after the rumormongers, false witnesses. There were false witnesses at Jesus' trial (Matt 26:59-61; Mark 14:56-57), and now they appear here as well. Any teaching against the temple was bound to provoke a strong reaction because it was holy, the center of their religion, and also for most in Jerusalem the center of their livelihoods. The coming of the Messiah was connected to the purity of the temple.

Both Jesus and Stephen predicted the destruction of the temple, and they did proclaim that Jesus would fulfill the law in himself, so in that sense this is not false. However, the claim that Stephen "never stops speaking against this holy place and against the law" exaggerates greatly and distorts the truth. Then when they add, "we have heard him say that this Jesus of Nazareth will destroy this place," that is a deliberate falsehood, for Jesus never claimed he himself would destroy it. Jesus predicted the destruction of the temple (Luke 21:5-6), but by God's judicial decree, not by him. Putting them together, Christ will not destroy the temple. The Father will do so because of national apostasy, but Jesus will replace it.

The last part of the rumor states that Jesus and Stephen will "change the customs Moses handed down to us," and this does have some basis to it, as the two most important areas of Torah, Sabbath laws and food laws, were altered; Jesus performed miracles on the Sabbath and allowed a great deal that the oral tradition prohibited (Luke 6:1-11; 13:10-17; 14:1-6). The early church was frequently criticized for ignoring the customs of the oral tradition (15:1-2; 16:21; 21:21, 28). However, in Matthew 5:17-20 he says clearly that he has come to fulfill the temple, not destroy it, and that the smallest part of the law will be intact in him. So these rumors were erroneous and intended not for truth but to turn the people against Jesus and Stephen.

Luke moves from the rumors that led to the arrest to the trial itself and remarks that when the Sanhedrin studied his face as the charges were swirling about him, "they saw that his face was like the face of an angel." This is reminiscent of Moses' face transfigured as he descended from Sinai (Exod 34:29-30). The verb (*atenisantes*) is the very one used of the disciples looking into heaven at the ascension of Jesus (Acts 1:10-11), with the obvious difference that the disciples were rapt in worship, while the Sanhedrin is intent on condemnation. Still, in both cases it speaks of a heavenly vision that has become real. God and his Spirit are filling the very countenance of Stephen as he prepares to speak.

————

This is an important section, for it shows that the unity of the church had its limits and describes the internal problems that began to plague God's people. Seeing how the Spirit guided the church to solve its own problems reveals important lessons that will improve our churches today as well. The first (vv. 1-7) dealt with the care of the needy, a major feature of the early church (2:43-47; 4:32-34). As the church rapidly grew, ethnic difficulties developed for which the church was not ready, here the care of

Hellenistic Jewish widows as well as Hebrew widows. Parallels with racial issues today are obvious.

At any rate, money needed for these widows was going to the Hebrew but not the Hellenistic widows. The apostles were in complete agreement that the situation called for change. However, they quickly realized that they needed to find more leaders, for they had neither the time nor the energy to make these necessary changes. The choice of the seven is definitely seen as the work of the Spirit. It is the exactly right move, once more bringing unity and staving off a fractured church. Church growth is a lot more than mere numbers. Here the church is growing in its leadership and in the well-oiled machinery running the church.

The second section (vv. 8–15) traces the ministry of the seven under the Spirit, centering on Stephen, whose ministry ends the Palestinian period and launches the universal mission the Spirit had intended all along for Christ's followers. He becomes the first great evangelist and apologist for Christianity, like Jesus combining the power of his works (signs and wonders) with the power of the word and fearlessly proclaiming the gospel truths. None of the Hellenistic Jewish leaders can stand up against him, and the gospel is triumphing in Jerusalem through him.

Since the Jewish leaders cannot defeat him in debate, they bring him down the same way they did Jesus, by sending out rumormongers to stir up controversy and then false witnesses to stir up opposition against him. They have him arrested and brought up on charges of blasphemy. This has happened to Spirit-empowered Christians in every age, and actually there have recently been more martyrs for Christ than at any other time in the history of the church. Hatred of and opposition to God's people will never cease so long as we live in a sin-sick world.

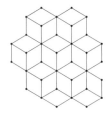

STEPHEN'S DEFENSE SPEECH
AND AFTERMATH
(7:1–8:3)

Stephen's speech draws the first section to a close, providing the final separation between the Jewish people and the followers of Christ. The church will no longer be a Jewish sect but a worldwide movement. We call this his "defense," but in reality Stephen takes charge of the scene and goes on the offensive against the thinking of the Jewish leaders. Nor is Stephen's speech anti-law. Rather, it is pro-Messiah, and the law is given the place God always intended when the Messiah arrived, as preparatory to his coming. The message is not, "We must do away with the law," but "The temple and law must be secondary since the Messiah is here." All of history is summed up and fulfilled in Christ. Interestingly, the name of Christ is never mentioned, yet he is in the forefront throughout. Stephen isn't defending himself so much as proclaiming the gospel.

The primary theme is that the presence of God is not limited to any land (promised land) or building (the temple) but is universal, covering all of God's creation. It takes the form of a recital of Jewish history from Abraham to Solomon and the temple, showing that God's chosen people have always tended to fall into sin and reject his chosen leaders, going their own way. The point then is that the current generation also fits that profile. They are a fallen people, and their only hope is Christ.

STEPHEN SPEAKS ABOUT THE PATRIARCHAL PERIOD (7:1–16)

THE HIGH PRIEST'S QUESTION (7:1)

The high priest (Caiaphas, in office until AD 36) led the Sanhedrin and was the natural one to finalize the charges. By asking, "Are these charges true?" he was challenging Stephen to refute the serious indictment if he could. It involved the charge of leading the nation into heresy and blasphemy, and if true would bring about the death penalty—stoning.

ABRAHAM (7:2–8)

Stephen's somewhat unusual address, "Brothers and fathers," looks at them as fellow Jews and out of respect as elders and models for him to emulate (so also Paul in 22:1). He begins with God's commission of Abraham, showing that God was at work long before there was any promised land. The emphasis is not on Abraham but on "the God of glory" who reveals himself by appearing to Abraham. The majestic God who manifests his **Shekinah** (sacred presence) to his people and remains with them through the exodus and wilderness wanderings is now personally involved with Abraham.

There is a question regarding when this glorious call came. Stephen places it "while he was still [in Ur] in Mesopotamia," from which his father, Terah, and family began their own wanderings as they moved to Harran (Gen 11:31–32). They lived there until his father died, at which time God sent him to Canaan. However, Genesis 12:2 places the call after the death in Harran. Both traditions existed side by side in Judaism. Stephen followed many who saw them as one tradition, but the call was twofold, first to Terah to move the family to Harran and then to leave Harran for Canaan.

The main point is that God took charge of the family and called it to migrate first to Harran and then to Canaan (7:3–4). The family was obedient to its calling. Stephen wants his hearers to understand the full history of the Jews as the people of God. The home God had purposed for them involved a migration that demonstrated their faith in God.

However, Stephen makes it clear that Abraham's call did not involve him receiving his inheritance but rather a promise (7:5). As we know from the book of Exodus, even his descendants did not set their feet on the promised land until Joshua. The inheritance was theirs, but they had to trust God's promise for generations. Abraham was a nomad throughout his life with no land to call his home, and he had only the distant idea of a future "inheritance" that would much later become their possession, the land that would belong to them.

The problem is that when Abraham received this promise of progeny and an inheritance, he still "had no child." So he had to have a twofold faith, in a future land and in future descendants (12:2; 15:2–6) to inhabit that land. Stephen's point is that Abraham's call was not centered on the possession of the land but on the promise of a future inheritance. The Christian life centers not on material or earthly possessions but on divine promises, as in Genesis 15:6: "Abram believed the LORD, and he credited it to him as righteousness."

In verses 6–7 Stephen draws from Genesis 15:13–14 and Exodus 12:40. The first is the primary text, predicting the four-hundred-year enslavement in a land where they will be noncitizens, or "strangers." The Exodus passage more exactly pictures 430 years for the sojourn in Egypt. There is no discrepancy, for Genesis is a general estimate and Exodus a more specific number. Yet God will vindicate his suffering people and "punish the nation they serve as slaves." The main thing is that God revealed to Abraham exactly what the future held and guided him and his descendants in fulfilling that calling. The stress on their being strangers or foreigners is also the point here, for that provides a parallel with the Christian movement and on being "foreigners and exiles" (1 Pet 2:11) as followers of Christ.

Israel would not only be vindicated but also rewarded for her patience. "Come out ... and worship me in this place" stems from Exodus 3:12, but Stephen substitutes "on this mountain" (Mount Horeb) with "in this place" (Canaan). This is the true destiny of God's people, worshipping and thereby sharing in the "God of glory." Stephen wants the Sanhedrin to know that he shares that central calling, and that he too lives to worship the Lord.

The special place of Abraham is finalized in verse 8 by centering on two of the blessings God bestowed on him, circumcision and descendants, and not just any descendants but patriarchs. The emphasis is on the fact that Abraham and his descendants are the covenant people of God, sealed by the rite of circumcision (Gen 17:9–14). This outward sign made them the special people of God.

For Stephen the covenant relationship lay behind the birth of the patriarchs, as the Greek has "and so [kai houtōs; 'so' is not translated in the NIV] Abraham became the father of Isaac." This was a direct and immediate answer to the promise of God and a covenant blessing. The movement from Isaac to Jacob to the twelve patriarchs intends to summarize them and allow Stephen room to develop the story further by centering on the youngest patriarch, Joseph, as a microcosm of Israel's struggles. He will go directly to Joseph in the next section. So Abraham's children were directly the children of covenant and a critical part of God's promises in which Abraham had faith. Stephen's point here is that all God's people must put their trust in him and obey him.

JOSEPH (7:9–16)

Joseph demonstrates further the extent to which God's people are not tied to a land. This section consists of two hardships, with each followed by divine deliverance. The first occurs in verses 9–10, in which Joseph is sold into slavery by his brothers. He was the youngest and his father Jacob's favorite (Gen 37), so out of jealousy they sold him to get rid of him. For Stephen this pictures the mistreatment of Israel by the nations throughout her history and especially the persecution of believers by the Jewish leaders.

God's deliverance of Joseph "from all his troubles" came as a result of God's vigilant care and orchestration of events. He "was with" Joseph and "gave Joseph wisdom" to interpret Pharaoh's dream (Gen 41). As a result he gained "the goodwill of Pharaoh," an understatement. In actuality, he was given Pharaoh's signet ring and placed in charge as second-in-command over Egypt. He went from imprisoned slave to "ruler over Egypt and all [Pharaoh's] palace" in one fell swoop due to God's rescue of him. Stephen likely sees himself in Joseph, rejected and betrayed by his brothers (the Jews) but with God on his side.

Stephen tells of a second crisis in 7:11–12. A wide famine crushes both Egypt and Canaan, and Jacob and his sons begin to starve. "Food" (*chortasmata*) in the phrase "not find food" can refer to animal fodder, meaning they could not even find food in the animal troughs to eat. The situation was desperate.

There was only one hope for survival. Egypt was the wheat capital of the Mediterranean, and there was grain there. So Jacob sent his sons there to obtain some (Gen 42). When they arrived, Joseph assuaged their desperate need but did not reveal who he was.

The food Joseph graciously gave lasted a short while but soon ran out, and that necessitated a second visit to Egypt (7:13–16). At that time (Gen 45) Joseph revealed himself to his brothers, stated that God had been behind all the events to provide a sanctuary for his family, and invited the whole family to move to Egypt as their home (45:8–15). Pharaoh discovered Joseph's background as a Hebrew and seconded that invitation (45:16–20). One question is Stephen's claim that "seventy-five in all" (7:14) moved to Egypt, when Genesis 46:26 tells us there were sixty-six people. The key is the "in all," as the **Septuagint**, the Greek version of the Old Testament, has seventy-five by adding the nine sons of Joseph to that number.

So the whole family came, took up residence in Egypt, and were well cared for the rest of Jacob's life. After Joseph's death, Stephen tells us that "their bodies were brought back to Shechem" in the promised land, their true home. Their final residence was in the very tomb Abraham had purchased for Sarah (Gen 23:16, for four hundred shekels of silver) and in which he was buried (Gen 25:9–10). Yet here there are further discrepancies, as Joshua 24:32 tells us Joseph was buried in Shechem on land purchased by Jacob. Several traditions have Jacob and the brothers buried at Hebron. Most assume Stephen is telescoping traditions together by way of summary, an unusual practice, while some believe Jacob repurchased the land at a later time. It is difficult to know. The main thing is that they were buried in the promised land.

STEPHEN SPEAKS ABOUT MOSES (7:17–43)

THE HEBREWS IN EGYPT (7:17–19)

After Joseph left the scene, things got tragically worse for the Jewish people in Egypt. The crises not only continued but also intensified. Yet Stephen interestingly says that this is when "the time drew near for God to fulfill his promise to Abraham." This is the promise to Abraham that his people would inherit the land God had purposed for them (see v. 5 above). This promise will be fulfilled in the actions of an oppressive king against the Hebrew people. The figure who turns everything around, of course, is the second great hero and Christ figure after Abraham, Moses. Joseph had led his people into Egypt to save them; Moses will lead them out of Egypt for the same reason. After Joseph, the Jewish people prospered. I prefer a more literal translation for verse 17 than "greatly increased"; rather, they "grew and multiplied," not just in numbers but in wealth and status as well.

However, that ended when "a new king, to whom Joseph meant nothing, came to power in Egypt" (7:18, quoting Exod 1:8). The Egyptians had always had a bias against the Hebrews. In Genesis

43:32 it says, "Egyptians could not eat with Hebrews, for that is detestable to Egyptians." This was even after Joseph had become a ruler of Egypt. So what the new Pharaoh decreed was not out of keeping with the times.

He attempted genocide against the Jewish people. He took advantage of his power over them and "dealt treacherously" with them, mistreating them terribly. The example Stephen uses is that precursor of Herod's slaughtering the innocents, the Egyptians "forcing them to throw out their newborn babies so that they would die" (7:19). The practice of exposure, in which unwanted babies were left out in trash heaps and forests to die, was frequently done in the ancient world and was widely practiced by the Greeks and Romans later. There has been a great deal of speculation about which Pharaoh actually set this plan in motion and stood against Moses and the Israelites. Most frequent suggestions are Thutmose I (1600–1514 BC), Seti I (1308–1290 BC), or Ramesses II (1290–1224 BC). It is impossible to know for certain, and the issue is bound up with the date for the exodus.

Moses' Childhood (7:20–22)

Stephen speaks of Moses' life in three periods of forty years each (vv. 20–29, 30–34, 35–43), possibly drawn from Exodus 7:7 (he is 80 years old when he confronts Pharaoh) and Deuteronomy 34:5–7 (he is 120 when he dies). Summarizing Exodus 2:1–10, these three verses speak of his childhood. God's hand is seen again saving and training the right man for the right job, as Stephen continues to stress God's sovereignty in redemptive history. Moses spent his first three months being hidden and protected by his mother so she wouldn't have to expose him. Stephen describes him as "well-bred," or "no ordinary child" (NIV), not just speaking of physical beauty but more spiritual upbringing. Both God and his parents were preparing him well for this future task.

When his parents "placed [him] outside," this was not exposure; rather, according to Exodus 3:3, they placed the baby in a papyrus basket and hid it "among the reeds along the bank of the Nile" (Exod 2:3), where Pharaoh's daughter found him and "brought him up as her own son." As a virtual member of the royal family, he no doubt enjoyed unimaginable childhood privileges. On this aspect the movies do not exaggerate. More importantly for his future role, he was "educated in all the wisdom of the Egyptians," an enormous advantage when he later had to face them down. Finally, even in his childhood he was "powerful in speech and action." This phrase, which the KJV translates "mighty in words and deeds," is reminiscent of Luke 24:19, where the Emmaus disciples described Jesus as "powerful in word and deed before God and all the people." Stephen definitely sees Moses as a type of Christ, and Luke probably would add that he typifies Stephen as well.

Rejection and Fleeing to Midian (7:23-29)

Moses' birth mother ended up being his wet nurse, and he was trained by her in his cultural and religious legacy (Exod 2:8-10). So he was Hebrew as well as Egyptian and never forgot his roots after he became an adult. Exodus 2:11 doesn't tell us his age, and "forty years" in verse 23 probably relates to the second block of time rather than Moses' actual age for this event. He decides he wants to get to know his birth people and starts to watch them, undoubtedly feeling sorrow for them and helpless to do much. As he observes them at hard labor, he sees an Egyptian beating a Hebrew laborer and intervenes. Drawing from Exodus 2:11-12, Stephen says that Moses "avenged him by killing the Egyptian." This begins the fulfillment of 7:7, where Abraham was promised "I will punish the nation they serve as slaves." This serves also as a harbinger for Moses' actions later as he avenges and liberates Israel from her oppressors.

In the next scene, however, Israel is decidedly ungrateful for what Moses has done. He had thought they "would realize that God was using him to rescue them, but they did not" (7:25). That was his purpose, and he expected them to know that. The Greek has "God was giving them salvation through his hand," looking to Moses as the savior of Israel. But they rejected Moses and wanted nothing to do with him, considering him more Egyptian than Hebrew and thus their enemy. The ignorance of the Israelites and their resultant lack of spiritual awareness is one of the hallmarks of Stephen's speech.

Moses was not only savior but peacemaker as well, as he next (7:26) tried to "reconcile" (*synēlassen*) two Hebrews fighting each other (Exod 2:13). His comment, "you are brothers," fits his situation as well, considering himself a "brother" of the two. In the Exodus story, one of the men is wronging the other, and the guilty party responds here, refusing Moses' appeal to bring peace and charging, "Who made you ruler and judge over us?" (7:27–28). He is actually rejecting Moses at both the earthly and the heavenly levels. As a member of the royal family, Moses had earthly power over them, and as sent by God Moses had divine authority as savior of Israel. So this Jewish man turned not just against Moses but also against God. The man "pushed Moses aside," thereby indicting himself and establishing another failure of Israel that will carry through Stephen's speech. Israel is not just ignorant but also rejects the very leaders (later the prophets) whom God sends to help them.

When the man adds, "Are you thinking of killing me as you killed the Egyptian yesterday?" (7:28 = Exod 2:14), he provokes real fear in Moses, for Moses had "hid [the body] in the sand" (Exod 2:12) and tried to keep the incident secret, lest he get in trouble with the authorities. He may have been an adopted royal, but helping a Hebrew slave and killing an Egyptian would not have been countenanced. In fact, Exodus 2:15 tells us that "when Pharaoh heard of this, he tried to kill Moses," so Moses' fear was founded in reality.

The Exodus account says he fled out of fear of Pharaoh's retribution, but Stephen has him fleeing due to being rejected by the Israelites, his true people. The man personifies the Hebrew people as a whole, rejecting God and his chosen messenger Moses.

There is also a **typological** connection here, as the people's turning against Moses is fulfilled in the rejection of Jesus and also of Stephen and the followers of Christ.

Moses fled to Midian on the east coast of the Gulf of Aqaba in Arabia and became a foreign resident, marrying Zipporah, daughter of a Midianite priest, bearing two sons, Gershom and Eliezer (Exod 2:16–22; 18:3–4). During this time he was protected from the wrath of Pharaoh and made ready by God for his later mission. God does not allow him to return until Pharaoh dies (Exod 2:23).

COMMISSIONING AT THE BURNING BUSH (7:30–34)

We now enter the next forty-year period (vv. 30–34). Stephen cites the event that ended that period: the burning bush and opening confrontation with Pharaoh took place when Moses was eighty and had spent forty years in Midian (Exod 7:7). As a shepherd he led his flock to Mt. Horeb (= Mt. Sinai), and there an angel appeared to him in a theophany "in the flames of a burning bush." When the bush was not consumed by the flames (Exod 3:2) Moses was amazed and went over to check out the strange sight. From the flames God spoke (7:32 = Exod 3:6), "I am the God of your fathers, the God of Abraham, Isaac and Jacob." Moses was not accepted by his own people, but he was by the God of his fathers, and this statement begins his commissioning as God's ambassador and messenger.

Moses' reaction is always the result of theophany, as he "trembled with fear and did not dare to look." Mere human beings do not look on the face of God and live (Exod 33:20), so this underscores the sacredness of the scene. Moses also becomes one of the few in history to whom God revealed himself directly.

The official commissioning of Moses occurs in 7:33–34 (= Exod 3:5–8), and with God's presence in the burning bush it becomes "holy ground," a precursor of the holy temple. This prepares for Stephen's later assertion that God's holy presence is not restricted to buildings (7:48). As God promised Abraham (7:7), here he says he will intervene and bring his people out of the place where they are enslaved. God says, "I have heard their groaning and have come down to set them free." Moses would become the God-sent envoy, commissioned to return to Egypt and liberate his people. Obviously, Stephen is also thinking of Christ who has been sent to redeem or set free sinful humanity.

FAILURE IN THE WILDERNESS (7:35–43)

The third forty-year block centers on the wilderness wanderings. The first section of this is verses 35–38, in which Stephen summarizes the commission Moses carried out for God and finalizes his rejection by his own people. Stephen begins with the basic theme, retelling their challenge against Moses, who is the God-appointed "ruler and judge" and then responding that God sent him to be "their ruler and deliverer." The term for "deliverer" is *lytrōtēn*, cognate of the term for "redemption," and as ruler and redeemer Moses was the type fulfilled in Jesus as "Prince" (5:31) and redeemer (Luke 1:68).

In verse 36 Stephen summarizes the period of confrontation, for the "wonders and signs in Egypt" are the plagues as well as the crossing of the Red Sea and the miracles in the wilderness. As such it is the perfect precursor of the life of Christ and the early church, with both also featuring signs and wonders along with the confrontation of evil and the liberation of those who put their trust in God. Moses and Jesus are the two primary biblical figures who were both ruler and redeemer, and Jesus is frequently in the Gospels (Matthew especially) seen as the new Moses, for instance in fleeing from Herod and the return from Egypt in Matthew 2 or the sending of the Twelve in Matthew 9:35–10:5a (= the commissioning of Moses; see vv. 30–32 above).

The Moses-Christ typology is made explicit in verse 37, where Stephen alludes to the prophecy of a prophet like Moses by citing Deuteronomy 18:15, "God will raise up for you a prophet like me from your own people." This is the third virtual title for

Moses—ruler, redeemer, and now prophet. Peter made a similar typological link in 3:22–23, but there is a new wrinkle here— Moses and Jesus are the prophets rejected by their own people. The people of Israel turn away from the leaders God sends to deliver them (as indeed they are also doing with Stephen).

The final section regarding Moses' ministry is verse 38, looking to Moses as the giver of the "living words" of the law. God had made him ruler or leader of the "assembly" or congregation (*ekklēsia*) of Israel, and in the desert at Sinai, Stephen mentions "the angel who spoke to him." Angels are not explicitly mentioned at Sinai, except in Deuteronomy 33:2, where Moses says of God, "He came with myriads of holy ones from the south, from his mountain slopes," but they simply accompany Yahweh as he descends on Sinai. This developed into a Jewish tradition that angels mediated the giving of the law at Sinai (as in Gal 3:19; Heb 2:2), which Stephen follows here. Here God is seen speaking through the angel, showing that all of heaven was involved with Moses at Sinai. The precepts of the Torah were "living words" because they brought life to God's people (Deut 4:1; 5:26; 30:15). So Moses in mediating God's redemption was the source of life.

God may have sent Moses to lead them and to give the law to them, but that didn't mean Israel would prosper through it. Stephen says in verse 39 that they "refused to obey him," and "instead, they rejected him." Stephen calls them "our forefathers," stressing the link with the apostasy of the present people of Israel. The children are like the father. It is hard to believe after all they had been through at the hands of the Egyptians, but "their hearts turned back to Egypt." They rejected God's revelation to Moses and refused to obey not just Moses but the God who sent him and spoke through him, preferring the Egyptian gods to the God of Abraham. The typological connection to Jesus as well as Stephen, which we have often seen, continues here.

The incident Stephen chooses (7:40–41) to illustrate this is the golden calf of Exodus 32, beginning with a quotation of 32:1, in which the Israelites tell Moses' brother Aaron to "make us gods who will go before us" (accusing God of abandoning his people). "As for this fellow Moses [note the disparaging tone] who led us out of Egypt—we don't know what has happened to him." Moses had actually ascended Sinai to receive the law on their behalf, but they refuse to recognize this and prefer to wallow in their own manufactured misery. In an act of ultimate idolatry, they created their own golden image of a god in the form of a calf (32:4), an animal used in sacrifices and considered by these apostates an image of Yahweh, fashioned by his people. Their celebration occurs in 32:6, and they consider this another of the Jewish festivals, now worshipping Yahweh as a calf. Thereby they were in control of God, had re-created him themselves, and could order him to do their bidding.

God's reaction is recorded in 7:42–43. Since they had "turned back to Egypt," God "turned away from them." Since they had fallen into the worship of "things," he "gave them over to the worship of the sun, moon and stars." "Gave them over" is the verb used in Romans 1:24, 26, 28, of the depravity of humankind to describe God's punishment of their folly. This is exactly what the phrase means here: they wanted it; now they've got it. The celestial phenomena stand for the worship of God's creation over the Creator, ultimate idolatry. Stephen quotes Amos 5:25–27 as from "the book of the prophets" because it is one of the Minor Prophets, which was looked at as a whole. The prophets are said to echo God's decision here that Israel must be punished severely for its sin.

The first point from Amos is that Israel's sacrifices have been falsified by its idolatry. Amos asks whether they had sacrificed to God in the wilderness, and the answer is no,[1] because in reality they had presented offerings to pagan gods. Molek was the Canaanite god of the sun and sky, and Rephan was the Egyptian

---

1. The particle introducing the question is *mē*, which expects the answer no— "You didn't, did you?"

god of the heavens. Later some Israelites offered infant sacrifices to Molek (Lev 18:21; 20:2; 2 Kings 23:10). They forsook the one true God and turned to pagan deities. The punishment was exile, with a significant part of their population deported "beyond Babylon." In Amos 5:27, which was written to the northern tribes of Israel, the deportation is "beyond Damascus," the first exile to Assyria of 2 Kings 17. Stephen changes this to the Babylonian exile of the southern tribes of Judah of 2 Kings 25 for effect.

STEPHEN SPEAKS ABOUT THE TABERNACLE AND THE TEMPLE (7:44-50)

The order to build a tabernacle for God was given on Sinai in Exodus 25, and instructions for building it came in Exodus 25-31. The model for the tabernacle was revealed on Sinai. It is called "the tabernacle of testimony" (NIV: "of the covenant law") because it bore witness to God's relationship with his people. God "testified" to the nation by revealing himself in his new home. It was constructed and spent its first years "in the wilderness," meaning it was outside the land, and it never dwelt in one place. It was intended as a portable dwelling for a nomadic people.

It entered the promised land with the Israelites under Joshua, but it still moved from place to place. Its first dwelling place was Shiloh, north of Jerusalem (Josh 18), and it remained there "until the time of David," when Solomon built the temple three hundred years later. Still, it was a tent and meant to travel around with the people. It was always temporary rather than permanent.

In 2 Samuel 6 David moved the tabernacle from Shiloh to Jerusalem and wanted to build the temple as a permanent dwelling place for God. Stephen echoes Psalm 132:5, speaking of David's vow to the Lord to "find a place for the LORD, a dwelling for the Mighty One of Jacob." He wanted a fixed, permanent home that would anchor God's covenant relationship with him and his people. However, in 2 Samuel 7:5-16 God told him it would be his family, not David himself, and so it was his son "Solomon who built a house for him," and the glory went to his descendants, not just to Solomon himself.

Rather than dwelling on the glory and ministry of Solomon's temple, as we would expect, Stephen turns immediately to one of his central points, "the Most High does not live in houses made by human hands" (7:48). It is important to realize that this is not a critique intended for the temple, as if Solomon made a mistake erecting it. In fact, Solomon himself made a comment very much like this in his prayer dedicating the temple in 1 Kings 8:27 when he said, "The heavens, even the highest heaven, cannot contain you," and when he declares that his true dwelling place is indeed heaven and not the temple (8:30).

Stephen's concern here is that when we contain God in a building like the temple, we can control him, and in reality he cannot be either contained or controlled by human power. He is applying the Jews' own polemic against idols to a misunderstanding of how the temple functions. Nothing "made by human hands" can encompass the Most High. Israel had stagnated into an idolatrous worship of the temple itself, when its true purpose was to facilitate worship of God. He finds corroborative evidence in Isaiah 66:1–2 (7:49–50).

This is the final chapter of Isaiah and is part of a section (Isa 63–66) contrasting God's faithfulness to Israel's faithlessness. These verses occur in a paragraph (66:1–6) demanding that brokenness must come before sacrifice, making the point that Yahweh dwells in the heavens rather than the temple and has created his "house." In fact, he created everything (his "hand made all these things"), so humility and obedience have priority over an elaborate "house" for God. Since God dwells everywhere and the earth is his footstool, his "resting place" cannot be confined to a building. With the earth as a mere footstool and his true home in heaven (also Matt 5:34–35), he cannot be restricted to a building. This is a point critical for our time as well, as too many Christians restrict their God-awareness to their time at church. We must at all times remember that God dwells everywhere.

STEPHEN CONCLUDES BY
INDICTING ISRAEL (7:51-53)

Stephen has been building to this climax throughout his speech. He is on trial but turns the tables on the Sanhedrin and indicts them before the court of God. The history of the nation and all its failures are being relived in the current generation. They are once again "stiff-necked" or stubborn people. The only way to worship and relate to God was stated down through the generations by Abraham, Joseph, Moses, and David, but they have failed to listen or obey. They have always turned away from God's appointed leaders (7:9, 25-29, 39, 41), and they have done the same with Jesus. They have tried to confine God to a building and gain control over him (7:48-50) and have refused to obey him.

As a result they are being indicted as "uncircumcised" people who have become just like the pagans. Their "hearts" have turned from him, and they refuse to listen ("ears") to the life-giving words of his Son. Like their ancestors described in Stephen's summary of Jewish history, they are characterized as resisting the Holy Spirit. In Isaiah 63:10 the prophet accuses his people of having "rebelled and grieved his Holy Spirit" and challenges them to "recall" the time of Moses when God "set his Holy Spirit among them" (63:11). The present generation is reliving the rebellion and failure of Isaiah's time.

Stephen then expands the list of those divinely chosen leaders whom the nation rejected by asking, "Was there ever a prophet your ancestors did not persecute?" A list of the prophets who were opposed and lost their lives is provided in Hebrews 11:32-38, and similar comments can be found in 1 Kings 18:4, 13; Jer 26:20-24; Luke 6:23; 11:47-51. The situation remains the same. The ultimate prophet, Jesus, has been rejected and slain, and now Stephen is on trial for his life. Those who "predicted the coming of the Righteous One" would be the messianic prophets like Jeremiah, who according to Jewish tradition was said to be stoned (4 Baruch 9:25–32); or Isaiah, who according to tradition was sawn in two (See Martyrdom and Ascension of Isaiah 5:1–15).

This has especially come to fruition in the fact that they "have betrayed and murdered" their own Messiah, Jesus the "Righteous One" himself. They betrayed Jesus when they condemned him and gave him over to Pilate, and they murdered him when they demanded that Pilate crucify him. They did indeed receive "the law that was given through angels" at Sinai (7:53, see on 7:38), a law mediated by all of heaven, with angels acting on behalf of God. They had this law and lived under it for centuries, and yet as so often in their checkered past, they "have not obeyed it." They developed a complex web of oral traditions to enable the people to keep the law, and yet in the single most important area, following and obeying their God-sent Messiah, they refused to obey it. Few have ever been so elaborate in their attempts to obey the law down to the smallest possible detail, and yet few have ever so completely turned against it in the most critical detail of all. They are utterly guilty of the very thing they are accusing Stephen of doing.

STEPHEN IS KILLED (7:54–8:1A)

Clearly Luke has two purposes in this passage, to narrate the death of Stephen and to present his successor, Saul. The leaders react harshly to Stephen's devastating indictment of them: "They were furious and gnashed their teeth at him." The trial quickly turns to a riot, and they forget all about legal niceties. Their fury is easy to understand, for he has accused them of apostasy and blasphemy and done so through what they would consider a completely biased account of their past. When he tells them they "always resist the Holy Spirit," that is the last straw.

We must remember that Stephen is "filled with the Holy Spirit" (6:3, 5; 7:55) and that Christ promised that he and the Spirit would

tell them what to say when they were under trial (Matt 10:19-20
= Luke 21:15). So what Stephen said not only is carefully planned
on his part but also is inspired by the Spirit. It is absolute truth.
That is strongly stressed here. In these last minutes of his life, he
"looked up to heaven and saw the glory of God." This is more than
a vision; it is an actual view of heaven and of Christ himself. As
"the heavens declare the glory of God" (Ps 19:1), heaven is the glory
of God, and Stephen actually gazes into it in its fullness and sees
Jesus himself there.

This is a great deal more than Stephen's last earthly sight
before going to be with the Lord. It is the true climax of his speech,
indeed of Acts thus far, for we see the actual extension of the
ascension of Jesus. After we saw Jesus himself ascending in the
cloud, we haven't viewed him again until now, and it is the last
time we physically see him in the New Testament until he returns
in Revelation 19. This then becomes the physical proof of the exaltation of Jesus, as through Stephen's eyes we see Jesus "standing at the right hand of God" in fulfillment of Psalm 110:1 (see
on 2:34-35). By his appearances we have known for a fact that he
was raised from the dead, and now we know he was exalted to
the right hand of God in glory.

Stephen words in 7:56 are significant. "I see heaven open and
the Son of Man standing at the right hand of God." "Open" is a perfect participle (diēnoigmenous), stressing a state of being, "standing
open," meaning the last days have truly begun and God in Jesus is
acting to bring an end to this evil world. In this, his transcendent
glory as Lord of all is powerfully evident. Moreover, it is the "Son
of Man" standing in all his glory, recalling Daniel 7:13 and the universal dominion this risen and exalted Lord enjoys. Heaven stands
open, and the exalted Son of Man stands as a divine Judge prepared to act precipitously, vindicating both Stephen in the present
and himself in the universal mission of the church that is about
to begin. Stephen's death is a fulcrum event that will launch the
fulfillment of the Great Commission ("Go and make disciples of

all nations," Matt 28:19) and Acts 1:8 ("You will be my witnesses ... to the ends of the earth").

At Stephen's words the anger of these leaders erupts and they lose control. Covering their ears with their hands, they are saying in effect, "We will hear no more of this blasphemy!" Screaming at the top of their lungs, "they all rushed at him," becoming a lynch mob. This latter point is debated, for several scholars wonder if the Sanhedrin would do such a thing. It would be like the Supreme Court justices losing control and hanging a particularly gruesome serial killer from a tree outside the justice building.

The truth probably lies somewhere in the middle. There is no legal verdict recorded here, but a hurried one similar to that at Jesus' trial (Luke 22:71) could have taken place, and in actuality they followed Jewish legal procedure for stoning a blasphemer. They "dragged him out of the city and began to stone him" for blasphemy in keeping with Leviticus 24:14 (see m. Sanhedrin 6:1). They could not follow the same Roman proceedings as they did with Jesus (nor did they want to), and their furious rage would not allow a lengthy procedure anyway. They did it the Jewish way, and the Romans allowed a certain latitude when it was a Jewish matter. It was very doubtful the Romans would care, so long as a real riot didn't break out. So it was not an official trial or an orderly execution, but neither was it completely disorganized.

The "witnesses" would have been members of the Sanhedrin who had heard Stephen's speech and the words at his vision. Removing their coats was not a formal action but rather their getting ready to throw the stones. The rules were for the witnesses to throw the first stones (Deut 17:7). We are now introduced to the figure who will dominate the rest of the book of Acts. Saul is described as a "young man," probably around eighteen years old or so. It is hard to know why he doesn't throw a stone. He may have been thought too young. By watching over the clothes, he was also probably an assistant to one of the members of the Sanhedrin, most likely Gamaliel, rather than an official witness.

As he is dying, Stephen states two things Christ also uttered at his death (7:59–60). First, he says, "Lord Jesus, receive my Spirit" (see Luke 23:46). He may still have been able to see Jesus himself with hands outstretched toward him. Jesus had called out to God; Stephen is looking at the "Lord Jesus" and so addresses him with these words from Psalm 31:5, confirming his belief that his impending death is merely a handing of his spirit over to the Godhead. It is not an end but a beginning, for then his real life will begin.

Second, with no more strength to stand on his feet, Stephen "fell on his knees," half in worshipful supplication, and repeats what Jesus says in effect in Luke 23:34, "Lord, do not hold this sin against them." The "sin" obviously is his own murder for telling the truth about the nation's relationship with God and about the person of Jesus. Luke presents Stephen reliving the powerful ministry and now death of Jesus. This continues another primary theme of Acts, the necessity of repentance and forgiveness for knowing Christ. Stephen is in effect praying for the conversion of his murderers.

Just after these two prayers, he "fell asleep," a euphemism for death (Deut 31:16; 1 Cor 7:39; 2 Pet 3:4). Here it hints at the fact that in the next instant he would wake up in heaven and see his Lord.

Saul had likely been present for the trial, accompanied his mentor to the execution scene, stood over the robes of the eyewitnesses as they stoned Stephen, and now "approved of their killing him" (8:1a), as Paul himself testifies in 22:20.

THE CHURCH IS PERSECUTED AND
THE MISSION BEGINS (8:1B–3)

Jerusalem at this time is a pressure cooker, with the leaders piling on more and more anti-Christian pressure until it finally explodes with the death of Stephen: "On that day a great persecution broke out against the church in Jerusalem." It was "great" in the sense that it was much more severe and widespread than those in chapters 4 and 5, affecting all the believers and not just the apostles,

and directed not just at silencing their witness but at eradicat-
ing their worship and the very existence of their movement. As
we will see, it led to many having to flee for their lives. Moreover,
it is also great because it initiates a lengthy time of persecution
that will last years. In Acts, it continues in the actions of Paul, who
is still conducting it when Christ reveals himself to him on the
Damascus road (ch. 9).

The result is that "all except the apostles were scattered
throughout Judea and Samaria." The saints were forced out of their
settled existence, thus fulfilling the prophecy of 1:8 that when the
Holy Spirit came, the believers would become "witnesses ... in all
Judea and Samaria," the first step in the worldwide mission. At this
beginning stage, they remained in the towns of Palestine, probably
moving in with friends or relatives in various places. The scene of
chapter 8 flows out of this, as Philip went to Samaria and so started
to witness there. Later he will move to Caesarea (8:40), and others
will eventually be scattered to Lydda (10:32), Joppa (10:36), and "as
far as Phoenicia, Cyprus and Antioch" (11:19). What the Christ followers did not understand about the Great Commission, that it
meant they would leave Jerusalem and Judea and go to the nations,
the Spirit would help them to accomplish by sending this "great
persecution" to scatter them out into the world.

There is a real question as to what "all except the apostles"
means here. It has often been said that the persecution affected
only the **Hellenistic** believers, since that is where Stephen ministered and where the persecution began. It may have started
there, but it is unlikely that the Jewish believers were unscathed,
and Luke says "except the apostles," not "except for the Jewish
followers." The Hellenist believers would have moved back to
their Roman places of origin, not primarily to Palestinian desti-
nations. So we can say it was especially severe for the Hellenistic
Jewish Christians but affected them all. The apostles remained
in Jerusalem because it was still the center of the church, not
because they were not included in the persecution. But many

Jewish followers were forced to flee as well, as seen in the ministry that took place in Palestine in chapters 8–10.

Luke returns to the immediate situation after the death of Stephen in verse 2 and then turns to Paul in verse 3, so recalling the situation in Jerusalem before moving to consider Samaria and the spreading mission of the church. The identity of the "godly men" who buried Stephen is uncertain. Many think these aren't believers, for then Luke would have said "brothers" or some such. Rabbinic law did not allow mourning for those stoned for blasphemy (m. Sanhedrin 6:6), and so the fact that they "mourned deeply" likely reflects strong disagreement with the Sanhedrin ruling and protest of their execution of Stephen.

Saul makes the persecution of the church virtually a full-time job. His actions are part of building a fence around the law in order to protect it from destructive heresies and evil practices. He would have believed that, so long as heresy is allowed in the land, the Messiah will not come. As a result, he became one of the leaders of the persecution, attempting to "destroy the church" (see also Gal 1:13; Phil 3:6). In doing so, he started "going from house to house" where groups of believers met for worship, and kept on dragging (the verb tense stresses ongoing activity) "both men and women" off to prison. In Jewish practice, the synagogue leaders formed a minor law court and could sentence miscreants, usually to beatings. Paul become one of these and was authorized to go to the illegal Christian house churches and arrest believers.

In Acts 26:9–12 he says he led the opposition that put many Christians in prison and led to several deaths. His goal was to eradicate Christianity, and when he started on his way to Damascus in 9:1–2 he asked the high priest for letters introducing him to the Damascus synagogues giving him the authority to arrest the Christians there and take them back to Jerusalem. He clearly believed that Jesus as crucified was under God's curse (Deut 21:22–23), and that Stephen's sentence of death was to be extended to all followers of this Jesus.

———

Stephen's incredible address to the Sanhedrin is one of the greatest speeches in Scripture and is a clarion call to repentance and conversion to Christ for the Jewish people of his day. This brilliantly conceived summary of Old Testament history is an evangelistic tract proving that Christ is indeed the only way to God, not the law or the land or any religious rite. The story of Abraham (vv. 2–8) shows that God's people do not depend on the land but on promise, for Abraham the promise of a future inheritance. Life with God centers on trust in him, and the patriarchs were the covenant children promised to Abraham as part of his reward for his faith in God. There is an important lesson in this for us too, as we are asked to wait on the Lord to fulfill his promises in his time, not in the time we wish.

Joseph (vv. 9–16) demonstrates that often the fulfillment of God's promise comes via hardship and sacrifice, as he had to overcome being sold into slavery by his own brothers and then imprisoned by his Egyptian benefactors. The lesson for us is that he watches over us like he did Joseph, who was not only rescued but rewarded, ending up a second ruler over Egypt and the rescuer of his very own family, who had earlier betrayed him. The point is that these promises of a God who is in control, turning the beleaguered Joseph into the redeemer of his people, apply to us as well as to him.

Stephen next turns to Moses. The story of his early years (vv. 17–29) illustrates that being chosen and empowered by God doesn't mean that following the Lord becomes easy. Both the Egyptians and his own people of Israel turn against him, and this one designated as savior and guide to free the Jews from the Egyptians has to flee for his life. One of the primary themes of Stephen's speech is the unfaithfulness of God's own people to him and his chosen messengers. Still, Moses' forty years among the Midianites prepares him for his future redemptive work.

The burning bush (vv. 30–34) shows Moses as a type of Christ, commissioned as God's agent to save his people and sent to suffer as a result. He will become the rejected deliverer (vv. 35–38). The third forty-year period is the wilderness wanderings. Moses is the messianic precursor, the "ruler and deliverer" over Israel who will free them. At the same time, the people of Moses' time are a type of the people of Stephen's day, refusing to obey God's messenger and preferring to go their own way. The golden calf incident (vv. 39–43) shows the idolatry this leads into, and God turns against his former covenant people in judgment.

This was Stephen's warning to the Sanhedrin of the implications of what it was doing. Even the tabernacle and temple (vv. 44–50) were temporary homes of God, and his true dwelling place is heaven rather than any earthly building. It was important that the Sanhedrin realize that while the temple contained God, he could not be restricted to it, for "the Most High does not live in houses made by human hands" (v. 48). He is everywhere, as critical a point for us as for the Sanhedrin.

Stephen's conclusion is very hard-hitting (vv. 51–53). While he is on trial for his life, he has turned his "defense speech" into a judicial indictment of Israel and of the Sanhedrin for refusing to obey God and for rejecting his chosen agents, first Moses and now Jesus. The Sanhedrin is guilty of the very same thing for which they have Stephen on trial, blasphemy and rejection of the true God.

Three things take place in rapid succession to end this first major section of Acts (1:1–8:3): First, Stephen looks up to heaven and actually sees the glory of the risen and exalted Christ standing in his glory at the right hand of God (vv. 55–56). Second, in their wrath these supreme justices of the Sanhedrin lose all semblance of decorum, yank him outside the city, and stone him themselves. What they did was completely legal and allowed by the Romans, but the intense anger and lack of control is where it went wrong. Like their ancestors, they turned against God as well as his own prophet (Stephen).

Third and finally, this launches the great persecution that itself initiates the outgoing mission of the church (8:1b–3). Saul in fact even at his young age becomes the leader of this severe persecution, obtaining authority from the high priest and the Sanhedrin to conduct raids of Christian house churches and arrest believers, placing them on trial and even leading to the execution of many. This terrible time, however, is used of the Spirit to force Christians to flee Jerusalem and scatter throughout Palestine and even further—many of the Hellenistic believers would have returned to their original homes in Gentile lands. So the universal mission is launched by the persecution.

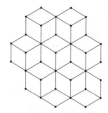

SAMARIA AND THE
ETHIOPIAN EUNUCH
(8:4–40)

The first major section of Acts (1:1-8:3) centered on the beginning of the church age, as the Spirit came from heaven and empowered the new messianic community to fulfill its calling and move out to the nations. However, the early church misunderstood[1] the call to go to the nations, interpreting it as the nations coming to them in Jerusalem, the Holy City, in line with the call to proselyte ministry in Isaiah and other Old Testament works. So they remained in the land, and the Spirit had to send a persecution to force them outward. So these early years could be labeled the Palestinian or Jewish Christian period. Stephen realized the implications, and his death spurred the impetus to move outward with the gospel. Estimates for how long this period was vary from two to five years. I would estimate that it was two to three years, and so perhaps AD 33 when the mission as we know it began.

---

1. It is important to realize the apostles were not disobeying the mission command. Rather, they misinterpreted it; and, in fact, God used that to anchor the Jewish Christian church in the two to three years they remained in Jerusalem. When they did begin the universal mission, they were a strong, united, and successful movement.

As the church moved outward to escape the persecution, witness continued to characterize its activity. Where the people went, the gospel accompanied them. Luke continually links this expansion with inspired, Spirit-driven leaders, from Peter to Stephen to Philip to Paul. Philip is hardly the only one ministering in this early period, but he is a critical stepping stone in following the program set out in 1:8 from Jerusalem (Peter) to Judea (Stephen) to Samaria (Philip), so Luke centers on him. As another of the seven, he also provides a link from the Palestinian period to the universal mission.

The next chapters provide a series of stages to the universal mission as the Spirit takes charge and guides the people of God into the will of God. There are six stages in all in chapters 8–11, with two geographical movements and three key individuals leading to the first Gentile church, Antioch: (1) from the Jerusalem church to Judea; (2) from Judea to Samaria; (3) the Ethiopian eunuch, the first pure Gentile, as the first transition; (4) the apostle Paul, the missionary to the Gentiles, as the second transition; (5) Cornelius as the final transition; (6) the church in Antioch as the archetypal Gentile church, leading to Paul's missionary journeys.

PHILIP MINISTERS IN SAMARIA (8:4-25)

Samaria lies between Judea and Galilee and so is the natural place to which refugees could flee from the persecution. However, it is somewhat unusual in light of the centuries of animosity between the Jews and the Samaritans. The Samaritans were the product of the Assyrian exile, when the Assyrians forced the Jews they had not deported to marry pagans, producing half-castes (2 Kgs 17:24-41). When the Jews returned from exile, they initially did not want these people to participate in rebuilding the temple, and later they divorced their pagan wives (Ezra 4:1-5; 9:1-10:44; Neh 13:1-3, 23-27). From that time onward, the Jews and Samaritans were enemies. However, Jesus had already conducted a successful mission to the Samaritans (John 4), setting the precedent for the church.

EVANGELISTIC MINISTRY AMONG THE SAMARITANS (8:4–11)

The account begins with a summary statement of Christian activity throughout Palestine by those forced to flee Jerusalem. It is noteworthy that they were not frazzled, confused people trying to establish new homes but immediately "preached the word." The church is now called "those who had been scattered," which had become a semi-technical expression in Judaism after the exiles and the Roman deportation labeled "the **diaspora**" (*hoi diasparentes*), referring to Jews dispersed in lands far from their homeland. This new Christian diaspora was the means by which the universal mission took place. Ironically, the persecution by which the Jews sought to eradicate the Christ movement was the single greatest factor in spreading it out to the nations.

Philip, one of the seven (6:5), went to Samaria, about forty miles from Jerusalem, and proclaimed Jesus as Messiah. John the Baptist had baptized in Bethany beyond the Jordan there (John 1:28), and Jesus had ministered in Sychar (John 4:6), so undoubtedly many people had been waiting for his followers to come back. They would have greeted Philip with joy. We don't know what city Philip visited, and Luke places his emphasis on the whole region rather than a particular town. Samaria in Acts is not really Jewish and yet not Gentile either. It is a stepping stone to the Gentile mission and begins the movement of the church to the nations.

The Samaritans considered themselves the true covenant people, followers of Abraham and Moses. Their holy mountain was Gerizim rather than Sinai, and they accepted only the Pentateuch as Scripture. They believed that their "messiah" was the prophet like Moses of Deuteronomy 18:15, and they called him the Taheb (restorer). This was a natural starting point for Philip's gospel message (used by Jesus as well in John 4:25–26).

Philip not only preached Christ but performed sign-miracles as well, so the crowds "paid close attention to what he said" (8:6). "They all" is a strong term in Greek, *homothymadon*, used also in 1:14; 2:46 for the deep oneness of the church, "one in heart and mind." So the crowd followed his preaching point by point and paid rapt attention to it all. The double whammy of great preaching and powerful miracles fascinated them all.

Luke then tells us what kind of miracles enthralled the people: power over the demonic powers and over various illnesses (8:7-8). The "shrieks" are not of pain but of frustrated defeat, as the evil powers turned out to have no power in the face of the overwhelming might of the Spirit in Philip. Demons are "impure" or "unclean" because they are filled with evil and taint everything they encounter. The "paralyzed or lame" are healed by both Jesus (Luke 5:17-26) and the apostles (Acts 3:1-10; 9:33-35). The natural result was "great joy in that city," not only because people had been healed and delivered, but also because they had found salvation in Christ. They have experienced both earthly and heavenly or eternal joy.

The power of Philip is especially seen when the people turn from Simon, the greatest sorcerer of his day, to follow Philip. Simon was a powerful magician but an equally strong self-promoter, calling himself "Simon the Great." You could call him the Barnum and Bailey of his day. Still, he was good enough at his craft that his fellow Samaritans were "amazed." He had earned his self-made title. The term for "practiced sorcery" or "magic" (*mageuō*, with a cognate used for the "magi" in Matt 2) refers to uttering incantations to gain control over the gods and getting them to do their bidding. Since Jews and Samaritans were famous for producing sorcerers (note the Jewish sorcerer Elymas Bar-Jesus in 13:6-11),[2] they applied this to controlling the angelic realm and thus God. Simon had become famous and had many followers due to his exploits, although Luke does not tell us exactly what they were. All we know is that they were spectacular enough to amaze the people.

Every person in Samaria, whether poor and ignorant or rich and knowledgeable, was captivated by him and gave him their

---

2. In actual fact, the Torah prohibited the practice of magic (Exod 22:18; Lev 19:26, 31; Deut 18:10-11), but many ignored this.

undivided attention. It is difficult to know for certain what he claimed about himself. The people all agreed with his self-asserted title that he was "the Great Power of God," but exactly what that meant is a real question. He could be claiming deity for himself like the emperors often did, translating it "great divine power" and stressing his own divinity. Or (more likely) he could be advertising himself as endowed with supernatural powers by God, probably equivalent to an archangel. Unlike Philip, he did not give the glory to God but took that glory on himself. He had "amazed them for a long time with his sorcery" (8:11), meaning he was a showman who went from place to place performing magic in order to enthrall the crowds.

The Conversion of Many Samaritans (8:12–13)

As with Jesus in Sychar in John 4, the evangelism of the community is quite successful, and many of the same people who had previously followed Simon now "believed Philip" when he proclaimed the gospel and "the name of Jesus Christ." By stressing "the name," Luke means both Jesus as Messiah/the Christ and that Philip demonstrated the power of Christ by performing signs and wonders (3:6, 16; 4:10, 30). He proclaimed that Jesus is the messianic figure expected by both Jews and Samaritans, that God's reign has begun and his kingdom has arrived. Then he proved his claims by exercising the power of Christ via miracles. This double authority in word and deed convinced large numbers that Jesus was indeed the Son of God. As in 2:38, the new converts then demonstrated their new faith by being baptized.

Even more amazingly, Simon himself "believed and was baptized," then "followed Philip everywhere," almost as an apprentice or disciple. The reason is just what we would have expected. He had found a power greater than his. In comparison to the healings and exorcisms of Philip, Simon's "great power" was rather ordinary, a bag of magic tricks. He wanted to learn how to do what Philip could do.

A real question is how sincere Simon's conversion actually is. In verses 18–24 he tries to buy this power for himself and is thoroughly rebuked for it. However, here Luke seems to present it as a genuine conversion. The reason for his conversion is that he was "astonished by the great signs and miracles he saw." If his belief was genuine, it was shallow and easily suborned by his greed. We can go no further than this. I would agree with those who see a parallel with John 2:23–25; his was a sign-based belief and must be questioned, as it will be in verses 20–24.

Peter and John Sent to Samaria (8:14–24)

The apostles were still the leaders and in charge of the Christian movement. They remained in Jerusalem after the persecution of 8:1–3 and needed to see this new thrust into Samaria for themselves in order to attest that God was indeed behind it.[3] They probably chose Peter and John because they were part of the inner circle (with James, John's brother). John was a good one to send because he had earlier wished to call fire down from heaven upon the Samaritans for their inhospitable attitude toward Jesus (Luke 9:52–55). This shows his change of heart well.

Receiving the Holy Spirit (8:14–17)

Part of the report that had reached Jerusalem was that while the new converts had believed and been baptized, the Spirit had not yet come upon them. That raised serious questions, and they had to examine what had taken place. It is hard to know why this occurred, but an educated guess could be that God wanted the apostles to be part of this important next step in the divine plan for the universal mission.

When Peter and John arrive (8:15), they immediately pray that these "new believers" might "receive the Holy Spirit." Paul

---

3. They will do the same for the Gentile mission when they send Barnabas to Antioch in 11:22.

in Romans 8:14-17 tells us that when a person truly believes, the Spirit immediately indwells them. However, Luke does not tell us how Philip and the others knew the Spirit had not come upon them. Does this indicate that glossolalia, speaking in tongues, was the initial sign? This strongly debated question is the subject of many books and articles. All I can say here is that there is nothing I see in the New Testament that makes that the case. I do think it is likely that they did speak in tongues (see v. 18 below and 10:45-46), but this was a fairly unique situation. My view is that it can be such a sign, but the Spirit must determine who does or does not receive that spiritual gift. I don't take it as a normative sign but do see it as a sign the Spirit can send to those whom he determines.

Still, the Samaritan converts had participated in the sign of baptism, showing that step of faith that signified they had been cleansed by the Lord. However, the Holy Spirit had not yet provided God's imprimatur that he had accepted them by giving the Spirit to them (8:16). So Peter and John accepted their faith commitment and immediately began praying for that critical step to take place. As they prayed, they laid hands on them (8:17), and at that time the new converts "received the Holy Spirit."

Is the laying on of hands normative? It seems to have been the method of the early church, for instance at Timothy's commission when he received his spiritual "gift" at the laying on of hands (1 Tim 4:14; 2 Tim 1:6). But nowhere is it seen as the normative method. In 10:44 (Cornelius) the laying on of hands is not needed.

There are three places where we are told the Holy Spirit comes down upon a group in a special way: here among the Samaritans, then at what could be called the Gentile Pentecost in 10:44-46, and then again upon the disciples of John the Baptist in 19:6. In each case a new group is welcomed into the church, and the Spirit indicates a new stage in salvation history. Each new stage moves the mission of the church into these new areas, and is signified by the sending of the Spirit to initiate first the Jewish Pentecost (Acts 2), then the Samaritan Pentecost (here), and the Gentile Pentecost

(Acts 10). By doing this, the Spirit is indicating that the Samaritans and then the Gentiles are now chosen by God to stand alongside the Jews as the covenant people of God, and the basis of that is now faith in Christ rather than keeping the law.

The Confrontation of Simon (8:18-24)

This incident is the basis of the term "simony," referring to the greedy attempt to purchase a spiritual reality falsely with money. Simon, formerly the greatest sorcerer in the land, has just been eclipsed by Philip, whose miracles were beyond Simon's power. Now he experiences the Pentecost phenomena of Acts 2 (perhaps all three—the wind, fire, and tongues, 2:4), and Simon just has to have that extraordinary power for himself. He had always bought whatever tools of sorcery he needed, and he now reasons that will work here as well. In reality this was a common practice, as seen in chief priests bribing Roman officials to receive a high office in the priesthood. His grave sin is to consider the power of the Holy Spirit nothing but another magic trick he can use to his own ends.

Simon's desire is that he like the apostles has the ability to impart the Spirit to "everyone on whom I lay my hands" (8:19). He thought God and the Spirit could be bought from the leaders of the church, and then he would control God and once more be "the Great Power of God." It makes me wonder how anyone who truly believes in Christ could have such a self-centered perspective. For years I have always thought he was a genuine believer who fell into an unfortunate error. However, more and more I am wondering if there ever was any true faith in him. Yet see further on verse 22 below.

Peter's rebuke in 8:20-24 is quite harsh, and deservedly so. As many have pointed out, this threat of divine punishment is also a curse, calling down divine wrath on so terrible a sin: "May your money perish with you." "Perish," to be eternally destroyed, is the biblical penalty for sin (Deut 8:19; Luke 13:3, 5). The Holy Spirit is a "gift of God" and not a commodity that can be bought and paid for to gain personal advantage. The Spirit can only be received from God and cannot be controlled and manipulated as a tool of human powers.

Next, Peter tells Simon he has "no part or share in this ministry" to the Samaritans (8:21). Simon likely had a vision of himself as the head of the church in Samaria, and Peter is telling him that is a delusion of grandeur, that his heart (his mind and his spiritual sense) is not "right before God," and thus he can have no "share" in God's work. He is not just in danger of being ostracized by the church but by God himself. The term translated "ministry" (*logos*) could also refer to the "message" of the gospel, thus meaning he will not share in the joy and blessings of the gospel. I prefer "in this matter" or "thing," because he will have no part in the work of the Holy Spirit. He is not right with God or the Spirit. Still, the language is of a failed and shallow believer rather than of an unbeliever. Peter never challenges his "belief" (8:13) here but rather his thought life. We could label him a "carnal Christian" rather than an unbeliever.

In 8:22–23 we see the demands Peter makes on Simon if he is to get right with God. This indicates his sin is not as severe as that of Ananias and Sapphira in 5:1–11, for repentance is possible. Peter tells him he must repent then pray for forgiveness "for having such a [wicked] thought in your heart." The problem is not just the action of trying to buy the Spirit but the very thought life that produced such a thing. The mindset lay behind the actions, and he had to cleanse his mind of such wickedness.

There is serious danger, and things must change. His fall into wickedness is anchored in the fact that he is "full of bitterness and captive to sin." His bitterness is probably not a reference to envy of Philip but rather the bitter poison of his heart of avarice and desire for power. This has chained him in the bonds of sin and taken over his life. If he doesn't turn his life around, the curse of verse 20 will come to pass, and eternal destruction will be the only destiny he has.

Simon responds in verse 24, and his prayer is that of a chastened, shallow Christian who realizes Peter is right and he is in real danger. There is debate regarding the sincerity of Simon's response, especially since he asks Peter to pray for him rather than uttering the prayer of repentance himself. Many believe that he does not truly feel remorse and is saying in effect, "Pray for me if you want, but I don't feel the need myself." It is also possible that he accepts the wrong he has committed but is more concerned with escaping its consequences than in truly repenting and getting right with God. However, I think that his request that Peter pray for him is due to feelings of unworthiness and that his repentance is genuine. Any of the three is viable for the context, but I prefer the more positive picture.

Several church fathers believed Simon Magus was the father of **Gnosticism** and heretical movements in the generations that followed.[4] The future of Simon can never be known for certain, for there are few sources. Our own conclusions depend somewhat on our estimate of the material here and whether there was genuine repentance in his life. I think there was and so am more positive about this future. However we take it, the story of Simon Magus is an important warning against allowing yourself to be a carnal Christian, for those who play games in their walk with Christ are in real danger of standing before Christ and hearing, "I never knew you. Away from me, you evildoers!" (Matt 7:23).

Summary: Ministry in Samaria (8:25)

While Simon dominates the Acts account, his was just one of several during the ministry of Peter and John in Samaria. Luke tells us three things, all general statements in an ABA pattern, with A = preaching the word and B = witness about Jesus. During their time

---

4. See, for example, Irenaeus, *Against Heresies* 1.23; Justin Martyr, *First Apology* 26.

there, "many" Samaritan towns and villages were evangelized. It is doubtful that Peter and John personally visited every town and village, for there were a great many in that part of Palestine. Still, their ministry was highly successful, as we have seen throughout this book.

PHILIP ENCOUNTERS THE
ETHIOPIAN EUNUCH (8:26–40)

The second stage on the road to the universal mission differs from the others in that this is an individual rather than a group, a wealthy aristocrat and Gentile proselyte on his way to Jerusalem to worship God in his holy city. It was commonly thought that Ethiopia was virtually the end of the world, so this is a foretaste of "the ends of the earth" in 1:8. Furthermore, as a eunuch his rights to worship were marginalized, as eunuchs could not enter the inner sanctuary of the temple or offer sacrifices (Deut 23:1). Since eunuchs could not be circumcised, they could never be fully Jewish. On a much more positive note, as a Nubian he would have been a black person and a further ethnic group entering the kingdom as part of the universal mission. So this also shows that the gospel is meant for every person and treats all equally.

THE SETTING: AN OFFICIAL ON THE ROAD (8:26–28)

Supernatural guidance continues to light the way for the gospel as it moves outward. Now an "angel of the Lord" appears to Philip and instructs him to head south from Samaria. This is definitely divine guidance, for we would have expected him to continue north from Samaria into Galilee and then Syria. But instead he bypasses Jerusalem and heads down the road south from the Holy City called the Gaza road. Angels often appear in Acts (5:19; 10:3, 7, 22; 11:13; 12:7–11, 23; 27:23) and continue the work of the Spirit in guiding the action in finding the will of God. Philip is filled with the Spirit (6:3) and is led by the Spirit here (8:29) here as well. So the angel and the Spirit supplement each other.

Gaza is the southernmost city of Israel, a major trade center rebuilt by the Romans on the route to Egypt. The mention of "the desert road" is a likely reference to the old city, destroyed by Alexander Jannaeus in 96–98 BC and lying mostly in ruins. This is the road on which he was to encounter the eunuch. As Philip was traveling on the road he met a wealthy eunuch returning home from worshipping in Jerusalem.

The "Ethiopian eunuch" would have been from Nubia, south of Egypt, the biblical land of Cush (Gen 2:13). Eunuchs were voluntarily castrated, usually because that would enable them to reach high office, as they were deemed less prone to pleasures and easier to trust. This had worked for him, and he had become a powerful official "in charge of all the treasury" of the land. "Kandake" ("Candace" in many versions) was not the name of the queen but the dynastic title she held; *kandakē* means "queen of the Ethiopians." So he was the treasurer of Ethiopia, one of the highest officials in the country.

He could not be a full proselyte (again because he couldn't be circumcised), but he was a God-fearer, meaning he was fully Jewish in belief and practice. Isaiah 56:3–5 promises a new name and a new place among the covenant people for foreigners and eunuchs in the new kingdom, and it is possible that Luke is saying that in the church this has now come to pass. He had traveled all the way to Jerusalem for the sole purpose of worshipping the Lord, probably referring to prayers in the outer court of the Gentiles.

He had finished worshipping the Lord in the temple and now was "on his way home." Due to his wealth, he is likely reading his own scroll of Isaiah (likely the **Septuagint** since he would be a Greek-speaking Gentile), undoubtedly quite a long scroll (perhaps more than one) due the length of the book. He likely had purchased it in Jerusalem on this trip and so is reading it for the first time. He had gotten as far as Isaiah 53 (as the Spirit dictated) when he met Philip. The "chariot" was not a military vehicle but a fairly luxurious carriage for such a high official, capable of carrying a driver and another person. As the trip took five months each way and was certainly a pilgrimage, the eunuch would not have scrimped on the carriage.

ENCOUNTER WITH PHILIP (8:29–31)

The Spirit once again takes over. An angel guided Philip in verse 26, showing the importance of this encounter, as all heaven is involved. The command is twofold for emphasis: "Go to that chariot and stay near it." The Lord wants Philip to hear what the man is reading (aloud) and then respond. Apparently he runs up to the carriage and then continues running alongside it. As he hears what the man is reading, he immediately grasps the opportunity for witness, as it is that portion in 53:7–8 that applies to Jesus as the Suffering Servant of Isaiah.

Since the Spirit has clearly made Philip bold even when talking to a high-ranking foreign official, he asks, "Do you understand what you are reading?" His very question imparts the offer to explain it if the man is confused (as he of course would be). The eunuch in effect asks for just that as he replies, "How can I ... unless someone explains it to me?" The verb (hodēgēsei) asks for someone to "show the way" or "guide" him to a correct understanding. The Servant of Yahweh could be a reference to the nation or to Isaiah himself. He recognizes his need for help and invites Philip to ride with him in the carriage so they can communicate more clearly. He is open and willing for it to take as long as needed so he can learn the truth.

THE GOSPEL FROM ISAIAH 53 (8:32–35)

The Isaiah 53:7–8 reading stems from the Septuagint, the Greek Old Testament that the eunuch was reading. It centers on the unjust suffering of the Servant of Yahweh, who is humiliated, mistreated, and killed while being innocent of any wrongdoing. The imagery of the slaughtered sheep and lamb looks at a sacrificial death that is "deprived of justice." The idea of atonement procured is not emphasized (it is in 53:5-6) but is still in keeping with Isaiah 53 and so implicit here. This Servant is God's own agent and yet suffered an unjust death inflicted by a wicked generation. God vindicating his Servant is also missing from these verses (it is in 53:10-12) in order to center on the guilt of this wicked generation and the fact that this took place because it was the will of God (53:10).

So the eunuch asks Philip, "Tell me, please, who is the prophet talking about, himself or someone else?" (8:34). Down through the centuries, this has been asked again and again as people try to identify this "Servant." Luke's readers (and we) ask the very same thing. There were three options, with the first two far and away the most widely held: Isaiah himself (whose message was rejected by the people), the nation (rejected by the nations around them), or a messianic figure (but they had no place for a suffering messiah).

This is the opportunity for which Philip has been praying, so he "began with that very passage of Scripture and told him the good news about Jesus" (8:35). Verses 7-8 were just the beginning, as Philip certainly went on into the rest of Isaiah 53 and proved to the eunuch that Jesus was the Suffering Servant and that his death involved atonement and resulted in his being vindicated by God (see above on vv. 32-33). After he had done this he would have shown the eunuch how all this applied to the issues of repentance, forgiveness, and salvation—the gospel, or "good news about Jesus."

THE BAPTISM OF THE EUNUCH (8:36-38)

Philip must have explained to the eunuch how baptism had become the Christian rite that followed conversion and signified that the individual had been cleansed from sin, with the immersion in the water signifying our death to sin and burial with Christ, then the coming out of the water signifying our being raised from death to life in Christ (Rom 6:1-4). So when he saw a body of water he exclaimed, "What can stand in the way of my being baptized?" This assumes that the man had come to faith in Christ a bit earlier and wants to fulfill 2:38, "Repent and be baptized." He had done the first and now wants to fulfill the second and complete his new faith journey.[5]

Philip agreed, and they stopped the carriage, walked down to the water, and he baptized the eunuch. The man would have been thrilled, for he was denied Jewish circumcision and recognition as a full proselyte due to his being a eunuch (see above) but now is finally fully an accepted member of the body of Christ. Quite a few commentaries discuss the question about the mode of baptism here—immersion, pouring, or sprinkling. However, this is not germane here, and Luke is not interested in the question. My own view is that immersion was the norm (Greek *baptizō* means "to immerse") but that the early church felt free to pour or sprinkle depending on the water supply.

THE CONTINUED TRAVELS OF THE TWO (8:39–40)

This second stage of the worldwide mission of God's people is now complete, so when the baptism had finished, "the Spirit of the Lord suddenly took Philip away." The Spirit had brought Philip, and now he "spirits" him away, fulfilling the adage from Job 1:21, "the LORD gave and the LORD has taken away." The conclusion in Job, totally apt here as well, is "blessed be the name of the Lord." Most likely this is meant as a supernatural disappearance. We don't know why. It is very clear, however, that the Spirit has orchestrated every detail of this significant event in the history of global outreach.

The eunuch never saw Philip again but "went on his way rejoicing." Joy is always the result of the coming of salvation (5:41; 11:23; 13:48; 15:31). We know nothing more about him, although Irenaeus (*Against Heresies* 3.12.10) and Eusebius (*History of the Church* 2.1.13) both said he was the first missionary to the Ethiopian people. That

---

5. Verse 37 contains a confession of faith on the part of the eunuch but is almost certainly a later addition to Luke's narrative. It is missing in the oldest and best manuscripts (𝔓45 𝔓74 ℵ A B C and others) and was added probably because later scribes felt a conversion experience was needed in the text.

would be remarkable, with the treasurer of the nation a missionary to the very nation he helped run. I would dearly love to hear his story!

Philip, in the meantime, was taken by the Spirit to the city of Azotus, Old Testament Ashdod (Isa 20:1), a Philistine city twenty miles north of Gaza. Philip seems to have become a traveling or pioneer missionary like Paul later became, as for the next while he preaches the gospel in all the towns and villages up the coast between Azotus and Caesarea (about fifty-five miles), where he then apparently settles (Caesarea is his home in 21:8, where he is described as an "evangelist" and has four prophetess daughters). The Word of God is indeed "alive and active" and "sharper than any double-edged sword" (Heb 4:12).

———

We are at a major turning point in Acts and in the history of the church, when it ceased to be a Jewish sect and became a worldwide movement taking the gospel to the nations. The next five chapters (8–12) will trace the steps to the Gentile mission. In the Great Commission (Matt 28:19; Acts 1:8) the Lord had called the church to the nations, but they misunderstood and believed they were to wait for the nations to come to them rather than go directly to the nations, which the Jewish believers were reluctant to do because the Gentiles were an unclean people. So God has just sent a "great persecution" (8:1) to force these believers out to the surrounding nations.

So first the fleeing saints moved into Judea and Samaria, taking the gospel with them. In Samaria (vv. 4–25), Philip spearheaded the mission both with mighty preaching of Christ and mighty miracles, so powerful that they led to the "conversion" of the leading magician of his day, Simon. He was probably an actual believer but a shallow one who tried to buy that miraculous power from Philip. He is a lesser version of Ananias (5:1–11), not an apostate but a carnal Christian who had to repent of his perfidy or face serious judgment from God. He is an example of the danger of self-centered Christians trying to use God to their own ends, something that goes on far more often than we think.

It was difficult for the Jerusalem church to accept the movement into Samaria, and so they sent Peter and John to authenticate it. It was the Spirit who did so, by reduplicating the Pentecost phenomena from chapter 2 and showing that God was indeed behind this expansion of the mission to the world. Their ministry there was as successful as Philip's had been.

The next stage is the Ethiopian eunuch (vv. 26–40), the first full Gentile convert, who would become the missionary to the Ethiopian people, another step in the worldwide mission of the church. He was returning from worshipping in the temple and reading an Isaiah scroll he had purchased in Jerusalem. The Spirit saw to it that he was at 53:7–8 when Philip arrived, perfect for preaching Jesus as the Suffering Servant and Messiah. The eunuch is converted and is then baptized by Philip, returning to his country as a full believer ready to take the gospel into Africa and become God's ambassador to those people. The Spirit's guidance here, as all the way through Acts, is perfect, and the mission of Christ as led by the Spirit continues to expand.

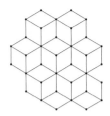

SAUL'S CONVERSION AND PETER'S MISSION
(9:1–43)

I n Luke's presentation the conversion of Saul/Paul is one of the critical steps for the universal mission of the church, for now the preordained missionary to the Gentiles comes to Christ and takes the mission a huge step forward. As in the ministry of Philip, God and the Spirit orchestrate every step of Paul's conversion. The power of the Godhead in the gospel is never more apparent than in the conversion of Saul, for he was the leading persecutor among the Jews and through his own initiative is tapped to take that persecution outside the confines of Palestine to the **diasporic** lands. His intention is to arrest as many Christ followers as he can and take them back to Jerusalem for trial. The gospel is mighty enough to break through that "dividing wall of hostility" (Eph 2:14) in Paul and not only bring him to Christ but change him so radically that the former despiser of Gentiles becomes the archetypal missionary to the Gentiles.

SAUL IS CONVERTED (9:1–30)

This event is so significant for the early church that there are four versions of it (Acts 9; 22; 26; Gal 1), which, for theological reasons, contain several differences in the details:

1. Between Luke and Paul
   a. The call: in Galatians 1 it comes on the Damascus road; in Acts 22:17–18 the call also comes via a temple vision in Jerusalem
   b. Second stage: in Galatians 1 Paul goes into Arabia after his conversion; in Acts 9 he goes to Jerusalem, omitting the time in Arabia
2. Between the three accounts in Acts
   a. In 9:7 the bystanders hear a voice and see no one; in 22:9 they see a light and hear no one
   b. In 26:14, a statement is added to Christ's challenge that "it is hard for you to kick against the goads"
   c. In 9:15–17 the commission to the Gentiles comes through Ananias; in 22:17–18 it comes through the vision in the temple; in 26:17–18 it comes on the Damascus road

These will be resolved as we come across them in the text, but they all reflect differing theological emphases rather than historical discrepancies. Chapter 9 is central in tracing the progress to the Gentile mission, so Luke stresses the voice of the commission in 9:7. Chapter 22 comes after the trip to Jerusalem and is Paul's defense before the Jewish mob, so there Luke stresses Jewish polemic and shows continuity between the Jewish temple (22:17–18) and the Gentile mission, in so doing highlighting the "light" of glory in the temple and in Paul's commission (very understandable to a Jew). Chapter 26 is Paul's defense before Agrippa, more Roman than Jewish, and it stresses the Gentile aspects. "Kicking against the goads" is a Gentile metaphor, perhaps turning a Hebrew phrase into a Gentile proverb for Agrippa.

Saul the Persecutor (9:1–2)

When we last saw Saul, he was going from one house church to another arresting believers and imprisoning many of them (8:3).

That continues as he is "breathing out murderous threats against the Lord's disciples."

As we will see in 26:10, he carried some of them out and delivered Christians up to their deaths. Moreover, according to 26:11–12 this was not the first time Saul had gone outside Palestine to "foreign cities." So Saul had spearheaded the persecution in Jerusalem and Judea and now was doing the same in Damascus and other diasporic cities. His goal was to establish the counterpart to the Christian mission to the world and start a worldwide pogrom of Christian communities. He wanted not just to breathe out murderous threats but also to carry them out and arrest as many believers as he could.

He decides to make Damascus his next target and goes to the high priest for letters of introduction to the synagogues there, establishing his official authority to conduct a program of destruction for this "heretical" movement. We should note that this goes against his mentor Gamaliel's advice in 5:38 to leave them alone and let God deal with it. He likely felt that advice would not work and more active measures were needed. He with these letters now has the authority to arrest believers and take them back to Jerusalem for trial. Synagogues had civil authority but not as broad a power as Paul needed, so the trials needed to be held back in Jerusalem.

For the first time, we see the title the Christians originally had for their movement, "the Way," taken from Isaiah 40:3, "Prepare the way for the Lord" (also 19:9, 23; 24:14, 22). They viewed themselves as proclaiming the "way" for Jesus as Messiah, and so theirs was the messianic arm of Judaism. In their minds there were now four Jewish sects—the Pharisees, the Sadducees, the Essenes, and now the Way (the Zealots would not appear as a sect until the 50s and 60s).

The Damascus Road Vision (9:3–9)

Saul would have traveled north from Jerusalem through Samaria then Galilee and into Syria, a distance of 136 miles (220 kilometers), which would have taken about a week. It was probably about the sixth or seventh day of the trip as he was nearing the city. Out of the blue (literally) he was suddenly enveloped in an incredibly bright light that "flashed" like lightning, and he fell to the ground. It was a "light from heaven," not an earthly phenomenon but a divine manifestation that "suddenly" came, possibly from a clear sky. It is a theophany, but unlike elsewhere it is Christ rather than God. From verse 7 we learn that only Saul saw the light and the vision that emanated from it. His companions saw nothing and simply heard a voice (without being able to distinguish words). The light was the **Shekinah** glory of Christ come to "dwell" (Hebrew *shakan*) with Saul. In 26:13 he will describe it as "brighter than the sun," saying it was "blazing around me and my companions." In other words, like at the burning bush (Exod 3), the whole area became sacred ground.

Luke does not tell us what Saul saw, but he was not one of the companions in verse 7. We learn from 1 Corinthians 9:1 that he had "seen Jesus our Lord," not in an ephemeral way but in an actual vision of Christ speaking akin to what Stephen saw in 7:55. In fact, Paul (in 1 Cor 9:1) anchored his authority to be an apostle in the fact that here he actually saw him, meaning that this was more than a vision but an actual appearance of Jesus, as in 1 Corinthians 15:3–7. So this vision/actual viewing was in itself a very important event in salvation history. For Luke it is a necessary preliminary event for the universal mission of the church because it provides for them the one who is to lead that mission. The light was so dazzlingly bright that Saul "fell to the ground," the normal reaction to a theophany (Ezek 1:28; 3:23; Dan 8:17; Rev 1:17).

He apparently does not yet see anyone but hears a voice stemming from the Shekinah light, "Saul, Saul, why do you persecute me?" The repetition of his name is for emphasis and parallels God addressing Abraham at the sacrifice of Isaac (Gen 22:11) or Moses at the burning bush (Exod 3:4). It certainly got Saul's attention. Contrary to some, he did not change his name from Saul to Paul when he became missionary to the Gentiles. Rather he used the Aramaic Saul when in a Jewish context and the Greek Paul in a Gentile context. In 22:2 we learn that the voice of Christ addressed Saul in Aramaic, and Saul was the name he went by in that context.

Jesus asks, "Why do you persecute me?" in the present tense, thus looking at his persecution pattern from the death of Stephen until now. Moreover, Jesus says, "persecute *me*"; when Paul persecutes Christ's followers he persecutes Jesus himself, for he is one with his people.

Needless to say, Saul is confused, wondering which of the many people he has been persecuting this voice could be, and both how and why it has addressed him this way. He asks, "Who are you, Lord," not knowing what kind of powerful, high official it might be. He may have in mind an angel or perhaps God himself in an Old Testament sense, but why a heavenly being would discuss his persecution of the church in this way would have been mystifying.

The voice responds, "I am Jesus," and it may be at this time when a figure emerged from the light and became distinct to Saul (1 Cor 9:1). This revelation would have shocked him to the core, and this alone would have needed the three days in darkness (v. 9) for him to work through the implications. He had been wrong for all this time! Moreover, as he persecuted the church he had been persecuting Jesus. This was a staggering truth. It was also a revelation of something equally astounding, that this Jesus whom the Jews had the Romans crucify and who had been buried outside Jerusalem actually had risen from the dead and was the exalted Lord of heaven.

This risen Jesus now orders Saul to "get up and go into the city, and you will be told what you must do" (9:6). He is truly "the Lord," in charge and expecting Saul to acquiesce completely, which he does. Saul is no longer head of the team headed to Damascus; Jesus is. Note the emphatic "told what you must [*dei*] do." This is the divine "must." Saul is to obey the divine directive he will be given in Damascus. We have no idea what happened to those who had been on the team with him headed for Damascus. They must have been completely confused by all that had happened. It will be interesting when we get to heaven to find out if any of them found Christ through this series of events.

In verse 7 Luke turns to the companions who had been part of his team (and likely others who had been traveling with them) and describes their involvement in the vision. Though they are present, they are not really a part of the event, which was only for Saul. So they "stood there speechless" because they "heard the sound but did not see anyone." Still, they were witnesses that this was not just a dream on Saul's part. God let them hear the sounds (but they could not distinguish words[1]) so they could testify that something indeed had happened. In fact, in 26:14 Paul tells us that the men had also fallen to the ground, so they would have been aware of an extraordinary event taking place. They would have been even more perplexed than Saul but were still witnesses at a secondary level.

In verse 7 we see the effects on the companions, and now in verses 8–9 we have the effects on Saul himself. The revelation itself now finished, he arises from the ground. When he opens his eyes, he is blind and needs his companions to take his hand and lead him into Damascus. He is unable to see for three days and uses that time to try to understand these astounding revelations. In 13:11 the sorcerer Elymas is also struck blind, but there it is judgment while here it is redemption, for it gives Saul the time to reorient his life and find Christ. His life is not just turned around 180 degrees; it is twirled completely around, and he has to become an entirely different person with an entirely new perspective on life and reality.

The combination of the brilliant light of theophany and the personal encounter with the risen Lord was too much for him (as

---

1. In 22:9 Paul tells the Jewish mob that these bystanders "saw the light but they did not understand the voice." Putting the two together, they saw a light but could distinguish no one and heard a voice but could not catch the words.

it would be for any of us). He was blinded spiritually as well as physically and needed spiritual healing more than physical. This was so wrenching an event that he "did not eat or drink" for the entire time. In one sense he was fasting, but in another his emotions were so high he did not want food or drink. A double miracle takes place, as both his eyes and his heart are opened when the light of God enters his life.

ANANIAS AND SAUL'S NEW BIRTH (9:10–19A)

We don't know how or when the gospel came to Damascus, but it was probably fairly early, perhaps following Pentecost when the converts of 2:41 (3,000 after Pentecost and Peter's sermon) returned home. Ananias was one of the believers there and was granted a vision and a mission by God. He was likely one of those tagged by Saul for arrest and transportation to Jerusalem for trial, but instead he is now chosen by God to go and finalize the conversion of the very one he has feared for a long time.

It is interesting to see that while Saul asked the identity on the one in the vision (v. 5), Ananias seems to know him (could he have been one of the pilgrims at Pentecost?) and responds, "Yes, Lord." He knows the Lord and is ready to do his bidding. Christ is very explicit, and Luke records the address ("the house of Judas on Straight Street") to show Jesus is in complete charge of all details. It is quite possible Ananias knew this Judas if he was a believer. But he could also have been the Jewish person Paul had originally been planning to stay with. Several point out that "Straight Street" was a broad thoroughfare, one of the major roads through the city. (It still exists today.) Saul is identified as "a man from Tarsus," pointing to him as a diaspora Jew from one of the major Roman cities of Cilicia. Saul grew up there, with pious Jewish parents of Pharisaic background but also wealthy citizens of Tarsus and therefore of Rome. (This will be important later in Acts.)

Saul is described as "praying" there in his blind condition (9:11), certainly meaning he is continually addressing God to understand the meaning of the vision he had received from Jesus. So Jesus now tells Ananias that he had given another vision to Saul that "a man named Ananias [would] come and place his hands on him to restore his sight" (9:12). Most likely Saul was also praying that this Ananias would shed light on the meaning of his vision, and at the same time he was undoubtedly seeking forgiveness for persecuting Jesus when he acted against his followers. Saul's conversion may have taken place during these three days, but most likely after Ananias had explained things to him. It is interesting that neither Saul nor Ananias are told that the greater purpose of his visiting Saul is for the man's conversion. Christ knew that this would come naturally and perhaps did not wish to add further complications to an already difficult situation.

In 9:13–14 Ananias gives voice to his greatest fear, his one demurral from what Christ is asking him to do. The church knew Saul was coming, and he had heard from many the havoc that Saul had wreaked on the saints in Jerusalem. This was a very fearful time, and it all centered on this Saul. He knew that Saul was in Damascus not for any good purpose but "with authority from the chief priests to arrest all who call on your name" (see also 9:1–2). To go and see Saul would be to place himself in the hands of the very man who intended to incarcerate as many believers as he could in Damascus. Many had certainly come to Damascus as a result of the persecution in 8:1–3 and would have brought reports of the terrible persecution that followed under the instigation of Saul. Ananias did not want to throw away his life on an impossible mission.

The Lord's response in 9:15 is to repeat the beginning command of verse 11—"Go!" For all the danger and potential for disaster, the orders are quite simple. In fact, they reflect the mission situation down through the centuries. The world will always hate the church, for darkness despises light, and the people of darkness hate the light "because their deeds [are] evil" (John 3:19–20). The people of God on mission are well aware of the grim possibilities but "go" anyway, for their God-assigned task is to take the light of God into the darkness of this world. This is at the heart of the missionary enterprise, the willingness to take the chance in a dangerous situation for the sake of the gospel.

The reason why Ananias is to go anyway is because "this man is my chosen instrument to proclaim my name to the Gentiles and their kings and to the people of Israel." There are two divine directives in the Damascus road vision and Ananias' visit—the conversion of Saul and his commission to go to the Gentiles. It is difficult to decide which is the more difficult step for him, for he was as anti-Gentile as he was anti-Christian.

Each of the three passages detailing the conversion of Saul gives a different time for when he received his call to the Gentiles. In 9:15 it came to him via Ananias; in 22:21 it came via a temple vision; and in 26:17–18 it came in the Damascus vision itself. This call was so radical for Saul that it took two corroborating commissions, three in all, before he could truly assimilate it. Ananias was step two after the initial call on the Damascus road. Note that he was not just to witness to the general populace but also to "their kings," as he will do before Felix, Festus, and Agrippa in Acts 24–26, and Nero during the Roman imprisonment. Further, he will not forego witness to his native siblings, "the people of Israel." Paul has a glorious future, and it is well worth taking a risk in order to bring him to Christ.

Ananias likely did not truly understand the final comment, "I will show him how much he must suffer for my name" (9:16), again with the divine "must" (*dei*; see also 9:6) marking this as Saul's predestined future. For Ananias, Saul was the one causing the suffering, not the one experiencing it. He didn't know what we know, that few have ever suffered more for Christ than he would (see 2 Cor 11:23–29).

In verse 17 Ananias realizes that Saul after his days in isolation and prayer has found Christ and so addresses him as "brother Saul." Taking courage, he enters the house where just days earlier his greatest enemy was lurking. In spite of the fact that he knows the Lord gave Saul a vision about his coming, he still feels it necessary to introduce himself by stating that he was sent by the very same Jesus who appeared to Saul on the road. This is the first time Luke has said that Saul actually saw Jesus.[2] Thus both Ananias and Saul had visions of Jesus and so were bound together in a very exclusive club. On entering, Ananias explains his twofold purpose, the earthly aspect ("that you may see again") and the heavenly, spiritual aspect (that you may "be filled with the Holy Spirit"). A double healing is taking place: physical and spiritual.

Ananias then performs his apostolic duty (though he is not an apostle, he is "sent" by Jesus with authority) and lays hands on Saul, so that these two miracles can take place. The laying on of hands imparted God's presence and power into a situation, so that at that moment, "something like scales fell from Saul's eyes, and he could see again." "Scales" may be more metaphorical than literal, referring to the fact that blindness had covered his eyes and is now removed, but most take this literally.

Paul's first act after getting out of bed as a whole person again was to be baptized. To Paul the spiritual aspect had priority over the physical. As we have seen often (2:38, 41; 8:12–13, 16, 36, 38) converts signified their new life in Christ by being baptized, and Saul continued that practice. He then took care of his earthly needs by "taking some food" and so he "regained his strength." He is now ready to begin his new life and reverse his mission, no longer acting against Christ's people but proclaiming Christ in Damascus and its environs.

Ministry in Damascus (9:19b–25)

Saul now begins to replicate Stephen's ministry in Jerusalem, proclaiming Jesus as Messiah and Son of God in the synagogues of Damascus. This is the first of two preliminary stages for Saul's

---

2. The Greek for "appeared" is *ophtheis*, "was seen by you."

future ministry to the Gentiles, his time in Damascus (and Arabia) in verses 19b–25 and then his time in Jerusalem in verses 26–30. In Acts another word for Christians is "disciples," which here refers to those believers he had planned to arrest and take back to Jerusalem for trial and is now staying with while beginning his ministry. We don't know what has happened to the Judas with whom Saul stayed while he was blind (v. 11). If he was a Jew who was unsympathetic to the Christian movement, Saul may have been forced to leave. If he was a believer Saul may have continued to stay with him during this time.

The Jews of Damascus were just as shocked at the change in Saul as the Christians had been. How could the well-known Jewish leader from Jerusalem who had come to arrest Christians have made so complete a turnaround that he had joined them and was preaching the very Jesus he had formerly despised so vociferously?

At this point there is a historical and literary discrepancy that must be studied. In Luke's account here, Paul ministers for some time in the Damascus synagogues, and when Jewish opposition arises he is secreted out in a basket and travels to Jerusalem. In 2 Corinthians 11:32–33 it is not Jewish plots but Aretas, king of the Nabatean Arabs, who plans to arrest Saul in Damascus. In Galatians 1:15–17 he goes first to Arabia and then returns to Damascus. How do we reconcile these three disparate accounts? Actually, it is not as difficult as many think.

Let's use the Acts account as the basis and see how the other two accounts fit into it. In verse 19b Luke says that Saul "spent several days … in Damascus," an indistinct number that would allow for Paul's ministry in Arabia, which he mentions in Galatians 1:17. Those to whom he would have been ministering in Arabia were the Nabatean Arabs, from whom Herod came and whose king was Aretas. There may have been more than one trip, for Damascus could have been Paul's central base. We are told in Galatians that Paul "went into Arabia … returned to Damascus, [and] after three years" went back to Jerusalem. This time in Arabia would be Paul's first foray into Gentile witness with his new Christian family in Damascus, and he could have spent intermittent ministry time between the two places. Paul would have studied Christian beliefs to understand those whose belief system he wanted to destroy. So he knew the gospel and Christian doctrine well, and in Arabia he put it together for an evangelistic ministry to Gentiles.

Then at the end of three years his powerful ministry in Arabia angered Aretas, who worked with the Jews in Damascus to arrest Saul. Both Acts 9:23–25 and 2 Corinthians 11:32–33 end with the necessity of sneaking Paul out of Damascus in a basket to save his life from the Jews and Aretas. Luke would have omitted the Arabia ministry from Acts to save space in a very lengthy book. He had to omit a great deal to cover thirty years of life and events in the early church. In conclusion, the three accounts when put together make a perfectly coherent whole, and there is no need to assume parts of the three are fictional.

Paul's ministry in Damascus (9:20–21) centered on preaching Jesus in the synagogues as Son of God (v. 20) and Messiah (v. 22). Needless to say, the Jews like the Christians earlier were "astonished" and perplexed at this. They knew the famous Saul who had "raised havoc" in Jerusalem and who had come to take Damascus believers as "prisoners to the chief priests" of Jerusalem. They were befuddled with the Saul who now was preaching the very person whose name he had previously wanted to destroy.

Yet during this time "Saul grew more and more powerful and baffled the Jews living in Damascus by proving that Jesus is the messiah" (9:22). He bewildered them in two ways, first by the very fact that he had made a complete turnaround and was a follower of Christ, and second by the power of his preaching and apologetic proof that indeed Jesus was the promised Messiah. He truly had become the successor of Stephen. This strength was both physical as he recovered from his blindness and fasting and (especially) spiritual as his ministry blossomed and grew. Like Stephen in 6:10 his reasoning provided irrefutable evidence (probably from

prophecy) of Jesus' messianic nature. Moreover, he was a powerful preacher and convinced many.

As with Stephen, when his Jewish opponents couldn't defeat
him in debate, they turned to plots to take his life. Confusion turned
into hatred. Saul learned of the "conspiracy among the Jews to
kill him" (9:23-24), the first of many he would endure. The "many
days [that] had gone by" would be the three years presenting the
gospel in Arabia and Damascus (Gal 1:18). This would not have been
widely known, similar to the Jerusalem plot later uncovered by Paul's
nephew in 23:12-16. Apparently, agents of King Aretas would make
the arrest, and this secret cabal would see to it that Paul was killed.

Saul somehow learns of the conspiracy (as God willed), and
he realizes he cannot leave by the city gates, since all exits are
patrolled by the enemy. Because of the danger he was in, his ministry there was over, and he would have to leave by a clandestine
route. Like all major cities back then, Damascus was encircled by
a great wall in case of war, so Paul's "followers" (he must have
had many who had found Christ through him) devised a plan that
worked. They found a large basket for transporting goods and used
it to lower Paul from a high window in that wall to safety. Thus he
made his way back to Jerusalem.

First Trip to Jerusalem (9:26-30)

Even though it had been three years and word of his conversion
had most likely got back to Jerusalem, Christians there were still
afraid of Saul. The reaction in Damascus is repeated here. How
could it have been otherwise? They had spent at least two years
being hounded, arrested, and some even killed under the hostile enmity of Saul. I estimate he had left for Damascus about
AD 34, and so now it would be AD 37/38, and not enough time had
elapsed for them to lower their defenses. They simply were unable
to believe he had really become a disciple of Christ. They were
afraid it was nothing but a plot to lure them to him and make it
easier to arrest them.

It is the Barnabas of 4:36–37, whose name means "son of encouragement," who saves the day and brings Saul to the apostles, though Galatians 1:18–19 tells us only "Cephas" (Aramaic for "Peter," the rock) and James were in town at that time. The other ten were certainly conducting missionary work elsewhere. Barnabas explains three things to them. First, he tells them how Saul was converted when he "saw the Lord" on the Damascus road, with the implication that he had been granted an appearance of the risen Lord. Second, he explains how "the Lord had spoken to him," including the call to salvation and possibly the call to the Gentiles. Third, he describes Saul's "boldly" (*eparrēsiasato*, see the noun cognate "boldness" in 4:13, 29, 31) proclaiming "in the name of the Lord." Paul is demonstrating the same boldness as a recent believer the church had found in chapter 4. This saved the day, and Saul received the apostolic blessing (Peter as before speaks for the others). In so doing, Barnabas becomes Saul's mentor, and they form a long-lasting partnership.

So Saul, now a trusted brother in Christ to the other saints, begins the same ministry he had conducted in Damascus (9:28–29), continuing his bold preaching, probably both evangelistic work among the Jews and a teaching ministry in the church. Stephen's previous ministry begins anew among the **Hellenistic** Jews (6:9–10), with the same results, as for the second time (with Damascus) his enemies "tried to kill him." The imperfect tense of "tried" tells us this took place over an extended period of time, but unlike with Stephen, it doesn't work. God has other plans.

Once again (see 9:24) their plot is uncovered, and now Saul is sent to Caesarea and then travels to his hometown of Tarsus (9:30). Caesarea was the provincial capital, a large port city about seventy miles to the north, a center of trade and politics. From there they "sent him off," most likely by boat, to Tarsus. Some think they did this because his mere presence was causing problems for them, but more likely it was for his safety. Jerusalem had become too dangerous for him. With all the Jerusalem church had gone through,

any difficulties resulting from Saul's ministry would just have been
added to a very long list.

He does not go to Tarsus in order to rest up with his family.
He is concerned for his own people and begins his Gentile mission there. Luke omits discussing his lengthy stay at Tarsus. In
Galatians 2:1 Paul tells us there were fourteen years between
Damascus and the second Jerusalem visit, the famine visit of
Acts 11:30 (= Gal 2:1-10). With the three years in Arabia, that means
ten to eleven years in Tarsus (AD 38-49). During that time, the ministry of Galatians 1:21-24 in Cilicia and Syria almost certainly took
place. This would have been a time of evangelistic outreach and
church planting very much like his time in Damascus and Arabia,
but now in a fully Gentile environment. At the end of that time
Barnabas came and brought him to Antioch, where the Gentile
mission proper begins in Acts (11:25).

PETER MINISTERS IN COASTAL CITIES (9:31-43)

While Luke highlights Peter's ministry in this passage, that is not
his major emphasis. Rather, Luke wants to emphasize that the
church continues to expand into new areas, now cities on the
Mediterranean coast. Also, the miracles recorded reduplicate Jesus'
signs and wonders, showing that the church is truly reliving the
life and ministry of Jesus, a major theological core theme of Acts.
It is clear that the primary requirement of miraculous attention is
need and not social status or fame. Aeneas and Dorcas were ordinary people who had suffered greatly. They were healed not for
their piety or wealth but because they needed help.

SUMMARY: A CHURCH GROWING IN PEACE AND NUMBERS (9:31)

There have been several summary passages, all showing that even
in times of tumult the church under the Spirit is flourishing (2:41;
4:4, 31; 5:14; 6:7). As persecution increases, the power of the Spirit
grows exponentially, and this verse shows all that has transpired.

This is also the first mention of ministry in Galilee. Luke has ignored it probably because it was nearly the entire focus of his Gospel, and he wants to center on Judea and Samaria now. Here he wants us to realize the church is growing at the same frenetic pace it is in the other two. There are five areas of growth.

1. This is a time of peace after all the tumult, so the persecution after the death of Stephen is temporarily over, and the saints can breathe a sigh of relief. Even more importantly, they have peace with God, as their future and eternity are secure in Christ.

2. They have been "strengthened" or "built up" (*oiko-domoumenē*) in Christ, who is the foundation for the edifice of God's people. This new building is in process of being erected by Christ and filled with the Spirit and so continues to grow in Christ. This is a major Pauline metaphor for the beauty and strength of God's people (Rom 14:19; 1 Cor 10:23; 14:3–5, 12; 2 Cor 13:10; Eph 4:12, 29), especially apropos due to Rome's predilection for huge building projects.

3. They are "living in the fear of the Lord," literally "advancing in awe" as they experience more and more of Christ. Here the metaphor is walking with Christ, advancing on the road to "the measure of the fullness of Christ" (Eph 4:13). Their church growth is in every area—not just in numbers but also in the spiritual and social arenas, and in their fellowship.

4. They are also "encouraged by the Holy Spirit" (*paraklēsis*), looking at the comfort provided by the Spirit in all life's troubles.

5. As a result, the church "increased in numbers" as more and more were added to the local assemblies.

LYDDA: HEALING A LAME MAN (9:32–35)

Peter, last seen in 8:20, 25, is visiting congregations around the region of Palestine (9:31) and arrives at Lydda, on the way to the coastal city of Joppa, about twenty-five miles north of Jerusalem. The town would have been visited earlier (perhaps founded) by Philip, as it was on the coastal road from Azotus to Caesarea (8:40). Peter is still the rock and functioning as the leader of the apostles and therefore of the church. Here he encounters a man named Aeneas (8:33), probably already a believer since it doesn't say he was converted after his healing (compare v. 35). He had been paralyzed eight years earlier, possibly from an accident, and thus was bedridden.

The healing is told simply, with no preamble: "Aeneas, … Jesus Christ [not 'I, Peter'] heals you. Get up and roll up your mat" (9:34). It should read "Jesus Messiah," for Peter is certainly emphasizing that it is Israel's Messiah at work. The man had not arisen from bed on his own in eight years, and his sleeping mat was no longer needed. "Roll up your mat" = "make your bed." He no longer needs help with simple tasks like this. His rehab took place in an instant, and he can return to the life he once led. Everyone who entered the house would have known a miracle had occurred. The healing and the man's compliance follow immediately, and undoubtedly he got up jumping around and shouting for joy.

The result (9:35) is the conversion of a great many of his friends and townspeople. "All those who lived in Lydda and Sharon" is another example of hyperbole, meaning "a great many." Freed from his bed, he probably walked all over the area for some time to come, and most of the inhabitants would have seen him jumping for joy and telling everyone of the great miracle. Many were converted. Sharon is the plain region north of the city including Joppa, so the believers evangelized an extensive region as a result of this miracle. The church continues to grow.

JOPPA: RAISING ONE WHO HAD DIED (9:36–43)

Joppa is another twelve miles northwest of Lydda, on the coast itself. A wealthy Christian woman named Tabitha (Greek Dorcas, both meaning "gazelle") was well known for her good works, in particular for almsgiving. She is another example of the emphasis on social concern in 2:44-45; 4:32-34. Luke uses an unusual term literally translated "woman disciple" (*mathētria*, the only time used in the New Testament) to stress her important place in the church.

She falls gravely ill and dies, and her family prepares her for burial by washing her and placing her "in an upstairs room," possibly until the mourners arrive for the funeral, but also possibly waiting for Peter to arrive. Since they didn't embalm bodies, burial always took place within twenty-four hours, so he had to have been in a nearby town to make it in time. They immediately send for Peter and ask him to come "at once." We don't know whether they are hoping for him to raise her up, or whether they want him simply to be part of the funeral. There are two such supernatural resuscitations in the Old Testament (1 Kgs 17:19-22; 2 Kgs 4:20-37), two in Luke (7:11-17; 8:49-56), and one in John 11:41-44. So they could have been thinking of this, but Luke gives no such indication. What we do know is that the church is taking its place among God's wonder-working people and especially is continuing the work of Christ, duplicating the miracles he performed.

When Peter arrives (9:39) the widows whom Tabitha had helped were in the room, weeping and wearing the "robes and other clothing" she had made for them. They wanted him to know how wonderful a person she had been. These were significant gifts, for most people could only afford one or two such robes throughout their lives. She had made a significant difference in many people's lives.

Peter follows the pattern of Jesus (9:40), asking everyone to leave (as Jesus had done with Jairus' daughter, Mark 5:40; also Elisha in 2 Kgs 4:33). He then got on his knees and prayed, asking Christ to give her back her life, then immediately turned and commanded, "Tabitha, get up!" There is no hesitation in Peter at all, and Christ's response is instantaneous. The woman opens her eyes, sees Peter, and sits up in the bed. He extends his hand, helps her stand, and sends for the others. The entire process took only a few minutes, but lives were forever changed.

As the bystanders and widows filed into the room, Peter presented Tabitha to them alive, and certainly the place erupted with shouts of wonder and joy (9:41-42). Needless to say, the miracle quickly "became known all over Joppa." It would have been the only thing talked about for weeks, and Tabitha would have become an instant celebrity. As with Aeneas, the major result was that many became believers. The mission expanded via powerful miracles, and accompanying that a powerful witness.

Peter must have had a fruitful ministry in Joppa, as he stays for "some time," probably due to the two miracles in this section and the growing number of believers who needed to be brought into the church. While there he stayed "with a tanner named Simon." A tanner worked with the skin of animal carcasses, and so tanning was not really considered an honorable profession, since tanners were constantly unclean as a result of their contact with dead animals. However, the main ones who would have serious problems would have been Pharisees. (Paul would have had a greater problem with it than Peter because he was one of the most rigid Pharisees.) However, Peter was a common fisherman and a Christian so almost certainly had no difficulty living at Simon's home. Still, it is interesting that Peter had no problem staying with a tanner and yet many scruples about entering the home of a Gentile (10:9-23). Inconsistency is the hallmark of being human.

———

The conversion of Saul (vv. 1-9) is one of the major events of the New Testament. Nothing demonstrates the power of the risen Lord or the truth of the old adage "the hound of heaven" better than this story. Saul began this with the desire to extend his personally led persecution of Christians to cities and diaspora Jews outside Jerusalem. His "murderous threats" against them (9:1) were getting worse. Yet in the midst of that, the light of God shone forth and turned his life completely around. The combination of the dazzling light and the actual appearance of Christ turned the absolute despiser of all things Christian into the greatest teacher and Christian leader of his or any time.

Moreover, a committed believer named Ananias was asked to trust God and be willing to walk into a very dangerous situation in order to confirm Saul's conversion (10–16). He was scared to death of the man. In fact, every Christian in Damascus was living in terror at the arrival of Saul, who before he would be done would have transported many of them back to Jerusalem for trial as blasphemers, which could carry a death sentence with it. Yet Christ had chosen him to go to this major enemy and preach to him the very good news he was trying to eradicate. Ananias was the model of the courageous missionary!

After three days in blindness, thinking and praying through the implications of his encounter with Jesus, Ananias now clears up much of Saul's confusion and brings him to Christ (vv. 17–19a). Saul is baptized and begins his new life (vv. 19b–25), starting with three years of preaching and evangelistic work in Damascus and Arabia, taking over Stephen's powerful ministry. Due to his huge success, the same kind of Jewish plots to take his life ensued, and both Aretas the king of the Arabs and the Jewish people of Damascus conspired to arrest and then kill him. Learning of it, he was lowered in a basket from one of the walls and returned to Jerusalem, his previous home for his adult life thus far.

Back in Jerusalem (vv. 26–30), Saul does not simply return to his home, kick off his sandals, and rest up after a strenuous three years in Damascus and Arabia. No, he has to build an entirely new set of relationships with the very people he was hounding and arresting, with many dying as a result of the persecution he had thrown at them. It was Barnabas who saved the day and got him together with Peter and James so he could share his story. With a still-frightened church able to trust and accept him, he began a ministry very much like what he enjoyed in Damascus, and it had terrific results until another plot forced him to flee again, this time to his old hometown of Tarsus, where he began an eleven-year ministry.

A wonderful little verse (9:31) comes in the middle of this chapter and in a sense sums up the results of all the steps to the Gentile mission in 8:1–12:25, telling us how wonderfully the church was growing in every area of its life due to the empowering presence of the Spirit as it expands to a worldwide mission and church. In fact, this is another of the summary passages in Acts, which show how the problems the church faced led them to depend more on the Spirit and as a result find greater strength (2:41; 4:31; 5:14; 6:7; 9:31). God is blessing them incredibly as he works in them and through them. Oh, that this could be said of all of our churches today! It should be turned into a barometer by which we each measure the true success of our own church in the eyes of God.

Finally, we see the ministry of Peter in the coastal towns of Palestine (vv. 31–43), and in a very exciting development we are treated to one of the primary themes of the book of Acts, that as the church continues to develop, it is reliving the life and ministry of Jesus himself. Peter performs two miracles during his ministry here, and each one reproduces a similar miracle in the life and work of Christ. In a sense, this is **typological**, as the church is the antitype reenacting the ministry of Jesus. Both the healing of lame Aeneas and the raising of dead Tabitha show that the work of Jesus continues in his church. This is further evidence that makes me doubt the view of some that the age of miracles is past. I don't see any New Testament basis for that position and think that God is still at work in this world through his people.

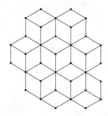

CORNELIUS: THE GOSPEL GOES TO THE GENTILES
(10:1–48)

This is the final stage of the movement to the Gentile mission, as afterward the first Gentile church is established in Antioch (in Luke's narrative). In Acts 8:4–9:43 Luke has taken us step-by-step from the persecution after the martyrdom of Stephen to the gospel in Samaria to the Ethiopian eunuch to the conversion and call of the missionary to the Gentiles, Saul, to the gospel moving upward along the coast (Lydda and Joppa) and now to the pure Gentile whose conversion will force the church to accept God's will to take the gospel to the Gentiles, Cornelius. We are in Caesarea as the mission has moved northward and is ready to break out into Antioch, the first Gentile church in Acts, and then the missionary journeys of Paul. Here the gospel has truly become universal and has fulfilled the promise of Pentecost.

CORNELIUS AND PAUL SEE
PREPARATORY VISIONS (10:1-16)

The Holy Spirit's absolute control of this event is seen in the fact that he sends visions to both the principal parties so they are ready and aware of the importance of this event. God directly intervenes at critical times in salvation history, and this is one of

them. The church will never look back from the perspective initiated here, that the gospel is meant for every people and is to be
contextualized for every culture. The importance of Cornelius'
conversion is illustrated in that it is the only other story in Acts
important enough to be narrated twice, in 10:1–48 and then again
in 11:4–17. These two stories, that of Saul and of Cornelius, will
change the history of the church and make its mission a worldwide movement.

The Vision of Cornelius (10:1–8)

Cornelius was a centurion, meaning he commanded a century
(officially a hundred, actually eighty men), six of which made up
a cohort (here labeled "the Italian cohort"), a tenth of a legion of
six thousand men. Judea had become a province in AD 6, but there
were no Roman troops stationed there until AD 70, so at that time
those there were local auxiliary troops rather than the regular
army. The Romans (like Cornelius) were in the provincial capital, Caesarea.

Cornelius' piety is described in four ways: (1) He and his family
(his wife and children shared his commitment) were "devout,"
devoted to God and worshipping him regularly. (2) He is a "God-
fearer" (see 10:22; 13:16, 26), a Gentile who believed and worshipped
Yahweh but was unwilling to (in his case, could not) become fully
Jewish by being circumcised. Likely he didn't follow all the precepts of the Torah either, nor did he regularly attend the synagogue. (3) He "gave generously to those in need"; centurions were
well paid, and he shared his largesse with the poor. (4) He prayed
regularly; the language here indicates a rich prayer life, not just
the expected official prayers but private prayers as well. Cornelius
is unusual even for a God-fearer.

At one of the Jewish times of prayer, three in the afternoon
(the ninth hour, see 3:1), he was probably praying (on the basis of
v. 2) when the Spirit sent a vision. He "distinctly," or clearly, saw

an angel of the Lord, identified later as "a man in shining clothes" (10:30). This angel comes up to him and addresses him, "Cornelius." That would get anyone's attention.

Like anyone who encounters a heavenly messenger in Scripture, Cornelius is initially terrified and asks (10:4, possibly expecting a rebuke), "What is it, Lord?" He realized that through the angel he was actually addressing God himself. His terror emphasizes the divine presence. As a centurion Cornelius would have seen a summons before God as more serious even than being called before Nero, the Roman emperor. He would have trembled anticipating the answer.

The angel's reply immediately assuaged his fears. His prayers and almsgiving have ascended to the Lord as a "memorial offering," an offering made as a tribute to God and pleasing to him (see Exod 7:14; Lev 2:2, 9, 16). In Psalm 141:2 they are likened to the evening sacrifice. So God tells Cornelius he is pleased with him and accepts his piety as an offering to himself.

Then the angel gives him his marching orders (10:5–6). He is to send men the thirty-seven miles along the coast to Joppa and get Simon Peter. He gives him the address of Simon the tanner (see 9:43) so there will be no need to search for him. His house is away from the town "by the sea" because as a tanner dealing with carcasses his house would have been unclean to Jews. Notice that the angel does not tell Cornelius why he is to do so. That will be told him later, when he meets Peter. We can only imagine how anxious he was as he waited to find out the Lord's will.

So Cornelius immediately obeyed, sending not just two slaves (*oiketōn*, household slaves) but also a "devout soldier," most likely a God-fearer like himself, who attended him as a member of his staff in the century. He "told them everything that had happened" so they would know how important their task was and what to do when they arrived. Then all he can do is wait the several days until they return with Peter.

THE VISION OF PETER (10:9–16)

As Cornelius' emissaries are on the way the next day and draw-ing near to Joppa, the same thing happens to Peter. He too is at prayer, this time at noon (the sixth hour), not the regular time for prayer (nine in the morning or three in the afternoon). To be by himself, he goes up the staircase at the back of the house (the normal Jewish home) onto the flatbed roof (equal to a family den today) and begins to pray to himself. He is hungry (perhaps an act of God for the sake of the vision). The Jewish meal times were mid-morning and late afternoon, so he must have missed the earlier meal. At any rate, while the food was being prepared, he "fell into a trance."

In this visionary state, he sees God opening heaven (a divine passive, "heaven opened"), an **apocalyptic** image that means God is acting decisively. A major event in salvation history is about to commence. This is an important image, for it adds perspective to the critical nature of the worldwide mission to the Gentiles. Then he sees a large sheet lowered to the earth "by its four cor-ners." He can't see the contents until it reaches the ground, and then he sees a mystifying sight—"all kinds of four-footed animals, as well as reptiles and birds," all of them unclean, meaning that, despite being famished, he dare not eat or he will be defiled (see Lev 11; Deut 14). God orchestrated his hunger to make the vision all the more powerful.

In the midst of this quandary, Peter hears a voice urging him, "Get up, Peter. Kill and eat" (10:13). He must have been completely confused, for the Torah told him he couldn't eat this meat, while this voice, which he surely assumed came from the Lord (probably the risen Lord Jesus) since it came from heaven, was telling him to do the very opposite. He probably thinks it is a test of his obedi-ence to the law and so responds, "Surely not, Lord! ... I have never eaten anything impure or unclean," certainly an overstatement but understandable in the context. His very emphatic "surely not" shows he is aghast at the suggestion. The purity laws were given to Israel as a basis for their holiness, to keep them separate from the pagan nations around them and centered on God. Observing these laws was thought essential for being faithful to God.

The voice's response is the turning point and key message of the vision: "Do not call anything impure that God has made clean." In the vision it relates to the unclean animals, overturning the laws of purity that governed Israel since Sinai. In the larger context it relates to God's acceptance of the Gentiles and Peter's unwillingness to enter an unclean Gentile home and share their food, even to present the gospel to Cornelius. The food laws are linked to Israel's relationship to the Gentile world, so Peter would have understood the connection. Christ had earlier done this (Mark 7:19, "In saying this [nothing entering the body can defile a person], Jesus declared all foods clean"), and now he is applying that new reality to the acceptance of Gentiles.

The laws of purity were needed in the old covenant, when Israel was to remain separate from the pagan nations and center on God. However, that time is past, and God's people are now commissioned to take the gospel to these very pagan nations and therefore to mingle and relate to them. The new age had begun, and the old ways now were creating a barrier to the gospel going forth to the Gentiles. In verse 16, the vision is repeated three times to make certain Peter realizes its implications. He still doesn't understand fully, but after his encounter with Cornelius he will tell it to the Jerusalem saints in 11:4–10, when he explains the extent to which the Lord was guiding his actions.

After the final repetition the "sheet was taken back to heaven," using the same verb (*analambanō*) that in 1:11 described Jesus' ascension. Peter is still somewhat confused but is now ready to meet with Cornelius and entertain the notion that nothing there will defile him. He is soon to learn that he can now associate freely with Gentiles as he takes the good news of salvation to them.

PETER ENCOUNTERS CORNELIUS (10:17-33)

THE MESSENGERS ARRIVE (10:17-23A)

As Peter is still contemplating the meaning and significance of the vision, the three men Cornelius sent to Peter (10:7-8) arrive. They have found the residence and stop at the gate, inquiring if Peter is there. The fact that this comes just as Peter is musing over the meaning of it all is God's timing. Their very presence further points him in the right direction. Their request will anchor the significance of the vision. We must realize that in one fell swoop this vision overturns what has guided Israel's eating habits as well as their relationships with the surrounding nations since the days of Moses. There is no way Peter or anyone else would come to grips with that easily.

Peter is still musing over his vision as they are about to enter the house, so now the Spirit adds his voice (10:19-20) to Jesus', telling him that in spite of his hesitation, he should go with Cornelius' agents. So now their request becomes a supernatural command, stemming from the Triune Godhead. Peter has heard verbally from both the risen Lord and the Holy Spirit, showing further just how critical this message is, not just for Peter personally but for the church as a whole from that time forward. He will be applying this revolutionary perspective immediately as he goes with three Gentile envoys into the home of a Roman Gentile centurion. The Spirit adds, "for I have sent them," indicating they are agents of God as well as of Cornelius. That is as radical as you can get, and Peter needs all the help he can find to enable him to handle what to him is such an outlandish situation.

Peter has been on the roof praying (10:9), so he goes down to meet the three and identifies himself to them, asking why they have made the lengthy trip to see him (10:21). Neither the Lord in the vision nor the Spirit has told Peter the purpose of their visit, so he is naturally quite curious to hear the answer.

Finally he learns the reason for all that has just transpired. They tell him they have been sent by Cornelius, an unusual centurion because he is "a righteous and God-fearing man, who is respected by all the Jewish people" (10:22). While he is a pure Gentile, he is a well-respected friend to the Jews, and he worships as a Jew. This certainly would have assuaged some of Peter's fears for considering such a request. He would have met many such God-fearers in various synagogues and been well acquainted with their type.

The next part went even further at convincing Peter to acquiesce to their request. The Spirit had also appeared to Cornelius in the same type of vision as to Peter, telling him to ask Peter to come. So he gets the Spirit's directive from both sides, Cornelius' as well as his own, to go to the man's house and meet him, obviously to present the good news to him. This he could do, and now the gospel will go directly to a Gentile as a Gentile, the final stage in the outward movement of the church's mission to the nations. Peter's scruples against going directly to a Gentile in his home have been removed by this triple message from Christ, the Spirit, and the three envoys from God. The last obstacle to universal mission has been overcome. Peter's surrender to the Lord's will is his invitation to the men to stay as his guests (it was too late to make the long trip that day) until they could leave the next day.

THE MEETING WITH CORNELIUS (10:23B–33)

When Peter realized the Lord had spoken to Cornelius as well as himself in visions, he knew it was indeed God's will that he accompany the men back to Cornelius. His conscience against such a thing was settled by direct commands from the Lord to both Cornelius and himself. More than a thousand years of separation has been set aside, and reconciliation will now become the name of the game. Peter took along his own representatives from Joppa to act as witnesses for the meeting.

They arrived in Caesarea after a two-day journey and immediately went to Cornelius' home. He had invited many relatives and close friends to meet the famous Christian leader, Simon Peter. He wanted them to share in the divine blessing and message that the vision indicated Peter would have for them. He would certainly have some inkling that it involved the Christian message he had heard a great deal about, much of it undoubtedly negative in the synagogues. Still, the vision would have alerted him that there was a great deal more to it, and he was anxious to hear and to have friends and loved ones share it with him.

When Peter walked in, his emotions overcame him, and as a result of the vision Cornelius "fell at his feet in reverence" (10:25). He treats Peter as if he were God's angel entering the room, and he is suitably embarrassed and aghast, quickly lifting Cornelius to his feet and exclaiming, "Stand up ... I am only a man myself." This is similar to 14:11–15. When the people of Lystra want to offer sacrifices to Barnabas and Paul, the two tear their clothes in horror.

As he addresses them, Peter shows he has come to understand the vision that had so perplexed him earlier. He realizes that most of the "large gathering" of Gentiles are God-fearers and fairly knowledgeable of Jewish customs and so simply highlights the important aspects behind his visit.

His very first sentence in verse 28 shows that he is no longer confused like he was previously (10:11, 17, 19). He now recognizes that the vision was more about Jew-Gentile relations than about food and so reminds the group that the law does not allow Jews "to associate with or visit a Gentile" (10:28), especially strong in Jewish tradition (Jubilees 22:16; Testament of Joseph 7:1). So his trip there was against the norm. The reason was well recognized. Even a devout God-fearer like Cornelius would have been in constant contact with foods and other things that would defile a practicing Jew. The only safe solution would be to avoid contact.

However, he points out, in the vision "God has shown me that I should not call anyone impure or unclean," including all those gathered in the room to meet him and hear his God-given message. The new age has arrived, and Peter has finally caught the implications, that Gentiles can now come to salvation without becoming Jews first, a debate that will consume everyone the next few decades.

It is significant that Peter has now come to this realization at nearly the same time as Paul. He wants Cornelius and his friends to understand why he is there and why everything has now changed. A Gentile could have become a Christ follower previously, and Peter could have brought him to Christ, but now Peter could do so while associating fully with him. Before this Cornelius would have had to come to Peter to be saved, but now Peter could even go into his house and participate in his life as a Gentile while bringing the gospel to him.

The only thing left (10:29) was the reason Cornelius had asked Peter to come. Peter knew he wanted to tell Cornelius and those gathered about Jesus and bring them to faith in him. But he wanted to hear it from Cornelius' lips and involve everyone there in his evangelistic goal. He is giving Cornelius the opportunity to share his side of the story and wants all the man's family and friends to hear it for themselves.

Everything started four days earlier when "a man in shining clothes"[1] appeared in a vision and told him God had responded to his prayers and almsgiving and to send to Joppa and fetch Peter (see 10:1–8). In the next two days his envoys would arrive, get Peter, and return to Caesarea. He adds here (v. 33), "It was good of you to come," recognizing what Peter had just revealed regarding the difficulty of a Jew coming to visit a Gentile.

On the fourth day they all have arrived at Cornelius' house and are gathered "in the presence of God to listen to everything the Lord has commanded you to tell us" (10:33). Cornelius recognizes his own unworthiness to receive such a visit either from the angel or from Peter and is shocked at the goodness of God and of Peter in granting him this blessing. It is remarkable to see this level of humility in one of the most grizzled individuals in the ancient world, a Roman centurion. It demonstrates the difference God makes in us when we open ourselves to him. Cornelius and

---

1. The appearance of an angel is too sacred a moment for Cornelius to share publicly, so he simply describes the heavenly being.

the others are waiting with bated breath to hear the instructions
Peter will bring from the Lord.

PETER GIVES A SERMON IN
CORNELIUS' HOUSE (10:34-43)

This is Peter's final sermon in Acts and takes the gospel in a new
direction, stressing the universality of the salvation God has made
available to all humankind. An entire history of racial division
is taken away in an instant. What a remarkable lesson this is for
us today!

THEME: THE IMPARTIALITY OF GOD (10:34-35)

He looks at this from two angles, that of God himself, who "does
not show favoritism" (actually he never has, as the Abrahamic covenant in Gen 12:3 shows) and that of God's creation, which "accepts
from every nation the one who fears him and does what is right."
Note it does not say "those who become proselytes and keep the
law" but "who fear [God]" (like Cornelius and the others).

The Jew-Gentile distinctions have disappeared, and the gospel
has opened up to all ethnic groups. People "from every nation" will
now make up the people of God, and the new Israel is an inclu-
sive entity open to every culture so long as they fear God and walk
rightly before him. Cornelius' prayer life relates to the first (fear
God) and his almsgiving to the second (do what is right). This
does not mean Cornelius has achieved salvation by this, for that
comes by faith, not works. But it does mean that he is accepted as
a candidate, and Peter is in the process of sharing with him and
the group what he must do now to have salvation. Their response
will not be narrated, but its effects will be seen in the coming of
the Spirit on them in 10:44-46.

THE MEANS: THE WORK OF CHRIST (10:36-41)

The perfect message for Roman soldiers, living under the facade
of the *Pax Romana* (the Roman peace), is that true peace is now

available in Jesus the Christ. This is the "word" (*logos*, "message") of *shalōm* given to Israel in the Old Testament (Isa 52:7; Ezek 34:25–29; Nah 1:15) and now to Gentiles in the new era (Luke 1:79; 4:18). What Cornelius and the others do not yet realize is that that peace will come to them "through" the life and work of Jesus, who is the expected Messiah and even more is "Lord of all." For those serving under the Roman emperor this is a critical concept. It is Jesus, not Caligula or Claudius, who is Lord of all God's creation.

They have all heard of the life and ministry of Jesus but are unaware of all that it meant. Peter wants them to know the truth behind the reports. Their information would have come from Roman channels, so they needed, as Paul Harvey would have put it, to hear "the rest of the story." "After the baptism that John preached" refers to the beginning of Jesus' ministry in Galilee and Judea. When the Baptist's work ended, Jesus' began.

The term "messiah" means "anointed one," and Jesus was "anointed" by the Holy Spirit at his baptism (Luke 4:14, 18). His was a ministry powerful in word and deed. So his was a ministry endowed by the Spirit, filled with power, and fulfilling all the Jewish expectations of the promised Messiah. In other words, he is the one awaited not only by the Jews but also by Gentiles like Cornelius and his friends.

Moreover, his whole life was one of good works, as he "went around doing good and healing all who were under the power of the devil" (10:38). His ministry traversed all of Galilee and parts of Syria. Wherever he went, he was "doing good," probably referring to healing miracles, and delivering people from the power of Satan through exorcisms. With the Messiah present, people being healed of infirmities, and Satan in retreat, the kingdom had definitely arrived and the age of salvation begun. Cornelius would have thought of this as an entirely Jewish affair, but now he recognizes how significant this is for him, a Gentile, as well.

In case any of his listeners have any doubts about what he is saying, Peter draws on two corroborating sources to demonstrate

these truths. First, "God was with him" (10:38c). Jesus had a supernatural ministry attended by supernatural forces. The power of
God lay behind everything he did. Second, "we are witnesses of
everything he did in the country of the Jews and in Jerusalem"
(10:39). Peter and the other apostles saw it all, so he wants these
Romans to realize he is not spouting Roman-style myths to them
in these stories about Jesus. He and the others were there and can
attest that all this really happened.

The events of verses 37-38 took place in "the country of the
Jews," considering Galilee and Judea from a Roman perspective.
The events of 40-41 would take place in Jerusalem. The heart of the
gospel is the sacrificial death and resurrection of Jesus, and Peter
highlights the Jews as both the recipients of Jesus' mighty ministry
and the executioners who had him killed. While the Romans nailed
him to the cross, Peter wants Cornelius to know it was the Jews
who "killed him by hanging him on a cross." Literally, Peter says
"hanging him on a tree," which from Deuteronomy 21:22-23 means
he died under the covenant curse, cut off from Israel. Obviously,
both Jews and Romans are guilty of the death of Christ, as are we,
for our sins put him on the cross.

However, his death on the cross was not the end, for "God
raised him from the dead on the third day." His humiliation led
to his exaltation (Phil 2:6-11), and seeming defeat produced glorious victory. Actually, he was in the grave about thirty-six hours,
but the Friday-Saturday-Sunday format led to the euphemism
"on the third day" (see Luke 9:22; 18:33; 24:6, 17; 1 Cor 15:3), likely
building on the theme of new (resurrection?) life in Hosea 6:2
and Jonah 1:17.

From resurrection Peter turns to the appearances and uti-
lizes a quite unusual way of saying it, beginning with the fact
that God "caused him to be seen" (10:40b). The purpose is to show
that the appearances—and Peter was one of the first eyewitnesses
(1 Cor 15:5: "he appeared to Cephas, and then to the twelve")—took
place on the basis of God's direct action.

It has been pointed out that Gentiles generally believed in the immortality of the soul rather than in physical resurrection, so Peter stresses the apologetic proof for the reality of Jesus' resurrection from the dead. God did not have Jesus appear publicly to all and sundry, to Jew or Gentile, but restricted the appearances to "witnesses whom God had already chosen" (10:41). These were the "eyewitnesses" of Luke 1:1–4, who were to provide the God-given evidence for the reliability of the reports as well as of the truth behind the Gospels and Acts. God especially used table fellowship, the sharing of meals, to anchor that personal involvement with the risen Lord (especially in Luke 24:30–31, 35, 41–43). The partaking of food proved to the disciples and now to Cornelius that the resurrection involved Jesus' physical body.

THE IMPLICATIONS: JESUS AS JUDGE AND SAVIOR (10:42–43)

As eyewitnesses, the apostles were "sent out" (the meaning of *apostolos*) with the task of preaching the gospel and witnessing to the person of Jesus the Christ, that God has ordained or appointed him "as judge of the living and the dead," an epithet for every human being who has ever lived (2 Tim 4:1; Heb 4:12; 1 Pet 4:5). The audience was originally the Jewish people, as in the early chapters of Acts. Of greatest significance is the fact that this is now expanded to include a worldwide audience, and this is the first of millions of sermons addressed to Gentiles and including them in the people of God, the new Israel. Peter describes this as "preach to the people." "People" in Luke-Acts tends to refer to the people of God, for centuries restricted to the Jews and now forevermore to include the Gentiles as well.

The content of the message is the appointment of Jesus as Judge, a theme found often in the New Testament (John 5:22, 27, 30; 8:15, 16, 26; Acts 17:31; 1 Thess 1:10; 2 Tim 4:1; 1 Pet 4:5; Heb 6:1–2). When we say Jesus is Lord of all, that encompasses his role as **eschatological** Judge, overseeing God's creation and bringing God's justice into this world. The title "judge of the living and the dead" highlights his role in producing salvation. "The living and the dead" is also an idiom for Christ's authority over life and death. Through his sacrificial death he alone can bring salvation, and he is also with the Father the Judge, who will assign eternal life or damnation at the final judgment of Revelation 20:11-15. Forgiveness of sins comes from him, and he will mete out eternal punishment as well.

The evangelistic element of this sermon comes in 10:43, where Peter tells Cornelius and his friends of the prophetic message coming out of the Old Testament that "everyone who believes in him receives forgiveness of sins through his name." The emphasis on "everyone" includes Gentiles as well as Jews. Salvation no longer comes through the law or via observance of rituals but only "through [believing in] his name." Moreover, all must have their sins forgiven, including the most pious observer of Torah. Salvation is not by works but by faith, as Paul will argue throughout his writings, especially in Galatians and Romans. "Believe" is in the present tense, stressing ongoing faith in Jesus as Judge and Savior. The Old Testament witness can be found in Isaiah 33:17-24; 55:6-7; Jeremiah 31:34; Ezekiel 36:25, 39:29; Joel 2:32, among others. Peter wants his listeners to be aware that all of Scripture is summed up in Jesus as Savior and Lord.

THE GENTILES RECEIVE THE HOLY SPIRIT (10:44-48)

The conversion of these Gentiles (probably of all who are there) is not recorded but assumed by the next thing that takes place. In Romans 8:14-17 the Spirit comes into the hearts of those who have found salvation in Jesus Christ, and that means that all these in Peter's audience have come to faith. Probably as Peter was explaining about faith-decision in verse 43, they found that heartfelt faith in Jesus. At that moment, as Peter was still speaking, "the Holy Spirit came on all who heard the message." The text implies that they heard and responded with faith. The actual language is that the Spirit "fell upon" (*epepesen*) them, a very dramatic description that recalls the Spirit descending on Jesus at his baptism (Luke 3:22).

This is often called the "Gentile Pentecost," the third one after the Jewish event in 2:1-4 and the Samaritan irruption in 8:17. The purpose was twofold—to authenticate the salvation of the Gentiles both for Cornelius and for the rest of the church and to facilitate the Gentile mission. It proves to anyone with an eye of faith that God is indeed behind the gospel's going directly to the Gentiles without forcing them to become Jewish first (as the Judaizers will soon be arguing in chapter 15). God is giving his imprimatur to the conversion of Cornelius and the rest who are present. This will settle the issue initially in 11:15-18 for those in the Jerusalem church, and there they will thank God that "even to Gentiles God has granted repentance that leads to life." We will see, however, that this acceptance is short-lived and soon opposed by many strict Pharisaic Jewish believers. Still, this is a momentous event in the history of the church.

Everyone knew this was a Pentecost-type event because the phenomena of Acts 2 were repeated (10:45-46a). The fire and wind are not mentioned (though they could well have been present), but the presence of glossolalia (speaking in tongues) was conclusive. The "circumcised believers" here are the Jewish Christians who accompanied Peter from Joppa (10:23). They would have understood this as further evidence of the Joel prophecy (Joel 2:28-32) but now "poured out even on Gentiles," an unbelievably significant event. No wonder they were "astonished" at what had just happened. It was impossible to miss the implications.

Needless to say, as these new Gentile believers are speaking in languages they have never learned,[2] they are praising God for

---

2. Charismatic and noncharismatic believers today debate whether the tongues were a Spirit language never spoken before or human languages that had not been learned by the tongue-speakers. That issue goes beyond the purview of this commentary, and I do not have room to delve into it. I myself believe that either is possible, and the Spirit decides.

all he has done. The view of tongues as a praise language fits the situation here. Cornelius and the others are overcome with joy at the salvation they have just experienced as well as the dramatic coming of the Spirit on them, and as at the original Pentecost they can't stop expressing that joy to all around them.

Peter is convinced that they have become believers, for they "have received the Holy Spirit just as we have" (10:47). He will say this again in 11:15, 17, and 15:8, 9. The presence of the Spirit in them is proof positive that (1) they must have "believed in the Lord Jesus Christ" (11:17) and (2) God "did not discriminate between us and them" (15:9), meaning that Gentiles can now be brought directly to Christ. A new age of salvation has begun.

So in keeping with 2:38, 41; 8:12, 36, 38, Peter argues that they should be "baptized with water" to signify they have been cleansed from their sins by the blood of Christ, resulting in the coming of the Spirit on them. They were baptized that same day (10:48). They ask Peter to remain with them for several days, and he does so, signifying his complete acceptance of them as fellow believers (and a total turnaround from his earlier position). They are now brothers and sisters in Christ, invaluable members of the church in Caesarea.

———

Centurions were the personification of toughness in the ancient world, yet Cornelius breaks the mold with his gentleness, love, and openness to the things of God. He is a God-fearer, known for his devout character and kind giving to the needy. So he was the perfect person to usher God's people into the new kingdom reality of salvation for all peoples and the gospel to include Gentiles as well as Jews. Every step taken by him and Peter was orchestrated by the Spirit, and it involved a rare pair of visions to both sides in order to navigate successfully the salvation-historical switch to a universal mission and good news for all people groups.

The vision to Cornelius (vv. 1–8) was pre-evangelism at its best, preparing him to listen to the peasant preacher Simon Peter from that upstart religion about which he had undoubtedly heard nothing good. By having him send for Peter, the angel involved him in the process and sounded a positive note for the initiation of the Christian message of salvation. Luke presents Peter's coming as a gift from God.

The vision to Peter (vv. 9–16) has a different purpose, to get him to realize that the food laws and laws of purity are no longer mandatory in this new age of salvation. This was very difficult, for these rules had been an essential part of the Torah since Moses and Sinai and were a key element of Jewish self-identity. For Peter to "kill and eat" any of these unclean animals went against everything he had ever done as a Jew. He was not a Pharisee and so was not rigid in his adherence to these things, but the food laws were very important, and he tried to keep them faithfully.

However, God's purpose was far more than this, for this was a symbol of the whole system of purity regulations, directed especially at Peter's willingness to enter the unclean home of Cornelius, an unclean Gentile. This was a central issue for the universal mission, for the gospel was to be taken freely to the Gentiles. It took Peter several days to understand its implications fully, for it changed everything for him. For us the parallel issue is racism, which has always been a barrier to missions. Many Western Christians have been raised feeling superior to more marginalized peoples and must learn to accept those to whom we take the gospel as equal to us in the eyes of God. All feelings of racial and ethnic superiority must go if we are to please God in our mission.

In the process of receiving the three envoys (from God as well as Cornelius) and agreeing to go with them back to Caesarea to meet with Cornelius (vv. 17–29), Peter finally understands the import of his vision, and both he and the Christian mission are changed forever. The salvation-historical switch now takes place, and the promise of Pentecost is realized, with the good news of

Christ now freely going to the Gentiles as equal participants in the new Israel, the true people of God.

Cornelius' acceptance of Peter (vv. 30–33) prepares for Peter's sermon (vv. 34–43), which presents the gospel via the newly emphasized doctrine of the impartiality of God to every nation and people. The key is that this new salvation comes not via covenant identity (as Israel) or faithful observance of the law but by the work of Christ (vv. 37–41). Jesus was the promised Messiah and came with both powerful preaching and mighty works, miracles that affirmed his supernatural origin. Moreover, Peter was the perfect one to tell Cornelius, for he saw all this firsthand and can witness to the truth of all he is saying. Even more importantly, Jesus was the Suffering Servant of Isaiah, who died for the sins of Cornelius and of all of us. The Romans executed him, but the Jews hung him "on a cross," so all humanity is guilty of his death. However, God raised him from the dead and chose eyewitnesses to whom he appeared and through whom he proves to all that he is indeed alive.

The result of Jesus' life is the recognition that he is Judge and Savior (vv. 42–43), who has brought salvation and forgiveness of sins to all humanity, Gentile as well as Jew. It is at this point when Cornelius likely found faith in Jesus, for immediately the Holy Spirit falls on him and the others (vv. 44–48), signifying their salvation (Rom 8:14–17). The Pentecost phenomena (possibly the wind and fire as well as the tongues) prove that this indeed is the Gentile Pentecost and that the new aeon does indeed include Gentiles as well as Jews as recipients of messianic salvation. Peter baptizes these new converts and stays with them several days, anchoring them in the church at Caesarea as full members. The movement to the Gentile mission is now complete, and the universal mission is ready to be unleashed under Saul's leadership.

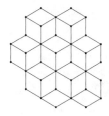

THE GENTILE MISSION: CORNELIUS AND ANTIOCH
(11:1–30)

With Cornelius God has made his intentions clear to the Jerusalem church, and the Gentile mission is now an established entity. Still, it is not a finalized movement, and many still have serious doubts regarding its legality according to the Torah. After all, the Gentiles are an unclean people, and they are not ready to jettison Jewish sensitivities on behalf of spreading the Christian gospel. So Peter has to return to Jerusalem, explain his actions, and justify his making Cornelius a convert before he had become a Jewish proselyte.

Note also that the story of Cornelius' conversion is here narrated for the second time. As with the story of Saul's conversion, the reason is the great importance of this event for the church's God-given mission. Luke wants every reader to be aware of these two world-shaking salvation-historical events for the future history of the church. Moreover, as a good narrator, Luke has saved certain details to make the second retelling more vivid to keep interest—he adds "wild beasts" to the list of 10:12 and mentions that "six" companions traveled with him to Caesarea.

PETER JUSTIFIES GENTILE CONVERSIONS
IN JERUSALEM (11:1-18)

CRITICISM OF PETER (11:1-3)

News of the conversion of these Gentiles quickly reached both the apostles and the believers not just in Jerusalem but throughout Judea, causing great controversy. So when Peter returned to Jerusalem after the conversion of Cornelius and the others in Caesarea, he faced several objections from the Jewish Christians there who were upset that "the Gentiles also had received the word of God" by being given the gospel and having been saved. These strict Jewish Christians were not opposed to their conversion but believed it should take place in two stages, first to Judaism and adherence both to the law and circumcision, then to Christianity as a Jewish proselyte. Luke calls them "circumcised believers" to highlight this central issue, whether the Gentiles should become circumcised Jews before they are given the gospel/word of God.[1] They insisted that uncircumcised Gentiles must be circumcised before given the good news about Jesus.

Their criticism of Peter centered on the issue behind his vision in 10:9-16, whether Jewish Christians can go into Gentile homes and share a meal with them (11:3). In their minds, that would render Peter and his party unclean.

---

1. Many think that these are a specific group of Pharisaic Jewish Christians who soon became the Judaizers who opposed Paul at the Jerusalem Council of Acts 15. This is on the basis of Gal 2:12, where "certain men [who] came from James" is identified with the Judaizers, but that is not actually the case. They pressured Peter to keep the law more carefully and to avoid eating with Gentiles, but they did not identify themselves in this way. I prefer the view, related here in the text, that they are simply Jewish Christians in general who want Cornelius and the others to become Jewish proselytes by being circumcised. Some of them later become the "circumcision party," but not yet.

THE GENTILE MISSION: CORNELIUS AND ANTIOCH   213

PETER RETELLS THE CORNELIUS STORY (11:4-17)

Since Peter's vision rescinded the food laws as binding on Christians, Luke retells it in great detail for emphasis. This was incredibly important for all Jewish Christians to understand, for it allowed Gentiles to come to Christ without having to jump through the Jewish hoop first. Christian rejection of Jewish food laws had implications far beyond this, for it also settled how Jewish Christians were to live their lives in the future. To Peter and Paul and the other apostles, the change made Christianity and Judaism separate movements. When Jewish people became believers, they joined Gentile converts as the new Israel, linked salvation-historically with their Jewish past but in the present free to follow Christ without being encumbered with Torah demands.

In the first two verses (11:5-6 = 10:9-12) Peter stresses the heavenly origin of the vision and the fact that the sheet with the unclean four-footed animals came down right "to where I was," thus involving Peter and his Torah convictions directly. The reader can feel his chagrin when he is told to "kill and eat" what would defile him before God. Then in verses 7-10 he retells 10:13-16 and relates the threefold repetition of the fact that the laws of purity have been removed by God from these formerly unclean animals and why it is now all right for him to consume them. The emphasis on the threefold command rescinding the nature of these animals as "impure or unclean" has implications far beyond the conversion of Cornelius, stressing the absence of the food laws as a requirement for Christians in line with Mark 7:19 ("In saying this, Jesus declared all foods clean").

The key phrase is in verse 9 (= 10:15), "Do not call anything impure that God has made clean." This affects both table fellowship with Gentiles and the taking of the gospel directly to the Gentiles and establishing relations with them as the good news is shared—the central aspect of the Gentile mission. It is this central fact that makes the universal mission possible. Moreover, one's walk with God is no longer to be centered on ritual observance and Torah obedience but on following Christ and being led by the Spirit. Here we are at the heart of the new aeon and the coming of the kingdom of God, the new age of salvation, into this world.

The purpose of 11:11–14 (= 10:17–33) is to show that God was orchestrating all the details and controlling every single step. Cornelius had been directed by an angel in sending to Joppa for Peter, and Peter had been told by the Spirit to go with them to Cornelius. Through this God's salvation came not just to the household of Cornelius but to Gentiles everywhere for all time. Every step from Joppa to Caesarea—the three envoys from Cornelius, the six brothers from Joppa, the coming of Peter, the proclamation of the gospel—changed the meaning of the salvation message forever. It no longer developed out of the Sinai law but out of the sacrificial death of Christ, and therefore it encompassed not just Jews but every person born into this world. It has truly become a universal gospel for a universal mission.

In the next verses, 15–17, Peter recounts the events of 10:44–46, using language ("the Holy Spirit came" from 10:44) reminiscent of the coming of the Spirit at Pentecost. So the Gentiles are affirmed by the Spirit as part of the people of God, and the same tongue-speaking as at Pentecost meant they were to receive salvation and the Spirit in their own language and culture apart from any Jewish heritage. Every people group stands equal in the eyes of God, and the gospel is to be proclaimed to them all.

In verse 16 Peter remembers the words of Jesus from Acts 1:5 (see also Luke 3:16), "John baptized with water, but you will be baptized with the Holy Spirit." This is not a statement about baptism. Peter had baptized Cornelius and his household (10:48). Rather, he is using it to emphasize the outpouring of the Spirit in the new age of salvation. The Gentiles are now a part of the new people of God equally with the Jews, and for all groups the measure of their inclusion to the people of God is no longer adherence to the law but salvation in Christ along with immersion in the Holy Spirit.

Gentiles are filled with the Spirit equally with believing Jews, and the two become one people in the Spirit, the new Israel. It is no longer adequate to think of them as morally unclean and unfit for the gospel until they have accepted and begun practicing the law. Jew and Gentile now stand equally before God and can come to Christ on their own.

Peter presents the implications of this in 11:17. God had given these Gentiles "the same gift"—the Holy Spirit—that he had poured out on the apostles at Pentecost. So, Peter asks, "Who was I to think that I could stand in God's way?" They had received the Holy Spirit apart from the law, and so Peter could not "stand in God's way" by refusing to accept them as converts and to baptize them. He will say this again at the Jerusalem Council (15:7–9), as it provides the final proof that God's will is for Gentiles to be accepted as they are and not required to accept Judaism before they can become Christians. To do so would be to become a hindrance or barrier to the will and work of God for Gentiles, and he dare not do that.

THE JEWISH CHRISTIAN REACTION (11:18)

The Jerusalem believers can clearly see that God was behind every step in this series of events, climaxed by the coming of the Spirit on the Gentiles, proving the reality of their conversion. All "further objections" are "silenced" (*hēsychasan*; NIV: "no further objections") by the overwhelming evidence that this is God's will, and all they can do is praise God, saying, "So then, even to Gentiles God has granted repentance that leads to life." Undoubtedly most of them did not truly want this (having grown up anti-Gentile), but they could not deny the absolute evidence proving this was God's will. He had done this, not Peter, and so they had to accept it. That is a great lesson for us. God will ask us to do many things we do not particularly wish to do, but uppermost in our minds must be God's will, and we must be able to acquiesce to it even when it goes against our personal desires.

It is crucial to note that they "praised God" once they knew it was his will. In so doing they needed to realize that God was behind it all. His granting repentance and eternal life to these Gentiles meant thousands more could freely come to Christ, and that had to be a source for joy. Note that repentance is not just a response on our part; it is first a gift from God. Every step of the salvation process is a divine gift, the result of divine mercy and love. Moreover, salvation means "life," which refers to spiritual life now and eternal life in heaven.

At some time in this period several developments took place in the Jerusalem church. Peter's mission work forced him to be gone from Jerusalem for long stretches, and it probably seemed clear this would govern the rest of his life. New leadership was needed, and at some stage James (the Lord's brother, not John's brother) took over as the head elder of the Jerusalem church. This will become clear in Galatians and Acts 15. Also, the letter of James was likely written near this time, given its strong Jewish flavor and the absence in it of any sign of the Gentile mission. Further, elders in the Christian churches began to assume leadership (following the Jewish pattern). Luke never tells us the origin of the office (11:30 is the first mention, though Jewish elders are found in 4:5, 8, 23; 6:12), but they more and more took administrative and day-to-day needs off the apostles' hands and gradually took over, with most of the apostles probably moving away to various mission fields.

LUKE INTRODUCES THE CHURCH
AT ANTIOCH (11:19-30)

Luke begins by telling us Antioch was one of the first churches formed by the exodus after the "great persecution" of Acts 8:1–3 following the death of Stephen. In chapter 8 Luke discussed the expansion into Caesarea, but here we learn that many of the scattered Christians went as far as Phoenicia (coastal cities in Syria, including Tyre and Sidon), Cyprus (a large island off the mainland and evangelized on the first missionary journey of 13:4–12), and Antioch (the capital of Syria). These, however, were Jewish Christians and so preached only to other Jews. The Gentile mission had not yet begun, and Luke traces the activity of Jewish believers in verse 19 and of **Hellenistic** Jews scattered after 8:1–3 in verse 20.

BARNABAS AND SAUL ARRIVE (11:19–26)

Some of the Hellenistic Jews who had moved to Jerusalem and joined the Hellenistic synagogues evangelized by Stephen were from Cyprus (11:19) and Cyrene (a region of Africa, see 2:10), and so when they were forced to flee they went to Antioch and began ministering to other Greek-speaking people there, the majority of the population. Antioch of Syria was the third-largest city (estimated from 300,000 to 600,000) in the Roman world after Rome and Alexandria. It was known for its Hellenistic culture but also for its idolatry (like Athens) and immorality (like Corinth).

The church was successful from the start, and "a great number" of believers came to Christ and joined the church. The "Lord's hand" may point to signs and wonders as well as proclaiming the gospel. At any rate, the church grew so fast that they soon needed to bring in mature leaders to take it to the next level.

When news of this growing church reached the apostles in Jerusalem, they realized the need and reacted as they had with Peter and John in Samaria (8:14), sending Barnabas to provide that leadership (4:36; 9:27). His task was not just to certify this new church but more to guide it and develop mature leaders to run it. In Samaria it was to solve difficulties that threatened the movement (namely, Simon Magus), but that was not the case here. It was all positive, and the church had grown so large that they needed a mature leader to guide it. Barnabas was just the right person for the task.

The first thing he did after arriving (11:23) was to commend and encourage them. He rejoiced in the evidence of "the grace of God" in their church, both in the number of converts and the maturity of the church as it grew. God's presence was evident at every level, and that brought him great joy. As the "son of encouragement" (the meaning of "Barnabas") he could only encourage them "to remain true [or steadfast] to the Lord with all their hearts." "All their hearts" in Greek is *tē prothesei tēs kardias*, "the devotion of their hearts," meaning that everything they do reflects how devoted they are to God and Christ. Barnabas' purpose is to anchor and strengthen them as they take the good news to the people of Antioch.

Luke then tells us why it was Barnabas they sent (11:24). He is described in language quite similar to Stephen in 6:5, 8. First, he is "a good man" clearly in every way: kind, compassionate, hardworking, helpful. He was both a giver and an encourager. Second, he was "full of the Holy Spirit," as Stephen was, adding the spiritual dimension to the ethical. Many think this relates especially to the prophetic gift, and that may be. Finally, he is "full of ... faith," meaning a deep and abiding trust in God and Christ, totally surrendered to him and dependent on the Spirit's empowering presence. With the church thriving, they need all these traits to help them stay on the right path.

The work became too much for Barnabas alone, and he thought the perfect assistant would be Saul, now eleven years ministering in the area around Tarsus and ready for a new challenge. He had just the right credentials. He had been trained as a rabbi under Gamaliel (22:3) and had a great deal of both teaching and evangelistic experience in Damascus and Arabia (Gal 1:15–17), in Jerusalem (9:26–30), and in the regions of Syria and Cilicia around Tarsus (Gal 1:21–24). Barnabas went to a lot of trouble getting him on board, traveling there (130 miles, a seven- to eight-day trip), and then having to search for him, as he was probably on a mission trip. Apparently, it wasn't hard to convince him to move to Antioch, and they both arrived there in due time.

For the next year they ministered in and around Antioch, strengthening the church and teaching the people, undoubtedly with evangelistic preaching as well, although Luke doesn't mention it. Their primary ministry seems to have been teaching in the church, most likely the life of Christ, the doctrines of the faith, and the teachings of the Old Testament. Jewish and Gentile believers probably met together; there is no evidence of separate Jewish and Hellenistic congregations like there was in Judaism. The church in Antioch would have resembled the Jerusalem congregations as described in 2:42–47. Luke emphasizes here the "great numbers of people" taught. Many think this is not teaching in the services of the church but evangelistic preaching outside the services. While possible, I think it better to see this as referring to the many who have become believers rather than large numbers of unbelievers.

It is here in Antioch where the Christ followers were first called "Christians." "Jesus of Nazareth" was often spelled *Nazarēnos*, so *Christianoi* would mean "those who belong to Christ," and it was only used by those outside the church.[2] There is no evidence until the second century that believers used this like they did "the Way" as a title for their movement. In fact, it is frequently said that this was a derisive title used to mock Christians, and that is certainly possible. All we can say for certain is that it was first used in Antioch.

The Famine Relief (11:27–30)

With John the Baptist and Jesus, the age of the prophets returned, and there were several who ministered in the New Testament church (Acts 13:1; 15:32; 1 Cor 12:28–29; 14:29–37; Eph 2:20; 4:11; Rev 22:6, 9). Both in the old covenant and the new, prophets were primarily "forth-tellers," delivering God's message to his people. However, they could also be foretellers, predicting future events and giving God's perspective on them. Barnabas wasn't the only person Jerusalem sent to Antioch; apparently, a group of prophets

---

2. Some translate "were called" as a reflexive, "called themselves," but there is too little evidence for this.

was headquartered in Jerusalem and traveled to various places to minister to churches. We don't know anything about such groups, but this one apparently traveled together in God's service.

"This time" likely means the year Paul and Barnabas spent ministering in Antioch, so in the early 40s, as Claudius reigned from AD 41 to 54. There were several famines during his reign, and most think this one took place around AD 44–45, so that Agabus' prediction would have come a couple years earlier, giving time for the relief efforts to develop. We don't know too much about Agabus or the prophetic circle he was a part of (see his second prophecy in 21:10–11). Agabus, Luke tells us, "stood up" at an important meeting of the whole church there and gave a message "through the Spirit." Most famines were local, but this would be an empire-wide failure of, most likely, the grain harvest.[3]

The purpose of the prophecy is to enroll the Antioch church in the relief effort for the poor churches of Judea. The church in Palestine (like the province itself) was poverty-stricken and had no resources to help it through the coming crisis. So in keeping with 2:44–45 and 4:32–34 the other churches would have wanted to intervene so there would be "no needy persons" there (4:34). When it says "the disciples" provided help, we must remember that this signifies not the twelve disciples of Jesus but Christians in general (as in 6:1, 2; 9:1, 10, 26). Every member was expected to contribute, but they did so "as each one was able," in proportion to their wealth. This was a precursor to the collection for the poor that dominated Paul's later ministry (Acts 24:17; Rom 15:25–28; 1 Cor 16:1–4; 2 Cor 8–9). "Provide help" is literally "send for service," indicating that this ministry of service to a sister church as a congregational care program is intended to minister spiritually through giving.

---

3. See also Josephus, *Antiquities* 3.320–21.

After collecting the money, they entrusted it to Barnabas and Saul,[4] who took this gift to Jerusalem. The church there was clearly to use it during the famine to purchase the food they needed for the congregation. Their trip is the second visit of Paul to Jerusalem, recorded in Galatians 2:1–10. They entrusted the monetary gift to the Jerusalem "elders," who have assisted the apostles with administrative help and perhaps have taken leadership of the Judean church when the apostles left, probably due to the persecution initiated by Herod in the next chapter.

———

The issue in this passage is far more important than most of us think. If Peter's explanation about the conversion of Cornelius to the Jerusalem church had failed, the way we conduct ministry and evangelize the world today would be vastly different. Ours would be a two-layered gospel. First we would convert to Judaism and the law, followed by conversion to Christ. We would still be living under the sacrificial system and the laws of purity as well as under Christ and the Spirit. Peter's argument as he retells the story (vv. 4–17) is decisive, with the central theme so critical, "Do not call anything impure that God has made clean" (10:15). Christ has removed the laws of purity as necessary for salvation (see also Mark 7:19), and so both our understanding of salvation and our religious observance are forever changed.

The key is Peter's emphasis in verses 11–17 that God and the Spirit orchestrated every detail in order to prove that Gentiles become believers not through Torah adherence but through the atoning sacrifice of Christ alone. This was completely proved by the Gentile Pentecost: The Spirit came down and repeated the

---

4. The order of the names shows that Barnabas was the leader of the team, with Saul his associate. We will see Saul, due to his extraordinary gifts, gradually rise to the fore.

Pentecost phenomena for the Gentiles to show that God is authenticating a new people group joining the people of God. So the new age has begun, and a new covenant reality governs a new world. The Jerusalem Christians could only recognize and affirm that God has "granted [the Gentiles] repentance that leads to life" (11:18).

The final step in the movement to the Gentile mission is the establishment of the mother church for that mission, to parallel the Jerusalem church for the Jewish mission (vv. 19-21). Antioch is the perfect choice, as it is the largest city east of Rome and was successful from the start. The church there grew so fast that the apostles in Jerusalem had to send Barnabas to oversee it (vv. 22-24), and he was so successful that he had to go and get Saul in Tarsus to help him oversee the church there (vv. 25-26). For a year they toiled there, and God blessed their ministry greatly.

A major episode during this time is the famine relief collection of verses 27-30. A group of itinerant prophets visited, and one of them, Agabus, predicted that a worldwide famine would take place soon. The sharing heart of 2:44-45 and 4:32-34 was demonstrated once again as the members of the Antioch church took up a voluntary collection, with each one giving in accord with their economic ability to ensure that the poverty-stricken Palestinian church didn't starve. This is an important lesson for us today about the fact that our churches dare never be thought worlds unto themselves who can ignore the church at large. Every church around the world is a sister congregation, and when they are in trouble we owe it to God and ourselves to alleviate their suffering.

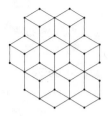

PERSECUTION UNDER HEROD
(12:1–25)

The peace and growth of the church that has dominated recent chapters comes to an abrupt end as Herod Agrippa I reenergizes Jewish opposition and initiates a major persecution centering on the apostles. We return to the difficult times of Acts 4 and 5. As it did there, the church does not retreat but forges ahead through suffering. As the believers face renewed opposition, they gain courage and Spirit-given strength, as Luke will highlight in the summary of 12:24, "the word of God continued to spread and flourish." In fact, God's hand of justice will reach down and give Herod exactly what he has earned, a terrible death that provides his just deserts.

This episode ends the first half of the book of Acts, what is often called "the Palestinian period" of the church. That categorization is somewhat simplistic, for 1:12–8:3 covered the Jewish Christian church, and then 8:4–12:25 covered the steps to the Gentile mission, as the Spirit moved the church step by step from being a Jewish sect to a worldwide religious force. Still, this chapter closes that period, and the rest of Acts (13:1–28:31) covers the development of the universal mission as it spreads throughout the Roman world.

JAMES IS MARTYRED (12:1-2)

James the Lord's brother has become the head elder of the Jerusalem church, but James the brother of John (and son of Zebedee) has remained ministering throughout the region as one of the Twelve. Meanwhile, Herod Agrippa I, grandson of Herod the Great, has just been named king of his grandfather's former realm by the emperor Caligula in AD 41. He will remain on the throne until his death in AD 44. The other Herods had jockeyed for this but had only been named rulers over a portion. Agrippa was the only one chosen to ascend the great man's throne.

The first thing he did after being named king was to initiate a persecution of the church.[1] This was not just an arrest and interrogation as by the Sanhedrin in 4:3. This was a violent situation; "persecute" here is *kakōsai*, "to do them serious harm." Luke names James as one of those who loses their life. He was one of the three who were especially close to Jesus (with Peter and John). He was beheaded like John the Baptist was, indicating a political crime to the Romans (akin to treason), but equally shameful as crucifixion to the Jews. In Agrippa's mind, this would have been the first of many such violent deaths.

PETER IS ARRESTED AND ESCAPES (12:3-19)

Clearly, Agrippa's purpose was to build his support base with the Jews. He was actually fairly popular with the Jewish people, and by killing James and a few others he was testing the waters to see the general reaction. When it met with approval, he went after Peter, undoubtedly intending to make him and James the first of many. With James he had apparently not bothered with a trial but just had him executed. Probably the hatred of the followers

---

1. This would be a flashback to a year or two before the famine-relief visit. These events with Herod Agrippa took place simultaneously with Barnabas and Paul's ministry in Antioch.

of Jesus had continued under the surface in spite of "the time of peace" (9:31). Now it rises again.

Arrest and Imprisonment (12:3-5)

Agrippa's intention with Peter was to have a showy public trial in order to garner further support, but he had to wait until the eight-day Passover and Feast of Unleavened Bread had ended, so he put Peter in prison awaiting trial, either the one in Herod's palace or the Antonia Fortress, where Paul will later be incarcerated (21:34).

Like Paul will be later, Peter is guarded by four squads of soldiers, and during the night they would have switched every three hours in order to remain vigilant. He was taking no chance of anyone trying to break him out, especially after the miraculous escape of 5:19-21. While all this is happening, the church, certainly still grieving over James, is "earnestly praying" that God will spare Peter (12:5). They have no idea how literally God will answer their prayer, as we will see.

Miraculous Escape (12:6-11)

Peter was constantly chained to two guards day and night, and the other two guards acted as sentries to watch for intruders, all this for a peasant preacher of an upstart religion. Herod was taking no chances. This continued for six or seven days, until the last day of the festival and the day before the trial was to begin. It is the final night, and Peter is asleep as he awaits the momentous events of the next day. He must have been trusting in the Lord to be able to sleep before what could be one of his last days on earth, but certainly he could not have been ready for what was about to transpire.

Suddenly (probably in the hours just before dawn) a bright light filled the cell, noticed only by Peter (12:7). The bright light may have been the same as that which appeared to Paul on the Damascus road, the **Shekinah** glory of God appearing in the cell, visible only to God's chosen one. Hebrews 1:3 speaks of Jesus as "the radiance of God's glory," and that is what we see here. The angel of the Lord (probably the same one as in 5:19; 8:26; 10:3) "suddenly" appears, and the presence of the Lord's glory is palpable for Peter, though he is completely confused as he expects nothing. He had already been rescued once (5:19), and the church is deeply in prayer for him, but neither he nor they are expecting anything miraculous to happen.

The angel "struck Peter on the side and woke him up." This is not just a touch but a strong blow. Apparently Peter is a heavy sleeper. When the angel tells him, "Quick, get up," the chains fall off his wrists. The guards, who are trained never to fall asleep, have been clearly put fast asleep by God. Let me paraphrase the next commands: "Get on your running shoes and fasten your seatbelt. We're making a run for it!" Peter like many prisoners must have been lying there wearing only a loin cloth, for he is to put on every article of clothing for walking—shoes, tunic, belt, cloak—and stay close behind the angel as he follows him out of the prison house.

The picture Luke paints is quite vivid (12:8-10): the bright light with the angel in its midst, Peter waking up after a heavy blow, his getting dressed one article of clothing at a time, his passing first one set of guards then the other, the gates opening as if on automatic power, and all the time Peter walking in a daze, thinking, "It can't be real; it must be a dream or vision." Everything is done by the Lord and the angel. Peter is barely functioning and is in shock. Only after they have passed "the iron gate leading to the city" and the angel has left him outside the prison a block later does he truly wake up. Every single step, everything that transpires, is a miracle sent from the Lord. This isn't a miraculous escape; it's an entire series of miraculous events enabling his escape. A dozen miracles, one after another!

When he is finally in control of his senses (12:11), he tells himself (and us), "Now I know without a doubt that the Lord has sent his angel and rescued me." The true situation has finally hit him that he has been rescued by the Lord a second time. This time it's a double rescue—"from Herod's clutches and from everything the

Jewish people were hoping would happen." It's not easy knowing that your countrymen want you dead, but he has been through that with Jesus and lived it for quite some time. For us it would be like the president and head of the Joint Chiefs of Staff instructing the FBI and CIA that they want us killed. That's a lot of firepower focused on ending your life, but God is on his side, and that's all that matters.

REACTIONS TO THE STUPENDOUS EVENT (12:12–19)

Peter knows the believers will be congregated for an all-night prayer meeting at the primary house church of Jerusalem, the home of Mary mother of John Mark. She is a wealthy woman with a house large enough to serve over fifty people. There were no separate buildings for churches until the time of Constantine, and every town had a series of homes that believers would call their local *ekklēsia*. The fact that no husband is mentioned means either that he was an unbeliever or that she was a widow. The fact that these prayers are going on through the night means they are praying for Peter's dire situation.

When Peter knocks on the door and proves God is still the God of miracles (12:13–14, actually a "gate" into the courtyard of an expensive home), a slave woman named Rhoda answers. Her great and joyous shock is seen in the fact that she leaves Peter standing at the gate and runs inside, shouting, "Peter is at the door!" What follows is a humorous and human scene. God has already answered prayer once before (5:19), and they have spent all night asking God to intervene for him, but when God's answer is standing right before them, they think he is a ghost! She hasn't even opened the gate, and Peter can only keep knocking and hoping someone responds.

When she keeps insisting it is actually Peter, they reply, "You're out of your mind. ... It must be his angel." Realize the implications. Their prayers for Peter have been interrupted by the announcement that he is standing at the door, but instead of saying that God has performed another miracle, they insist that any such assertion can't be rational because he must still be in prison.

Nowhere is such an angel used as a name for a person's ghost, so it must mean his guardian angel (see Ps 91:11; Dan 3:28; Tobit 5:22; Matt 18:10; Heb 1:14). Many have noted a rabbinic text, Genesis Rabbah 78 on Genesis 33:10, as demonstrating the belief in some circles that such angels can resemble the people they watch over. At any rate, their prayers are clearly marred with strong doubt that God could (or would) do such a thing, even though he has done so already once before. Possibly they have prayed only for protection rather than release, but I don't think so. They have been praying but not really believing that God would answer them.

All this goes by the boards when they actually open the gate, seeing Peter standing there. Needless to say, they're astonished, their doubts swept away. We can guess the chaos that ensued, with everyone talking at once. Peter then motions them to be quiet (12:17) and proceeds to tell them everything that happened. They must have laughed with him as he was telling them how long he was walking in a trance behind the angel, not believing it could be happening. God continually surprises us with his loving care.

Two things follow. Apparently the other apostles and the elders of the church are not present at the prayer meeting, so he tells them to let "James and the other brothers" know about his miraculous escape from prison. There were many such house churches in Jerusalem, and he could not visit them all. This is also further evidence that the apostles are not in Jerusalem any longer, and that the Lord's brother James has taken over leadership of the church there (as we will see in 15:13–21; Gal 1:19; 2:9). The "others" could be other Christ followers but more likely refers to the other elders of the church.

The second thing Peter does is leave "for another place." We don't really know what this "other place" is. It almost certainly is not just another prayer meeting in another house church. Peter is in serious danger if he stays in Jerusalem, for the authorities will be looking everywhere for him. If they catch him now, his life will be over. So he most likely joins the other apostles in itinerant missionary work and goes on the road from place to place, but now leaves for his own safety as well as for the church's mission.

In verse 18, the soldiers from whom he escaped are scared out of their minds and frantic over what has happened to Peter. As we will see in the next verse, Roman law says that a guard who allows a prisoner to escape will have to pay the same punishment as the prisoner would have received, in this case execution. If they fail to get Peter back, they will die. So Luke's "no small commotion" is actually an understatement.

Herod organizes an area-wide search for him, but to no avail. He is gone and far out of the area. So he calls in the guards and thoroughly interrogates them (probably using torture to get at the truth), then executes them, actually a legal decision and not just anger at their ineptitude. He probably also suspects they accepted a bribe to set Peter free. He would hardly have accepted a miraculous escape at the hands of God. Herod had come to Jerusalem for Passover and now returns to his home in Caesarea (9:30; 10:1) and the Herodian palace there.

HEROD AGRIPPA DIES (12:20–23)

Herod will now face the very end he had ordered for the guards earlier. He had flaunted his own authority over that of God himself, and now he must face the consequences. Divine retribution for sin is the theme of this section, and Herod will receive what his arrogant self-centeredness and deliberate flaunting of his authority will bring down on his head. As Rome-appointed king of the entire region, he controlled the issues that arose.

Tyre and Sidon were free Phoenician coastal cities and depended on trade with Galilee for their grain supply. They had a dispute with him regarding this supply. This is not attested in any Roman or Jewish records, so we don't know exactly what it was, but they need to get Herod's goodwill over this and get him to release his embargo against them. They had bribed Blastus, Herod's chamberlain or chief of his household (a political as well as domestic office). This works, and reconciliation is effected.

The next events are found also in the Jewish historian Josephus (*Antiquities* 19.343-50), and the two accounts mostly agree. At the treaty banquet, which Josephus says are the Roman games to honor the emperor, Herod is dressed in all his royal finery, and as he readies himself to speak, the crowd erupts with high praise normally used of Caesar, "This is the voice of a god, not of a man." Luke tells us that Herod accepted the acclamation without "giving praise [Greek: "glory"] to God," which constitutes blasphemy on his part. His hubris brings divine judgment down on him, and immediately "an angel of the Lord struck him down, and he was eaten by worms and died." Josephus tells us he died after five days of intense intestinal pain. The main thing is that God took his life for his blasphemy and breaking of the first commandment.

THE CHURCH CONTINUES ITS MISSION (12:24-25)

As we have seen often, the result of crises in Acts is the awakening of the power of God in the church. One of the most persistent themes in the book is the fact that every difficulty the church faces is an opportunity to find a deeper faith and watch the Spirit work. Summary passages like this seem to come after the church has come through serious afflictions and show how through them the church grows stronger both in numbers and spirit (2:41; 4:4, 31; 5:14; 6:7; 8:25; 9:31). In these passages, the "word of God" becomes an epithet for church growth, meaning that the preaching of the gospel has led to numerous converts. In the midst of extremely severe difficulties, including the death and imprisonment of two of the Twelve, the mission of the church continues to thrive. Once more, there is truth in Tertullian's famous saying that "the blood of the martyrs is the seed of the church," and the presence of the Spirit turns everything around.

As part of this expansion of "the word of God," Barnabas and Saul return from delivering the famine-relief money to the Jerusalem church (11:30). With them they bring the son of Mary, whose large home became one of the leading house churches, as we saw in 12:12–17. John is his Jewish name, and Mark his Greek name. He is very much like Timothy in 16:1–3, a young, dedicated believer and son of one of the leading families in the church who wishes to join the team as an assistant and engage in ministry. He will help in Antioch and accompany the team on the first missionary journey (see also 13:13; 15:37–39).

———

This final chapter in the Jewish Christian period of the church shows again the bitterness and opposition of the Jews to all things Christian. There had been a time of relative peace and unprecedented growth in recent chapters, but that ends here. Herod is trying to curry favor with his Jewish subjects by instigating a pogrom against the Christ followers, and he begins with James (vv. 1–2), arresting and then beheading him. He manages to arrest Peter as well, but there isn't time for an official trial, and he must incarcerate him until after the Feast of Unleavened Bread (vv. 3–5).

Peter's miraculous escape shows how God works in spite of our lack of faith. Neither Peter nor the church that has an all-night prayer meeting on his behalf expects God to do anything, and Peter treats every step of the angel's orchestrating his miraculous release as part of a dream-vision (vv. 6–11). Then when he arrives at Mary's house church and greets the believers as they are at prayer, they believe it's not really him but just his guardian angel (vv. 12–17). This is a lesson regarding answers to prayer and our faith in a God who works on our behalf. It tells us that we should be open and ready for God to do great things.

Herod is livid at his escape and the ruination of his plans to set the Jews further against the Christians. This has served instead to make the Christians even more famous due to another miracle. He executes the guards and returns to his palace in Caesarea (vv. 18–19), and another attempt to thwart the will of God goes down the drain. In Caesarea he receives the just consequences of his foolish actions. After allowing himself to be worshipped as a god, he is struck down by God and dies a painful death (vv. 20–23). The lesson is that arrogance and actions against God will always receive their just reward.

Finally, God uses these murderous attempts to make the church even stronger, and as a result there are further conversions and power in their witness (vv. 24–25). Barnabas and Saul return from Jerusalem with John Mark, and the church is poised for the next step in its Spirit-driven movement to the universal mission.

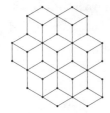

PAUL'S MISSION IN CYPRUS AND GALATIA
(13:1–52)

This episode marks the midpoint of the book and the goal to which we have been pointing since the promise in 1:8 that the gospel will go "to the ends of the earth." It is common to label this Paul's "first missionary journey," but we have already seen at least three other extensive missionary times—Damascus and Arabia in 9:19-25 and Galatians 1:17; Tarsus and Cilicia in Acts 9:30 and Galatians 1:21-24. Antioch could be called a third mission period, and so the one in Acts 13 could be thought of as a fourth missionary journey. Someone may demur, "Surely Antioch isn't a missionary 'journey' but a settled ministry." However, it resembles closely the so-called third missionary journey, which was a settled ministry in Ephesus for over two years.

Nevertheless, this first of the three is a momentous event, and Luke portrays it in this book as launching the worldwide mission of the church. The same Holy Spirit who descended at Pentecost in Acts 2 spearheads this move and is behind every stage, as he was behind every step of the Gentile mission in 8:4-12:25. The Antioch church becomes the supporting church and Paul's headquarters for his missionary journeys.

In this opening salvo of Paul's journeys outward from Antioch, they will first go to Barnabas' homeland, the island of Cyprus, and then into southern Asia Minor to a series of cities where Paul's pattern of "first to the Jew, then to the Gentile" of Romans 1:16 will be established.

PAUL AND BARNABAS TRAVEL TO CYPRUS (13:1–12)

A COMMISSIONING SERVICE (13:1–3)

Luke stops using the name Saul in 13:9 and begins using Paul, probably to symbolize that he is now missionary to the Gentiles, as Saul was his name when among Jews and Paul his name when among Gentiles. Paul will continue ministering to both peoples, and in fact wherever he goes he will center on the Jewish populace first; but he will at all times personify the Gentile mission. These three verses are used to conclude the focus on Antioch in the book of Acts and to launch the central theme of the rest of the book, the worldwide mission of the church.

We don't know what kind of meeting this was, but it consisted of "prophets and teachers," perhaps comprising the leadership of the church at Antioch, which with the city being the capital of the province of Syria would have been the leading church of the region. New Testament prophets would have been similar in some ways to their Old Testament counterparts, men and women called by the Lord to be his mouthpiece and deliver messages directly from him. As evidenced by Agabus in 11:28, this at times involved predicting the future. The teachers would be tasked with instructing the church by immersing the believers in biblical and theological truth. Many of the creeds and hymns of Scripture were likely written by these teachers.

Along with Barnabas and Saul, three of the men are present for this meeting. Simeon called Niger (which means "black") would have been a black man from Africa (like the Ethiopian eunuch). Lucius was from Cyrene (like Simon who carried Jesus' cross) and

may have been one of the believers from the **Hellenistic** synagogue of 6:9 who was forced to flee in the great persecution of
8:1–3. Menaen, we are told, had been "brought up with Herod the
tetrarch," namely, Herod Antipas, tetrarch of Galilee. He may have
been connected with Chuza, Herod's steward, whose wife, Joanna,
was part of Jesus' team in Luke 8:3. Luke does not distinguish who
was a prophet and who a teacher. Barnabas and Saul would at various times hold all three offices (as well as apostle).

As they prayed and fasted, the Spirit took over and commanded,
"Set apart for me Barnabas and Saul for the work to which I have
called them." This was undoubtedly a prophetic message, and the
God-appointed "work" was the Gentile mission, finally coming to
fruition. Paul's earlier ministries in Arabia, Cilicia, and Antioch
were preparatory. Antioch would provide the home base, and
the mission would move out from there to the rest of the Roman
world. The two primary movements that readied the church for
the Gentile mission were the conversion of Cornelius and this commissioning event here. So this is a critical moment in the history
of the church. The Spirit has directed every stage from Stephen
to Philip to Peter and now in the decision of the Antioch leaders
to "set apart" the two pioneer missionaries chosen by the Spirit
to take the mission to its next level.

Their call takes place in the midst of prayer and fasting (both vv.
2 and 3), so it is immersed in worship. The leaders want to make certain every detail flows from the Lord and glorifies him. The laying on
of hands (see on 6:6; also 8:17, 19; 9:12, 17) is a worship event as well
as a commissioning service. It is important to realize this becomes
not a call to a new ministry but rather to a new phase of the ministry both have already embraced. The new aspect is the itinerant nature of the work they will be doing as they take the gospel
to pioneer fields that have not heretofore been exposed to Christ.
Furthermore, witness is seen as an aspect of worship. This is how
I always feel when I minister in a new setting. When I preach I am
inviting the people to join me as I worship the Lord. Both preaching

and witness flow out of worship and are types of worship activities. Barnabas and Saul are "sent off" within a worship atmosphere.

Mission in Cyprus (13:4-6a)

They are commissioned by the Spirit, and they are sent by the Spirit. Barnabas is a native of Cyprus (4:36), and Cyprus had already been preevangelized by some who fled the persecution of 8:1–3 (11:19). So Barnabas as head of the mission team and led by the Spirit determined that that would be a good place for them to begin their new ministry. They go to the major port city of Seleucia (sixteen miles away on the coast) and sail the short distance to Cyprus (about sixty miles by sea). They disembark at Salamis on the east side of the island, the largest city on the island and the center of commerce. Cyprus is a large island about 140 miles long and 60 miles wide, with the two major cities at the eastern tip (Salamis) and the western tip (Paphos).

As they will do everywhere they go, they first "proclaimed the word of God in the Jewish synagogues." There was a large Jewish community there and several synagogues, so they spent a bit of time there (we don't know how long). Implicit in the tone here is the success of their initial mission on the south part of the island. John Mark (12:25) at this early time is a helpful assistant and probably worked at integrating new converts into the movement and dealing with practical matters like food and lodging. While the church was certainly already present in Salamis and elsewhere (see 11:19), the ministry of Barnabas and Saul seems to be primarily evangelistic rather than teaching in the church.

They did not restrict their ministry to Salamis but "traveled through the whole island" presenting the gospel in town after town. The two main cities were about a hundred miles apart, so Luke is summarizing a fairly extensive amount of time evangelizing that many cities and towns. Luke has decided to do what he did about the ministries in Arabia and Cilicia: say nothing in order to have room for those portions on which he wishes to center.

THE ENCOUNTER WITH ELYMAS BAR-JESUS (13:6B–12)

They eventually arrived in Paphos, a new Roman city replacing an older town destroyed by an earthquake in 15 BC. It had been made the capital of the province that same year and was named after a Syrian goddess. As such it was the center of several cults including Aphrodite, with a famous temple in the old city. Soon after arriving, they encountered the second sorcerer/magician of Acts (after Simon Magus in chapter 8; see also 16:16–18; 19:13–20). He was probably the royal astrologer of the proconsul Sergius Paulus and is called here "a false prophet," meaning one who advertised himself as a prophet but served only himself and earthly profit.

Jews and Samaritans became well-known sorcerers because of their extensive angelology, which the Romans would have linked with their extensive pantheon of gods. However, the Roman gods were capricious, never the friends of people, while the angels were seen as messengers of Yahweh who helped the people of God. This gave them status in the world of magic. There is special irony in his name "son of [*bar*] Jesus." In a sense, the two Jesus figures squared off with each other, and Paul would be shown to be the true prophet.

They encounter this court sorcerer in the praetorium of the Roman proconsul Sergius Paulus. Cyprus was a senatorial province, run by the Roman senate and so governed by a proconsul appointed by that self-same senate.[1] Luke has nothing but good to say about him, calling him "an intelligent man," probably meaning he always sought the truth and was open to the Christian message. As will happen again in Athens, new preachers and teachers were required to speak to the authorities to ascertain whether they were worthy to set up shop in the province. So Sergius Paulus asks the

---

1. These were generally peaceful provinces that didn't require the presence of the Roman army. Judea, on the other hand, was an imperial province and needed a great many troops due to anti-Roman sentiment. It was governed by a legate (for instance, Pilate).

two missionaries to come speak with him. Some think that Luke's "wanted to hear theword of God" means that he is already positive toward the Christian message, but that is not necessary here. He was probably neutral at this point.

Elymas saw them as a serious rival. He felt he owned Sergius Paulus, not due to his Jewish faith, for he had long abandoned that, but to his Greco-Roman magic. He rightly saw that the Christian faith was unalterably opposed to all the pagan ideals he had bought into, and as Paul spoke to his master Sergius Paulus, he recognized the attraction the gospel had to him. The battle had been joined, and he had to act quickly, so he "tried to turn the proconsul from the faith" (13:8). "The faith" refers to both Christianity as a religion and Christian truth as a set of doctrines. Paul was proclaiming Jesus as the expected Messiah and salvation by faith, and it was clearly attracting the proconsul. Elymas realized if that were to come to pass, his influence and power would be over.

The battle now enters its final phase. In verse 9 the name Saul appears for the last time, and he is named "Paul" from this point forward. As missionary to the Gentiles and "filled with the Holy Spirit," he pronounces God's curse on Elymas as "a child of the devil and an enemy of everything that is right" (13:10). The man had given himself over to the evil powers, and his power came from Satan, not from God. He has become the opposite of his name Bar-Jesus ("son of Jesus"). As one who is filled with evil rather than good, he is "full of all kinds of deceit and trickery," and his incantations are proved to be nothing but magic tricks.

Clearly, Paul wants Sergius Paulus to see the absolute contrast between such falsehood and the truth of Jesus Messiah. He is "perverting the right ways of the Lord" by using his power as a false prophet to twist God's "straight path" or "right ways" (NIV) into a set of lies. As such, he has come under divine judgment, and "the hand of the Lord is against you." He has become God's enemy, and he will thereby pay the price. Now like Peter in 5:5, 10, with Ananias and Sapphira, Paul becomes God's avenging angel and strikes Elymas "blind for a time" so that he is "not even able to see the light of the sun" (13:11). This is a limited curse (like Zechariah in Luke 1:20 or Paul in Acts 9:9), probably meant to allow the man time to repent and get right with God.

The result (13:11b-12) differs for Elymas and Sergius Paulus. The false prophet is enveloped in "mist and darkness" and can only grope his way around, with others leading him by the hand. His spiritual darkness is now compounded by physical darkness, but we have no indication that he ever repented of his sins. The proconsul, on the other hand, saw and believed. He was "amazed at the teaching about the Lord" and certainly amazed at Paul's superior power over his court sorcerer. So Paul is confirmed both by the powerlessness of Elymas and the conversion of Sergius Paulus, who rightly is brought to the Lord more by Paul's teaching (for that is what Luke mentions) than by his mighty power.

PAUL AND BARNABAS TRAVEL TO PISIDIAN ANTIOCH (13:13-52)

The Journey from Paphos to Pisidia (13:13-14a)

The team decided to move on from Cyprus back to the mainland, and Luke again abbreviates the travel part, moving inland up to Pisidian Antioch in just two verses. Their first stop was Perga in the province of Pamphylia, more than a hundred-mile boat trip. They probably preached the gospel while there (they did so on their way back, 14:25), but Luke mentions only the departure of John Mark and his return home to Jerusalem and his mother Mary. He doesn't tell us why John Mark did so, but it was not a good separation, for when Barnabas wanted to bring him back for the second mission trip, Paul opposed it so strongly (Luke calls it desertion) that it split the team (15:37-39). We never learn why Mark deserted. He could have been homesick (though that seems weak as a later reason to split the team), or perhaps he strongly opposed Paul's growing leadership and strategy for reaching the

Gentiles. Whichever, it was severe enough to be called a "desertion" in 15:38.

Pisidian Antioch, the major city of the region and a military
center, was another hundred miles north, this time by land on a
major Roman highway called the Via Sebaste. This missionary
journey is dictated by this major trade highway, which covered
the eastern half of Asia Minor. All the towns of Acts 13–14 are situated on this highway. The city lay in the Taurus mountain range
near the border of the region called Pisidia, and so it is called that
to distinguish it from the many other towns named Antioch (like
Syrian Antioch in chapter 11). They apparently went around several major towns, and Luke could simply have omitted those details.
Some think Paul had contracted malaria in the low elevations of
the coast and needed to go higher—Antioch was 3,600 feet above
sea level; see Gal 4:13, "because of an illness"—while others believe
Sergius Paulus on Cyprus had contacts in Antioch and suggested
Barnabas and Paul go straight there. It could also simply have been
the Lord's leading to go that route. All the cities in chapters 13–14
were in the province of Galatia, and so the team spent the next
year or so in that region.

PAUL'S SERMON IN ANTIOCH (13:14B–41)

The setting: the synagogue (13:14b–15)
As would become his regular practice, Paul and his companions
went to the synagogue and ministered there first. It was common
for the heads of the synagogue to invite visiting rabbis to speak,
and apparently the leaders[2] had learned who Barnabas and Paul
were, so they asked them to share "a word of exhortation" (a
common idiom for a sermon) during the service. Their intention
was to worship on their first Sabbath in the city, but that was not

---

2. The leaders (*archisynagōgoi*) are lay officials, often the patrons of the synagogue, who are in charge of services and practical affairs in the synagogue.

to be. Services usually began with the Shema (the confession combining Deut 6:4–9; 11:13–21; and Num 15:37–41) followed by a reading from the Law and the Prophets (as here). A last-minute request to distinguished visitors was not unusual. Paul accepts, stands to speak, and motions with his hand to get their attention.

Survey of history from the patriarchs to David (13:16–22)

Paul first addresses the congregation as "fellow Israelites and you Gentiles who worship God" (NIV), but it would be better to read "fellow Israelites and you God-fearers," for the God-fearers were a religious class in the first century, as we have seen (10:2, 22). This group consisted of Gentiles who believed and worshipped as Jews but were unwilling to be circumcised and become full Jewish converts. Most likely there were degrees in which that was true among the Gentiles here, from interest to sympathy to actual belief.

The allusion to the patriarchs stresses their election to be the covenant people (13:17; see Deut 4:37; 7:7); the Jews are the chosen people. This continued in Egypt as God "made the [chosen] people prosper" and then "led them out." The Gentiles would have appreciated "the mighty power" that he exerted on behalf of his people. The language is quite strong—literally, he "exalted them" and delivered them "with uplifted arm," strong military language all Romans would have enjoyed.

Further, God put up with their failures and "endured their conduct" during the forty years "in the wilderness," emphasizing his forgiving their terrible conduct and delivering them ultimately. Then he went before Israel in their conquest of Canaan by being the Divine Warrior who "overthrew seven nations[3] in Canaan" and gave their land "to his people as their inheritance" (13:18–19, see Josh 14:1–2). This parallels Rome's rise to power exactly and would have again appealed greatly to his audience. I doubt they had ever

---

3. Deut 7:1 lists "the Hittites, Girgashites, Amorites, Canaanites, Perizzites, Hivites and Jebusites, seven nations larger and stronger than you."

heard this view of Israel as the precursor to Rome. The "450 years" would parallel the 700 years of Rome's history. It is a round number for the period of the sojourn in Egypt plus the wanderings in the wilderness and the conquest of Canaan.

Paul then turns to the period of the judges (13:20b) but says little about them, simply relating how they ruled until the monarchy began under the ministry of Samuel the prophet. The judges were more military deliverers of the people than judicial heads, and that is probably the emphasis. When the people demanded a king, God gave them Saul, whose reign lasted forty years, a detail not found in the Old Testament but which was the traditional length of his reign.[4] In the context Paul is likely thinking of his namesake's failure in the end.

Finally (13:22), after Saul is taken from the scene, David is made king, and he has God's approval who testifies, "I have found David son of Jesse, a man after my own heart; he will do everything I want him to do." Two NIV translations could be improved. "After this" is actually "After he was removed" (metastēsas), stressing Saul's failure. "Made king" is literally "he raised up [ēgeiren] David as king," using the same verb as was used for Jesus' resurrection in 13:30, 37. Saul symbolizes failed Israel, and David is a type of Jesus the Messiah.

God's "witness" to David is built on a collage of three texts: (1) "I have found David" recalls Psalm 89:20, "I have found David my servant; with my sacred oil I have anointed him," stressing David as the messianic (anointed) king. (2) "A man after my own heart" points to 1 Samuel 13:14, where Samuel is rebuking Saul and preparing the way for David as the true "ruler of [God's] people." (3) "He will do everything I want" goes back to Isaiah 44:28, which speaks of Cyrus as "my shepherd [who] will accomplish all that I please"; he is the one who will deliver God's people as another precursor for Jesus Messiah.

---

4. Compare Josephus, *Antiquities* 6.14.9

Paul intends this rehearsal of the history of the nation to prepare the way for his message about Jesus as the one who fulfills not just the messianic prophecies but the entire history of Israel as the chosen covenant people.

Fulfillment in Jesus and John the Baptist (13:23–25)

Now Paul introduces his main topic, Jesus as brought forth "from this man's [David's] descendants" as royal Messiah. As Messiah, Jesus is the "Savior" whom God "promised," fulfilling all of this history in himself. The promise has to be the Davidic covenant of 2 Samuel 7:12–14: "I will raise up your offspring to succeed you … and I will establish his kingdom." Jesus is the royal Messiah, and the final kingdom has arrived with him. He alone could fulfill the Davidic promise, for David's dynasty ended, and only Jesus, the Davidic Messiah, could fulfill the promise of an eternal kingdom. So he and he alone is Savior, the one who "will save his people from their sins" (Matt 1:21).

John the Baptist is the messianic forerunner (13:24–25) and prepared for his coming by proclaiming "a baptism of repentance" (NIV: "repentance and baptism"), which signified repentance and salvation from sins (see Luke 3:3). Paul is mentioning this here because it is a perfect segue to Jesus as the basis of our salvation. The Baptist represents repentance for the forgiveness of sin, and belief in Jesus and his sacrificial death is the basis of salvation. "All the people of Israel," including those at the synagogue in Pisidian Antioch, must repent and turn to Jesus. For John, this repentance was to be symbolized by baptism, which signified cleansing from sin.

It is important that the listeners know John was not the Messiah but rather prepared for his coming. So Paul relates how the Baptist pointed to Jesus and said, "There is one coming after me whose sandals I am not worthy to untie" (13:25, found in Luke 3:16). The Baptist is stating that he is not good enough or important enough even to be Jesus' slave. Since the feet signified all the dirt of life clinging to a person, slaves were not required to loosen the ties on their master's sandals. Jesus is Lord of all, and John is nothing compared to him. Paul is telling them to place all their attention on Jesus and come to him alone for salvation.

Further fulfillment in Christ (13:26–37)

In a sense, this is the second half of Paul's sermon, for he addresses his audience again (see 13:16) as "fellow descendants of Abraham and God-fearers" (my translation). He wants to stress especially how everything he has said in verses 16–25 pointed to Jesus as God's gift to humanity to provide salvation for all people. The "message [*logos*] of salvation" is first of all Jesus as "the word of God" and second, the gospel message about him. As descendants of Abraham, they are one with him, and as he pointed to Jesus the Christ, they too must come to their Messiah for salvation. This word is "to us," yet also "for us" (*hēmin*), for our benefit and salvation.

In verse 27 Paul sums up passion week, when the residents of Jerusalem and their leaders "did not recognize" Jesus in spite of all the evidence right before them. The emphasis is on their guilt, for it was not an inadvertent failure to realize who he was but a studied and deliberate rejection of all he was. The leaders (Greek "rulers") were the scribes and Pharisees, the chief priests, and especially the Sanhedrin, which made the final decision to have Jesus executed. So they condemned him to death, yet in so doing so, Paul emphasizes, they in reality "fulfilled the words of the prophets that are read every Sabbath," referring to the messianic prophecies in passages like Psalm 22:6–7; 69:2; 118:22; Isaiah 52:13–53:12. God knew of it long beforehand, and he had it completely under his control. Paul's point is that these people in Antioch read the passages every Sabbath and like those in Jerusalem failed to "recognize" their significance.

Paul's next point of emphasis is on the fact that they "found no proper ground for a death sentence" and still turned him over to Pilate, asking that he be crucified (13:28). This is from a

Roman perspective. They condemned him as a blasphemer, but that was only by Jewish law, and Pilate as a Roman found him innocent. Still, they demanded his death and would not accept Pilate's no (Luke 23:18, 21, 23). Paul here stresses Jewish guilt, arguing that in Jesus' crucifixion they "carried out all that was written about him" (13:29) in the prophecies regarding the death of the Messiah (see v. 27). Paul then mentions one of these prophecies, from Deuteronomy 21:22: how "they took him down from the cross [literally, 'tree']" (see Acts 5:30; 10:39). Apparently, the "they" who "laid him in a tomb" does not refer to Joseph of Arimathea or Nicodemus but to the authorities who killed him, specifically Pilate, who gave permission to bury Jesus.

Paul wants his listeners to realize not just his claim that God raised Jesus from the dead but the fact that this can be proved by eyewitness testimony. Not only has sin been defeated on the cross, but also the death that came on humankind as a result of sin (Rom 5:12–14) has been nullified by his resurrection. Death no longer rules over this world, for when God's people die they immediately are transformed and transported to heaven to be with their Lord.

Moreover, this can be accepted as more than a claim by a few isolated followers, because "for many days he was seen," and his glory was evidenced by his followers from Galilee. Of course, Paul is alluding to the appearances of the risen Jesus for forty days (1:3–8). If his listeners wish, they can look up the many who witnessed the risen Lord firsthand and hear their stories. Paul in a sense was one of them through the Damascus road encounter with the risen Jesus. These people, Paul stresses, are even "*now* his witnesses to our people," encouraging them to look into the truth of Jesus' resurrection.

From the fact of the resurrection, Paul now turns to its implications, especially that through the resurrection God's "promises" in the Old Testament have been "fulfilled for us," in particular the promise (it is singular in the text) made to David in verse 23 that one of his descendants would sit on his throne forever. This came to pass in Jesus and especially his resurrection, when he ascended into heaven and assumed his eternal throne. Paul uses three prophetic passages to make his point.

The passage he believes especially signifies this is Psalm 2:7, "You are my Son; today I have become your father." The psalm is about the nations' rage over God's anointed, and this verse celebrates how God has accepted him as his son. Jews took the "today" in the psalm as the enthronement of the king, especially the royal Messiah, and it is used this way at Jesus' baptism in Luke 3:22. In the early church this passage is seen as referring to Jesus' entire incarnate existence, from his birth to his resurrection as an enthronement to his status as royal Messiah. In this passage it is his resurrection in particular when his eternal "throneship" is made evident.

From Psalm 2 Paul turns next to Isaiah 55:3 and Psalm 16:10 to demonstrate that Jesus the promised Messiah (Isa 55:34) would never see decay (Ps 16:35). The point is that Jesus is Son of David as well as risen Lord, and that his resurrection was unlike all the other raisings from the dead in Scripture. They all returned to a human body that would still see death and decay (like Tabitha in Acts 9:36-43), but Jesus received an incorruptible body that would never again see decay.

Isaiah 55:3 shows that God has given to his people "the holy and sure blessings promised to David," which Paul links to Jesus via the Davidic covenant in 2 Samuel 7:14-16. As the Son of David, Jesus Messiah also inherits these blessings, and through him they are made available to God's people. So there is a twofold fulfillment here, first to the risen Jesus and then through him to God's new Israel, the true covenant people. These promises are "holy and sure," and they come to us through faith in Jesus, Son of David and Son of God.

Then in Psalm 16:10 (13:35) we see the other side of the promise, that God "will not let your holy one see decay." This is similar to Peter's use of Psalm 16:10 in Acts 2:27-31, that this passage could not refer to David since his body remains in a grave. Rather, it can only be fulfilled in Jesus, who was given a resurrected body. Paul has the same argument in verse 36. The first three aspects of David's life paralleled Jesus—he "served God's purpose" by obeying God with his life; he died; and he was buried. The fourth aspect is hugely different—"his body decayed." Jesus was raised from the dead and given eternal life with no decay. That concludes this section: "The one whom God raised from the dead did not see decay" (13:37). He is alive forevermore and is the only hope for salvation, for he is royal Messiah, Son of God, and Savior.

Call to repentance and faith in Christ (13:38–41)

This section consists of two parts, the promise (vv. 38–39) and the warning (vv. 40–41). The promise is that "through Jesus the forgiveness of sins is proclaimed to you." This proclamation becomes a call to repentance on the part of the people in the synagogue. In Jesus God provided salvation through his death and resurrection for us. Forgiveness of sins is now made possible, and it is theirs via repentance and faith in Jesus.

The law of Moses was inadequate for justifying sinners. The sacrificial system and the purity laws could only care for one sin at a time, and they could not solve the sin problem. The reason is that the Torah could identify sin but could not "set [the sinner] free" from "*every* sin." It was a temporary instrument, adequate only until the next sin was committed. Justification is a legal concept, describing God as the judge on his throne declaring the sinner to be righteous and right with him, defined well in Romans 3:21–26, with the results in Romans 5:1–11. True righteousness and forgiveness can be attained only for those who "believe" in Jesus the Messiah, and it is obtained only "through him," not through the law. Salvation comes by faith, not works; by trusting in him, not be observing legal regulations. We could not achieve forgiveness for ourselves, but he did through his atoning death on the cross.

Then Paul gave the synagogue audience a warning in verses
40–41. They dare not scoff or treat with disdain what Christ has
done on their behalf like the Jews of Jerusalem did. "Take care"
is *blepete*, "beware," and refers to a serious danger that will have
disastrous consequences. He cites Habakkuk 1:5, in which the
prophet warns the Israelites who have turned against God that
God is about to do something that they will not believe and that
will cause them to be filled with "wonder" but that will also cause
them to "perish." The Babylonian armies will invade Israel as judgment for their utter sinfulness and apostasy. The warning here
is far more serious than the one in Habakkuk, for "perish" here
is eternal punishment in hellfire, not just death at the hands of
an invading army. "Something" in the NIV is somewhat of a weak
translation, for the literal meaning is "I am working a work [*ergon
ergazomai*] in your days, a work that you would never believe," and
that work of God for Paul is the death and resurrection of Christ,
the sole basis for the faith-response that can produce forgiveness.
In these verses Paul is letting them know that only repentance and
faith in the saving work of Christ can suffice for them to receive
God's forgiveness and salvation.

RESULTS: DIVISION AMONG THE PEOPLE (13:42–52)

The sermon had positive results, as those who attended were
intrigued and asked Barnabas and Paul to speak further on the
next Sabbath. This is somewhat unusual, for that was normally
handled by the president of the synagogue. It shows the incredibly high interest the "people" had in the Christian message. At this
stage there is nothing but positive reactions. In fact, after the service Luke tells us that both Jews and Gentile proselytes "followed"
and continued to discuss the sermon with them. For the rest of
that Sabbath day, evangelistic challenge followed the gospel message from the service. During that time Paul and Barnabas (Paul's
name is now first, as he has taken over leadership on this occasion) "urged" their listeners to "continue in the grace of God" by

PAUL'S MISSION IN CYPRUS AND GALATIA   249

moving from interest in the gospel to faith-decision in Jesus. The implication is that many are converted. By "God's grace" they are forgiven and become believers in Christ.

The result is that interest continued to grow during the days leading up to the following Sabbath, and when it rolled around, "almost the whole city gathered to hear the word of the Lord." Of course this is hyperbole, but the synagogue is packed with people who have come to hear of the remarkable things Paul had shared the week before. Some think this may be more literal and that a few thousand gathered, with an open-air meeting perhaps described here. The "word of the Lord" is the gospel message (8:25; 11:16), and again the implication is that there were many conversions the following Sabbath as well.

As a result, Jewish "jealousy" arises because of the success of the gospel in their midst. The term (zēlou) is translated "zeal" by some, meaning that the success of Paul forced them to look carefully at their own set of beliefs and made them even more "zealous" for the law of Moses (also 21:20; 22:3), leading to their studied opposition to the Christian reinterpretation of its place in God's plan. I see this as containing a double meaning, being the first of several places (with 14:2; 17:5) where the gospel's success with Gentiles and God-fearers leads to jealousy from the Jews who have only limited success with Gentiles, and then that bringing about an even greater zeal for the law that leads to increased persecution of Christians.

The two apostles respond fearlessly with the same boldness displayed in 4:13, 29, 31, and 9:27, 28. This will come to characterize his preaching (14:3; 19:8; 26:26) and is an important lesson for us today. Too many preachers say only what they think will please their congregation and end up with weak, shallow messages that will never please God. Paul refused to worry about negative reactions and spoke what God led him to say. That should be our goal as well.

God had led Paul and Barnabas (anagkaion, divine necessity) to proclaim the gospel truths ("word of God" = "word of the Lord"

in v. 44) "first" to the Jews, as will be seen in every city they come
to in their missionary journeys (see Rom 1:16). The chosen people,
the Jews, the children of Abraham, have a certain priority in God's
covenant and plan. However, here in Pisidian Antioch, they "reject
it and do not consider [themselves] worthy of eternal life." The
second clause is the result of the first, meaning in effect, "with
the result that they have rendered themselves unworthy of eternal life." The critical phrase is "eternal life," for it is available only
upon responding to the gospel call to repentance and faith in the
risen Lord. It is resurrection life these Jews are throwing away
when they refuse the gospel message.

In their preaching, Paul explains (13:47), they are obeying the
challenge of Isaiah 49:6, "I have made you a light for the Gentiles,
that you may bring salvation to the ends of the earth." Paul realizes now that this was God's intention all along and not just after
Jesus' Great Commission of Matthew 28:18–20 and Acts 1:8. God
told his messengers long before that they were to bring God's salvation to "the ends of the earth," so these Christian messengers
are simply following the divine directive. The Jews are first, but
that means they are a first step to reaching the nations for God.

The people of the old covenant rejected the call of the
Abrahamic covenant (Gen 12:3; 22:18) and the call of Isaiah 49:6,
and we with Paul and the people of the new covenant age are chal-
lenged by the Lord to take up that clarion call and respond by being
a part of the universal mission to reach the world. Paul is considering his mission to the Jews and then the Gentiles to be a second
return from the exile after the one predicted by Isaiah. As such he
and Barnabas are "a light for the Gentiles" and are initiating here
the universal mission to the ends of the earth.

There are two results to the sermon, the positive reaction of the
Gentiles (vv. 48–49) and the negative reaction of many Jews (v. 50).
This will become a pattern played out in town after town in the
missionary journeys to follow. The former were "glad and honored

the word of the Lord," meaning they received the gospel message with joy. "Honored" is "glorified/brought glory to" (imperfect *edoxazon* to stress the ongoing nature of the honor) the gospel reality. In other words, for the rest of their lives they praised and honored God's saving truths.

Luke's description of God's saving activity is striking: "All who were appointed for eternal life believed." "All" is *hosos*: "as many as" were destined or chosen to have their sins forgiven, their hearts cleansed, and to inherit eternal life. This emphasizes God's sovereign control over salvation and would be connected with Romans 9 and 10 in showing God's power over the process of divine election. This is certainly a debated issue, and for myself I try to maintain a balance between God's predestination of his people and the parallel fact that they come to Christ on the basis of faith-decision. It is God who writes the names of his people in the heavenly book of life (Ps 69:28; Dan 12:1; Rev 3:5; 13:8; 17:8), and at the same time all believers turn their hearts to Christ.

In another summary passage, Luke stresses the results—"the word of the Lord spread through the whole region" (13:49). Luke highlights this several times throughout Acts (2:41, 47; 4:4, 31; 5:14; 6:7; 8:25; 9:31; 11:24; 12:24) to demonstrate how even the most difficult of times can be used of the Spirit to "spread" the gospel. Since Pisidian Antioch was the major city of that part of Asia Minor, it became the center for evangelizing the many towns and villages of that region, and the growth of the church there was entirely successful.

In contrast, the Jews, as was the case throughout the life of Christ and the development of the church's mission, instigated a serious persecution (13:50). They incite two groups from the synagogue and then the community to turn against Paul and Barnabas—a group of influential women who were God-fearers (see 10:2; 13:16) and several "leading men of the city." The first group was apparently several prominent women who on their

own (their husbands did not follow their lead) had been attending
the synagogue. The "leading men" were not attenders but probably were convinced by the influential women.

So there are three stages of opposition—the synagogue officials convincing these wealthy and powerful women who then in
turn convince the city leaders that Paul and Barnabas are dangerous and must go. Their argument would have been the same one
we will see again and again—the vast number of conversions will
divide the city and threaten the balance between Jew and Gentile,
which thus far had been peaceful. Especially in danger because
of these Christian preachers is the primary god of the region
ironically named "Men," and as a result Paul and Barnabas were
"expelled ... from their region." Yet still their mission had been a
success, and a sizable church was left behind in the region.

After being forced to leave, the two missionaries "shook the
dust off their feet," a symbolic curse Jesus taught his disciples in
Luke 9:5; 10:10-11 to signify that "even the dust of your town we
wipe from our feet as a warning to you." Because they have rejected
God, he is rejecting them, and they have become as unclean as the
dirt on their streets. So the mission team moves ninety miles east
to the town of Iconium in Galatia.

As we have seen often, in the midst of the rejection and persecution, they do not react with gloom and sorrow. Rather, "the disciples were filled with joy and with the Holy Spirit." In 5:41, this
rejoicing came about "because they had been counted worthy of
suffering disgrace for the Name." That continues here. The Spirit
fills the void left by the rejection, and the result is even greater joy.

We are at the cusp of history here, when the relationship of God's
people to the world of unbelievers is changed forever, and God's
message is taken directly to the nations. Never again will they wait
for the nations to come to them. Antioch is now called to step in

for Jerusalem as the mother church of the Gentile mission, and Paul, who was called on the Damascus road for this very purpose, is now set apart and called to be apostle to the Gentiles along with Barnabas (vv. 1–3). In so doing they are setting the tone for our future as well, for all of us are called to be sent to the nations in some fashion or another.

The first place they visit on their itinerary, that which inaugurates the worldwide mission, is Cyprus, where Barnabas grew up (vv. 4–12). The two traverse the island and have a successful ministry throughout. It is clear that God is behind their journey and blessing the gospel as it moves now into purely Gentile lands. In Paphos they encounter Elymas Bar-Jesus, a false prophet and court magician/sorcerer who opposes them and tries to turn proconsul Sergius Paulus against them. However, the Spirit-given power that resides in Paul renders the evil man sightless to show that he is entirely part of the world's darkness. This show of Paul's mighty deeds linked with his mighty words brings Sergius Paulus to Christ and provides the perfect initiation of God's mission to the nations.

From there the team entered Asia Minor and initiated the next step of the universal mission. It is clear that the Spirit guided them step by step on their itinerary. The primary disappointment was John Mark, who for unknown reasons deserted and went home (vv. 13–14). The human factor will always be present in ministry, as we all have to work with our maturity and level of faithfulness to our calling as we minister. Mark failed, but in the end he made up for his lost years. His story is a lesson for us all that we can make up for past failures and find not only forgiveness but also great success due to the Lord's presence in our lives.

In Pisidian Antioch (vv. 14–41) Paul's method is established as the team ministers first in the synagogue, with Paul preaching his inaugural sermon in Acts. He begins by detailing the history of Israel from the patriarchs to David (vv. 16–22), establishing two things. First, the history of God's people parallels that of Rome itself, showing they were the original intended world power.

Second, the entire history of God's people was intended as prep-aration for its fulfillment in Jesus Messiah. He brought together all God's intentions in himself.

In the central section (vv. 23-25) Paul presents Jesus as the royal Messiah fulfilling all the hopes of the nation in himself. Even so important a figure as John the Baptist realized he was nothing in comparison and prepared the way for Jesus. The central part of every sermon in Acts is the salvific effects of the death and resur-rection for humankind (vv. 26-31). The Jews (not just the Romans) are guilty of both rejecting Christ and taking his life on the cross, but he died for the sins of the very ones who executed him, and he was raised so that they may have life. Paul uses three passages to show the implications of Jesus' resurrection (vv. 32-37). First, Psalm 2:7 shows that Jesus is enthroned in heaven as the eternal Son of God. Second, in Isaiah 55:3 the "holy and sure blessings" of David are given first to the risen Lord and then to the new Israel as the covenant people of God. Third, Psalm 16:10 points to his indestructible body, which would never "see decay" as proof of the eternal nature of the promises made to his people.

The result, as we would expect, is both a promise and a warn-ing calling on the listeners (vv. 38-41) to repent and turn to Christ. There is more at stake than they could ever begin to understand, for both promise and warning relate to eternal life, which will either be attained or lost by their decision. Nothing could be more important than their response to this call to salvation.

The first response to the message is positive (vv. 42-47). For two Sabbaths the people flock back to hear more, and many are con-verted. However, the other Jews become jealous of their success and oppose them even more severely. Yet that leads to increased boldness on the part of Paul and Barnabas. What a lesson for us! Too often we react to the displeasure of others by watering down our message, but the early church was so centered on Christ and the Spirit that increased persecution was met with even greater intensity in their ministry.

In the final analysis (vv. 48–52), the mission team is expelled from Pisidian Antioch, yet they do not leave in defeat but in victory, for even as they experience "participation in his sufferings" (Phil 3:10), God is at work bringing souls to himself, and they are leaving behind a strong and growing church. They will be back (14:21–23), and God will continue to use even the opposition for his glory.

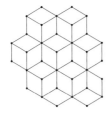

PAUL'S MISSION IN
GALATIA CONTINUES
(14:1–28)

Paul and Barnabas continue on the major Roman road called Via Sebaste, which they took from Perga to Pisidian Antioch in 13:14. It continues to the east, and the mission team follows it. Their goal is to establish the church in eastern Asia Minor, and the three cities they choose (Iconium, Lystra, Derbe) are intended to be centers for the spread of the gospel in the region in the same way that Pisidian Antioch became in 13:49. They passed through many other towns[1] on this trade route, but these are the three they have chosen to be centers of Christian activity.

PAUL AND BARNABAS TRAVEL
TO ICONIUM (14:1-7)

Iconium was the most important city of its region both economically and politically. It lay on a plateau about 3,300 feet above sea level in a mountainous region of modern-day Turkey. As a judicial center as well as a trade center, it was an important town with a good-size Jewish population.

---

1. As I have said before, they may well have ministered in some of these towns, but Luke has decided to cover only the main three.

The team followed the same pattern it had established ("as usual," see 13:5, 14), going first into the synagogues and evangelizing the Jews. Their proclamation of the good news is so effective that not only are a good number of Jews brought to faith in Christ but several Greeks as well. These were probably God-fearers in the synagogue service and possibly pagan Greeks in the evangelistic activity in the days that followed. At any rate, the encouraging results that they have had elsewhere continue in Iconium.

The positive response did not continue long. Those Jews who refused to respond with belief did not let it rest there but stirred up the Gentiles (the majority of people in Iconium) and "poisoned their minds against the brothers" Paul and Barnabas (14:2). Apparently, they spread malicious rumors about them and turned the minds of the town against them.

While the team had left Pisidian Antioch due to persecution, they decide to spend "considerable time" in Iconium (14:3) evangelizing and establishing the church among the converts. During that time, they continue "speaking boldly," one of the themes of Acts (see 13:46). As with Jesus, the more severe the opposition became, the greater the bold response. Probably the "considerable time" meant weeks and perhaps months, as they made certain the church was strong enough for them to go on to the next town. As we have seen throughout this book, the Lord "confirmed the message of his grace by enabling them to perform signs and wonders" (14:3; see 2:22, 43; 3:10; 4:14, 30; 5:12; 6:8; 8:6–7). Their mighty words are accompanied by mighty works. Undoubtedly that made them even more popular with the general populace, who would have figured the gods were especially on Paul and Barnabas' side. The Jewish people would also have been thrilled, believing that the age of Elijah and Elisha had returned.

The result, as we have seen so often, is division in the city: "Some sided with the Jews, others with the apostles" (14:4). The debate must have gone on for some time whether to allow them to continue preaching and especially to perform miracles or to force them to leave. Note that Paul and Barnabas are called "apostles" here and in verse 14. Paul argued for that office on the grounds that he had "seen" the risen Jesus on the Damascus road (1 Cor 9:1-2; 15:8-10), but here Luke is not equating them with the Twelve but rather saying that they have been authorized and "sent" by direct edict from God.

In the end, the opposition won. A consortium of opponents, "Gentiles and Jews, together with their leaders," formed a plot to "mistreat them and stone them." "Leaders" could mean a combination of civic officials for the Gentiles and synagogue leaders for the Jews. The main thing is that the plot covers the religious and social spectrum and so is quite serious. Among the Jews, stoning was the penalty for blasphemy; this did not involve any kind of trial but rather mob action. Paul and Barnabas conclude that it is no use fighting to remain in Iconium. It is best to leave and continue with the mission, so they hurriedly flee to Lystra (twenty miles from Iconium) and Derbe (fifty-five miles away) in the region of Lycaonia. They were not sister cities, and in fact the two were ninety miles from each other. Still, their goal continued to be met, as they "continued to preach the gospel" but now in these two distinct areas.

PAUL AND BARNABAS TRAVEL
TO LYSTRA (14:8-20)

Instead of following his normal pattern of narrating the team's first going to the synagogue, Luke turns to a miracle story primarily because of the startling events that follow. This functions as a conclusion to the towns visited on this mission trip, demonstrating the powerful effect Paul and Barnabas had on the people to whom they ministered. Their power due to the presence of the Spirit in them was such that the pagans thought they were gods. Paul and Barnabas are mortified, needless to say, but the fact of God's power in them is made all the more evident.

The Healing of the Lame Man (14:8–10)

Lystra was a recent Roman colony founded about 25 BC, when Galatia was reformed as a province, and it was a fairly wealthy town commercially. This is the third such healing (Luke 5:17–26; Acts 3:1–10), and unlike the man in chapter 3 this man had been crippled from birth and had never walked. Also unlike the earlier episode, this man, Paul realized, "had faith to be healed" (*sōthēnai*, "to be saved"), with a double meaning that says he was ready to be healed both physically and spiritually.

Luke is not saying Paul could only heal the man if he had the faith to accept it. This is not a psychosomatic healing but a supernatural miracle. It does mean, however, that the man is touched spiritually as well. The crippled man is listening as Paul proclaims the gospel there in the marketplace at the center of the city, and he responds. Paul observes his growing faith-response and is led by the Spirit to stop his message, look the man in the eye, and command, "Stand up on your feet!"

Both healings, of the body and of the spirit, take place simultaneously. We must remember he had never in his life stood up, and many of the people would have known him, for he had undoubtedly been begging there all his life. Can you imagine the reaction of the onlookers when they saw what they had never expected ever to observe, this man with withered legs standing on his feet? The tenses stress that after leaping to his feet, he began walking around the marketplace, undoubtedly leaping for joy, for some time. Moreover, the faith of the man allowed him to be an active participant and not just a passive recipient in the miracle; he thus experienced the spiritual as well as physical results of the healing. That would have been quite the sight as he went back and forth from the physical delight to the spiritual joy.

The Reaction of the Crowds (14:11–13)

Lystra was in the region of Lycaonia, and they spoke a language called Lycaonian, one of several indigenous languages spoken in that part of the world. They would have known Greek and Latin, but their common everyday speech was Lycaonian. This is a key to the scene, explaining why Paul and Barnabas didn't understand what was taking place until it was too late. This is a great example of missionaries who often aren't prepared sufficiently for the people to whom they're sent. Paul and Barnabas thought the people were responding to the gospel and being saved, because the response came to them "in the Lycaonian language," which they didn't understand.

The actual response is quite tragic, for the people see the miracle and assume that "the gods have come down to us in human form," calling Barnabas, the leader of the team, Zeus (the king of the gods) and Paul, the spokesman for the team, Hermes or Mercury (the messenger of the gods). This was a common response. We might remember Simon Magus in 8:10 calling himself "the Great Power of God," labeling himself a demigod. Powerful sorcerers were thought to be descendants of the gods, and this concept was part of the crowd's reaction.

So the apostles had inadvertently become the cause of blasphemy. They didn't know the main legend of that part of the world that drove their reaction. Long ago, the myth went, Zeus and Hermes (likely in actuality the main gods of the region) visited their valley and walked from one end to the other asking to be put up for the night. They were turned down everywhere until they reached the far end, and an elderly couple had mercy on them. That next morning the gods laid waste to every home, built a great temple to Zeus, and made the elderly couple priest and priestess of it. From that time on the entire region was waiting for the gods to return so they could make it up to them. They assumed Paul and Barnabas were giving them that chance.

So as a result, the priest of Zeus, whose temple (as in many cities, like Ephesus with the famous temple of Diana) lay just outside the city gates, shocked the two to the core when he suddenly brought out bulls with wreaths on them to offer as sacrifices to these two "deities" who have given them the honor of visiting them.

THE RESPONSE OF PAUL AND BARNABAS (14:14–18)

Needless to say, the two "apostles" (see 14:4) are horrified at what they have inadvertently allowed. Tearing the clothes is an expression of grief, and they are thinking God will bring judgment on them for causing such blasphemy. They run into the crowds, shouting at the top of their lungs for the people to desist.

Paul's message is important, for it is one of two in Acts (with the Mars Hill address of chapter 17) addressed to a purely Gentile audience and centering on natural revelation (God's creation) rather than special revelation (God's revelation in his word). These were pagan Gentiles with no knowledge of Jewish Scriptures or theology, so what would work with Jews (Jesus as expected Messiah) would not work here. As such this message has important implications for apologetics.

The first point (14:15a) is that Paul and Barnabas are "only human, like you." They're not gods, and it is blasphemy to worship them as such. Their entire purpose is not to be lauded as gods but to proclaim the one true God, "bringing you good news, telling you to turn from these worthless things [idols] to the living God." Zeus and Hermes and all such "worthless things" like bulls and wreaths that have no lasting value must be jettisoned. The lame man had never been healed by such things, nor could he be. This would have been a serious charge, for it would mean rejecting the ancestral gods of the Romans as well as all the religious life surrounding them and turning to a God they are just hearing about for the first time. However, it was this God who had the power to heal the crippled man and who cared enough to get involved with the human dilemma. The gods of Mount Olympus would never do so, for they are dead idols and not the "living God."

The second point (14:15b) is that this "living God" is the Creator God who sustains all his creation, who "made the heavens and the earth and the sea and everything in them." The point is that the God of the Jews and Christians is not aloof but participates in human affairs. He created everything in this world but controls it on behalf of his people, in whose lives he is deeply involved. This is exemplified in his healing of the lame man.

Third, in Christ he has changed his approach to the nations (14:16). By bringing these people the good news, God is now bringing salvation to the nations that formerly were left to "go their own way," worshipping the pantheon of gods, building pagan temples, and engaging in empty rites. No longer. The one true God has turned to the Gentiles and brought them the good news, meaning he will no longer overlook their futile religion and empty practices.

Fourth, God has provided a witness (NIV: "testimony") to himself by showing them his kindness and generosity in sending "rain from heaven and crops in their seasons" (14:17). The seasons are a great benefit, for through them God "provides you with plenty of food and fills your hearts with joy." So long as the nations go "their own way," they will never know this joy because they can only react to the day-by-day happenstance changes in creation. They can never experience the loving Creator and see his hand in all the good things he provides. But this God is revealing himself in the gospel message, and as they hear it they ought to recognize the God of creation who cares for them. So now this joy is theirs to enjoy.

Luke's final point here (14:18) is that even with the good news they were proclaiming, "they had difficulty keeping the crowd from sacrificing to them." This is one of the few times the good news is not effective. These superstitious people have spent their lives immersed in their idolatrous religion, and they will not leave it easily. This too provides an important lesson for us all. We cannot expect instantaneous results on every occasion. Quite often, as here, people are not easily convinced to turn their lives around. God is patient, and so must we be. People do not make an about-face easily, and we must allow them the time they need to make such a switch.

REJECTION AND STONING (14:19-20)

Another thing we will be seeing as we continue through Acts is how Paul's opponents follow him from town to town to turn the people against him and force him to leave. This will occur again, as in Thessalonica in 17:6-7 and in Caesarea in 24:1. Jewish opponents from Pisidian Antioch and Iconium come all this way to turn the people against the Christian messengers from God. It works, and they stone Paul, undoubtedly for blasphemy in preaching this Jesus. We don't know why it is just Paul and not Barnabas. Perhaps he is not with Paul on this occasion, or perhaps to them Paul as the spokesman is seen as the true danger to the ancestral religion.

At any rate, they intend to kill him, and the stoning is vicious enough that they think him dead and leave. Now comes one of the truly great miracles in Acts. A stoning so strong that Paul is left for dead has to be pretty horrible. Paul would have been unconscious, possibly in a coma, and definitely with broken limbs and so on. He remains in that condition long enough that everyone leaves, thinking their nemesis dead. Yet as soon as they are gone, with his friends gathered around him mourning, he suddenly just "got up and went back into the city." That set of injuries would have had any normal person in bed (for us, in the hospital) for quite some time, whereas Paul is on his feet, walking back into Lystra, and on a long journey (likely walking) the very next day. That says only one thing to me—miracle. All of the broken limbs, head injuries, and so on are healed. He may have been brought back to life! Can you imagine the people who stoned him as he walked by them that evening? Wow—hard to imagine.

PAUL AND BARNABAS MINISTER IN DERBE AND THEN BACKTRACK TO ANTIOCH OF SYRIA (14:21-28)

FOLLOW-UP IN THE THREE CITIES (14:21-23)

Luke probably says little about their ministry in Derbe because it is without incident and at the same time very productive with a

great many converts and a settled church in the end. The opponents from Lystra are probably so shocked at the miraculous recov-
ery that they back off and don't follow him there. Derbe is actually quite a ways, about ninety miles from Lystra (see on 14:7) and
also a central city in its region. They had the time to stay in Derbe
long enough to make many disciples (not just win them but deepen
their walk), and apparently there was little opposition there.

From there the mission team decides to head back to the
mother church, Antioch of Syria, but to do so the long way around.
Actually, Derbe is reasonably close to that city (in 16:1 they come
back this very way), but the believers aren't quite anchored in the
churches they had evangelized on this journey, so they believe
they need to revisit them and do follow-up ministry in each. They
reverse their direction and visit Lystra, Iconium, and Antioch,
spending some time with each church to help it mature and grow.
Luke describes them all at the same time, so I will cover what Paul
did in all three (14:22–23):

1. "Strengthening the disciples": These recent converts
   needed good teachers and time to grow in Christ. That is
   the problem in many churches today, teachers who are not
   deep or mature enough to disciple the members properly.
   So having Paul and Barnabas to teach the teachers and take
   the people deeper into the Scriptures would have been an
   incredible blessing.

2. "Encouraging them to remain true to the faith": "Faith" here
   is both the Christian faith, remaining immersed in the
   truths of the faith, and persevering in trusting God more
   deeply in their lives. Faithfulness and vigilance are needed
   in every age.

3. Passing through "many hardships to enter the kingdom
   of God": This builds on the challenge to persevere and
   reminds me of Psalm 23:4 and "the valley of the shadow
   of death" (I still prefer this KJV translation). God is always

with us as we endure our pilgrimage through life, but this doesn't mean everything will be easy. Hardships are the building blocks of discipleship and force us to depend on him more deeply. If everything went the way we wanted it to, we would become narcissists who lived only for ourselves. Trials help us to center on God and his presence in our lives and enable us to be kingdom people. Notice the imperative, "we must" (*dei*), meaning the Lord deems it necessary that we learn endurance. Here the "kingdom of God" is not so much the present kingdom that arrived with Jesus as the final kingdom that we will "enter" at death. The difficulties of life are the obstacles that we must endure in order to attain that heavenly kingdom (see Matt 5:20; 7:21; 18:3; Mark 9:47; 10:23–25; John 3:5), and they become building blocks to spiritual maturity.

4. Appointing "elders ... in each church": The early church decided to designate the leaders of local churches "elders," which followed Jewish practice for the most part. Rabbis did not function at the local synagogue level, and so elders were the natural choice. The term designated more their spiritual maturity than their age. The term "elder" is synonymous with "shepherd" and "pastor" in the New Testament, referring to the person in each church who fed the flock and watched over it, but there is also a plurality of elders who guide the church. Paul and Barnabas are using their apostolic authority in appointing these leaders. After the choices are made, they with the church prayed and fasted over them and "committed them to the Lord," in what sounds like a special service of commitment. They have "trusted/believed" (*pepisteukeisan*) in the Lord at their conversion, and now they are living a life of trust in him and can entrust or commit their chosen leaders to him as well.

MISSION ACTIVITY IN PERGA (14:24-25)

From Pisidian Antioch they retrace their steps south through Pisidia and then Pamphylia, coming to Perga (the capital city of Pamphylia), where they begin their mission work on the mainland in 14:13. Luke never mentions any evangelistic work there, only that this is where John Mark abandoned them. So this is either the first time spent in ministry there or further follow-up as in the other three. It is strange that Luke says so little, for Perga is the second-largest city Paul has visited (after Pisidian Antioch) and a very cosmopolitan town. It probably was just like the others, and Luke had said all he had intended regarding this mission trip. It was probably a successful time like the others had been.

At the end of that time, the mission team left and went down the few miles to Attalia, the port city of Pamphylia. Their sole focus was on returning to the mother church in Antioch of Syria with the good news of their successes and the new churches they had established, so there they booked a ship. They had apparently decided not to revisit Cyprus, probably because they felt it had previously been evangelized and already had fairly mature churches (though Barnabas will return later with John Mark, 15:39).

THE RETURN TO SYRIAN ANTIOCH (14:26-28)

Their report back to the sending church of Syrian Antioch (see 11:19-21 on this church) was quite successful overall. Luke wants us to realize that just as Paul and Barnabas had "committed" the elders to the Lord in verse 23, they too had previously been "committed to the grace of God" by the church in Syrian Antioch. This type of committal service (13:1-3) has down through the centuries become the common practice of virtually all churches and a necessary part of our dedication to the Lord's work.

In this second half of the journey Barnabas and Paul are moving into Galatia and start with the important city of Iconium (vv. 1–7), which becomes almost a test case for the others, as their ministry sets a pattern they will continue to follow. Their opening ministry in the synagogue is again quite successful, but in the end the combined opposition of Jews and Gentiles overwhelms them, and they are forced to flee to Smyrna. Still, as before, the more intense the persecution, the greater the boldness of God's envoys.

The healing of the lame man (vv. 8–10) is especially meaningful, for it is an excellent example of the combined physical and spiritual healing that takes place when faith is involved. The palpable joy that would bring would truly be a sight to behold. The aftermath is a truly interesting story (vv. 11–13), for it shows the tragic results that can ensue when we are unprepared for the people to whom we are sent. Paul and Barnabas did not know the Lycaonian language and so failed to realize they had inadvertently caused blasphemy by leading these people to think they were gods. When they saw the bulls and sacrificial paraphernalia, they were mortified.

Still, it led to an important message, showing how the early church proclaimed the gospel to pagan Gentiles who did not know the Scriptures (vv. 14–18). The emphasis on natural revelation and God's creation, showing his love for these people, is very helpful in our own witness. Paul's point is that the living God of the Christians who created this world cares for them much more deeply than their false gods, and they should turn to him.

However, opposing Jews came from Antioch and Iconium and stoned Paul, leaving him for dead. Then an incredible miracle took place: he got up virtually from the dead, returned to Lystra, and then led them to Derbe (vv. 19–20). There could be no more spectacular affirmation of the power and reality of Paul's message. God is truly in control.

They decide to retrace their steps through the cities of Galatia (vv. 21–23) and follow up with the churches they had founded to strengthen them spiritually and appoint good leadership to guide them into the future. This is an important principle for all evangelism programs, making certain that new converts are discipled and begin to grown into mature believers.

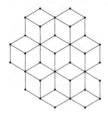

THE JERUSALEM COUNCIL
(15:1–35)

I n Acts 11 the issue of Gentile inclusion seemed to be a settled issue, as Peter's narration of Cornelius' conversion convinced the assembled believers in Jerusalem that God wished for Gentiles to be free of the law and able to come to belief in Christ apart from legal observance (11:1-18). However, there apparently were many who had not attended that meeting—believers from Judea with a Pharisaic bent who continued to believe that Gentiles must embrace the law before they could become believers and that they must follow the demands of the law after they become Christians. This party in the early church were called "Judaizers" because they wanted to turn the Gentiles into Jews before they could convert.

One central issue in this is the relationship of Galatians to Acts 15. Many believe that letter was written during the third missionary journey, but I follow those who think it is written just after Paul returned to Syrian Antioch.[1] As I discussed in the last chapter at 14:28, it is very likely that when he returned, he learned that the Judaizers had sent a group that had visited the churches in Galatia, telling them that Paul and Barnabas were wrong and that they had

---

1. See "Recipients and Date" in the introduction to the Galatians volume in this series.

to embrace Judaism. The Galatian letter is Paul's response, and he considered the Judaizing position heresy (Gal 1:6-9). Paul's return, writing of Galatians, and the Jerusalem Council took place in AD 48, and the journey itself took place in AD 45-47. This is another central episode in the history of the church, and in fact it is the central chapter in Acts.

Galatians is a manifesto on faith and freedom. A key issue in the letter is which Jerusalem visit Paul is discussing in 2:1-10. If it is the Jerusalem Council, then this was written after that event and doesn't apply here. But if it is the famine visit of Acts 11:27-30, which I think is more likely (see my Galatians commentary in this series), then it fits exactly in the situation here. If Paul had written the Galatians commentary after the Jerusalem Council, there is no way he would have failed to mention it. The silence of Galatians about that council must mean the letter was written before that meeting. Galatians was written in the months leading up to the events of Acts 15.

Paul argues in Galatians that the other apostles accepted him as the apostle to the Gentiles, and as such Titus, a Greek believer, did not need to be circumcised to be a Christian or a member of Paul's team. Then in 2:11-14 he describes the incident when he confronted Peter over his capitulation to "certain men ... from James" who demanded he not share meals with Gentiles. A major question is whether James himself had become the leader of the Judaizers, and how this jibes with Acts 15:13-21, where he clearly is on Paul's side. Probably it is best to say that he had questions about how far Paul was going in accommodating himself to Gentile ministry but still agreed with Paul's proclamation of the gospel for Gentile conversion. The main thing is that Galatians is a critical document leading up to the issues addressed at the Jerusalem Council.

ANTIOCH SENDS A DELEGATION
TO JERUSALEM (15:1-5)

The "certain people" were the Judaizers, who arrived claiming to be sent by James (Gal 2:12), and thus seemingly with an apostolic directive demanding that the Gentiles in Antioch submit to the Mosaic law: "Unless you are circumcised, according to the custom taught by Moses, you cannot be saved." Needless to say, the die is cast. Either Paul is right and Gentiles can come freely by faith and accept Christ, or these strict Jewish Christians are right and Gentiles must become Jewish proselytes before they can turn to Christ.

Several have called these "new" requirements, but in actuality Paul's claims were newer. As I have said earlier, the Jewish Christian name for their movement is "the Way," and they considered themselves a messianic sect within Judaism. So it was commonly accepted in the Palestinian church that new converts would continue to keep the law. Still God had made it clear, and in 11:1–18 the Jerusalem church had accepted it, that Gentiles would come to Christ apart from the law. Now these strict Jewish Christians were disputing these developments, and so the leaders of the Jerusalem church called a council to settle the issue.

The argument is that there are two demands on all converts— that males be circumcised, and that all converts follow "the custom taught by Moses," meaning the Mosaic ordinances in the law. "Cannot be saved" is a divine passive meaning "God will not save you." He is the author of salvation, and he demands the Torah be kept if he is to recognize a person as saved. So there are two issues—whether for sinners to find salvation God demands that Gentiles must embrace the law and be circumcised before becoming a believer; and whether the Christian life must be a combination of walking in the law's regulations as well as of walking with Christ.

In Antioch, there was a lengthy period of vociferous debate as Paul and Barnabas fell into "sharp dispute and debate" with the Judaizers (15:2). In Galatians 2:11–16 the Judaizers convinced Peter and even Barnabas to stop sharing meals with Gentile Christians. Paul had denounced that as hypocrisy and won the day. In Jerusalem, similar debates convinced the apostles and elders that the previous consensus (Acts 11) had reached an end, and another council on the issue of Gentile conversion was necessary. So they called for a full gathering of the church and invited Antioch to participate. The Antioch church was overjoyed at a full council to decide the issue once for all.

Wisely, they appointed Paul and Barnabas to lead the delegation. The implications of this are quite important. The Jerusalem church was still considered the mother church of all others, including the Gentile churches like Antioch. Of course, this makes a great deal of sense, for that is where the apostles still reside, but they also accept the leadership of the Jerusalem elders.

Antioch is about 250 miles from Jerusalem, so instead of traveling straight there, they decide to stop at churches in Phoenicia (on the coast of Syria; Tyre and Sidon were in Phoenicia) and Samaria (between Galilee and Judea) and report on the recent advances in Gentile ministry they had experienced. The term for "conversion" (only here in the New Testament) is *epistrophē* and means a "turning" to Christ from the pagan gods. This report on the success of the Gentile mission results in great joy in all the churches, showing that the rest of the church not only agreed with Paul but also was thrilled at the prospect of full participation by Gentiles in the church. The Judaizers are clearly the minority position in the church as a whole.

When the delegation arrived in Jerusalem, they were "welcomed" by a church that was glad to hear from them (15:4). Clearly the mood is positive to them, and the Acts 11 decision to accept Gentiles is still held by most. Their report covered "everything God had done through them," which means the events in Galatia as well as Antioch. The report would have covered not only Gentile conversions but also the establishment of churches and appointment of elders in those cities as found in 14:23. The report seems to have been well received by the majority there. Notice the emphasis on what "God had done through them." This is the key issue, as it was in 11:17–18. If indeed this was God's work, the issue is settled. Those who accepted this were distinctly on Paul's side, and most of the general believers in Jerusalem seem to have done so.

The mention of the three groups who met the delegation and led them into the council meeting is also significant—"the church and the apostles[2] and elders." This is critical for the issue of whether the leaders make the decision or the church as a whole. Here all three are involved—the leaders make the initial decision (15:6), and this decision is ratified by "the whole church" (v. 22).

The issue is brought to the fore by the same group of Jewish Christians who "belonged to the party of the Pharisees" (I called them "Judaizers" at the beginning of this chapter), who believed that "the Gentiles must be circumcised and required to keep the law of Moses." The Pharisees were the primary opponents of Jesus, but quite a few had become followers as well. They had carried their strict understanding of the law into their Christian beliefs. So at this initial meeting with Paul and Barnabas they give voice to their demands, protesting the freedom Paul gave Gentile converts to ignore the law and its restrictions.

PETER GIVES A SPEECH AT THE COUNCIL (15:6–11)

The two sides, Paul and the Judaizers, apparently argued back and forth on the issue for some time, with the leaders of the church as a whole, the apostles and elders, adjudicating as they "consider this question." The goal was clearly to come to a final position that would become the policy of the church as a whole. The result would not just be the status of Gentile converts but the look of Christianity as a whole. Will the movement continue as a Jewish sect alongside the Pharisees and Sadducees, or will it become a separate religion entirely? Will Christians keep the legal regulations of the Torah or be free to work out their own set of moral and ethical norms? A great deal was at stake in the decision to be made here.

---

2. The apostles had likely fled after the persecution by Herod Agrippa (12:1, 17) but have now returned, perhaps still considering Jerusalem their home church at least for this critical meeting.

Three speeches (Peter [vv. 7–11], Paul and Barnabas [v. 12], and James [vv. 13–21]) sum up the daylong deliberations. Note they come after a lengthy amount of discussion in which undoubtedly the arguments were given lengthy presentations. Finally, Peter stood up, the first of the major respondents because his time with Cornelius initiated and at the same time finalized the position of free Gentile inclusion in the church.

Again, Peter stresses, it was not he but God who chose that the Gentiles hear the gospel directly from Peter's lips, not mediated by the law, so that they can hear and believe directly. As God's choice, there is no debate (divine election). He of course is especially thinking of his vision (10:9–16), which proved to him that God has declared the Gentiles clean and able to come to Christ without converting to Judaism first. "The message of the gospel" is the good news that Gentiles too can simply repent and believe in Christ as Messiah and Savior in order to be saved and have their sins forgiven.

Then Peter adds a further point (15:8), that God not only chose Cornelius to be saved but also demonstrated his acceptance of Gentiles "by giving the Holy Spirit to them, just as he did to us." This, of course, is the Gentile Pentecost of 10:44–46, accompanied by the speaking in tongues and possibly the other phenomena of 2:4, the wind and the fire. He explains that this was not a mistake, for God "knows the heart" and knew that Cornelius and the others in his party had been genuinely saved and cleansed from sin. So both God and the Spirit ratified Cornelius' true conversion and with the Pentecost event gave their imprimatur that Gentiles stand alongside Jews as equals in his kingdom.

His conclusion is also clear: in doing so God "did not discriminate between us and them" (15:9). Both come to Christ on the same basis, repentance and belief and not via the law. There is a complete absence of any distinction between the two people groups, for both the means of salvation and the results of salvation are the same—repentance, belief, and cleansing from sin. The hearts of both Jews and Gentiles alike are "purified ... by faith," not by the works of the law. Purity in the eyes of God is no longer achieved by following the laws of purity or the food laws, but entirely by a heart-change via believing in Christ and finding forgiveness of sins via his sacrificial death on the cross.

Instead of protecting the law, the Judaizers are actually testing God by "putting on the necks of Gentiles a yoke that neither we nor our ancestors have been able to bear." This "test" uses the same verb as in Hebrews 3:9 of Israel testing God in the wilderness and calling down his wrath. This is much more than just questioning his decisions; it means standing in the way of his will. Implicit is the wrath of God falling on them as a result of their perfidy.

When they demand that Gentiles be circumcised and submit to the Mosaic injunctions, Peter argues, they in actuality are placing a yoke on their necks resembling what oxen have to endure. The yoke is an interesting image, for we have grown up thinking of it negatively, but several scholars argue that in Judaism and the Old Testament it was used positively (Jer 2:20; Lam 3:27). Yokes united two oxen and enabled them to help the farmer plant his crops, so connoting a good harvest. So it spoke of the "yoke of wisdom" or the yoke that united God and Israel (Jer 2:20; 5:5). However, the yoke also stands negatively for servitude and bondage (Lev 26:13; 1 Kgs 12:9–10). That is more likely how it is used here, to describe bondage to the law. This is a reversal, for to these Pharisaic Jewish Christians the yoke of the law was entirely positive, but to Gentiles it was a burden they could not bear (Matt 5:20; 6:1–18). That is the point here.

So by forcing this burden on the Gentiles, these strict Jewish Christians were "testing" or "trying" God like Israel did in the wilderness. This constituted disbelief, for they refused to believe or accept God's clear choice of Gentiles and so existed in dispute not just with Peter and Paul but with God himself. God and his Spirit had clearly shown their will, but the Judaizers refuse to receive it.

Moreover, Peter adds, "neither we nor our ancestors have been able to bear" this yoke. The Pharisees had added a lengthy list of oral traditions to enable people to keep it, but that had just made matters worse. Throughout its history Judaism had struggled to keep the regulations, and the point, Peter argues, is that if it is virtually impossible for the Jewish people who have grown up with it, what chance do the Gentiles have of keeping it? It becomes an impossible burden for them.

Finally, in verse 11 he applies this to the concept of salvation, stating that God never intended that the law become the instrument of salvation either for Jews or Gentiles. No, it is always "through the grace of our Lord Jesus that we [the Jews] are saved, just as they [the Gentiles] are." It is neither by circumcision nor by the Mosaic regulations that salvation is effected. Rather, it is by "the grace of our Lord Jesus" who gave his life as an atoning sacrifice on the cross and who was raised from the dead so we could find new life. In this new covenant age legal observance cannot suffice, only the grace of God through the work of Christ.

BARNABAS AND PAUL SPEAK AT
THE COUNCIL (15:12)

Peter's story, one that most of them had probably heard before at the first Jerusalem gathering in 11:1-18, was so conclusive that the entire assembly, even the Judaizers, "became silent," for there was nothing more to say. It's not that the Judaizers were convinced they had been wrong, but they didn't know how to overturn that powerful story. They were probably feverishly trying to think of something to say but couldn't find the words.

In that silence Barnabas and Paul (note the return to the original order of names, as the council still thought of Barnabas as the leader) intervened and told their story, which settled the issue even further. The "signs and wonders" would not just be the miracles they performed, though they were certainly impressive enough, but the miraculous sequence itself. The greatest wonder was the way God had worked in city after city. Still, the blindness of Elymas, the many healings, Paul's walking away from being stoned, the healing of the lame man, and the near worship of Paul and Barnabas at Lystra clearly presented proof that God was behind their ministry among the Gentiles.

JAMES SETTLES THE ISSUE (15:13–21)

The third and final speaker is James, the Lord's brother and chief elder of the Jerusalem church. His is the voice that settles the issue. He has clearly been listening throughout the day and now becomes in effect the concluding opinion that settles it all. He first shows his agreement with "Simon" Peter that in him God "intervened to choose a people for his name from the Gentiles."

His first point is agreeing with Simon that God orchestrated the entire incident and chose the Gentiles to be his people. That is truly the deciding point. Once anyone agrees that God did it, they have made their decision and are on Paul's side. So as God intervened and chose the progeny of Abraham to be his chosen people, as he intervened to redeem them from Egypt, as he intervened to give them the promised land, so he also is intervening to add the Gentiles to believing Jews in forming new Israel, the community of the new covenant. These people have now been chosen "for his name"; they have become "Christ-ians," and God's people now includes Gentiles.

James undoubtedly spoke extensively, using scriptural proof to support Peter and Paul's thesis, and Luke chooses to include Amos 9:11–12. God had sent Israel into exile, but there would be a new exodus, and a new restoration that would include the Gentiles. This passage occurs near the end of Amos and narrates the destruction of apostate Israel and its restoration when it is rebuilt and the Davidic/messianic line restored.

James is using the **Septuagint** form in which "the rest of mankind"[3] seeks the Lord, therefore referring to the conversion of the Gentiles in the messianic age. The early church believed it

---

3. The Hebrew Masoretic text has "the remnant of Edom" (see Amos 9:12).

was the messianic community inhabiting the inauguration of that age. The opening line ("After this I will return") might be taken from Jeremiah 12:15, which says God would "uproot" his disobedient people along with the nations but return and restore both the nations and Israel, thereby strengthening the point in Amos.

Thus James is saying that the Gentile mission, instituted by Jesus in the Great Commission of Acts 1:8 (and Matt 28:18-20; Luke 24:47), fulfills the prophecies of Amos 9 and Jeremiah 12 regarding the conversion of the Gentiles in the messianic age when the Davidic line is restored in Jesus the Davidic Messiah. That age has begun with the death/resurrection of Jesus and the arrival of Pentecost. The "fallen tent" has been rebuilt and the "ruins" restored in these events, and now with Cornelius and the missionary journey of Barnabas and Paul, the "rest of mankind may seek the Lord." Once again the emphasis is on "the Lord, who does these things," meaning God, not Peter or Paul, is behind the conversion of the Gentiles and is the one authenticating it. His point is the same as in 11:17-18, "even to Gentiles God has granted repentance that leads to life." There is no disputing what God has shown to be his will.

James sees the entire process of mission to "the ends of the earth" (1:8) as a fulfillment of Amos 9. The rebuilding of "David's fallen tent" is the church as the new "temple" of the messianic age, and the restoration of the "ruins" takes place in the institution of believing Jews and Gentiles as the new Israel of that age. During this time the Gentile mission fulfills the prophecy of the "rest of mankind" seeking the Lord. These Gentiles will join the Jews as the new people of God who "bear my name." The important point here is that they will do so as Gentiles and not as Jewish proselytes. As Paul says clearly in Romans 11:17-21, the Gentiles will be grafted into God's olive tree along with the Jews to become a single people of God.

The phrase "things known from long ago" echoes Isaiah 45:21, another prophecy that the nations would turn to God in fulfillment of ancient prophecy (before Isaiah), perhaps the Abrahamic covenant that God's choice of Israel as his covenant people would be meant to bring his blessings to the nations (Gen 12:3; 22:18; 26:4; 28:14). So the Gentile mission was intended virtually from the very beginning of Israel as God's people.

In the messianic age both Jews and Gentiles have the same basis for salvation—faith in Jesus, but not the works of the law or circumcision. So James concludes "that we should not make it difficult for the Gentiles who are turning to God," meaning not to impose on them the Mosaic regulations like the Judaizers are trying to do. God has authenticated Gentile conversion in the Cornelius incident, the Spirit has anchored this by sending the Gentile Pentecost, and now the mission of Paul and Barnabas in Galatia has proved that the proclamation of the law was not needed to bring Gentiles to Christ. The Amos 9 prophecy has finalized the process, so circumcision and keeping the law are no longer to be seen as requirements for conversion.

The council of apostles and elders has one stipulation to add to their decision in the matter: a letter to be sent to all established Gentile churches telling them of their new freedom from the law and from the demands of the Judaizers but asking them to abstain from four things that stem from their constant contact with Jewish believers and their settled convictions. These are particular issues that will come up and endanger the full fellowship of Jews and Gentiles in the church.

There are important questions regarding the meaning and intent of this letter. Two extremes can be ruled out: first, that they relate to cardinal sins of idolatry, immorality, or murder/blood. Blood probably relates to food laws rather than murder, and "things strangled" does not have a cardinal issue in mind. The other extreme is that these are merely pragmatic and relate to fellowship between Gentiles and Jews in the church. This is part of the issue but not the whole. It is more serious than this.

Two aspects account for these four instructions. The central problem of idolatry and participating in pagan temple worship is definitely part of it, and the regulations in Leviticus 17–18 regarding Gentiles who live in Israel parallel the situation in the early church. It was common for Jews and Gentiles to inhabit the same churches, and that often caused serious relational difficulties as they followed quite different cultural and religious practices. So these four areas are an attempt to build bridges between the two. This letter gives the Gentiles freedom in coming to Christ and in worshipping apart from the Mosaic regulations but asks them to respect Jewish Christian sensitivities and avoid practices that would offend them. These four are requests rather than requirements and meant to apply only to churches that contain both Jewish and Gentile Christians trying to live together in harmony. Still, Luke considers them quite important and restates them here and in the letter at 15:29. Let's consider each item in turn:

1. Food polluted by idols: Much of the meat consumed in the ancient world came from sacrifices in temples. They provided the butcher shops and the restaurants, so it was common to eat this meat normally even at home. The difficulty is harmonizing the prohibition here with 1 Corinthians 8:1–8, where Paul says idols are nothing and seems to be okay with eating that meat. I would link this prohibition in Acts 15 with the second point of 1 Corinthians 8:9–13, which states that one should not eat that meat if it would cause spiritual harm to a weaker believer in their midst. Similarly, the prohibition here is not absolute but applies only when with a Jewish Christian who could be offended (see also Rom 14 on this). Participation in the idolatrous temple banquets, which would also invoke the blessings of the gods, is probably also prohibited. These are prohibited in 1 Corinthians 8 and 10 as well.

2. Sexual immorality: This refers to any kind of sexual relations outside marriage, thus not only adultery but

prostitution, homosexuality, incest, or pornography. All of these were both allowed and practiced freely in the Gentile world (and sadly in our society as well) but were serious sins in the Jewish-Christian setting.

3. The meat of strangled animals: This was a common way of killing animals in the ancient world, but it was not allowed in Jewish contexts because the blood could not be properly drained from such animals (Exod 22:31; Lev 17:14). Blood is sacred and is a symbol of life, and to eat undrained meat was considered a serious offense in Judaism.

4. From blood: Some think this is a euphemism for murder (shedding blood), but far more likely is a continuation of the food laws. The same kind of "blood pudding" was available then as it is in many countries today, but needless to say, this was not allowed in Jewish contexts (Lev 17:10–11) for the reasons just noted in the third item.

James's rationale is expressed in 15:21: "For the law of Moses has been preached in every city from the earliest times and is read in the synagogues on every Sabbath." This is somewhat obscure but probably means that the Gentiles should respect the Jewish Christian sensitivities because Gentiles all around the world did so. There is evidence of some cities requiring their butcher shops to carry kosher meats for the Jews living there.

THE COUNCIL WRITES A LETTER TO THE GENTILE CHURCHES (15:22–29)

It is difficult to know if "with the whole church" means the apostles and elders deliberated separately and then presented their decision to the congregation, or whether the church as a whole was part of the proceedings all along. The language of verses 6 and 22 make the former more likely. Luke doesn't tell us what happened to the Pharisaic faction after the decision of the council went against them. Did they remain and take part in the decision to send the letter, or did a schism occur and these believers separated themselves from that point on? I think the latter was the case, for Paul considered them to be heretics (Gal 1:6-8). Still, they were likely a minority faction, and we don't know how it all turned out.

The decision to send the letter seems unanimous, and the final decision was undoubtedly well received. Along with the letter, they decide to send two representatives to accompany Paul and Barnabas to Antioch and obviously the other churches they will visit: Silas and Judas Barsabbas (= "son of the Sabbath").[4] They are called "leaders among the believers," prominent men in the congregation. In verse 32 we will learn they were both "prophets" like Agabus (11:26-30) and could speak for the Jerusalem church. Judas is Jewish and Silas is Roman. The latter becomes a trusted associate of Paul (Acts 16:19, 25; 17:4; 1 Thess 1:1; 2 Thess 1:1; 2 Cor 1:19).

It is addressed to the churches Paul will be visiting in the provinces of Syria (Antioch is in the north of it) and Cilicia (near Tarsus, Paul's home where he spent 10-11 years, Acts 9:30; 11:25; Gal 1:21-24), which had Antioch as their hub. In 16:4 Paul will deliver the letter to many churches in Asia Minor as well at the start of the next journey. It is interesting that the churches of Galatia are not in the address, when those were the churches the Judaizers visited that started the whole controversy. However, Paul would not be going that far, so they were not mentioned here.

Initially, the Jerusalem church learned of the problem from the debates in Antioch when Paul and Barnabas returned after the missionary journey. Interestingly, they don't actually describe the controversy, probably assuming the churches know of it, but instead talk of the underlying problem—"Some went out from us without our authorization and disturbed you, troubling your minds by what they said." This clears up one question that we had. In Galatians 2:12 they are described as "certain men ... from James," and there was a real question about James's part in sending the

---

4. Is he related to the "Joseph Barsabbas" who was one of the candidates for apostleship in 1:23? It is an interesting possibility.

Judaizers out. This makes clear he had no part in it and they used his name because he had some concerns about Gentiles and the food laws that were similar to theirs. That everything they did was without his authorization.

The effects of their teaching in Syria and Cilicia (and Galatia as well) were twofold—the churches were "disturbed," or deeply confused, and the people's minds were troubled, or very distressed by their demands. How could it be otherwise when they were being told they had to undergo circumcision and begin following the Mosaic injunctions like the food and purity laws?

With this letter, the council and the Jerusalem church decided to send two official representatives to clear up the confusion. They would accompany their "dear friends" (Greek: "beloved") Barnabas and Paul to deliver the letter and explain further. These two would aid the apostles and clarify the final decision of the council. It is not that they distrust the two apostles but that they wish to make certain the churches know they were behind the message and agreed entirely with it. In case these churches didn't know Paul and Barnabas, the letter added that they were "men who have risked their lives [a vast understatement!] for the name of our Lord Jesus Christ." There was no one who had more of a right to speak than they.

The purpose of Judas and Silas (see v. 22 above) is to give verbal witness to the contents of the letter and to supplement the report of Barnabas and Paul. The letter is the official statement of the position of the Jerusalem church on this essential issue, and the two representatives provide word-of-mouth witness to the entire process that led to the letter.

The decision is preceded by the formula "It seemed good to the Holy Spirit and to us." It was God's decision revealed by the Spirit to the mother church and passed on by them as the decision of the Jerusalem Council. The Pharisaic believers had placed serious "burdens" on the Gentiles, described in 15:10 as a "yoke" on their necks, the two categories of which were circumcision and the Mosaic regulations. Those restrictions are no more, and Gentile converts are free of both. Their salvation is secure in Christ.

All the council asks of them is to observe four "requirements," or "necessary things" (*epanankes*), discussed in verse 20 (also 21:25). They are mandatory or essential because they relate to the cardinal sin of idolatry, and fellowship between Jews and Gentiles in the church depends on taking care regarding these issues. The order of the four here—food sacrificed to idols, then blood, strangled things, and immorality—follows that of Leviticus 17–18, emphasizing the question of Gentiles and Jews living together as God's people. So the question of fellowship and unity is uppermost.

THE LETTER IS RECEIVED IN ANTIOCH (15:30-35)

The four official representatives of the Jerusalem Council— Barnabas and Paul, Judas and Silas—arrived in Syrian Antioch and delivered the letter to the whole church there, which met in a sacred conclave. The statement that "the people read it" does not mean it was passed from person to person. The verb is *anagnontes*, meaning it was "read aloud" to all the people together, and the people were both overjoyed and encouraged by its contents. As James had said, the burdens were now lifted, and the people could begin building their life as the body of Christ together. Obviously the four "requirements" of verse 29 were not seen as a burden, since by observing them the Gentiles cemented their relationship with the Jewish Christians in the church.

The encouragement of the Antioch Christians was enhanced by the two official delegates from the Jerusalem church, Judas and Silas (15:32), who ministered to them, both comforting and strengthening these believers by what they said. They had been commissioned by the apostles and elders to verbally "confirm" (15:27) the decision of the council, and they did so with obvious delight. Clearly their ministry was more than just affirmation of what had transpired. Luke adds that these two were also "prophets," filled with the Spirit to reveal messages directly from God to the church (see 11:27-28). They clearly had a preaching and teaching ministry in churches while they were in Antioch and built up the people spiritually.

Judas and Silas minister for a time (apparently brief) and then return to Jerusalem (15:33). They undoubtedly help to cement the relationship of the Jewish and Gentile sides of the church, proving the wisdom of James and the other leaders in choosing both a Jewish (Judas) and a Gentile (Silas) envoy to represent the Jerusalem church. The "blessing of peace" is both the traditional greeting (shalōm) and an exceedingly wise choice because this "Jerusalem letter" has done more to bring peace to the church than they ever could have imagined. Their decision had pulled the messianic community back from a potential schism.[5]

Paul and Barnabas remain in Antioch and "taught and preached the word of God," enabling the people to grow further spiritually and work out what a united church looks like. As we see from the Pauline letters (see Rom 14-15; Eph 2; Phil 3), unity was a very difficult thing to accomplish and took literally decades. Of course, it is no easier in our day, and the human propensity to look down on people who are different in any way is always there to magnify our prejudices and hinder harmony in our churches. We must at all times work very hard to make the unity within the Godhead the basis of our acceptance of each other.

———

This chapter is not just the literary center of Acts; it is the historical core as well. In every sense the results provide the Magna Carta of the Gentile church, giving these believers freedom to join believing

5. Several ancient manuscripts add a verse 34, "But Silas decided to remain there," likely added by a later scribe to explain why Silas is present with Paul in verse 40. However, the majority (𝔓74 ℵ A B Byz and others) do not have the verse, and it was probably added later.

Jews as the people of God with freedom to worship him as Gentiles and not just as Jewish proselytes. The process began in 11:1–18, when the Jewish Christians in Jerusalem realized that now "God has granted repentance" to the Gentiles to join the Jews in the church.

However, the orthodox believers, who came to be known as "Judaizers" (for turning Gentile converts into Jews), demurred and refused to accept that conclusion, demanding that Gentiles be circumcised and become Jewish followers before they can become Christians. This continued through the months after Paul returned from what is called the "first missionary journey" and led to the Jerusalem Council decision in this chapter. So the first section (vv. 1–5) describes how the Antioch church decided to send a delegation to Jerusalem to present the case before the elders and members of the church. On the way they reported the good news about Gentile conversions and were received everywhere with joy. This joyous acceptance continued when they reached Jerusalem.

The council meeting (vv. 6–21) centers on three speeches—by Peter, by Paul and Barnabas, and by James—and has become for us a perfect model for deciding both doctrinal and ecclesial debates in the church. Peter's opening address (vv. 6–11) came from his own experience as the one who in Acts 10–11 first encountered God's will for the Gentiles. His two proofs were convincing—God's elective will was shown in his "choice" (v. 7) of the Gentiles to be converted directly as a result of Peter's gospel message, and he gave the Holy Spirit to them (v. 8), proving that Gentiles are saved by the same grace as the Jews (v. 11). The Judaizing claims were exceedingly dangerous, for they were testing God (v. 10) and bringing a judgment like the wilderness generation had to endure for going against the divine will.

Paul and Barnabas then told of the "signs and wonders" God had performed among the Gentiles (v. 12), the greatest of which was the sign of their conversion. This led to James' concluding message (vv. 13–21), which settled the issue and proved that God did indeed will for the Gentiles to be counted inclusively with the

Jews in the church. James finalizes the arguments and provides another model for decision-making by consulting Scripture itself before deciding what is God's will in the process. James turns to Amos 9:11–12 and links the conversion of the Gentiles with rebuilding "David's fallen tent" (16–18), where the purpose of bringing Israel back from exile is not only the restoration of Israel to God but is also "that the rest of mankind may seek the Lord, even all the Gentiles." This goes back to the Abrahamic covenant and convinces James that the very choice of Israel to be God's people was so that they would take God to the nations and bless them as well. So the Judaizers are terribly wrong to put obstacles in the way of Gentile conversion, and the church should continue the earlier practice of proclaiming salvation to the nations (vv. 19–21).

There were still two areas of concern (vv. 22–29)—the Gentiles committing idolatry due to their ignorance of the law, and of their offending Jewish Christians when they worship together with them. So the Jerusalem church writes to all the Gentile churches and asks them to respectfully avoid four things: (1) food sacrificed to idols in pagan temples; (2) sexual immorality, that is, sexual relations outside marriage; (3) consuming animals that were strangled when sacrificed or prepared for consuming, because the blood could not be sufficiently drained from them; (4) meat from animals in which the blood was not sufficiently drained before it was butchered. These last two were important because blood is sacred and symbolic of life and as such should not be consumed. The goal of this letter and its requests was to enhance the quality of fellowship between Jews and Gentiles in the church.

The letter and news of the results of the council were extremely encouraging to all the churches, not just in Jerusalem but in Antioch and other places as well (vv. 30–35). The four delegates returned to Antioch with the good news. After a short time, Judas and Silas returned to Jerusalem while Paul and Barnabas remained in Antioch for a while, both preaching the gospel and teaching the people in the churches.

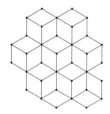

MISSION IN MACEDONIA
AND ACHAIA, PART 1
(15:36–16:40)

The results of the Jerusalem Council greatly enhanced the church's vision to embrace its Spirit-driven mission to the unreached peoples of the world. While the Judaizers were creating havoc in the churches of Palestine, Syria, Cilicia, and Galatia, the universal mission was at a standstill, for until the philosophy of mission could be worked out, it would be impossible to move forward. If Gentiles would have had to become Jews, the gospel would have to move forward at a snail's pace because it would be encumbered by all the legal restrictions from the Mosaic regulations.

Now that Gentiles could freely come to Christ and be saved by faith rather than by the works of the law, the mission of the church could explode to the nations. That is exactly what this journey does, almost leapfrogging the previous journey in its haste to move forward to reach the lost. Paul is proving his dictum of Romans 15:20, "It has always been my ambition to preach the gospel where Christ was not known." Those churches today that have little interest in the worldwide mission of God are simply disobedient and unwilling to listen to the Spirit, for it is impossible to be a Spirit-filled believer and fail to care for the unreached. Certainly we are not all called to be missionaries, but we are all called to pray, give for

God's mission to the world, and in some way be a part of God's reaching out to those who so desperately need him.

Acts is a compendium of the step-by-step process by which this universal mission bloomed like a rose, with one petal after another opening up to the light of God shining on a world of darkness and pouring down on it the new life in Christ that he has made available. From the Palestinian period in which God's church became anchored in Christ (1:1–8:3), the church's task was gradually revealed, following the blueprint of 1:8 and moving out first to Samaria, then to the Ethiopian eunuch, and finally to Cornelius as God's people became aware of his intentions to bring his salvation to the nations, the whole world of humankind.

So through Peter, then Paul, and then James, the Spirit revealed through his chosen leaders that the church is God's army bringing his true peace (unlike the *Pax Romana*, or "Roman peace") to the whole world of sinful humankind. The extent to which this is true is seen in all of its splendor in this missionary journey, as the gospel moves at breakneck pace from province to province. It simply cannot be stopped as it moves from Syria to Cilicia and through all of Asia Minor (16:1–10), then by divine fiat (the Macedonian vision) beyond even Paul's imaginings to Macedonia (16:11–17:15) and then Achaia (17:16–18:17).

PAUL AND BARNABAS SEPARATE (15:36–41)

After spending some time in regular ministry in Antioch,[1] Paul wants to move on and do follow up work in the churches he had established in Galatia (undoubtedly to deliver the Jerusalem letter to them as well). His wants to revisit "all the towns where

---

1. Some time had elapsed, for Silas returned to Jerusalem (16:33). Yet when Paul leaves on his journey in 15:40, Silas is back in Antioch and joins his team. We don't know why and how that took place, but the process would certainly take quite some time. Silas may have already made that decision and just returned to Jerusalem to say goodbye to family and friends.

we preached the word of the Lord and see how they are doing," a task they had already done once in 14:21–28. At that time they had appointed elders and strengthened them spiritually, and he wanted to make certain these churches were well aware that the Judaizers who had tried to change the parameters of the gospel had been very wrong and were no longer in the picture. My daughter several years ago was part of a team that experienced major evangelistic success in several villages in central India, but in all the time she was there they never went back to anchor the gospel in the lives of those people. I have always believed this was a major mistake. Paul would certainly never have failed to do that.

A serious disagreement ensues (15:37–38) when Barnabas wants to take along John Mark, his cousin (Col 4:10) who had abandoned the team in Perga (13:13). We don't know why Mark did so and why Paul felt he was not ready to rejoin the team. Whatever they were, Paul felt very strongly that Mark had "deserted them in Pamphylia" and was not yet ready to return. Some think this is a continuation of the conflict recorded in Galatians 2:11–14, when Paul accused Peter and Barnabas of hypocrisy over their treatment of Gentile Christians, but that is a separate incident and prior to this event, occurring before the Jerusalem Council.

The result is such a "sharp disagreement that they parted company" with each other (15:39). The term (*paroxysmos*) could denote anger between them, but we don't know. Most likely Barnabas thought Mark deserved forgiveness and a second chance, while Paul believed that the ongoing mission was too important and serious to warrant having an immature assistant along. The two could not agree, and Barnabas felt strongly enough that he took his young cousin and protégé and returned to his home in Cyprus (see 4:36) in order to do follow-up work there (see 13:4–12). Mark is later fully reinstated and accepted by Paul (Col 4:10; Phlm 24; 2 Tim 4:11) and of course writes the Gospel that now bears his name. Paul and Barnabas also reconcile (1 Cor 9:6).

The process was quite painful, but in the end with the Spirit in control it ended well for them both. A certain amount of good did result from this split, for there were now two mission teams working among the Gentile lands, and the help Barnabas gave John Mark was essential for his later, highly successful ministry.

Paul then chooses Silas, the Roman believer (see 16:38) who had been part of the delegation from Jerusalem (15:22, 27) and had returned to Antioch, probably for this very purpose of joining Paul's team. He becomes the first of three (with Timothy in 16:3 and Luke, the "we" of 16:10) to join Paul for this lengthy mission trip of about three years (AD 49–51).

The Antioch church likely supported both Paul and Barnabas in their separate mission journeys (Luke just mentions the one for the sake of his narrative flow) and "commended [his team] to the grace of the Lord," praying over them that God's grace would go before them on each stage of the coming mission. The mission begins in Syria and Cilicia, covering churches Paul had founded in his time in Tarsus (Gal 2:11–14) and Antioch, the churches to which the letter was addressed (15:23). "Strengthening" once again (14:22) refers to churches that grow into spiritual maturity.

There is a good lesson in this paragraph. Luke does not assign blame or take one side over the other. There are times when sharp disagreement is unavoidable and teams do split up. When that happens we should fall on our knees, examine ourselves as deeply as we can, and let the Lord lead us. In this instance, good came of both sides, though the split was definitely not optimal. However, with human beings such things do occur, and we like Paul must do the best we can.

PAUL REVISITS GALATIA AND IS JOINED BY TIMOTHY (16:1–5)

Paul takes the route from Antioch to Galatia that he didn't take earlier when he went back through Galatia (14:21–23). This time they went overland north through mountainous terrain from Tarsus to Derbe then Lystra (where Paul had been stoned). There he met an extraordinary young man from an exceptional family, Timothy, whose grandmother was Lois and his mother Eunice (2 Tim 1:5, both dedicated believers), and whose father was Greek (Acts 16:1). The fact that his mother married a Greek shows his family is syncretistic and at home in the **Hellenistic** world, possibly for several generations. Still, we know from 2 Timothy 3:15 that he had been steeped in God's word "from infancy" (his mother was Jewish) and that both his grandmother and mother had a "sincere faith" in Christ and were converted during that earlier mission in 14:8–20. They with Timothy had been growing in Christ from that time on, and Timothy was ready to spread his wings.

Timothy had a solid reputation in the church (16:3), and he was known and respected even as a young man as far away as Iconium, so Paul decided to add him to his team. Since Timothy was the product of a mixed marriage, he hadn't been circumcised. Paul felt it important to have him circumcised so he could minister in Jewish as well as Gentile settings. At first glance this may seem strange or even wrong since Paul had denied the place of circumcision in salvation. But that's the key. This was not done for the sake of his spiritual state but for the sake of ministry among the Jews. As such it is a rather remarkable concession for ministry and shows Timothy's level of dedication. Luke tells us it was done "because of the Jews who lived in that area, for they all knew that his father was a Greek." With a pagan father and being uncircumcised, he would have been mistrusted by the Jews, so Paul wanted to regularize his status. An uncircumcised Jew was untenable. Judaism traced descent through the mother's line, so a Jewish mother made him legally Jewish. Now no Jew could object to him ministering in their midst.

The ministry of the team in Lystra and Derbe (and probably Iconium and Pisidian Antioch as well) was the same as it had been in Syria and Cilicia. They told of the decision of the Jerusalem Council (16:4), read them the letter and told them of the four requirements the Jerusalem leaders had set down, and strengthened the churches spiritually (16:5; see also 2:41, 47; 4:4, 31; 5:14; 6:7; 8:25; 9:31; 12:24). Undoubtedly the churches in Galatia were just as thrilled with the results of the council as those other churches had been. Luke tells us that it affected their evangelistic success as well, relating how the church "grew daily in numbers." So the church was strengthened both in size and in their spiritual walk.

IN TROAS, PAUL IS CALLED TO MACEDONIA (16:6–10)

This is a favorite passage of mine, for it shows the direct guidance of the Spirit in Paul and demonstrates as well how sensitive Paul is to the leading of the Spirit. The Spirit wanted the team in Macedonia ASAP, but Paul and his team weren't ready for that, so both in Galatia and again in Mysia he prohibited Paul from going south into the province of Asia the first time (v. 6) and north into Bithynia the second time (v. 7). Then when they reached Troas, the Spirit sent a vision to propel them into Macedonia (v. 8). Moreover, these two messages may have come via neither an audible voice nor a vision but apparently by way of a Spirit-sent inner conviction. There are many times we must be open to "a still small voice" (like Elijah received in 1 Kgs 19:12 KJV) in finding the Lord's will. At the same time, it may have come through a prophet, and Paul or Silas may have been that prophet. We simply do not know.

Paul had his ideas regarding the direction the team should take, and as they moved through the region, he first wanted to travel to the province of Asia in the western half of the peninsula. He doesn't seem personally ready to go into Macedonia, probably because the western half of Asia Minor (Turkey today) had not as yet been evangelized. Most feel he wished to preach the gospel in Ephesus (in the province of Asia), but the Spirit had reserved that for the next missionary journey. The seven cities of Revelation 2–3 were in that province, so it later became one of the most thriving Christian centers in the world. Luke doesn't tell us how the Spirit prevented that from happening, as I discussed above. It is absolutely clear, though, that the Spirit wished the gospel to move into Europe (Macedonia and points west) immediately, not later.

As they continued toward Troas and Macedonia, Paul next wanted to travel north (16:7). Mysia is at the northwesternmost point of the peninsula there, and he intended to go northeast of it to Bithynia and evangelize that territory. The city of Byzantium was there, which later became Constantinople and the capital of Christianity in the East. For a second time the Spirit said no, and so there was only one thing left, to finish the journey through Mysia and go the short distance left to Troas (16:8).

Troas was a major port at the northwestern tip of Asia Minor near the ancient city of Troy, with just a short boat ride from there to Macedonia. We don't know whether Paul was still reluctant to go there. Some think he at this stage intended to take that route, and the vision was confirmation of that decision. Again, we cannot know for certain. What we do know for sure is God's intention to take his gospel into Europe at this point.

On one of the first nights there the Spirit sends him a vision of a Macedonian man who calls out, "Come over to Macedonia and help us" (16:9). Now it becomes very clear as to the purposes of the Spirit in verses 6–8. God has destined the team to continue to push outward with the gospel. At the very beginning of the church's mission, God wants them to move out to the Greek provinces near the area of Rome itself. He wants this sooner rather than later. Churches today that ignore international missions and believe God has called them exclusively to their "Jerusalem" are wrong. He is a God for all the nations,[2] and we are all meant to be involved in some way. "Help us" in this context means to bring the gospel of salvation and help them find life.

---

2. The Abrahamic covenant shows this was God's intention all along. He had chosen Israel not to restrict his mercy to one people but so that they could take his blessings to all the nations (Gen 12:3; 22:18; 26:4; 28:14).

Macedonia is the northern half of Greece (with Achaia to the south), and it was home to Alexander the Great as well as the greatest set of philosophers and medical practitioners the world had ever seen.[3] The mission team immediately obeyed the divine call (16:10) and felt propelled to leave, concluding that preaching the gospel in the Greek lands was indeed God's will. So these verses (6–10) are a wonderful example of an important spiritual truth, that God is involved in our lives guiding us to find his will. He certainly doesn't always make it clear, and I personally prefer to understand verses 6–7 as a growing conviction rather than a vision. We should always assume that God is involved, and we are not strictly on our own. He cares, and it is our task like Paul here to seek that "still small voice" (see on v. 6).

We should take note of the centrality of "we" here, the first of many of the "we" passages in Acts (16:10–17 with 20:5–15; 21:1–18; 27:1–28:16) indicating events in which Luke himself takes part. Luke probably joined the team here at Troas, and so there are now four on the team (with Paul, Silas, and Timothy). God will change the world as they knew it as a result of these four, for the church from that point on will follow their lead and plant the gospel in land after land. There is only one criterion—obedience to the heavenly vision.

PAUL MINISTERS IN PHILIPPI (16:11–40)

This has been the goal all along. Even though for a long time Paul was not ready for it, the Spirit had other plans, and now finally they all realize what they are to do and the team is by now completely on board.

---

3. That is still true. The only parallel is Florence in its golden age, but that was focused more on the visual arts (especially the work of Michelangelo and Leonardo da Vinci).

THE TRIP TO PHILIPPI (16:11–12)

They set sail from Troas and first travel to Samothrace, a small island and town with a huge five-thousand-foot mountain on it on the northern side of the Aegean Sea. They stayed there that night and then sailed to the port city of Neapolis on the northern coast of Macedonia. Due to favorable winds, they made it across the Aegean Sea to Neapolis in just two days (it took five days coming back, 20:6). From there they traveled ten miles on the Roman road Via Egnatia (the "Ignatian Way," the major east-west road through the province) to Philippi.

Philippi was a thriving town of about ten thousand inhabitants, labeled here "a Roman colony," meaning it had been adopted by Rome, and its citizens were Roman citizens. It was just an unimportant small town until 42 BC, when Mark Antony (Julius Caesar's chief supporter at the time) and Octavian (Caesar's nephew who became the emperor Augustus) defeated his assassins Cassius and Brutus near there and made Philippi a Roman colony and home for retired soldiers from their army. With its wealth and importance as a center of Roman life, it became a "leading city." Normally *prōtos* means it was the capital city, but Thessalonica was the capital city of the province, and Amphipolis was the administrative center of the district (there were four in the province) of which Philippi was a part. So the title "leading city" refers not to its status as an administrative center but its status as a major Roman colony.

It is strange that Luke describes their mission there simply as "stayed there several days," for it was likely a few weeks/Sabbaths. This turned out to be an important stay in what became an important city for the Christian cause, as Paul's Letter to the Philippians will show.

THE CONVERSION OF LYDIA (16:13–15)

Philippi was a religiously diverse town but only with regard to various Greco-Roman cults. There were few Jews due to prejudice against the Judeo-Christian God, and Philippi will become a byword for persecution and animosity. When Paul's team arrived they went outside the city to "a place of prayer" near a river. This could mean there was no synagogue, and that would mean there were fewer than ten Jewish males in the city.

That is quite debated, for many believe this was "a house of prayer," a synagogue described in terms of its primary purpose (prayer). I have my doubts and tend to prefer the traditional view since Luke (1) does not use the term "synagogue," (2) mentions only women at the meeting, and (3) has the setting outside the city. The main problem with this scenario is that there are several women but no men, highly unusual for the ancient world. So I go back and forth on this but generally prefer the more natural conclusion given the language Luke uses, that there were not enough men for a synagogue. When he says Paul spoke "to the women who had gathered there," that must mean no men were present.

Luke centers on one of the women, Lydia (16:14), a citizen of Thyatira—a city known to us as one of the seven churches of the book of Revelation (Rev 2:18-29). The city was in the district of Lydia, so some scholars think her name is simply meant to say she is "a Lydian woman," but she is named this throughout, so that is unlikely. As a "dealer in purple cloth," from a region famous for its luxurious cloth, she would have been a wealthy merchant who catered to the extremely wealthy. The purple dye came from small shellfish in the Aegean and was very difficult to extract, so few could afford such clothes. Further, she was a God-fearer like Cornelius (10:2, 22) and so worshipped and practiced as a Jew.

Lydia was "listening" (the imperfect tense may point to a lengthy presentation) closely as Paul presented the gospel, and we are told, "the Lord opened her heart to respond to Paul's message" about Jesus as Messiah and Savior of Israel. She is converted along with "the members of her household" (16:15), which could mean her slaves but probably means her children. The fact that no husband is mentioned indicates she is either widowed or divorced. If widowed, that also explains how she is at the head of the family business and is master of her own house. So she and her whole family are baptized, possibly along with others who are not mentioned here.

Her invitation is interesting: "If you consider me a believer in the Lord [Greek: 'to be faithful to the Lord'] … come and stay at my house." She wants them to know she is not a charlatan or opportunist but genuinely wants to be a part of their ministry. Her home becomes not just a place to stay or a center of the mission to Philippi; it becomes the first house church in Europe (16:40), the center of worship for the growing number of believers in Philippi. This also tells us she was wealthy, with a home large enough for over fifty worshipers.

The Possessed Slave Girl (16:16–18)

Luke doesn't say much about the ministry of the team in Philippi and never mentions reaching out to the Gentiles, though the tenor of the story assumes that this is likely implicit. Given the description above, there were virtually only Gentiles in Philippi, so Luke doesn't have to be explicit. The second incident (after Lydia) takes place one day as they were headed for "the place of prayer," probably to address those still not converted there. On the way they were met by a demon-possessed slave girl. The demonic "spirit" who possessed her was named Python (Greek: *pneuma pythōna*) after the dragon god of Greek mythology, the god of divination and ventriloquism. The men who owned her made a huge profit as she foretold the future (one of the earliest "fortune-tellers") and made oracles or pronouncements protecting people from harm. Such activity is clearly condemned in Scripture (Lev 19:31; Deut 18:10–11; 1 Sam 28:8; Isa 8:19; Ezek 12:24).

Apparently Paul did nothing when he passed here this first time, and he failed to cast out the demon "for many days" afterward. During that time she virtually became Paul's public relations person, telling everyone how important he was: "These men are servants [slaves, *douloi*] of the Most High God, who are telling you the way to be saved." There is a certain ambiguity here, for "Most High God" could be taken as a supreme God like Zeus, and "the way to be saved" could be seen as one among many. So listeners would think this was one of the Greco-Roman cults or even a mystery religion. Still, for Paul this would have heightened interest and got people to listen to what he was saying.

For quite a few days she followed him everywhere, telling the townspeople why he had come. It is possible it was God's will to use her this way, but Paul might also have found it humanly convenient for her to gain attention for his ministry this way. This is definitely the only story like this among all the exorcism stories of Scripture. The situation rather than the tragedy of the demon-possessed young girl seems to be driving Paul's response.[4]

Finally, Paul becomes "so annoyed" or disturbed at the spectacle (16:18) that he can no longer let the situation continue, so he commands, "In the name of Jesus Christ I command you to come out of her!" The "name of Christ" is featured throughout Acts (see 3:6, 16; 4:10, 12) and is the basis of Paul's power as well. The evil spirit does not quibble or fight back; it is overwhelmed and immediately leaves her. In this instance we do not learn whether she ever becomes a believer. It is the aftermath that concerns Luke.

THE JAILING OF PAUL AND SILAS (16:19–34)

The owners of the slave girl are out a lot of money now that the source of their income has been healed by Paul, and needless to say they are not happy. They pretend their reasons are religious (they are Jews) or legal (causing a riot), but Luke tells the truth—it is entirely financial. They perform what could be called a "citizen's arrest" and drag the Christian leaders before the magistrates in the agora, or central marketplace. Still, their complaint to the

---

4. The first "we" passage ends here (16:10–17), and the next doesn't begin until 20:5 (see on 16:10), so most believe Luke stays in Philippi and doesn't rejoin the team until they are in Troas after the final missionary journey.

authorities centers on the fact that these men are despised Jews (though in reality they are both Roman citizens) and are "throwing our city into an uproar," a blatant lie but quite serious, since the primary duty of magistrates in every city was to maintain order and keep things on an even keel.

The further charge is that they are "advocating customs unlawful for us Romans to accept or practice" (16:21). The emphasis on "us Romans" appeals to the basic prejudice against Jews in that city. It wouldn't matter that there was no proof of riots or unlawful customs, because they would be suspicious of Jews in every way. By advocating a Jewish way of life, all Jews in Philippi (and all God-fearers) could be charged with this. Adding Christian ideas to Jewish beliefs and practices would simply be seen as further evidence of the seditious views these missionaries embrace.

That the crowd "joined in the attack" (v. 22) doesn't mean physical violence but rather that they joined their voices to the owners in verbally accusing Paul and Silas before the authorities. This would explain the actions of the authorities better, for there doesn't seem to be any judicial trial before the beating. The magistrates likely thought the evidence was certain and went straight to the beating and imprisonment. One wonders in this serious situation why Paul and Silas didn't claim their rights as Roman citizens. Yet that would have occasioned a great deal of time and effort (getting the proof from Tarsus, Paul's hometown, lengthy court proceedings, and so on) and increased the animosity between them and the citizens of Philippi. So Paul, as he often does, refrained from demanding his rights, even with the severe consequences. Furthermore, the action here somewhat resembles mob action, and there may not have been time to do so.[5]

---

5. Compare this with the later scene in 22:22–29, when he does assert his citizenship rights. That involved scourging, not just beating with rods, which could have killed him or left him crippled for life. When it does come out here that they are Roman citizens (16:37–39), the authorities are alarmed, for

They are stripped of their clothes (with just their loincloths left) and then beaten with rods, called the *admonitio* (English: "admonition"), for it was intended as a warning against future illegal activity.

Paul was truly amazing. In 2 Corinthians 11:23–27 Paul notes five times the thirty-nine lashes, three times being beaten with rods like here, and many other severe penalties he had endured for Christ. He could have easily deserved his own chapter in *Foxe's Book of Martyrs*. No wonder he had such a powerful effect on those around him. In Paul God truly had a spiritual giant who should serve as an inspiration for us all.

With their backs undoubtedly bloody after the severe beating and their clothes simply thrown back over their wounds, they are chained to the filthy wall of the Philippian prison, their feet in stocks, and just left there (16:23–24). It would be hard to imagine anything more discouraging, with their wounds uncared for, their backs bloody, and chained in the cell of one of the filthiest places imaginable. They are being treated as the lowest of criminals and virtually left to rot. Still, these two Christians at the very least had disturbed the public peace, and that was a punishable crime. It's hard to know why the jailer would put them in the "inner cell," usually reserved for hardened criminals, but he had been told to guard them "carefully," meaning it was a serious situation. Possibly because of their display of miraculous powers, they were judged to be dangerous sorcerers and so needed special care.

It must have amazed everyone in the prison, jailers and prisoners alike, that these severely wounded prisoners, rather than groaning and crying out in their pain,[6] were "praying and singing hymns to God" (16:25) in the total darkness and misery of the night.

---

citizens were not supposed to be beaten, and these magistrates were in serious trouble.

6. They had been several hours sitting on the floor with their feet in wooden stocks and their bleeding backs against the filthy stone wall of the cell.

No wonder everyone was "listening to them." Nobody else there had an ounce of happiness in them! Their bodies may have been devastated, but their spirits were soaring in worship to the God who had "counted [them] worthy of suffering disgrace for the Name" (5:41). Instead of questioning God for allowing them to get into this predicament, they are thanking God for the privilege. Of course, I am not saying they were glad to be there and were like medieval monks looking for opportunities to suffer more. Their prayers certainly included a request to be set free and continue their mission, but they still rejoiced in the Lord in the midst of their dilemma.

Suddenly, everything was turned upside down. A "violent earthquake"—Macedonia and Asia Minor (modern-day Turkey) are in a severe earthquake zone—shook the very foundations of the prison, so severe that cell doors were opened and chains broke free (16:26). Of course, God, not nature, was behind all that transpired. The fact that *every* prison cell was opened and *every* chain broke loose was a supernatural event. God was behind every detail. This is the third example of a miraculous escape from prison (after 5:19-20; 12:6-10), and in all of them, the power of the gospel is enhanced by the divine intervention.

If a prisoner escapes, the jailer is not just disgraced but as good as dead, for he will have to fulfill the sentences of the escaped criminals, as we saw in 12:19, when Herod executed the guards that allowed Peter to escape. So when the jailer awoke at the time of the earthquake and saw the cell doors open, he was going to take the honorable way out by committing suicide rather than wait for Roman justice to take place.

We don't know how Paul became aware of the jailer's intentions; it could have been the Spirit who intervened, or Paul, in the center of the prison, may have somehow heard the sounds (the jail was in total darkness) of the man getting ready to take his own life (16:28). At any rate, he immediately is led to cry out, "Don't harm yourself! We are all here!" How Paul knew no prisoner had run away is also a mystery. There were probably not too many prisoners in a town of ten thousand, and they would all have been kept in the general vicinity of Paul and Silas. The main thing is God is orchestrating the action to protect the jailer from execution (and certainly to bring him to Christ).

The jailer calls for torches so they could evaluate the situation, and uncharacteristically (when has a jailer ever done this?) he then "rushed in and fell trembling before Paul and Silas" (16:29). He had undoubtedly been listening and was aware of who they were, so he was prostrating himself before the Lord and his chosen envoys. Paul actually had taken over as the one in control at this juncture, and the jailer was throwing himself at his mercy (and that of the God who was behind him).

Paul had perhaps presented the gospel to the other prisoners, and the jailer had heard it, so he asks, "Sirs, what must I do to be saved?" (16:30). Paul had just rescued him from death, and that made him desire to be rescued from ultimate death as well. "Saved" here does not mean kept from the consequences of escaped prisoners, for that has already happened. We don't know how much of the gospel he knew, but there is a spiritual sense of the language reflected in his request. I doubt if at this stage he was highly aware of it all, for all he had to go on was what he had heard Paul and Silas say to the other prisoners. But he knew something supernatural had transpired, and he wanted to be right with the God who had done that.

Paul and Silas' response was undoubtedly much longer than what Luke narrates here, but this is of course an accurate summation: "Believe in the Lord Jesus, and you will be saved" (16:31). This is one of the central message of the book (2:21, 38; 4:12; 5:14; 9:42; 10:43; 11:14, 17; 13:39; 15:11), and both Jews and Gentiles find salvation the same way—faith in the Lord Jesus. Jesus is Lord not just over this world as his creation but over the process of eternal salvation as well. Paul must have explained to the man the sacrificial death of Christ on the cross and the forgiveness of sins attained by believing in his penal substitution for sin.

The jailer's family was present and listening as well, for Luke adds, "you and your household," then tells us, "Then they spoke the word of the Lord to him and to all the others in his house" (16:32), probably meaning wife, children, and slaves. It is remarkable that in the midst of the chaos caused by the earthquake, collecting all the prisoners, and establishing order after all this, Paul and Silas would have the time to proclaim the gospel in some depth to the jailer and his family. Only God could have enabled them to make the time in all this confusion. It was common for a family to follow a "patriarch" in his religious stance, but clearly each one of the members came to faith along with him.

Four things (16:33–34) show the reality of his conversion: (1) He "washed their wounds," showing kindness and mercy to prisoners over whom he had the power of life and death. Jailers were notorious in the ancient world for their wanton cruelty. He was truly a changed man. (2) He and his family were baptized, thereby making a public announcement of their conversion. I wish I could know how the rest of his life went. It is certain that he proved a valuable member of the Philippian house church. (3) He brought Paul and Silas into his home and fed them. This was actually dangerous for his career, for jailers would never be allowed to do either one. But now he and the mission team were brothers in the Lord, and he treated them exactly like family. (4) He and his family rejoiced at his newfound faith. As believers their lives had meaning and a security Rome could never provide. He had seen enough evil in his lifetime; it was time to enjoy the goodness of God and the kind of friendships he would never have believed possible.

FREEDOM AND DEPARTURE (16:35–40)

An amazing amount has happened in less than twenty-four hours' time. Paul casts the demon out of the slave girl, and in the next few hours Paul and Silas are accused, arrested, severely beaten, and shut up in a filthy prison. That very night at midnight they are singing hymns when a massive earthquake knocks the prison off its foundation and frees every prisoner. In the next few hours before daylight all the prisoners are secured, the jailer is rescued from committing suicide, he and his whole family become Christians, and they form a new family with Paul and Silas.

Now, early the next day at dawn, about eighteen hours or so after it all started, the order comes through to free Paul and Silas (16:35–36). This was a very serious official order, for they sent the "lictors" ("officers" in the NIV) with the message. These at all times accompanied magistrates and were both police officers and symbols of their authority (they carried the wooden rods for the magistrates). We don't know the reason for the about-face. Many think they may have seen the earthquake as a sign of the displeasure of the gods at their hasty decision regarding Paul and Silas and want to get them out of their hair.

But Paul will not "go in peace." It is at this point that he reveals that they are both Roman citizens and complains that the city had no right to beat them without a trial (required when dealing with citizens). We don't know how Paul would have proved his citizenship; it was not common to carry such documents around. Still, the simple fact that he could have may have been enough in this instance. So the magistrates could be in serious trouble for mistreatment of citizens. His response is quite harsh: "And now do they want to get rid of us quietly? No! Let them come themselves and escort us out" (16:37). He has allowed his frustration to build up for some time and is now erupting with indignation at the unfairness of it all. He demands that they admit their culpability in the whole situation.

Here we see the human Paul once again. He even says something about it in 1 Thessalonians 2:2, "We had previously suffered and been treated outrageously in Philippi." There were times when he was willing to give up his rights (1 Cor 9:12, 15, 19), but this was not one of them. He had been publicly beaten and humiliated. Now they want to get him to leave "in secret" or "quietly," and he will have none of it. So he demands that they both come to the prison themselves, in a sense with their hat in their hands, and give him and Silas a personal escort (with honor) out of the city. They had treated Paul and Silas like peasants; now the two are demanding to be dismissed with the dignity and honor they deserve. They want a public acknowledgment of the wrong done to them.

The magistrates are filled with alarm (16:38–39), for they had been too hasty in accepting the complaints of the owners of the slave girl and had failed to allow due process to these visitors, who should have been treated with the honor of Roman citizens. There was no excuse for their ignorance of the citizenship of the two, and any proper court process would have discovered that. They would be in a world of hurt if Paul and Silas were to press their claim. To head off this danger, they immediately came and tried to appease the two, to escort them from prison, and to beg them to leave without accusing the magistrates before a higher court (in Thessalonica, the capital of the province). This was a classic example of the demand for justice at work. The magistrates must capitulate to the victors, Paul and Silas, and be willing to allow them to recover their dignity.

Their honor returned to them and some level of protection won for the believers in Philippi, Paul and Silas have just one act left (16:40). They go to the house church meeting at Lydia's house, encourage the believers there, and say goodbye. So even though somewhat brief, the time of Paul and Silas in Philippi is highly successful, spawning at least one house church there. From the letter to the Philippians we know that was just the beginning, and they became the congregation that remained closest to Paul throughout his ministry.

———

This wonderful and bold journey to the lost peoples of the world was truly world-changing, for it moved at breakneck pace, far beyond even what Paul could have conceived as it moved not just into the rest of Asia Minor but into Europe, taking the team through both Macedonia and Achaia in one fell swoop. It set the pattern for the church's mission for all of history, presaging others like the apostle Thomas's mission to India and China. Paul had wanted to go to Ephesus and the province of Asia (16:6–7), but God wanted to establish the worldwide parameters of the church's mission and so had them cover an incredible amount of space, reserving Ephesus for the next journey (chapter 19).

The journey begins on a negative note (15:35–39), with Paul and Barnabas splitting up the team and going their separate ways over the question of allowing John Mark to rejoin them. It is a good example of the human factor in missions. I think it likely that both men were guilty of spiritual failure in this instance, but the Spirit was in charge and worked it out for good in the end, as two mission teams resulted and God was at work on both sides.

As the team moves out to Galatia, two things take place. First, an outstanding young man joins (16:1–5), Timothy, who is what Mark wasn't, deeply spiritual and a team player. The product of a strong upbringing, he adds youthful zest and energy to the others. Then as they move west through Galatia and Asia Minor, the Spirit takes over (vv. 6–10) and illustrates for us the depth of details in which God is involved in all our ministries. He is not an aloof God but guides us step by step to what he intends is the optimal path of our ministries. He takes the team straight to Troas and then from there to Macedonia very swiftly, for even with this haste, it will take three years to finish this journey, and so the Lord wants to "waste" no time getting here.

In Philippi (vv. 11–18) two significant things take place, both involving women. The positive side (vv. 13–15) is the conversion of Lydia, a wealthy dealer in purple cloth whose home becomes the first house church in Europe and who becomes the major patron of Paul's team while in Philippi. The negative side (vv. 16–18) is a demon-possessed slave girl who for several days becomes the primary advertisement drawing people to Paul as she tells everyone about the Most High God he is proclaiming. He finally gets annoyed (a very human picture of him) and liberates her of the demon, which turns her handlers against Paul and the team.

The magistrates trusted the trumped-up charges and, ignoring the time-consuming process of a trial, just beat them with rods and threw them into the innermost depths of the prison, their feet in stocks and their backs against a filthy wall (vv. 19–24). Yet Paul and Silas are singing hymns and rejoicing in the Lord over the privilege of suffering with and for Christ when an earthquake comes (vv. 25–26). Thinking his life is over because of prisoners escaping, the jailer is about to commit suicide when Paul saves him first from having to kill himself and them from the eternal consequences of his sins (vv. 27–31). He and his family become believers and make Paul and Silas part of their family (vv. 32–34).

The final scene (vv. 35–40) shows the complete victory Paul and Silas won over the magistrates of the city when they demanded their rights as Roman citizens and forced these officials to come hat in hand to them and admit their guilt in the affair. This shows that missionaries do not have to be mice and allow pagan officials to heap whatever indignity they wish on them. There are times when ministry demands justice, especially when it means finding protection for other believers in the future. Paul and Silas left the church somewhat protected, although theirs was always a severely persecuted church.

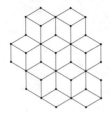

MISSION IN MACEDONIA AND ACHAIA, PART 2

(17:1–34)

The team (Paul, Silas, Timothy) will take one of the most famous routes in antiquity, the Ignatian Way through Macedonia to Achaia. Their first stop is Thessalonica, about one hundred miles away, but as they travel on this Roman highway along the north coast of the Aegean Sea, they pass through Amphipolis, the capital of the Macedonian district of which Philippi is a part, and also Apollonia. It is possible that Paul didn't stay to minister in those two because neither city had a synagogue. We don't know. At any rate, Thessalonica was the capital of Macedonia and a city of about fifty thousand, with a Roman proconsul and a council of a half dozen officials called "politarchs" (17:6; NIV: "city officials") governing it. It had a major harbor and was both a commercial center and a pro-Roman city.

PAUL MINISTERS IN THESSALONICA (17:1-9)

They spend the first three Sabbaths there ministering in the synagogue. Luke says Paul "reasoned," or "dialogued" (*dielexato*), with them, meaning he not only taught the people but also argued logically, proving that the Scriptures pointed to Jesus as Messiah and Savior (as we see in v. 3). This includes both synagogue preaching and wide-ranging debates on evidence from prophecy. So this refers to the weeks they were discussing the issues with the people.

The subject matter is Jesus Messiah, and Luke says Paul for this three-week period was "explaining and proving" three things (17:3): (1) Jesus is the expected Messiah promised in the Scriptures; (2) as Messiah he "had to" (*edei*) become the Suffering Servant of Isaiah and the Psalms; (3) he also "had to" rise from the dead. Undoubtedly Paul opened nearly all the Old Testament texts we have already seen used in Acts to convince the people that Jesus was indeed the God-sent Messiah who came to bring salvation to his people. Behind this short verse is a world of meaning, as it declares that the entire gospel was intended to bring people to repentance.

The results were encouraging, with some Jews, a great many God-fearers, and even "quite a few prominent women" coming to Christ and establishing the first house church at the home of Jason in the next verse (17:4–5). Luke tells us they were "persuaded" or converted and "joined" Paul and Silas; the Greek "joined" (*proskleroō*) means to "form an association" or "join a community" with a common purpose. Behind both verbs is the work of God, who brought them into Jesus' new kingdom.

We are told here that there were "some" Jews converted, but 1 Thessalonians 1:9 indicates very few, and most of the converts were God-fearers and pagans, with this a predominantly Gentile church. The "prominent women," as in 13:50, were probably also God-fearers and the wives of the leading men of the city, so they had more freedom of movement than most other women.

"Other Jews" (the many not converted) are "jealous" (see also 5:17) of the success of Paul and Silas on several fronts—their success in winning converts from Jew and Gentile alike, the money from wealthy Gentiles that used to go to Jewish causes, and the number of God-fearers and proselytes who have joined their ranks. So they went into the agora, the market square where "bad characters" or what we would label "gang members" loitered about, and organized a mob riot, the one thing the Romans would not tolerate. This mob of lowlifes rushed to the main house church that had been formed, belonging to a certain Jason (see Rom 16:21), hoping to drag Paul and Silas out to the crowd and probably beat them.

The two aren't there (17:6), so they grab Jason and a few believers and drag them before the city council (the "politarchs" mentioned in v. 1) and loudly accuse them of having "caused trouble all over the world." This is not really hyperbole, for riots had ensued almost everywhere Paul had been, though we don't know how much of that they knew. Just the year before (AD 49) the emperor Claudius had expelled Christians from Rome due to the riots of many Jews against them. We will soon meet Priscilla and Aquila, two Christian leaders who moved to Corinth due to that event (18:2). So the Thessalonian officials would naturally be on edge regarding such charges. Their accusation of Jason's opening his home to such dangerous agitators would have carried weight. He could be accused of sedition, which would carry the death sentence.

Added to this is the further charge that they are "all defying Caesar's decrees" by declaring "another king, one called Jesus." This is exactly the charge against Jesus, one that Pilate declared false (Luke 23:3-4). Rome had been a republic for hundreds of years[1] but became an imperial monarchy when Gaius Octavius, Julius Caesar's nephew and heir, became the emperor Augustus in 27 BC. So this charge was even more serious and would have been interpreted as treason if it could be proved. Yet that would only be so if it was a political claim, while in reality it was a religious and spiritual claim.

Their ploy worked to an extent. Both the crowd and the officials were "thrown into turmoil" as they believed the charges and were afraid of the consequences to their city (17:8-9). They would have been terrified of Roman intervention and even of Roman

---

1. They refused to have a king who reigned for life and instead were ruled by a series of "consuls," two of which were elected each year.

displeasure. As an extremely pro-Roman town, they depended on their benefactors virtually for everything. So such a potential catastrophe was extremely disturbing, and they weren't certain what to do. Still, Jason apparently answers the charges satisfactorily, and they do not give in to the crowd's demands. They simply have Jason and the other Christians "post bond," that is, pay bail, to secure their promise that Paul and Silas (and they themselves) will not commit any such seditious acts in the city, then they "let them go."

PAUL MINISTERS IN BEREA (17:10-15)

That very night the believers bow to the pressure, find Paul and Silas, and send them "away to Berea," forty-five miles from there on the Ignatian Way. In 1 Thessalonians 2:17-18 it is clear that the mission team did not leave of their own accord but were forced (by the crowd and officials) to do so. In fact, Paul and the others tried again and again to get back to them, but Satan kept creating obstacles that thwarted their desires. Still, they found a much better environment for presenting the gospel in Berea. They as usual begin by going to the Jewish synagogue, but here they receive a much better reception.

Verse 11 is one of my favorite passages, as it expresses how everyone, believer and nonbeliever alike, should approach the Scriptures. The Jews in that town "were of more noble character than those in Thessalonica," meaning they were tolerant and open to what the team was saying without allowing prejudice to cloud their judgment. In fact, they were not just willing but "eager" to hear what Paul and Silas had to say. Clearly they had a deep desire for truth and wanted to judge for themselves. The Spirit had made them ready for the gospel message, and they gladly listened. Like them, we all should seek truth and be open to what the text is actually saying, not read into the passage what we want it to say.

As they listened, they "examined the Scriptures every day to see if what Paul said was true." They prayerfully listened and judged point by point what they were being told. As before Paul reasoned and interacted with them "every day," and they were always eager to hear more and assimilate the truth content after examining it. Synagogues were not just places of worship but centers of study as well, so they never reacted against the scriptural proof Paul elucidated but rather thought carefully and openly to ascertain the logical message it contained. They at all times wished to determine whether the points made were "true."

As often before (16:14; 17:4) many became believers, even a large "number of prominent Greek women and many Greek men" (17:12). They could have been God-fearers, or perhaps this means the team proclaimed the gospel in the marketplace as well. At any rate, there is noticeable success from the start there. As so often, the message of Christ and salvation appeal across the social spectrum to the elite as well as the poor.

However, once more the success is short-lived. The Thessalonian Jews hear of their success, and just as with Antioch and Iconium in Galatia (14:19) they then travel to Berea, "agitating the crowds and stirring them up" (17:13). Their opposition had worked once; they assume it will work again, and it does. As often, "the word of God" is the gospel message, for while it is not Scripture itself, every word is based on Scripture.

The Christians capitulate once more (17:14), not wishing to stir up more persecution than they have to. This time, though, only Paul leaves, for the Bereans are a young church and need to be better grounded in their faith. So they send Paul to the coast, accompanied by several of the faithful (v. 15) who apparently want to place him on a ship to be taken to safety. Because Mount Olympus stands in the way of traveling by land, the regular way for going to Athens is by sea (a two-hundred-mile journey). Luke assumes his readers will know this and doesn't mention the sea journey here. Paul's escorts bring him to Athens (17:15), and when they return shortly after, Paul sends a message to Silas and Timothy to join him there as soon as possible.

From 1 Thessalonians 3:1-2 we see that the two do rejoin
Paul in Athens briefly, but Timothy is sent back to Thessalonica
to "strengthen and encourage" the Christians there while Silas
is apparently sent on an errand somewhere in Macedonia (perhaps Philippi). The persecution in Thessalonica has become quite
severe, and the Christians there need all the help they can get.
They finally rejoin him for good in Corinth (18:5). Nothing is ever
said about Berea again, and we don't know why. The people there
were so receptive, and on the surface it seems an ideal town for
producing a strong church. Moreover, Silas was left there to help
the church there to grow mature. It might just be chance that Paul
never mentions Berea again. It is one of those mysteries that will
ever go unsolved.

PAUL MINISTERS IN ATHENS (17:16-34)

Paul reaches the province of Achaia and begins in Athens by himself, with no one from his team accompanying him, due to the
situation at Thessalonica. Paul seems strangely reluctant, seemingly almost too shy to proclaim the gospel in this hometown of
thinkers and philosophers. As an intellectual and yet superstitious city (with all the temples and idols), the populace knew
little about Judaism, so the sermon here is brilliantly conceived
(worthy of Athens in the quality of its reasoning) and shows
Paul's undoubted training in Greek rhetoric from his growing up
in Tarsus. He deeply understands the pagan mind and crafts a
well-reasoned presentation of the Creator God and his relationship with humankind.[2]

---

2. However, it is also common to think Paul could not have written this,
and that it is a creation of Luke himself, because the pessimistic tone of
Romans 1:18-32 and the optimistic tone here are too dissimilar. However,
when we look at the Romans passage in the context of Romans 1-3, it is not
so pessimistic as people think, for the total depravity there makes way for
God's work of salvation in the larger context. Paul was a brilliant thinker who

It is very difficult to ascertain Paul's intentions in going to Athens. Was it on the planned itinerary all along, or was he there only as an accident of timing as he waited for his associates? It has been common for scholars to think he was there only by happenstance and did not plan to establish a church in Athens. The tone is quite different from that which he uses in the other towns on this missionary journey, and the fact is that no local *ekklēsia* resulted from his time in Athens, although the results were generally encouraging. (The two converts named here is a higher number than in any of the other towns on this trip.) Athens is mentioned only once more in the New Testament (1 Thess 3:1: "we thought it best to be left by ourselves in Athens"), and so the same mystery that attends Berea surrounds attempts to determine the success or failure of Christianity in Athens. I agree with those who see limited success. Paul did not fail in Athens, and this message deserves its place in the pantheon of brilliant sermons.

Setting in the Synagogue and Marketplace (17:16–17)

At the start Paul seems passive, just "waiting" for Silas and Timothy. I doubt that he planned to leave as soon as they arrived, and in fact that did not happen, for he immediately sent them on other errands (see on 17:15 above). He was probably waiting to begin ministry there together with the other two (but needs in Thessalonica and Berea interrupted that as well). At any rate, while he is waiting he notices how the city is "full of idols." Athens was for five hundred years considered the intellectual center of the Greek world, and virtually every great philosopher either was born there or migrated there. It was a city of only thirty thousand inhabitants, but it may have had two to three times that many statues and idols in it. Paul had grown up in another major city, Tarsus, but never

---

contextualized the gospel perfectly for different cultural and intellectual contexts, and this Areopagus address is a perfect example of that.

imagined a town with that many idols and temples. So Paul is greatly "distressed," even annoyed.

Paul's ministry plan is interesting. In most towns he would go to the Jewish synagogues and spend some time there and only then go into the agora, or marketplace. Here, however, he proclaims the gospel in both at the same time, probably in the synagogues on Sabbaths and then in the marketplace during the week, reaching out to Jews, God-fearers, and Greeks together. Yet Luke never discusses the results of his synagogue sermons, centering entirely on his time with the **Hellenists** and philosophers of Athens. The agora was the central square of the Hellenistic city, and all visiting philosophers and teachers gravitated there to speak to the citizens who came both to shop for goods and to listen. It was the commercial and entertainment center at one and the same time. These speakers provided some of the primary entertainment of the day and drew large crowds.

DEBATES WITH PHILOSOPHERS AND THE AREOPAGUS (17:18-21)

It was common in the central plaza for the various philosophical schools to "debate" or discuss various issues that arise from the differences in their outlooks, and these became quite popular for the people of Athens. The two main schools of thought in the first century are named here. The "Epicureans" (followers of Epicurus, 341-270 BC) were the agnostics of their day, believing that the gods had nothing to do with human affairs and just found happiness by themselves. So pleasure or happiness is the highest good and means remaining free of excess living and of fear, avoiding tension and pain. The Stoics (followers of Zeno, 340-265 BC) were materialists and pantheists who believed the world consisted of material objects infused by divinity that held everything together. The rational side of humankind is the highest faculty and virtue is the highest good. To achieve that people must live in harmony with nature and make good, rational choices.

Their reaction to Paul's preaching is not very positive. Many considered him merely a "babbler," a term that builds on the image of birds scavenging for seeds, picturing Paul picking up bits and pieces of ideas and throwing them together in haphazard fashion. Others are closer to Paul's actual teaching when they accuse him of "advocating foreign gods," recognizing the religious content but failing to realize its origin. They could not understand the Jewish background even though there were synagogues in Athens. They considered the Jews unworthy of their attention. It is possible, as some surmise, that they didn't consider Yahweh a foreign deity because of this presence of Judaism in Athens, and that they thought Paul was introducing two new gods—Jesus and Anastasis (resurrection), seen in the added comment, "They said this because Paul was preaching the good news about *Jesus and the resurrection*." This is quite possible but difficult to prove. Either way, they do not understand what Paul is talking about and can't put his message into any system of thought they know.

The laws were quite strict against endangering the traditional gods of Athens by introducing "foreign gods," so those who were gathered there had to bring Paul before "a meeting of the Areopagus" to ascertain if he had broken any laws (17:19). This was not an arrest. It was a required meeting to see if the city should allow him to continue proclaiming his foreign deities. The Areopagus was not just the name of the district of the city (Mars Hill) but the name of the major administrative council of the city that met there and decided civil and civic issues as they arose.

The council had two questions for him, both of them related to the "new teaching" and "strange ideas" that were being propounded. It is hard to distinguish whether this is a positive scene, with the people wanting to hear more, or negative, with the council judging the legality of this preaching as well as the competence of this new unknown speaker. Probably it was a little of each. There is more curiosity than animosity on this occasion; it is not a trial but a hearing.

Luke's parenthetical comment about the Athenian propensity for centering on "new things" (NIV, "latest ideas") points us to a more positive view of the scene here. Scholars are divided whether this is a critique denigrating them as the true "babblers" rather than Paul or a more neutral comment showing that they are open and interested, truly curious about the new teaching. Once more, there are likely aspects of both at play. Athenians were famous for their love of innovation, but at the same time this was a serious examination by the city council to determine if these "latest ideas" should be allowed in Athens.

THE AREOPAGUS ADDRESS (17:22–31)

Paul is often pictured standing on the brow of the hill with the crowds below him, but he is actually standing in the middle of the council itself and addressing the members. His introductory "men of Athens" is addressed to the council, which was composed entirely of men, but there were both men and women in the crowds, so I agree with the NIV, "people of Athens." The first comment was recognized often by outsiders. The adjective *deisidaimonesterous* can mean "very religious" or "very superstitious." In this instance the positive side is stressed, referring to the incredible number of temples, altars, and idols throughout the city.

Paul has the perfect sermon intro: "For as I walked around and looked carefully at your objects of worship, I even found an altar with this inscription: TO AN UNKNOWN GOD." They wanted to make certain that no god could be offended by being ignored in their city, so any god not mentioned in the city is "unknown" and can now feel included. The vast number of idols and altars are meant to be comprehensive, showing the extreme piety of the Athenian people. So with that altar the people no longer need to worry that a god might be offended.

His next point is critical: "So you are ignorant of the very thing you worship—and this is what I am going to proclaim to you." He is defining his "foreign god" as the actual "unknown god" on the altar, a brilliant ploy, saying in effect, "the unknown god is Yahweh, the God I am proclaiming to you, the Christian God I am going to tell you about. You don't know him, but now I am going to introduce him to you." The Athenians are being pictured as searching, and Paul wants to lead to the one who will satisfy their longing.

In verses 24–25, Paul makes four declarations about the personhood of God. First, he is "Lord of heaven and earth," seen in the fact that he "made the world and everything in it." This is monotheism at its best, the truth of the one God who alone created "heaven and earth" and governs it as its Lord. The emphasis on "everything" shows how false the Greek view of the pantheon of gods actually is. For them, each god is one aspect of nature, but the Christian God is Lord of every single thing in this world. Still, the Stoics had similar ideas, as the gods created this world and ruled over it. So Paul is building on some parallels.

Second, this God who is Lord of all "does not live in temples built by human hands," the same point Stephen made in 7:48. The Stoics would agree with this, but at first glance it would seem to contradict Solomon's temple as God's house. The point of both Stephen and Paul is still valid, however, for God's omnipresence cannot be *restricted* to a temple. God is not dependent on anything human beings can do; he is sovereign Lord over all creation.

Third, God "is not served by human hands, as if he needed anything" (17:25). We mere mortals answer to him; he doesn't answer to us. This is closely connected to the previous point. He needs nothing that we can provide. Scholars often note the liturgical language here, pointing to sacrifices and offerings by which we give service to God. He does not need our worship; rather, it is our privilege and joy to give him our worship.

Fourth, he "gives everyone life and breath and everything else." The Creator God sustains life in this world and is the source of all we need for life. The breath of life is in keeping with the Stoics but obviously stems from Genesis 2:7 and the robust creation theology of the Jews.

In verse 24 God is Creator of everything in the world, and in verse 26 he is Creator of humanity. Paul doesn't allude to Genesis 1:27-28 or mention Adam, but all he says obviously stems from there. The idea of all humankind stemming "from one man" has no parallel in Hellenistic thinking or mythology, so this is truly "new" (v. 21). Paul adds that it is from this common ancestor that "all the nations" have their unity as well. So every nation and every person inhabiting them is brought together in the one God Paul is espousing.

Moreover, as the human race inhabits the whole earth, God "marked out their appointed times in history," meaning the "seasons" or established times. Paul likely has two things in mind, the seasons of the years as every person passes through life, and the seasons or epochs by which God governs and controls the nations and their appointed time on earth.

Paul adds that God appoints the "boundaries of their lands," not only when but also where they exist on earth. This is the doctrine of divine providence, held by the Greeks as well as the Jews. Each and every nation and each and every person inhabiting draws their very existence from the mercy of the God who governs how they live and where they live. Genesis 10-11 discusses how God orders the nations, and in the Song of Moses the Most High "divided all mankind" and "set up boundaries for the peoples" (Deut 32:8). Corporately as nations and individually as people, life is initiated and governed by God. On this second point, the Stoics would agree with Paul.

The next verse (17:27) is also a distinctly Christian (and Jewish) point, that God's providence does all this "so that they would seek him and perhaps reach out for him and find him." The gods of the Greeks were not social beings in terms of seeking fellowship with their creation. They were capricious, often aloof and overall indifferent to humanity. The progress of thought here is significant, moving from seeking to reaching and then finding God. This is the gospel message, picturing God reaching out and humankind finding him.

In fact, the flip side is actually the main point. Paul assumes that these council members and all who are listening are actually searching for and wanting to find God. As God seeks humanity, humanity at the same time seeks him. The Jews thought of this social side of salvation as unique to them: God was their covenant God, as defined by his relationship with his people. God is near, and he asks only that people reach out for him as he cares for them. Paul is offering that possibility to his listeners. They have always experienced God through his creation, and now it is time that they be reconciled and experience him personally.

This social God who created this world and who desires that his creation seek and find him must be understood by his created beings. Paul grounds this in two quotations in verse 28. First, Epimenides of Crete (600 BC) states that our very being is defined in him: "In him we live and move and have our being." Paul is saying that it should be a simple thing to seek and find God, for in reality our entire existence is caught up in him. He is near in every way it counts, so all any human being has to do is open one's self up to life in its fullest, and they will find him. Every aspect—we are living beings, we move about of our own free will; we "have our being," or exist as autonomous creatures—is a reality because God is there and makes it possible. In this sense we don't have to work at finding him. He is there always, and we relate to him by the very fact that we are living beings. The council would have understood the "in him" in a pantheistic manner, as it was a key aspect of Stoic thought.

Second, Aratus of Cilicia (300 BC) said, "We are his offspring," going further to say we are not only near to him but related to him as kin. Since we belong to the human family, we belong to God and are his children. Again, those present would have understood this in a pantheistic sense, that God is in all of us. Paul, however, understood it quite differently, in terms of the Old Testament doctrine of creation. He wants to build on common ground and erect larger truths on the foundation of partial truth here. They understood it in terms of the spark of divinity in all of us, Paul in terms of the creation of the "one man" (v. 26) from whom all others came. It is not divine essence but divine creation that defines our existence.

Paul then applies this (17:29) to the rampant idolatry that offended him earlier (17:16, 23) and uses this observation to conclude this second part of his address: "Since we are God's offspring, we should not think that the divine being is like gold or silver or stone—an image made by human design and skill." While this is directed at the idolatrous overkill of Athens, his listeners would have largely been in agreement. The fact that we are God's offspring should put the lie to any thought that God can be confined to human-made objects of mere precious metals or stone, a stance that all Epicureans and Stoics agreed with, although they accommodated the prevalent idolatry in practice. Paul with his Jewish background is more consistent and less hypocritical than his philosophical counterparts here, and they too did not wish to think this way, though in actual practice they did.

The final point of his address is no longer merely theoretical in nature but hortatory, a call for repentance. This would have been surprising to the council, who were expecting to decide whether to allow Paul and his brand of rhetoric into Athens. Instead, Paul calls them to become followers of his religious movement. They were not expecting a prophet who would speak for the God he represents. He is saying that this Creator is also a Judge, and that the gods the Athenians worship are not gods at all. This God has "overlooked such ignorance" as found in Athens (the city that more than any in the world prided itself on the depth of its knowledge!) but no more. Now he "commands all people everywhere to repent." Paul is no longer worried about their decision regarding the "foreign gods" he supposedly preaches (v. 18), for the God he proclaims is the one God and Creator of everything in Athens, the only God who exists or matters. To the Athenians this would have been a new cult like any of the mystery religions, but for Paul this is supreme truth, and he asks the council and other onlookers there not to vote to accept him but to repent and turn to this one God.

Everything that the council represents partakes of the "times of ignorance" (*tous chronous tēs agnoias*; NIV: "such ignorance") that God has allowed in the past but will no longer overlook. In the speech thus far Paul has allowed his listeners to misconstrue what he has said, but now he demands that they realize the implications of the one Creator God and the one man through whom all humankind came. The "times of ignorance" have now become "times of repentance," for God will no longer fail to punish them for their failure of awareness.

The time of accounting has come: God "has set a day when he will judge the world with justice by the man he has appointed" (17:31). The mission God has launched to the world is not just a presentation of the possibility of salvation but also a rescue from and a warning of what will happen to those who fail to repent. To "judge the world with justice" is very strong language for the day of final judgment, a Jewish doctrine that the Athenians would not have understood. They had the Furies and wraiths of judgment but not a final day set in the divine calendar of history. The "appointed times" of verse 26 includes a time of final judgment in which every person will give account of their lives to the divine Judge on his *bēma*, or throne of judgment. So there is a new seriousness to the call for repentance, with eternity at stake.

The appointment of "the man" and the proof given "to everyone by raising him from the dead" would also have been entirely foreign to these Hellenists. The Greeks did not allow any concept of physical resurrection, and the after-death thinking they entertained was completely connected to the idea of the immortality of the soul but not of the body. The Athenians would have been aghast at Paul's suggesting such a thing as the resurrection of Jesus' body from the dead. Still, Paul argues not just that it has taken place but that it proves Jesus is the one appointed with authority to judge all humankind. The council members must have been reeling, as Paul never developed or explained all this about Jesus but just expected them to assimilate it.

REACTION AND AFTERMATH (17:32–34)

As one would expect, the idea of physical resurrection from the dead caused many of those in the audience to sneer and scoff, for such was actually offensive to the Greek assumption that after death only the soul passed on and crossed the River Styx to the Elysian fields. The body was evil, and when it died, it was gone. The council was tracking with him until this point, but now many of them ridiculed him for this offensive suggestion. To them death should be the final end. Still, there were a few others who remained curious for more and said, "We want to hear you again on this subject."

Paul at that point leaves the council, and we never hear what the final vote was. Still, it doesn't appear to have been negative, and he and his Christian followers were probably allowed to continue in Athens. No church is reported to have been founded there, but the number of followers is fairly remarkable in comparison with elsewhere. As a result of his ministry there, several "became followers of Paul and believed," which may indicate implicitly that a house church was formed. The Greek says they "joined" Paul (*kollēthentes*), which could imply they became not just "followers of Paul" but joined the church as well.

In addition, two distinguished converts are mentioned, the one "Dionysius, a member of the Areopagus," or council. Eusebius later said he became the first "bishop" of the church there (*Ecclesiastical History* 3.4.10). Second, a prominent woman named Damaris believed. It was not normal for women or wives to attend such gatherings, but there is a chance she was a wealthy woman or wife of some standing in the city and was there.

The main thing is that Luke ends the narration of Paul's time in Athens by pointing to limited success and perhaps the beginnings of a church there. However, the lack of any mention of a house church and the note in 1 Corinthians 16:15 that the household of Stephanas in Corinth constituted "the first converts [firstfruits] in Achaia" could indicate that no actual house church came into being there. My own feeling is that in 1 Corinthians Paul was discussing the immediate environs of Corinth and not Athens, and that there is a good chance there was a house church established in Athens. But I can go no further.

———

Under the leading of the Spirit, the mission team continues to bring the gospel to Macedonia, continuing the promise of 1:8 to be witnesses "to the ends of the earth." Following the superhighway the Ignatian Way, they move out first to Thessalonica, the capital of the province, and we get a glance of the early church's evangelistic method (vv. 1–9).

They begin with the Jewish people. Paul spends several weeks in synagogues both preaching in services and reasoning there and in homes the rest of the time, proving that the Scriptures point forward to Jesus as the Jewish Messiah, and that in light of these they must repent and believe in him to receive new life from God. This goes well at first, but the unbelieving Jews stir up the rabble against the Christian evangelists, and after the riot they are forced to flee before they are ready. Much of the next few weeks (even while in Athens) are spent trying to anchor the Christians of Thessalonica in their faith.

Paul then goes to Berea (vv. 10–15), where the Jews are quite different from the Thessalonians and remain open to the true message of Scripture. The church is formed there easily and begins to grow, but troublesome Jews appear from Thessalonica and again Paul is forced to leave, going by ship to Athens, where he waits for them to join him.

Paul spends the first days in Athens waiting for Timothy and Silas to arrive, but he cannot remain silent for long (vv. 15–21). The incredible proliferation of idols and shrines perturbs him, and he has to speak out. The early interaction is mixed. Some think him a mere seed-picker and uninteresting, but others are ready to hear more and take him before the Areopagus, the city council, to determine how worthy he is.

The speech itself (vv. 22–31) is brilliantly conceived, as Paul begins (vv. 22–23) by using a statue dedicated to "an unknown god" and telling them that he plans to unveil the identity of that God. The main body of his speech consists of relating that this God is the Creator God who is sovereign over everything and gives breath to all living things (vv. 24–25). He then turns to what this God does: he is not the aloof god of the Greeks but the covenant God of the Jews and Christians, reaching out so humankind can find him (vv. 26–27). This would indeed have been a foreign idea to the Greeks.

Paul now uses two quotations to prove his point (vv. 28–29). From Epimenides of Crete he proves that humankind finds God in the very process of moving through life, as he is an integral part of our very existence. Then from Aratus of Cilicia he establishes the truth that we are actually related to him as kin, being part of God's family. There is thus no need for idols of wood or stone, for we relate to God directly.

His conclusion (vv. 30–31) would have been startling, calling for repentance on the part of every listener in light of the fact that God (and Jesus) is the eternal Judge and that a day of final judgment is coming. The latter was not part of Greek thinking, and the idea of Jesus physically rising from the dead would have been even more foreign.

The aftermath and future of the church in Athens are difficult to determine, for Luke tells us little (vv. 32–34). The results of Paul's speech were positive, and the two distinguished followers and positive tone in general likely means Paul was allowed to stay, and that there was at least a house church established there. We can go no further, and it is strange that Athens is not really mentioned again.

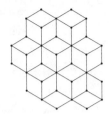

MISSION IN CORINTH
AND AFTERMATH
(18:1–22)

C orinth, the other major city of the province of Achaia (with Athens), receives the same length of treatment as Athens. This is the final city that ends this particular missionary journey, and it becomes the thorn in Paul's side, giving him an enormous number of headaches due to their opposition to him and secular approach to church life. Paul spent about eighteen months there in AD 50–51, and Corinth became the center of church life for Achaia in the same way it had been named capital of the newly established province in AD 44. After a rebellion, the Romans destroyed it in 146 BC, and there was no city until Julius Caesar resurrected it in 44 BC and colonized it with retired veterans. It became a thriving commercial center of about 100,000 (though some estimates range as high as 200,000 or even 300,000) and, while statements of its rampant immorality were overblown, it was a very secular place, and its outlook made it a difficult church to lead, as Paul found out.

PAUL SPEAKS IN THE CORINTHIAN
SYNAGOGUE (18:1-4)

Corinth was about fifty miles from Athens and lay at a cross-roads for trade goods to be shipped into the province. It was a

natural destination for the mission team and contained a great
many resources for church growth. Shortly after arriving Paul met
two leading Jewish Christians, Aquila and Priscilla, who had been
expelled by the emperor Claudius the year before (AD 49) along
with many others due to riots by the Jews against the Christians
there. They were originally from Pontus, which with Bithynia
became a single Roman province. Paul most likely met them as a
result of his tentmaking and leatherwork. In Corinth they owned
the business in which he labored. He often supported himself, as
rabbis had been taught to do, with the cloth and leatherworking
that his home area of Cilicia was famous for (see 1 Cor 4:12; 2 Cor
11:7; 1 Thess 2:9). In all three cities where they worked beside Paul—
Corinth, Ephesus (18:18-19), and then back in Rome (Rom 16:3, 5)—
their large homes were used as house churches. They returned
to Rome when Claudius died in AD 55 and his edict was no longer
in effect.

At the outset Paul followed his basic plan, speaking in the synagogues every Sabbath and "trying to persuade Jews and Greeks"
(18:4). This likely went on for quite a while and was successful.
By "persuade," Luke means both to convince them of the truth
of the gospel message and to bring them to Christ. What we don't
know was whether Paul's ministry with Greeks referred to those
who were a part of synagogue life (God-fearers) or an evangelistic ministry in the agora alongside the one in the synagogues on
Sabbaths. I expect the latter, for his secular work was always connected to his gospel ministry.

PAUL IS REJECTED AND TURNS
TO THE GENTILES (18:5-8)

Silas and Timothy have been gone for some time on errands to
Berea and possibly Philippi (see on 17:15), but they finally return.
They bring much-needed financial help from the Macedonian
churches (2 Cor 11:9; Phil 4:15), enabling Paul to leave secular work

for a time, and he "devoted himself exclusively to preaching" and ministry, once more trying to persuade people that Jesus was indeed the Messiah the Old Testament said would come.

As always, Jewish opposition began to erupt (18:6), and it became vicious and "abusive," with scurrilous attacks. They caused increasing trouble to the point that synagogue ministry became a virtual impossibility. So Paul followed Jesus' prescription from Luke 10:11 (and Acts 13:51) to shake the dust off his clothes as a prophetic curse of judgment (Neh 5:13) showing that they had brought it down upon themselves: "Your blood be on your own heads! I am innocent of it." Paul bore no responsibility for the divine judgment that would pour down on them. Part of the judgment will be the absence of any opportunity to repent, for "from now on I will go to the Gentiles." The time of the Jewish people in Corinth is past, and it is time for Gentile repentance.

Paul then put that judgment into practice and left the synagogue (18:7), moving his teaching ministry next door (so that all could see the meaning clearly) to the house of Titius Justus, a God-fearer who had become a believer. He had made his home available to serve as a house church and center for the gospel in Corinth. The Jews who had rejected Paul could see the results of their foolishness every day as Paul turned the gospel ministry over entirely to converting the Gentiles.

At the same time, the Jews lost the president of their synagogue, Crispus, who with his entire household came to faith in the Lord (17:8). He would have been the leading and most pious Jew in the region. His conversion is important enough that Paul mentions baptizing him in 1 Corinthians 1:14. He undoubtedly was just as important a leader in the church as he had been in the synagogue. Finally, Luke tells of "many ... Corinthians," probably Jews as well as Gentiles, who "believed and were baptized." In other words, in spite of all the troubles, Paul began with a successful ministry in Corinth.

PAUL RECEIVES AN ENCOURAGING
VISION (18:9-11)

There had been enough negative signs that Paul was beginning to get discouraged, especially after his difficult time in Athens. In 1 Corinthians 2:3 he says, "I came to you in weakness with great fear and trembling." All the opposition and rejection he faced in Corinth didn't help, and compounding this was probably trouble in the churches as well. So God sends him an encouraging vision: "Do not be afraid; keep on speaking, do not be silent. For I am with you, and no one is going to attack and harm you." Paul is enduring tremendous pressure and under serious danger, but with the Lord on his side there is no need to fear.

The command to stop being afraid reminds me of Joshua, Israel's great general, who knew no fear militarily but was terrified to take over for Moses. God told him several times, "Have I not commanded you? Be strong and courageous. Do not be afraid; do not be discouraged, for the LORD your God will be with you wherever you go" (Josh 1:9; see also Deut 31:6; Josh 1:5-6, 7, 18). Jeremiah comes to mind as well, as God at his commissioning responded to his feelings of inadequacy by telling him, "Do not be afraid of them, for I am with you and will rescue you" (Jer 1:8; also 15:21). Every great leader must fight through terror and find courage. Like Joshua and Paul, we must all make ourselves aware of the presence of the Lord in our lives when we face seemingly insurmountable odds.

Paul was weary of the continued attacks and opposition against his ministry, so Jesus (the Lord here) commands him to "keep on speaking" and refuse to be "silent" in the midst of it all. Corinth must continue to hear the gospel, and the verbal attacks are irrelevant in light of that. Christ and his Spirit indwell him and will empower everything he says and does. The Lord's words "No one is going to attack and harm you" should be translated "When people attack you, they will not harm you." Slander and lies will always be spread against us, but nothing they say will matter. As 1 Peter 4:14

says, "If you are insulted because of the name of Christ, you are blessed, for the Spirit of glory and of God rests on you." God does not tell us that there will never be hatred and suffering, but rather that they will come to naught. As 1 Peter 1:11 puts it so well, this concerns our sharing in "the sufferings of the Messiah and the glories that would follow."

Then Jesus adds, "I have many people in this city." Paul so far has just begun tapping the spiritual resources in Corinth, and there are many conversions yet to come. The result is that Paul receives the strength to continue ministering there (Acts 18:11), and he stays eighteen months, "teaching them the word of God." This pattern will be repeated in Ephesus as well (19:8–10). Strong opposition, as we have seen throughout Acts, produces even stronger divine reaction and results in a strengthening of gospel resolve and even greater numbers coming to the Lord.

PAUL APPEARS BEFORE THE PROCONSUL GALLIO (18:12–17)

The vision was perfectly timed, for the opposition was increasing in intensity. The Lord had promised that no lasting harm would result, not that no charges against Paul would be raised. The animosity of the Jews reaches new heights, and they try a new strategy, going to the Roman proconsul rather than to the rabble. In other words, now Paul is facing legal opposition, as his opponents bring up official charges similar to Jesus before Pilate. Rather than bring him to trial before a city ruler, which would affect the immediate area alone, they realize a Roman governor's decision would have ramifications for the entire province. This was a senatorial province and so was ruled by a proconsul appointed by the Roman senate (see 13:7). Gallio was the brother of the philosopher Seneca and was proconsul from AD 51 to 52, one of the settled dates that allow us to work out the dating of events in Acts. He was very popular with both his coworkers and the people of Achaia but had to leave early due to illness.

The Jews probably reasoned that a new governor would be more amenable toward their charges and so tried a "united attack," feeling numbers would impress Gallio. Again, this was a legal attack not a physical riot. They "brought" or hauled Paul before the *bēma*, or "place of judgment." This was an actual judicial bench in the city forum where cases were held.

Their charge (18:13) is difficult to ascertain with precision, for when we read "persuading the people to worship God in ways contrary to the law," we must ask whether they are speaking of Jewish or Roman law. One would think Jewish in light of those making the charge, but Gallio wouldn't have heard any Jewish cases, for his entire concern was Roman law. Yet his response in 17:15 shows he understands the charges as Jewish law. I think it likely that both "laws" are meant. These Christians were threatening the Jewish right to worship the way they pleased, and the riots in Rome, with which Gallio would have been quite familiar, exemplified the threat to public order that Paul now represented.

However, when does worship constitute sedition, especially since the many Roman cults and the mystery religions were allowed? Later Christianity was called atheistic and outlawed at times because they didn't believe in the Roman gods, but at this early stage they were considered a Jewish sect and allowed because Judaism was exempted from coerced worship of the Roman gods. Perhaps the Jewish leaders were trying to disconnect Christianity from themselves and get it condemned as an "illicit religion" (not a *collegium licitum*). This makes some sense.

This was a pretrial hearing in which Gallio listened and decided whether he would hear the case, so all the details have not yet come out. Still, he interrupts Paul and responds immediately (17:14–15). He doesn't need to hear anything else, so he renders his verdict now. If it concerned "some misdemeanor or serious crime" against Rome (literally a "serious case of fraud" against the government), he would hear the case and proceed to trial. But it is neither. It is nothing more than "questions about words and names and your own law," namely, issues about Jewish laws and theological debates. There is nothing here, he is saying, that infringes on Roman legal issues, so this has nothing to do with him.

This is a very important legal verdict, for it establishes the Roman precedent that Christianity should be treated as a Jewish sect and have the same rights and privileges that Jews have in Roman law. Moreover, problems with mainstream Judaism are to be treated as internal issues to Judaism and to be decided by their own courts, not Roman law. The Corinthian Jews had taken a chance and lost big time. This verdict was the complete reversal of their hopes to brand Christianity as an illicit religion.

Two anti-Semitic acts follow, showing that Gallio's verdict was not entirely attributable to his legal wisdom. First, he didn't just dismiss the case, showing respect for both sides. He "drove them off." The language shows disrespect. Second, the **Hellenistic** crowd grabs Sosthenes, president of the synagogue, and beats him right in front of Gallio, who "showed no concern whatever." Sosthenes was probably the one who succeeded Crispus as synagogue ruler and who headed the delegation that brought the charges against Paul before Gallio.[1] So some think the crowd consisted of Jews who were angry at Sosthenes for his poor handling of the case. While possible, I don't think that makes as much sense as this being a scene of anti-Semitic behavior.

PAUL TRAVELS TO EPHESUS, JERUSALEM, AND ANTIOCH (18:18–22)

Paul remained in Corinth only "for some time" (Greek: "a number of days"), possibly, as some think, until the weather cleared and he could travel by boat. (During winter the winds were unfavorable.) He had decided it was time to get back to Antioch of Syria

---

1. It is possible to equate this Sosthenes with that believer in 1 Cor 1:1 who had a part in the writing of 1 Corinthians. If so, that would mean that he later also became a Christian.

and report, plus he wanted to visit Jerusalem. He must have left Silas and Timothy in Corinth, for he traveled only with Priscilla and Aquila. Likely the problems that dominate the two Corinthian letters were beginning, and Paul wanted to leave them to try to gain some control in that most difficult church. Luke does not spend a lot of time on this, so we cover about 1,800 miles in just a few verses.

Preaching the gospel there was quite successful, and there was a sizable number of believers in Corinth. However, there were also quite a few elite, educated, and wealthy among the converts, and many of these were caught up in Greek rhetoric and sophistry, thinking that Paul was an inferior teacher and preacher because he didn't match up to the Hellenistic traditions of logic and language.[2] They were what we often call "carnal Christians," more secular than Christian in outlook and thinking, and they denigrated Paul at every opportunity.

So Paul ends his lengthy stay and leaves for Antioch, also planning a quick visit to Jerusalem due to the vow he will be making at Cenchreae. This was the harbor and port city of Corinth, only a seven-mile walk from there. A church had apparently been founded there during the stay in Corinth (Phoebe was a deacon, Rom 16:1), and Paul decides to take a vow there, probably in light of the trip ahead but possibly also in thanks for God working things out in Corinth. I think both aspects were behind the decision.

We don't know for certain what kind of vow this was. It could have been a simple thanksgiving for all God did in Corinth, but more likely it is a Nazirite vow (Num 6:1–21) in light of the comment that "he had his hair cut off." This was a vow of dedication asking God to intervene and protect him, and it involved not only cutting the hair (at the outset then at the end, giving that hair as an offering to God in Jerusalem) but also abstinence from wine and

---

2. Many think these problems did not arise for a year or so yet. If that is the case, Silas and Timothy are simply left behind to stabilize the new church there.

fermented drinks, staying away from dead bodies, then presenting sacrifices and offerings to the Lord in Jerusalem.

So they sailed first to Ephesus, across the Aegean and a little
north. Priscilla and Aquila[3] have also decided to move and apparently are planning to take residence in Ephesus and start a
church there. That is the reason for the stop in that city. They
either already own a home there or purchase one after arriving.
It becomes a house church for the growing number of converts
(1 Cor 16:19).

Paul clearly did not plan to stay too long but went into the synagogue and "reasoned with the Jews," language that means to present Jesus as the Jewish Messiah and debate the Jews there over the
truth of that claim (see 17:2, 17; 18:4). Presenting the gospel involves
both evangelistic preaching and apologetic reasoning. Ephesus
was another great city of the Roman world, with about a quarter
million inhabitants, the incredible temple to Artemis/Diana (one
of the seven wonders of the ancient world), and a major center
for trade and commerce.

The Jews there ask him to remain longer (18:20); this is surprising, as it is one of the few times they don't severely oppose
him and try to get rid of him. However, he is anxious to make it
to Jerusalem for Passover and then return to Syrian Antioch and
greet the churches there. So he declines, promising to return as
soon as God wills (18:21). As we know, that would be quite soon
and would dominate the next missionary journey (chapter 19).

He covers nearly a thousand miles in one verse (18:22), traveling by ship the six hundred miles to Caesarea then going down to
Jerusalem to greet the congregations there and then very quickly

---

3. The order of names in a list is usually based on status and importance. It
is quite unusual for a wife to be named first, but in the six occasions they are
mentioned Aquila is first twice (Acts 18:2; 1 Cor 16:19) and Priscilla four times
(Acts 18:18, 26; Rom 16:3; 2 Tim 4:19). We don't know why; some think Priscilla
came from a more important family, but possibly she had the greater ministry of the two of them.

going back up to Antioch in Syria (a 335-mile trip). He may be history's first jet-setter! He probably fulfilled his Nazirite vow while in Jerusalem and also reported on the exciting developments in the Gentile cities of Macedonia and Achaia. Then he quickly returns to Antioch in Syria, the mother church from which Paul and Barnabas were officially commissioned to begin the Gentile mission (13:1-3). Luke doesn't tell us what Paul did there, but it was certainly a report of all the exciting developments as the gospel spread quite strongly from Asia Minor to Macedonia and then Achaia. He stayed for "some time" (18:23), perhaps as much as a few weeks, and then left to resume his mission.

———

The Corinthian ministry began exactly like others, as Paul joined with two Jewish Christians from Rome, Priscilla and Aquila, and together conducted a successful time in the synagogues, producing many converts. There were several encouraging signs until opposition overflowed. This time the rejection was so fierce that Paul shook the dust off his feet (vv. 1-6) and turned to the Gentiles, going next door to the home of Titius Justus (vv. 7-8). Especially meaningful was the conversion of the Jewish leader there, Crispus.

At this time the Lord, knowing Paul needed encouragement, spoke to him in a vision and told him the Lord would watch over him and protect him (vv. 9-11). The principle is quite profound. As we unite more and more deeply with Christ, it means we will participate "in his sufferings" (Phil 3:10), but suffering is the path to glory, so the more we go through, the more we experience Christ in our lives and God's protective presence.

Here in Corinth the Jews try another tack, not rioting against the Christians and using the rabble to cause mob action, but instead bringing up charges against them in a Roman court of law with the proconsul of Achaia, Gallio (vv. 12-15). However, this backfires when Gallio considers it merely a Jewish issue and dismisses the case. Moreover, he shows his own true colors when he allows a couple of anti-Semitic events (vv. 16–17), including the beating of Sosthenes.

Paul wants to get to Jerusalem for Passover and so leaves Corinth, travels 1,800 miles in just a few verses, ends one missionary journey (vv. 18–22), then begins his last missionary journey (v. 23), to Ephesus. To begin the trip, he takes a Nazirite vow at Cenchreae, dedicating his travels to the Lord as a thank offering.

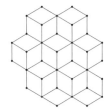

MISSION IN EPHESUS
(18:23–20:1)

Paul intended for this trip from Antioch through the churches of Asia Minor to Ephesus to be simply another step as he brought the gospel to the Roman world. He planned to make a fourth journey after this to Rome and then to the western half of the Roman world (Rom 15:23-24). However, in God's higher purposes this was to become the final missionary journey before Paul was arrested in Jerusalem and sent to Rome in chains, fulfilling God's will in an entirely new way. It would be the church as a whole and not just Paul and his team who would fulfill this call to a worldwide push toward all the nations. Still, this extended stay (two and a third years) in Ephesus was a critical part of the Gentile mission and demonstrated with a certain measure of finality the power of God and Christ over the pagan ways of the Roman world. As a center of magic in that part of the world, Ephesus became a powerful foretaste of the triumph of Christ and the mission of the church in God's universal mission to the world.

PAUL ENGAGES IN PRELIMINARY
MINISTRY (18:23-28)

The next missionary journey (commonly called the "third missionary journey," but see the introduction to chapter 13) begins when Paul leaves Antioch for the return to Asia Minor. He once again visits the churches he had established on his first journey into Asia Minor, his third follow-up visit overall (with 14:21-28; 16:1-5). Paul's concern to make certain the churches he had founded continued to grow is amazing. I remember being taught in college and seminary that when a pastor left a church they should cease all contact with it. I understand the reason for this but doubt the wisdom of it. Luke doesn't say, but on his way to Galatia, Paul likely also visited the churches of Syria and Cilicia (Acts 15:42; Gal 1:21-24). This adds another 800 miles to the travel itinerary, meaning 1,800 miles in two verses (18:22-23).

A remarkable young Jewish Christian named Apollos arrived in Ephesus shortly after Paul had been there in 18:19-21. He came from Alexandria, the second largest city in the empire, with 500,000 inhabitants, as many as 100,000 of them Jews. His résumé was impressive; he was well-trained and learned, adept in handling the Scriptures. Philo was from Alexandria, and it is likely that by "thorough knowledge," Luke means that he knew how to show the Old Testament expectation and promise of the coming Messiah as pointing to Jesus. Both in sermons and debates he used Scripture well.

We don't know how or where he was "instructed in the way of the Lord," but his training was also thorough. Some think he had emigrated to Judea, come into contact with the Baptist's followers, and been converted there. We will discuss this further below. Next, Luke tells us he "spoke with great fervor and taught about Jesus accurately," which could refer to his fiery enthusiasm when preaching. However, the Greek is "fervent in spirit," which some think is "fervent in the Spirit" (due to the articular *tō pneumati*), and would mean the Spirit had particularly gifted him for his ministry. The majority of scholars doubt this because it conflicts with the following "he knew only the baptism of John," obviously meaning "not the baptism of the Spirit." However, that is related to Apollos' knowledge while this is related to his spiritual gifts. So I think "fervent in Spirit" is the proper reading.

One wonders how it could have come to pass that Apollos was unaware of Pentecost and the gift of the Spirit. The best answer, suggested above, is that he had indeed found Christ in a group of the Baptist's disciples like those we will see below in 19:1–7. It is also possible that after the Baptist's death some of his disciples migrated to Alexandria, and it was they who had brought him to Christ. We simply cannot know. Some have doubted that he was a believer at this point, but the description of him in these verses definitely supports his having saving faith but somehow being unaware of Pentecost. To teach "about Jesus accurately" would have to include his sacrificial death and resurrection.

When he arrived in Ephesus, he like Paul went immediately to the Jewish synagogue and "began to speak boldly" about Christ (18:26). Priscilla and Aquila were present for his talk, realized his deficiency, then took him aside and "explained to him the way of God more adequately." His **Christology** and understanding of the gospel had been sufficient, and now his pneumatology and doctrine of spiritual gifts are more than sufficient as well. He now knows the full gospel.

Apollos' desire is to travel to Achaia and proclaim Christ. This likely means he didn't want to become a pastor of congregation(s) in Corinth but probably wished to become an itinerant missionary, taking the gospel to cities throughout that province. However, according to 1 Corinthians 1:12; 3:4–6, 22, Apollos did become in a sense the pastor of the Corinthian churches. The Christians there in Ephesus were very encouraging and even wrote letters of introduction to the churches in Corinth and the rest of the province so he would be welcomed.

Upon his arrival in Corinth he had a very successful ministry and proved "a great help to those who by grace had believed" (18:27). Luke wants us all to know that we have not become believers on our own initiative but are saved only by the grace of God. Apollos has become another grace gift of God to the Achaian Christians.

Both becoming a believer and growing in Christ are possible only on the basis of God's empowering presence.

That aid the church experiences from him is especially seen in his gospel ministry, as he "vigorously refuted his Jewish opponents in public debate" (18:28), re-creating the ministries of Stephen and Paul among the Jews. They have few answers as he peppers them with his knowledge of and facility with Scripture to support his claims that Jesus is indeed Messiah, Suffering Servant, and Savior. The verb for "refuted" (*diakatēlencheto*) means that he "overwhelmed" them in debate. The public nature probably refers to synagogue preaching on the Sabbath and reasoning in the synagogues during the week.

PAUL MINISTERS IN EPHESUS (19:1–20:1)

As Apollos was making a huge impact on the Jews of Corinth probably early in AD 52, Paul was on his way to Ephesus. The "interior" area of Asia Minor means the elevated regions and mountain passes of the Roman highway Via Sebaste through Galatia and Phrygia (18:23; see Acts 14). Paul was becoming quite familiar with this terrain and these cities.

THE DISCIPLES OF JOHN THE BAPTIST (19:1–7)

There he meets "some disciples" who are more seriously deficient than Apollos, for when Paul asks in verse 2, "Did you receive the Holy Spirit when you believed?" they respond, "No, we have not even heard that there is a Holy Spirit." Luke does not identify them, and there is significant debate as to their origins. Are they converts of Apollos before he was set right by Priscilla and Aquila (believers), or are they Jewish followers of John the Baptist (unbelievers)?

On the basis of their being called "disciples" (a term for Christians in Acts) and Paul's saying "when you believed," many conclude they were Christians but with a very strange background. However, they are completely ignorant about the Holy Spirit. It

is hard to conceive that this means the very existence of the Holy
Spirit, for Judaism knew about the Spirit (Isa 32:15; Ezek 39:29;
Joel 2:28–32), but they knew nothing else. Therefore many others
doubt very much that they could truly be believers, as their ignorance went beyond that of Apollos in 18:24–26. Paul was assuming
they were Christians, but most likely they weren't. The only baptism they had received was John's, so they were his disciples rather
than Jesus'. "What baptism did you receive?" is literally translated
"Into what were you baptized?" so they were unaware of Christian
baptism as well.

What Paul says next (19:4) shows his realization that he had
been wrong, for he presents the gospel with it, "John's baptism was
a baptism of repentance. He told the people to believe in the one
coming after him, that is, in Jesus." These "disciples" were unaware
of repentance (Luke 3:3, 8) and faith in Jesus (Luke 3:15–17), meaning they were not believers. Paul convinces them that their discipleship status was inadequate, and they apparently at this point
are converted and experience both repentance and faith-decision.

Their conversion is implicit here (Luke often does this), and
he reports the aftermath, that they are "baptized in the name of
the Lord Jesus" (19:5). The original description of baptism in the
Great Commission of Matthew 28:19 is "in the name of the Father
and of the Son and of the Holy Spirit," meaning "in union with
the Triune Godhead." Frequently it is abbreviated as here, but it
is more than just a formula. In baptism we become one with "the
Lord Jesus," and he becomes sovereign over our lives. In baptism
we are immersed in the Trinity and here in the lordship of Christ.

After their baptism, Paul lays hands on them (see 6:6; 13:3), and
"the Holy Spirit came on them," with the result that "they spoke in
tongues and prophesied." Romans 8:14–17 tells us the Spirit enters
every person when they come to faith and are converted, but this
is one of the special events initiating a new group coming into
God's family. In 8:17 it constituted the Samaritan Pentecost, and
in 10:44–46 it became the Gentile Pentecost. Here it may well be a

message to the many other followers of the Baptist who have not come to Christ, showing them that that is the true next step God wants them to take.

The fact that there were twelve men in all (19:7) is probably not meant to symbolically constitute a new "Twelve." Most likely it signifies a large new group joining the church, especially since twelve men were sufficient to start a new synagogue. The people of God continue to grow in significant ways.

Two Years of Ministry in Ephesus (19:8–20)

Paul's first three months followed his usual pattern of ministry in the synagogue, both preaching the gospel and defending the truths about Christ and the kingdom that has arrived with him. His message is that God's reign has begun in a new way with the coming of Jesus Messiah. This time he had a lengthy time of "freedom" to proclaim Christ, and once more it was quite successful, as many seem to have been persuaded. As usual, however, it ended when some of the Jews "became obstinate" (*esklērynonto*, "hardened themselves") and "maligned" (or "insulted"; literally, "spoke evil of") "the Way" (what they first called themselves, see 9:2). We have seen this with Jesus and Stephen too. Paul's opponents spread lies about Paul and the church, trying to turn people against them any way they could.

As Paul had done numerous times before, he turned his back on these hardened opponents and "left them" (as prescribed in Luke 10:11; Acts 13:51). In 18:7 he moved across the street from the synagogue to the home of Titius Justus. Here he and his "disciples" moved from the synagogue to a Gentile lecture hall owned by a Tyrannus. Such halls were equivalent to movie theaters today. They were places where people went during rest breaks from work, siesta, or free time in order to be entertained with lectures given by philosophers or speakers like Paul.

The Western family of manuscripts (for instance, Codex Bezae [D]) added the hours eleven in the morning to four in the afternoon, a logical period that fit the normal hours they would break from work due to the sun's heat. Luke didn't add this to his text, but most agree it makes sense and is more than possible. If Tyrannus was primary lecturer as well as owner of the building, this time during the heat of the midday would probably have been when he took his break as well, so Paul used it during this time.

This pattern of mornings and evenings working at his trade of tentmaking, and free time speaking at the lecture hall, Luke tells us, went on for two years (19:10), probably late AD 52 to 54/55. This lengthy period of uninterrupted, unopposed ministry bore incredible fruit. With his team and added workers like Epaphras (Col 1:7; 4:12) as well as Tychicus and Trophimus (Acts 20:4; Col 4:7-8), numerous house churches were established and the entire province evangelized, as seen in letters to Colossae, Ephesus, and Philemon. Probably the seven churches of Revelation 2-3 were evangelized now as well, and Paul's letters to Corinth and Rome were written at the end of this period.

Luke tells us that "all the Jews and Greeks who lived in the province of Asia heard the word of the Lord." This is not overly hyperbolic, for a similar explosion of the gospel has occurred in recent years in China, where about 6 million believers in the early 1980s grew to at least 67 million Christians thirty years later.[1] The stories in China are undoubtedly like those in Asia here, as the good news spread like wildfire.

During this time God also sent signs and wonders to confirm Paul's ministry (19:11-12). These "extraordinary miracles" would not only confirm that God was behind Paul's ministry, but also, as was the case with both Jesus and Peter, would make Paul very popular and draw people to hear him speak. Pieces of clothing—handkerchiefs and pieces of work aprons—were passed around and used to heal the sick and cast out demons, much like Jesus' cloak

---

1. Eleanor Albert, "Christianity in China," https://www.cfr.org/backgrounder/christianity-china (accessed July 30, 2018).

in Mark 5:27–29 and Peter's shadow in Acts 5:15. This sounds like popular magic, but God did use such things in the ancient world, and they had a mighty and positive effect. This does not provide a biblical basis for "healing cloths" today, for it was God who used it for his purposes, not the healer himself who sought to profit from such extravagant signs. The Spirit sovereignly decided when to use it, not the miracle worker.

Ephesus was a center for magic in the ancient world, and there is a deliberate contrast between Paul's miracles in verses 11–12 and the magic tricks of sorcerers in this section. In 13:6–11 we read of Paul's conflict with the Jewish court astrologer and sorcerer Elymas Bar-Jesus, and I noted that many such came out of Judea and Samaria due to their preoccupation with angels and heavenly powers. Moreover, magic was a source of entertainment back then just like philosophers and other soapbox speakers, so groups of them would band together and go town to town performing tricks and "driving out evil spirits." They were the Houdinis of their day.

One of the common methods used to force these demonic powers to leave the people they had possessed was to invoke the name of a particularly powerful god, or for the Jewish exorcists, of Solomon or an archangel. The name of a person contained their inner essence and had power. The Beelzebul incident of Luke 11:15, 19, is an example of this. The name of Jesus, due to his power over the demonic world, was considered particularly powerful, so these Jews attempted to use it to force evil spirits to do their bidding.

Some of them may have heard Paul use the name of Jesus to cast the evil spirit out of the slave girl (16:18; also Peter in 3:6, 16; 4:10, 12, 30) but especially in every sermon he proclaimed. They had seen the powerful miracles he performed and figured they could have that power as well if they used the name of his God. Moreover, his power seemed effortless, while most magicians wearied themselves with strenuous gyrations and complicated incantations with far less effect. So they wanted his ability for themselves.

In particular, Luke names one itinerant group, the "seven sons of Sceva, a Jewish chief priest" (19:14). This would be one of the leading priestly families, often seen in the Gospels and constituting those from whom the high priest would be chosen (for instance, Annas and Caiaphas, Luke 3:2; John 18:13, 24). We have no idea how the sons of such a powerful family would be here doing this, but some think their claim was not true but was just used for PR, or that they were "sons" in terms of being distant cousins. Whatever their origins, they try to use the names of Jesus and Paul to their own ends.

The evil spirit responds directly through the person he is inhabiting, a common practice seen even today in instances of demon possession. Being a member of the spirit realm, the demon "knows" the resurrected Jesus, and he "knows of" Jesus' envoy and follower, Paul. However, the sons of Sceva do not belong to Jesus and so have nothing to do with him, and the evil spirit asks, "but who are you?" These Jewish magicians have no connection with the Jesus of Paul and so have no source of power.

To prove their complete lack of power, the "man who had the evil spirit" jumps on them and single-handedly overpowers all seven of them (19:16). The superhuman strength of the demon-possessed was seen in the Gerasene demoniac of Mark 5:3–4 and Luke 8:29, where the unfortunate man was able to break his chains and subdue his guards. So here the man attacked all seven and "gave them such a beating that they ran out of the house naked and bleeding." The effect is immediate. The powerlessness and failure of Paul's opponents is proved dramatically, and the name of Jesus is shown to possess a power the people have never seen.

The whole city is filled with awe. The noun *phobos* in verse 17 combines the ideas of fear and awe, and both are connoted here. Both Jews and Greeks felt these emotions as they saw the power of the God of Paul and his Son Jesus (the Greeks would have linked this with Zeus and Apollo). Both feared this powerful God of the Christians turning on them, especially since they have been treating his emissary Paul so poorly. Their awe came as they glimpsed the actual power that lay behind Paul.

In all that had transpired, "the name of the Lord Jesus was held in high honor," meaning that he was not only shown to be powerful but was also proved to be the Lord of his creation. It is likely that "Jesus was held in high honor" (or "glorified") means that numerous conversions occurred as a result of this incident. If he had power and control over the demonic realm, he would also be sovereign over his creation as well and salvation is to be found in him. His lordship had been proved to be total, "Lord of all." This becomes another summary passage showing how crises and opposition often stimulate the power of the gospel and its witnesses, resulting in many conversions (2:41; 6:7; 9:31, 42).

This is proved further by another critical event, as many sorcerers are converted as well (19:18-19). When they found faith in Jesus, two things resulted: they "confessed" (*exonologoumenoi*) their sins, and they "disclosed" or "admitted" (*anangellontes*) their magical practices (NIV: "openly confessed what they had done"). The second is an extension of the first. The occult was a part of everyday life in Ephesus (and, to a lesser extent, all over the Roman world), and they now realize the satanic realm is behind every part of it. But these are not regular people. As we will see in the next verse, these are sorcerers, those who make a living from it (like Elymas in 13:6-11).

Incantations were not public knowledge but were secret and private, intended for the use only of the sorcerers themselves. So the magic scrolls were viewed as the source of their power and were closely guarded. Without them the exorcist was powerless, and they were worth a great deal of money. Such an event as this had likely never been seen in Ephesus before, when an entire group of magicians got their magic scrolls together in a single pile, let alone burned them.

One would think that instead they would sell the books and use the profits like Barnabas in 4:36-37 or the Seven in chapters 6-7 to care for the poor. However, they did not want Satan's profits, and they wanted to ensure that the occult formulas in these scrolls were never used again, so they had to burn them. To do so publicly told all of Ephesus that such practices were evil and that the name of Jesus had absolute power over such. The amount they were worth, 50,000 drachmas (silver coins that were a basic unit of currency), was a princely sum, worth 50,000 days of labor (one drachma or denarius for a day of work), or about 167 years (working 6 days a week or 300 days a year).

The result of these great victories over the magic of Ephesus was that "the word of the Lord spread widely and grew in power" (19:20), another of the many summaries in Acts that shows how every confrontation with evil and the crises that resulted actually served to strengthen God's people and cause his word to reach out all the more powerfully to win the lost to him (see 2:41, 47; 4:4, 31; 5:14; 6:7; 8:25; 9:31; 12:24; 16:5).

Plans to Visit Jerusalem (19:21–22)

Two years had now transpired, and Paul felt it was time to leave Ephesus to others and begin once more his pioneer missionary work, this time going to Jerusalem but revisiting Macedonia, Achaia, and then Rome on the way. As always, these are ambitious plans, involving time and expense, but he obviously felt it was the Lord's will. The task of establishing the church in the province of Asia was greatly successful, and he had good local leadership to whom he could entrust the work there. "All this" refers to the recent victories of verses 17–20 and the strong church that emerged as a result. The NIV "Paul decided" is actually "resolved in spirit/Spirit" (*etheto en tō pneumati*). It could read "resolved in his spirit" (so KJV, NET, NJB), but it could be an emphasis on the Spirit's guidance, "resolved in/by the Spirit" (NASB, NLT, ESV, NRSV, CSB, LEB). I would agree with the latter.

Paul placed his hopes before the Lord, seeking to ascertain what the Spirit decided "must" (*dei*) come to pass. He decided the

Spirit wanted him to do follow-up visits in Macedonia and Achaia on his way to Rome, and then to travel from there to Jerusalem. The Spirit had indeed led in part, but Paul's own desires led him to get part of it wrong. This is very human, and all of us will make this error at times. We trust the Lord to work out his will (like Paul) even when we fail to ascertain it.

Paul was writing 1 Corinthians at this time, with Romans and 2 Corinthians written during his three-month visit to Macedonia and Achaia (20:1-3). During this latter part of his time in Ephesus he had actually written three letters—a "previous letter" (1 Cor 5:9-11), 1 Corinthians, and a "severe letter" (2 Cor 2:6-9, 7:12)—and had also visited Corinth once (the "painful visit," 2 Cor 2:1; 12:14, 21; 13:1-2).

He has also been gathering a collection for the poor in Jerusalem, as indicated in 1 Corinthians 16:1-4 and 2 Corinthians 8-9. His visits to the churches in both provinces included collecting money and representatives to go to Jerusalem with him (see 20:4-5 for a list). In Romans 15:23-29 Paul explains that his visit to Rome will have the added purpose of initiating the next great mission push, this time covering the western half of the empire from Rome to Spain. Of course, these are Paul's hopes and plans. Everything will be turned upside down with his arrest in Jerusalem and series of trials first in Caesarea and then in Rome itself.

Paul is not quite ready to leave Ephesus yet, so he sends his "assistants" or "helpers" (NIV), Timothy and Erastus, ahead to Macedonia (19:22) to prepare for his coming. Timothy is the better known to us, as he worked alongside Paul for so long, but Erastus is by far his social superior. He was probably the Erastus who was treasurer over all of Corinth (Rom 16:23; see also 2 Tim 4:20). That such a high official would come to Ephesus in order to assist Paul in his ministry shows the incredible change the gospel made in people. For one of the highest officials in Corinth to work side by side with a mere young man of no special societal status was even more unusual then than it would be today. Their task was undoubtedly to prepare the churches for Paul's coming and to start arrangements for collecting the gift for the Jerusalem poor. The reasons for his remaining in Ephesus for a time are unspecified but are certainly related to the needs of ministry there.

THE RIOT IN EPHESUS (19:23-20:1)

Just as things seemed to be jelling for Paul, another crisis erupted, once more because the success of the gospel was ruining the profits of those making money off of the status quo (as at Philippi, 16:19). This time it was the silversmiths causing "a great disturbance about the Way" (on this, see 9:2; 19:9).

Demetrius and his speech (19:23-28)

The riot was caused by a successful silversmith named Demetrius, "who made silver shrines of Artemis" (Roman Diana), goddess of fertility and of the hunt. As a result he "brought in a lot of business for the craftsmen there." They sold silver replicas of the temple, one of the seven wonders of the world, four times the size of the Parthenon, 425 feet long, with 127 60-foot marble columns around the base. It was the largest building in the Roman world, and the Artemis cult was among the most famous. Needless to say, it had an enormous amount of economic as well as religious power behind it.

Demetrius was most likely the dean of the guild of silversmiths and possibly the leading manufacturer of the miniature shrines. He had a great amount of clout, and when he spoke, things happened. His speech informs us in very helpful ways about the impact Paul was making on the city as well as the religious establishment. It could almost serve as a summary of the success of the mission in Ephesus. It's clear from what he says that the gospel is making a huge impact. He begins with the fact that these craftsmen are making a very good living indeed from the artifacts they are selling (19:25). The language reflects that many of them have become wealthy from the sales.

Paul and the other Christian missionaries have "convinced and led astray large numbers of people" not only in Ephesus but across the whole Asian province. This tells us that his mission teams that have branched out from Ephesus have not just been occasional ventures but systemic, saturating the many cities and towns with the gospel. Those who think the early church struggled and made little impact should read Acts again. The province of Asia was the wealthiest province in the entire Roman Empire. For instance, all but one of the seven cities of Revelation were large and fabulously wealthy, and the other, Thyatira, was still a bustling manufacturing town. For all of them to have a thriving church was quite an accomplishment in just two years.

Paul's argument as verbalized by Demetrius is not new. We've seen it before: "Gods made by human hands are no gods at all" (19:26; compare Isa 46:1-7; Acts 7:48; 1 Cor 8:4-6). Once people realize that there is no power behind an idol and it is just a piece of wood or stone, the idol business is finished. The gospel message is making a huge difference in Ephesus. Obviously, sales have dropped off drastically throughout the province, as many have been converted and others have serious questions.

In fact, Artemis herself and her temple are seriously endangered in three ways (19:27): (1) The "trade" in copies of the idols and shrine is in process of losing "its good name." It is being unmasked as nothing but a dead idol. People will not buy effigies of nondeities that they no longer revere. (2) The temple itself will be "discredited" (literally, "considered nothing"), for what good is a temple that worships a useless idol? All that beauty and grandeur will lose its value if there is nothing behind it. (3) The goddess Artemis herself is in danger of being "robbed of her divine majesty," with the verb *kathaireō* meaning her divinity might be "destroyed" if people listen to this Paul. At present she is worshipped not just in Ephesus but in all the province and even worldwide. She was honored to much the same degree as Zeus and Apollo, but that might cease if these Christian preachers are not stopped.

With this final warning, the place erupted with fury as the crowd started screaming (19:28), "Great is Artemis of the Ephesians!" This became a virtual war cry, for the city identified itself with their patron goddess and viewed Paul's preaching as an attack on the virtual life and prosperity of Ephesus itself. The anger and excitement grew, and soon the whole city was enveloped and in an uproar against these Christians. Jewish persecution had now evolved into pagan opposition as well. Chaos reigned, and a riot erupted. The crowds seized two of their leaders, Gaius and Aristarchus, "traveling companions from Macedonia" and coworkers at Ephesus (see 20:4; 27:2).[2]

The riot erupts (19:29–34)

Paul and his companions are in great danger from the angry mob, and when the crowd rushes into the theater together, it could easily have become the Christians' tomb. This was a large amphitheater that could hold 24,000 people and was used for official as well as popular assemblies, so it was a natural place to go. Paul, without thinking clearly in the heat of the moment, at first wanted to make an appearance to the angry crowd, but wiser heads prevailed (19:30–31), including some city officials who had become friends with him and possibly Christian supporters. Paul wanted to intervene to save his coworkers and friends, but they convinced him that he would forfeit his life in the process. These officials are called here in Greek "Asiarchs," high officials who organized the games of the city and proposed important legislation to the city council. They were wealthy and very influential in the city, and Paul would definitely have listened to them carefully. God

---

2. Aristarchus is from Thessalonica. The Gaius of 20:4 is from Derbe in Galatia, so this is unlikely to be the same Gaius. Another Gaius is from Corinth (1 Cor 1:14; Rom 16:23), but that is in Achaia. So this Gaius is probably not mentioned elsewhere.

intervened, and it is certain that even the two who had been seized had also somehow survived the riot.

The chaos increased, and there was no order at all in the theater (19:32). Mob thinking prevailed, and everyone was shouting and yet had nothing to say. As Luke says, many "did not even know why they were there." They just thought all the tumult looked like fun. The term "assembly" normally refers to a church meeting (*ekklēsia*) and in this context to one like the regular monthly city "assembly" that met in this amphitheater, but here it is a rag-tag mob of total confusion.

A Jewish leader named Alexander is pushed forward (19:33), apparently to make sure the tumult isn't blamed on the Jews, and asks for silence so he can speak. It doesn't work, and he ends up creating more chaos, because as soon as they realize he's a Jew (probably by his clothes), they begin shouting "Great is Artemis of the Ephesians" all over again, and they keep it up for two more hours. They apparently see the Christians as Jews and think he is linked with Gaius and Aristarchus (v. 29). At least there is no more confusion, for every Gentile present is caught up in acclaiming Artemis. It is amazing that no believer was killed in all this.

The city clerk speaks (19:35-40)

Finally, the one person they would listen to stepped forward, the city clerk (something like the chair of the city council or mayor today). He was the arbitrator between the civil authorities and the Roman imperial rule and spoke for both sides. His message is an official speech (19:35-40) with four parts, and finally the mob is quelled as people begin to listen:

1. The *exordium*, or introduction (v. 35), reminds the crowd that "all the world" knows that their city has the honor of being the "guardian" of both the temple and the image of the goddess Artemis. The term *neōkoros*, or "guardian," was a special title marking the glory of being a temple-warden city and hosting the goddess herself. The description "her

image, which fell from heaven" most likely is based on a meteorite that purportedly fell from Zeus, who gave this stone idol to Ephesus for safekeeping.

2. The *propositio*, or thesis of the speech (v. 36), is the call to "calm down and not do anything rash." Since Zeus himself has authenticated the temple, there is no reason to fear these upstart Christians and cause any disturbance of the peace. Their goddess is safe, so disband and go home. If this reckless action continues, they will be sorry, for the Romans will intervene and people will die.

3. The *probatio*, or argument meant to prove his point, takes place in verses 37–39 and consists of two parts. First, these Christians have committed no crime and have never acted against the goddess or the temple. They have proclaimed their God, Jesus Christ, rather than opposing the goddess. They are not temple robbers seeking to steal sacred (gold or silver) objects from the temple, a capital offense in the ancient world. Nor are they blasphemers who slander or mock the goddess. This latter could have been argued, but Paul's friendship with several Asiarchs (v. 31) probably means he had already talked to officials and satisfied them on this issue. The clerk realizes that an unprovoked attack on a Roman citizen like Paul could be disastrous for the Ephesian officials (see the parallel in 16:37–40).

In light of this, he tells the crowd that Demetrius and the other silversmiths had better change their approach, warning them against precipitate action and commanding that they bring such charges before the city courts and the Roman proconsuls (19:38). This illegal action is going to get them in serious trouble. There was a single proconsul[3] over the province (see 18:12), and he ruled on behalf of the

---

3. The plural "proconsuls" is probably due to the fact that they changed every year or two. We could translate, "There are people like proconsuls to hear cases."

Roman senate and had charge of the army stationed there. If they don't want to take the issue to the Romans, the silversmiths could take it to the "legal assembly" of Ephesus itself (19:39). Either is vastly superior to what they are doing now.

4. The *peroratio*, or conclusion, attempts to instill fear by warning the crowd about the danger of "being charged with rioting" (19:40) and thus causing Roman military intervention. In that case, everyone would suffer. There is "no [logical] reason" that could explain satisfactorily what they have done, and they had better disband immediately or face the consequences, not only Roman military action but also the loss of privileges the Romans had extended to Ephesus.

The two results (19:41–20:1)

Luke ends this episode rather suddenly, with the city clerk dismissing the crowd and Paul's abrupt departure from Ephesus. The city clerk sends the silver guild packing, and all the people in the crowd go home. It had been a seriously dangerous situation, and he had only saved the day at the last minute. If the guild wished, they could have appealed to the official courts, but for now Paul and the other believers were safe. Undoubtedly, Gaius and Aristarchus (v. 29) were released, and no further action was taken.

I will feature 20:1 in both this and the next chapter, for it is a transition verse, both concluding Paul's time in Ephesus and initiating his trip first to Macedonia (20:3) and then to Jerusalem for the Sabbath and to take the collection for the poor to Palestine. He seems to have left immediately after the episode, probably so the silversmiths won't have time to bring him (and the Ephesian church) up for charges before the city courts. He barely took time to encourage the saints, he was so concerned to leave and defuse the terrible situation.

This had been a far more traumatic experience than we would surmise from the language of Acts. In 1 Corinthians 15:32 Paul says he "fought wild beasts in Ephesus," an ancient metaphor for human riots and obstinate people. Some interpret this from the standpoint of the theory that Paul was in prison in Ephesus (2 Cor 11:23: "in prison more frequently"), but that is quite unlikely.[4] Also, 2 Corinthians 1:8–11 speaks of affliction experienced in Asia, when Paul despaired of life itself. In addition, Paul experienced despair over the church at Corinth, with four letters, the first three from Ephesus (see on 19:21), and several visits. The leaders of that church were almost as bad as the Ephesians, totally caught up in themselves and their secular ways. So this was a very difficult period in Paul's life.

———

This next phase of Paul's ministry begins with a fascinating figure, Apollos, an Alexandrian believer who is especially gifted in knowing and using God's word to prove that Jesus is Messiah, Son of God, and Savior. Yet even someone as gifted as he can have serious deficiencies, and God uses Priscilla and Aquila to fill in the gap in his understanding about the Spirit (18:24–28). Like him, we often have such gaps, and we need to work at getting a good education that can prepare us to serve God and his church well.

Luke then introduces a second group, followers of John the Baptist rather than of Christ. They know nothing about the Holy Spirit, and Paul has to bring them into the orbit of Christ, help them to find faith in him, and see to it that they are baptized into the Holy Spirit, the third such after the Samaritans (8:14–17) and the Gentiles (10:44–46). The universal mission continues to move outward to embrace group after group.

One of the truly remarkable two-year periods in the history of the church ensued, as the church in Ephesus thrived and the

---

4. See the introductions to my commentaries on Ephesians or Colossians in this series.

large and wealthy province of Asia was wholly evangelized, with churches placed in countless towns and villages (19:8-12). The power of the Spirit moved mightily, and signs and wonders proliferated. Ephesus, due to the presence of the temple of Artemis, was a center of magic and sorcery, and many encounters with the occult took place there (vv. 13-20).

Luke relates two examples of this conflict with magic at Ephesus. First, one of the many groups of Jewish sorcerers (vv. 13-16) is traveling about portraying themselves as sons of the high priest Sceva, giving them the appearance of powerful magic. But the demon-possessed man jumps on them and gives them a thorough beating, showing that they do not have the power of either Jesus or Paul behind them. Second, as many of these sorcerers are brought to Christ (vv. 17-20), they begin to gather their secret magic books. Rather than sell them and use the devil's money in the church, they decide to burn them all as a witness in Ephesus of the greater power of the Christian God. The reality of spiritual warfare is demonstrated powerfully here, and too many today pretend the dark powers don't exist or at least live as if they don't exist. This is Satan's great strategy, getting Christians to look the other way as he works in the world and in the church. We must realize that we are in a far more serious war with the forces of evil than we imagine, and must "put on the full armor of God" (Eph 6:10-17).

Paul has been in Ephesus over two years and is beginning to realize it is about time to leave (vv. 21-22). His desire is to visit Jerusalem, take them his collection for the poor, and embark on a new missionary journey to Spain, which will begin an entirely new epoch in his life and ministry. However, before he can carry out his plans, a riot erupts (vv. 23-28), as a leading silversmith sets Ephesus into a frenzy by stirring up animosity against Paul and the Christians due to the success of the gospel and its results, the diminution of the profits Artemis has brought the idol trade. This tells us a lot about the impact the gospel made on ancient society. So many came to Christ that even their economy was endangered.

The riot becomes a very dangerous situation (vv. 29–34), and Paul comes about as close to being killed as he can get and still live. He wanted to appear before them, but that would certainly have meant his demise, and wiser heads prevailed. The riot kept getting worse until finally the city clerk, the highest official in the city, appeared and took the wind out of their sails. He told the mob that Artemis was not in danger, but that they were in a lot of danger from Roman intervention unless they disbanded (vv. 35–39). That finally did it, and the riot ceased. This must have been one of the most frightening times in Paul's life. With that he was ready to end his Ephesian mission and head for Jerusalem (v. 41).

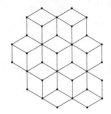

PAUL'S RETURN TO JERUSALEM, PART 1

(20:1–38)

After the extremely tense and difficult end to his lengthy time in Ephesus, Paul has two goals: to revisit the churches he had founded on his mission tours and to make it to Jerusalem to deliver the gift from the Gentile churches for the poverty-stricken believers there. There are six extended stays in this trip—in Corinth (20:3), in Troas (20:7-12), in Miletus (Ephesian elders, 20:17-38), in Tyre (21:4-6), in Ptolemais (21:7), and in Caesarea (21:8-14). The emphasis is on the importance of community life and church fellowship among the Christians.

The second emphasis, which will take us through the rest of Acts, is on opposition and plots against Paul's life. Clearly Luke wants his readers to be ready for the struggles of being a light-bearing Christian in a dark, sin-sick world. The message is a difficult one for the church today—do not expect the Christian life to be easy. The shallow prosperity gospel that too often proliferates leads to disappointment, for that is not God's will. Christ's "yoke is easy" (Matt 11:30), but it is still a yoke, and it is easy only when we rely on Christ.

PAUL TRAVELS THROUGH MACEDONIA
AND ACHAIA TO TROAS (20:1-6)

Luke covers Paul's time in Macedonia and Achaia remarkably quickly. Paul follows the pattern of recent follow-up visits, encouraging the people in Christ and probably strengthening the leadership in the churches, traveling the Ignatian Way through Macedonia from Philippi to Thessalonica to Berea, and possibly going northwest as well to the province of Illyricum (Rom 15:19). While Luke gave this trip short shrift, Paul considered it quite important, mentioning it often (1 Cor 16:5; 2 Cor 1:16; 2:13; 7:5). He was especially thrilled with the Thessalonian response and the model they set with their sacrificial giving for the poor in Jerusalem (2 Cor 8:1-5). During this time, he writes 2 Corinthians, where some of the issues are resolved, and prepares to visit the city.

He spent three months in Achaia (southern Greece, 20:3), possibly over the winter of AD 56-57, when it is difficult to travel. Besides Corinth, he would have visited churches in Athens and Cenchreae (18:18; Rom 16:1). During this time he writes Romans, finishing a virtual "trinity" of three of the most powerful treatises ever written in a one- to two-year period (the two Corinthian letters and Romans). Certainly this was a time for consolidating the issues in Corinth that had produced so much heartbreak and for moving the church in the right direction.

Luke provides no details about the plot that Paul learned about just as he was set to sail for Syria. It must have involved killing him on the ship itself, for he changed plans and instead went overland back through Macedonia to Troas. With representatives of the churches traveling with him (v. 4), this change of plans would have been quite complicated.

It is odd that Luke lists seven travel companions (20:4) but never tells us much about them or why they are with Paul. They clearly represent the power of the gospel in those cities where Paul and his team have ministered. The prevalent opinion is that they are taking the collection for the poor from their churches to the mother church in Jerusalem as a personal thank-you for their sending the gospel to the Gentiles. Paul viewed the collection as a salvation-historical link binding the Gentile and Jewish churches together, thereby producing much-needed unity among the communities. The Jewish churches have supplied the "spiritual blessings" (the knowledge and truth side); the Gentile churches have supplied the "material blessings" (the earthly and financial side, Rom 15:25-27, 31; see also Acts 24:17; 1 Cor 16:1-2; 2 Cor 8-9). The result is that the two become one in Christ.

The seven delegates come from and represent the three provinces of Macedonia (Sopater from Berea, Aristarchus and Secundus from Thessalonica), Galatia (Gaius from Derbe, Timothy from Lystra), and Asia (Tychicus and Trophimus). Strangely, no one from Philippi or Corinth is named. This doesn't mean these two cities have failed to contribute or send delegates. Most think Luke (who is writing this list[1]) comes from Philippi and represents that city, and Corinth could be represented by Titus or by Paul himself. Philippi has regularly supported Paul financially, and the most detailed instructions anywhere can be found in 2 Corinthians 8-9. It is highly unlikely that they refused to participate.

The seven delegates went ahead of them and traveled by ship from Corinth to Troas (20:5). Paul wanted to share Passover and the Festival of Unleavened Bread with the Philippian churches and so traveled by foot the 450 miles to Philippi, where Luke had apparently been ministering. So he rejoined Paul there. The "we" passages designate where Luke is part of the team, and they begin here. Luke had remained in Philippi from 16:17 to 20:6 here. Passover was in early April that year, and Pentecost, at which time they hoped to be in Jerusalem, was fifty days later, so they

---

1. The "we" passages ended with Luke at Philippi in 16:17, and it is likely that he remained there until now, as the "we" material begins again here in 20:5-6 as they sail from Philippi. Either Philippi is Luke's home, or he has stayed to minister there for this time.

had seven weeks to get there. When they had sailed from Troas to Philippi in 16:11-12, it took two days due to favorable winds. With the winds reversed, it now takes five days.

EUTYCHUS FALLS FROM A WINDOW AT TROAS (20:7-12)

Each stop on this trip is a combination of follow-up with encouragement and farewell, as Paul was planning to spend the rest of his life taking the gospel to the western half of the Roman Empire (Rome to Spain, Rom 15:15-29). His week in Troas (probably due to the shipping schedule) began on the "first day of the week," which probably would have been Sunday on the Christian calendar (1 Cor 16:2; Rev 1:10), to "break bread." This could have been the regular Christian worship service[2] or a special meeting due to Paul's arrival, more likely the latter due to the proceedings indicated here.

The group assembled and shared a fellowship meal (breaking bread, Acts 2:42, 46; 1 Cor 10:16). Paul preached a sermon and taught for some time, then likely also began filling them in on his ministry and with news from the other churches. He had so much to say that he went on from early evening until midnight, with the room lit by many lamps (20:7b-8). You can only guess how stuffy it became, for the room was probably packed with people. Still, it was exciting as they heard story after story like the ones we have just read in Acts 17-19. I'm sure that every time Paul seemed to slow down due to the lateness of the hour, the people egged him on to keep talking. No one would have wanted him to stop. Moreover, Paul planned to leave the next day and so wanted to say it all in that single meeting.

---

2. Early Jewish Christians met twice, on Saturday at the synagogues and Sunday for the Lord's Day worship. They were not allowed (by the Jews) to attend synagogue services from the 80s on.

He was still going strong at midnight (probably after five or six straight hours of speaking) when tragedy struck. A young man (perhaps fourteen to eighteen years old) named Eutychus[3] had been sitting in a window well, and apparently the meeting room was on the third floor. We don't know whether this was a large, wealthy home or a tenement building, but the boy had been nodding off and finally fell fully asleep, falling backward out of the window and plunging the three stories to his death.

Paul rushed to the boy (20:10) and fell over his body, wrapping his arms around him and declaring (undoubtedly under prodding by the Spirit), "Don't be alarmed. ... He's alive!" Paul didn't mean that the fall failed to kill him. Rather, as a result of the Spirit's quick work, the boy had been raised back to life. There have been several such resuscitations in Scripture. Paul's reaction of throwing himself on the boy is reminiscent of Elijah and Elisha in 1 Kings 17:19–24; 2 Kings 4:23–24. In addition, such raisings from the dead have been performed by Jesus himself (Luke 7:11–15; 8:49–56; John 11:38–44) and by Peter (Acts 9:36–41).

Luke tells the story as if it were just a regular occurrence (perhaps with Paul it was). The young man has just come back to life with the whole group watching in awe, and all he says is, "Then he went upstairs again and broke bread and ate" (20:11). Ho hum, another day in the life of Paul the apostle! It sounds almost like just another regular occurrence. This is the middle of the night, and everyone is hungry after the strain of seeing a youth brought back to life. It is hard to decide whether "talking until daylight" means he resumed teaching or sat and talked to the people in general. I suspect the latter. Paul was busy answering questions and telling more stories. This went on until dawn, and he departed Troas soon after.

---

3. Interestingly, his name means "lucky one."

PAUL SAYS FAREWELL TO THE ELDERS
FROM EPHESUS (20:13–38)

Paul wanted to go south to Assos overland by foot (we don't know why), so Luke and the rest of the team boarded a ship and picked up Paul there for the trip to Miletus. By this time Paul was in a bit of a hurry, as his main goal was to reach Jerusalem by Pentecost. Assos was 30 miles south, a two-day trip. The ship was a coastal vessel and stopped at all the main ports. By boat, Miletus was another 125 miles south, beginning with a journey to Mitylene on the island of Lesbos. The next days they went to the islands of Chios, then Samos, and finally arrived at Miletus at the mouth of the Meander River 20 miles south of Ephesus (20:14–15). It was a major port city and the natural place to meet the Ephesian elders so as to lose as little time as possible getting to Jerusalem (20:16). It was important to avoid stopping at Ephesus itself, for the harbor was silting up and there could be major delays getting in and out. Moreover, ships that stopped there would be doing major trade, and it would have taken even more days loading and unloading goods.

To save time, Paul made arrangements while in Miletus for the elders to travel down there to meet him. He needed to get away to Jerusalem as soon as possible. It was a 60-mile journey through rugged terrain, so about four days each way. This is Paul's only speech recorded in Acts to a Christian audience. He knows this will be his last time with these friends from Ephesus, though not for the reason he thinks, and so this is a farewell speech. He believes he will be going on to Spain and doesn't realize what will begin in Jerusalem, though he has an inkling it could be bad (see his request for prayer in Rom 15:31).

He begins by rehearsing the two-plus years he spent with them, defending his conduct and reminding them of his service and sorrows when he first arrived. He had "served the Lord with great humility and with tears and in the midst of severe testing by the plots of my Jewish opponents" (20:19). He wants them to rejoice in those years, for he shared the gospel, brought them to Christ, and anchored them in the faith. He lived among them, not making demands but living in humility and service to them. "Served the Lord" is *douleuōn tō kyriō*, meaning "becoming his slave," bringing in all the imagery that begins many of Paul's letters, "Paul, slave of Jesus Christ" (my translation of Rom 1:1; see also Gal 1:10; Phil 1:1; Titus 1:1). Paul rejoiced in being set free from the slavery of sin so that he could become God's slave (Rom 6:20–22).

In serving both God and the Ephesian people, he had to learn to embrace suffering and sorrow, for as in virtually every city in which he ministered, he had to endure the "plots of my Jewish opponents." This "severe testing" (*peirasmōn*, "trials") hurt deeply, for his one desire was to bring them to Christ, while their one desire was so often to rid the earth of him. In fact, it was a plot that had resulted in Paul's being in Miletus in the first place, for he had been about to go by ship from Corinth to Syria in 20:3 when a plot to kill him on board the ship forced him to go overland back through Macedonia to Troas and down to Miletus.

Finally, in 20:20–21 he recapitulates his preaching ministry with them. The primary characteristic was boldness in proclaiming the whole gospel both "publicly and from house to house." He held nothing back and refused to worry about plots or persecution. No one would ever be able to accuse him of watering down the reality of sin and salvation in order to curry favor from the listeners (unlike all too many today!). There is no "I'm okay, you're okay" theology from Paul. The declaration is very clear: "They must turn to God in repentance and have faith in our Lord Jesus." In other words, warnings of death and eternal damnation as well as the realization that there is no salvation by good works but only via repentance from sin and faith in Jesus' atoning death are all present.

In light of the many plots against him, Paul realizes his plans to visit Jerusalem do not seem overly bright, but he wants them to know that he is "compelled by the Spirit" to do so. All through Acts, the Spirit has directed the actions of the leaders of the church (1:8; 4:8; 5:32; 6:3, 5; 7:55; 8:29, 39; 9:31; 10:19; 11:12, 28; 13:2, 4, 9; 16:6–7;

19:21). As the incredible number of passages shows, this is a predominant theme in the book. Paul has no idea what is going to transpire; all he knows is that it is the Lord's will. In Romans 15:31 he asks for prayer that God will keep him "safe from the unbelievers" in Jerusalem but never that God will keep him from going. We will see this issue again (Acts 21:4, 10-14).

Paul's understanding of all these warnings is found in verse 23, "I only know that in every city the Holy Spirit warns me that prison and hardships are facing me." Notice it is not "warns me to stay away from Jerusalem." The Spirit is readying him for the extremely difficult time awaiting him but *never* tells him not to go. In fact, he is under the Spirit's compulsion that he *must* go. So in other words, he doesn't know, but the Spirit does and wants him to be ready for "prison and hardships." He has faced that very thing in Philippi (16:19-40), Corinth (18:12-17), and Ephesus (19:28-41), and now he will go through it again in Jerusalem. He is informed by the Spirit that God's answer to his prayer of Romans 15:31 will be a no. He will not be delivered from the hands of his enemies, but he will be spared and allowed to continue his ministry, albeit in a different way.

Paul has only one goal (20:24). It is a beautiful testimony and a great sermon in itself. He refuses to allow his dire prospects to bother him, for "I consider my life worth nothing to me." As God's slave (v. 19), his life is nothing, for it belongs entirely to God. The Greek is "not worth a single word," an idiom meaning "less than nothing." This is similar to Philippians 1:20-21, "that now as always Christ will be exalted in my body, whether by life or by death. For to me, to live is Christ and to die is gain." If Paul loses his life in Jerusalem, praise the Lord. All that matters is the Lord's will.

He states that his "only aim is to finish the race and complete the task the Lord Jesus has given me—the task of testifying to the good news of God's grace." I am writing this on the opening day of the Winter Olympics, and the imagery of "finishing the course" or "race" is a powerful one, seen in events ranging from the brief sprint of short-track speed skating to the marathon of the Summer Olympics. Paul must have been a sports fan (how can anyone not love the Olympics!), for he used this image often (1 Cor 9:24; Phil 3:14; 2 Tim 4:7) for the idea of "fulfilling" or "completing" (*teleiōsai*) the destiny God had for his life. All his energy and effort were focused on the tasks God had placed before him. This was not just a short dash but a marathon race that demanded perseverance and long-term commitment. The proclamation of the gospel was everything, and he had dedicated his life to that task.

So Paul is saying a final farewell to his friends in Ephesus— "none of you ... will ever see me again." This is not a prediction of his death but a revelation of his future task, his belief that the Lord wanted him to spend the rest of his life ministering to the lost in the western half of the Roman Empire, from Rome to Spain (Rom 15:24, 28). We know differently, though many think he did get to Spain briefly after his Roman imprisonment.[4] He may also have visited Ephesus again, for due to future problems in that area he returned to Macedonia and Troas (1 Tim 1:3; 2 Tim 4:13). He sent Timothy there (1 Tim 1:3) and later added Tychicus (2 Tim 4:12). He sums up his ministry once more as "preaching the kingdom" that arrived with Christ (1:3; 8:12; 14:22; 28:23, 31).

In light of his faithful ministry, he wants them to know "I am innocent of the blood of any of you" (20:26), a solemn pronouncement that sounds very strange, as if he were saying, "I have neither hurt nor killed any of you," obvious in light of the fact that he has never been a soldier or a criminal. Certainly he means that as a result of his consistent gospel witness no one who has heard him can say he was responsible for their eternal damnation.

The reason he is innocent is that he has "not hesitated to proclaim to you the whole will of God" (20:27). This is critical for us as well. When each of us stands before God, we will be examined by the eternal Judge as to how faithfully we have fulfilled

---

4. See my Romans commentary in this series at 15:24.

our calling. All of us who are preachers and teachers will face the reality of 2 Timothy 2:15, "Do your best to present yourself to God as one approved, a worker who does not need to be ashamed and who correctly handles the word of truth." Those who have watered down the gospel truths and preached a shallow message will have to hang their heads in shame as they answer to God for their half-hearted messages. That was not Paul, who at all times fearlessly proclaimed *truth*.

Paul is worried for their future. He has been their apostle and evangelist, but now he takes on the role of prophet and predicts dire times ahead for the Ephesians. The Spirit has told him of the invasion of false teachers. The elders will have to take charge of their church, for Paul won't be around. As elders, "the Holy Spirit has made you overseers" (*episkopoi*), those who are guardians of the flock and called to spiritual vigilance over it. There were three synonymous terms for the pastoral office—elder, overseer, pastor. Since as elders they oversee the church, they must "keep watch over yourselves and all the flock." The spiritual safekeeping of God's people is their responsibility. The term was often used for the leaders of Israel, both military (Judg 9:28; 2 Kgs 11:15) and civil (Isa 60:17). It is a natural term for the leaders of the church (1 Tim 3:2; 1 Pet 2:25) in terms of their responsibility to be vigilant over themselves and the church.

The third term builds on the leader as elder and overseer: "Be shepherds [pastors] of the church of God." These three primary New Testament terms for pastoral leadership—shepherd, elder, overseer—are combined here, as well as in 1 Peter 5:1–5 and the Pastoral Letters to describe the divinely chosen leader of a church as an elder who shepherds the flock and oversees the people in discharging their office. The image of the shepherd stems from God as a shepherd in Psalm 23 as well as Psalm 100:3; Isaiah 40:11; Ezekiel 34:12–16. The task of a shepherd is vigilance, protection, guidance, in general taking care of God's flock. There are two areas of focus, first watching over one's self, and second over God's people. The emphasis is on "all the flock," every member, both Jew and Gentile.

The threefold reason is quite powerful: every one of these leaders has (1) been given these responsibilities by the Holy Spirit, (2) is part of "the church of God," and (3) is "bought with [Jesus'] own blood." Note the trinitarian thrust—from the Spirit, from God the Father, from Christ the Son. The connection between the latter two elements is quite significant. The church belongs to God as his special possession because of the incredible purchase price, "bought with his own blood." The blood payment is the redemption price for the forgiveness of our sins (seen in Rom 3:25; 5:9; 1 Cor 10:16; Col 1:20; Eph 2:13).

The danger is profound (20:29-30). Paul is soon to depart, and a major source of their protection will be gone. There will be a double invasion, with false teachers coming from outside and from inside the group. The external threats are seen as "savage wolves" who will "not spare the flock." This is similar to Luke 10:3, where Jesus said he was sending the disciples out "like lambs among wolves." Wolves were natural enemies, predators who stalked and killed sheep, are often used throughout the Old Testament as a metaphor for the enemies of God's people (Jer 5:6; Ezek 22:27; Hab 1:8; Zeph 3:3). The shepherd has as one of the primary duties protecting the flock from being torn to pieces by such creatures, and this applies quite well with spiritual shepherds rescuing God's flock from "savage" false teachers (John 10:11-12; 2 Cor 11:4, 13-15).

The external source of invading heretics will be matched by internal schism, as "from your own number men will arise and distort the truth in order to draw away disciples after them" (20:30). These will be deliberate liars who will pervert the truths of the gospel about Christ and salvation through him. Jesus spoke about this in John 8:44, when he accused his Jewish opponents, "You belong to your father, the devil. ... He was a murderer from the beginning, not holding to the truth, for there is no truth in him. When he lies, he speaks his native language, for he is a liar and the father of lies." The false teachers in Ephesus will be Satan's children, consciously distorting the truth in order to gain followers who have "itching ears" (2 Tim 4:3) and flock to (pun intended) their innovative ideas. In Romans 16:18, "by smooth talk and flattery they deceive the minds of naive people."

This prophecy was fulfilled in four stages. First, what is called the Colossian heresy began about three years after this event (AD 61) and spread to other parts of the province (Col 2:4, 8, 20). Second, in the Pastoral Letters (1 Tim 1:18–20; 4:1–3; 2 Tim 2:14–19; 3:1–9), false teachers had gained some control over Ephesus and other parts of the province (AD 64–65). Third, in the Johannine Letters (1 John 2:18–19; 4:1–6; 2 John 7–11), false teachers were even more in control (early 80s). Fourth, in Revelation 2:1–7, 18–29, false teachers like the Nicolaitans and Jezebel created havoc for the church. One could say the province of Asia became the epicenter of false teaching for the early church.

In light of the extreme danger, Paul tells these elders to "be on your guard" (20:31, repeating v. 28) by keeping spiritual vigilance over the church and remaining on high alert, ready for these false prophets and teachers to appear. These pathological liars worm their way into congregations. They are experts at camouflage and appear kosher when in reality they plan to destroy the church and get rich in the process. Heresy has long proved to be a get-rich-quick scheme, incredibly effective at both destroying truth and making a lot of money doing it. I think of a preacher several years ago whose goal was to have a Rolls Royce for every day of the year and was well on his way when he was unmasked and deported. So it is up to the mature leaders who know their theology and can smoke out the charlatans.

Paul uses his two-and-a-half-year sojourn with them as his example. During that time "I never stopped warning each of you night and day with tears" (20:31). As we remember from all of chapter 19, he fought a constant battle against sorcerers, opponents from Jewish and Gentile backgrounds, and dissension in their own ranks (for example, in Corinth). He never let down his guard and stayed on top of issues, and the Lord awarded him for his bold leadership. Very few have ever gone through as much as he did in serving the Lord with faithfulness and courage (see 2 Cor 11:23-29, written shortly after the Ephesian ministry). He realized, however, that he could not protect them by himself. To safeguard the church, all the members were to follow his lead and admonish each other to remain faithful to Christ.

Verse 32 would be a wonderful theme verse for a worship service. To "commend" (*paratithemai*; NIV: "commit") a person means to "place them before" or "entrust them into the care" of another. Paul gives them over to God, and to his great gift to us, "the word of his grace." Our loving and compassionate God will provide for us his care and protection via his divine word, given to us as his grace-gift. Here we see the true rationale for serious Bible study and what it will do for us. This is how God watches over us and rescues us from the savage wolves of verses 29-30. It is his word that unmasks their lies and reveals the truth about their false teaching. God's grace is the saving grace of the gospel and the deep theological truths regarding Christ and his salvation.

There are three results when God's word governs the life of our churches and of each one of us: (1) We are built up or edified, meaning we ourselves as individuals and a corporate whole are God's great construction project. Then (2) we are the recipients of Christ's "inheritance," one of the beautiful themes of Scripture, referring to the future and final blessings God has for his people in Christ (Eph 1:14, 18; Col 1:12; 3:24; Heb 1:14; 9:15; 1 Pet 1:4; 3:9). Finally, (3) we are placed "among all those who are sanctified," or "made holy," thereby becoming "saints" who have been set apart for God and are called to live apart from sin and the world (Acts 26:18; Rom 15:16; 1 Cor 1:2; 6:11; 1 Thess 5:23; 2 Thess 2:13).

In the rest of this paragraph (20:33-35), Paul wishes to set the record straight as to his personal finances and accountability. Itinerant speakers, being a major form of entertainment in the first century, were notorious for their greedy desire for personal gain. In a major city like Ephesus this would have been especially true, so he wished to emphasize that "silver or gold or clothing," compensation of any kind, never interested him. Popular speakers back then spent a great deal of time cultivating well-healed patrons with deep pockets, but Paul would have none of that. Moreover, elders of churches would be tempted to raise money for themselves as much as for their churches, and he wished to avoid that as well.

Rather than receiving financial gifts from others, Paul always demanded to pay his own way as he ministered so that he could never be accused of any such thing (v. 34). This is why he worked as a tentmaker (Acts 18:1; 1 Cor 4:12; 1 Thess 2:5-9; 2 Thess 3:8-10). It is true that he accepted gifts occasionally, but only later after he was no longer present in the church, and those gifts were for his ministry, never just for him personally (2 Cor 11:7-10; Phil 1:5; 4:15-18). He was not against others receiving support (1 Cor 9:1-6), but he surrendered that right in order to guard himself from false charges.

Instead, he wanted the monetary results of his "hard work" to be used to "help the weak," and used this as a "show-and-tell" strategy (*hypedeixa*), providing a model or guide to others as to what proper ministry looks like. His goal was always to enable those who lacked his opportunities and were destitute to receive the help they needed. We are back to this guiding principle of the early church, to seek to get to the place where "there were no needy persons among them" by sharing their own possessions with the poor (4:32-34; see also 2:44-45).

It is very interesting that Paul in support of this cites a *logia jesu* (word of Jesus) not found in any of the Gospels: "It is more blessed to give than to receive." This denies the principle of reciprocity, "Give so that you can receive," and teaches the need to give without thought of return, to give entirely for the sake of helping others. I remember a prosperity preacher once teaching the principle of giving more in order to get more from God, making it virtually a get-rich-quick scheme. That is a travesty of truth and must be soundly condemned.

Jesus provides here another beatitude like those in Matthew 5:3-12. True eternal blessing comes from a giving heart, not through accumulating possessions. Those who hoard their wealth live for the temporary and surrender the permanent. As Jesus said so well in Luke 16:9, "Use worldly wealth to gain friends for yourselves [by helping others], so that when it is gone, you will be welcomed into eternal dwellings." There are two guiding principles: use your resources to make other people's lives better; and when you do so, those possessions will be banked in heaven and come back to you as eternal reward.

The final farewell was a scene of tears and sorrow, for Paul had revealed to them that he believed "they would never see his face again." At the end of his speech, they all knelt down together and prayed, commending each other to the Lord in their respective ministries. The four gestures—kneeling, embracing, kissing, weeping—show the deep ties between God, the elders, and Paul. Many see this as primarily a solemn moment, but I see it primarily as a loving moment. Paul is their spiritual father, and the thought this might be the last time they would ever see him is overwhelming.

Paul prayed for strength for the future dangers he had just outlined, and they likely prayed for his two requests stated in the recent letter to the Romans (15:31)—safety from the plots of the Jews and blessing for the contribution he is taking to Jerusalem. The "holy kiss" was a common greeting and farewell, more a Jewish than a Greek custom (Gen 27:26-27; 31:55; Luke 7:38, 45; Rom 16:16; 1 Cor 16:20; 1 Thess 5:26).

The elders (and Paul) were especially grieved because they thought he would never be back. They didn't realize he would be back in Asia Minor after his Roman imprisonment due to problems there (see on 20:25). After their farewell, they "accompanied him to the ship" to begin his journey again to Jerusalem.

———

The missionary journeys are now finished, and Paul begins that fateful trip to Jerusalem that will change everything for him for the rest of his life. He had hoped to begin the next missionary journey, this time to the western half of the Roman Empire, but that is not to be. Still, he leaves Ephesus for the first part of his travel plans, follow-up visits to the churches he had founded in Macedonia and Achaia (vv. 1–6). He has a very fruitful time, writing key letters (Corinthians and Romans) and solving serious issues (Corinth).

An important lesson regarding flexibility in planning is found here. Paul had planned to sail straight to Syria, but a Jewish plot against his life forced him to make serious changes involving a lengthy overland trip all the way back through Macedonia to Troas. Yet that also enabled the events at Troas and the very important farewell to the Ephesian elders to take place. When we are seriously inconvenienced by events out of our control, we must leave them to God and trust that, as here, enormous good will come of it.

The week in Troas (vv. 7–12) demonstrates the new unity in the church, as Paul talked on and on about goings-on in the other provinces, and the people were enthralled to hear the stories. They deeply cared about their fellow believers and what was happening elsewhere, a far cry from too many churches today that only care about what is happening within them. The raising of the young man was remarkable, but equally shocking is the way everyone seemed to take it in stride as just another event in the life of the church. We need more expectations of God at work among us, and these believers provide quite a model of the "normal Christian church."

Paul's farewell speech to the Ephesian elders begins with his ruminations of his time with them (vv. 17–21), recalling the joy even in the midst of hard times and opposition. Paul was convinced that sharing the gospel was worth all the plots and hatred directed his way and was filled with joy at the privilege of serving the Lord and seeing souls enter the kingdom. Paul's prospects from our perspective would be quite dim (vv. 22–27), as they center on danger and plots and struggles. In fact, it was doomed to be worse than Paul knew, for the years of imprisonment ahead would not be easy. He is a great model to follow, for he refuses to worry about the difficulties and focuses entirely on finishing the course God has set out. It is not comfort that matters but serving the Lord faithfully.

In the next section (vv. 28–31) Paul took on the mantle of prophet and warned them of false teachers that would enter the church both from without and within the congregation. These would rend the flock like savage wolves and tear apart congregations. To counter these destructive, satanic individuals, the leaders needed to be mature (elders), vigilant (overseers), and spiritual guides (shepherds) to God's flock. This is even more important today, for there are far more false teachers and movements disseminating falsehood to contend with. Our churches must become bastions of truth and keep our people centered on God and Christ.

In the final part of the speech Paul first sets the record straight about his finances (vv. 32–35). He sought nothing for himself but cared only to serve the Lord and help others. He was the model Christian leader—living not for himself but for the God he served and the people to whom he ministered. The farewell itself (vv. 36–38) was poignant, for it showed how deeply he and the elders cared for one another. Yet it was also joyful, for they commended one another to the Triune Godhead and knew he would make all things right.

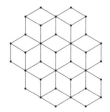

PAUL'S RETURN TO JERUSALEM, PART 2
(21:1–36)

The final missionary journey has now finished, but Paul hasn't realized it, thinking he is going to head for Spain after his visit to Jerusalem. He had asked for prayer in Romans 15:31 that God would deliver him from the Jews who were plotting against his life. God answered that with a "yes-and-no" response, delivering him from the plot against his life but not from arrest and trial. He would indeed go to Rome but in chains rather than on a mission. In fact, the rest of Acts will detail that "trip" to Rome and the legal attempts by his Jewish enemies to get him condemned and killed by the Roman authorities. That ploy worked with regard to Jesus but not for Paul.

PAUL CONCLUDES HIS JOURNEY
TO JERUSALEM (21:1-16)

Luke couches the travel narrative here as a series of meetings with the saints in several key cities on the way—Tyre, Ptolemais, and Caesarea. These meetings combine the theme of unity and community with the increasing pressure on Paul resulting from the plot against his life and the question as to whether he should go to Jerusalem. This provides an enduring lesson for us on discovering the will of God and the leading of the Holy Spirit when there are signs and interpretations that point in more than one direction.

The "we" passages begin again in verse 1 (see on 16:10), indicating that Luke has rejoined the team here for the trip to Jerusalem (21:1–18). The ship they had boarded in Troas now continues from Miletus, and they round the peninsula (where Turkey is today) then travel between it and the island of Rhodes (the seat of another of the "seven wonders," the Colossus of Rhodes) to the city of Patara. There they change to a grain ship (for leaving the coast and sailing east). This was a much quicker trip than following the coast around, and they would have made it in five days. The ship travels south of Cyprus and across the Mediterranean to Tyre on the coast of Syria, where it would "unload its cargo," which took seven days.

They stayed at the homes of the believers in Tyre for the seven days the ship took to unload. There would have been some who had become "disciples" when Jesus was there (the Syrophoenician woman, Mark 7:24–30; see also Luke 6:17), others when the expanding mission of the church reached there in Acts 11:19. Probably there was a fairly developed church in Tyre.

During that time the Spirit sent them a prophetic word via the believers there "not to go on to Jerusalem." This is very difficult because earlier (20:23) the Spirit warned him not to stay away from Jerusalem but rather than when he went, "prison and hardships" awaited him. Then later in Caesarea (21:13) he interpreted the Spirit's warning to him in chapter 20 that he should go and willingly face the hardships that would entail. So the best way to understand the prophecy here in verse 4 is that the Spirit warned them that hardships awaited Paul in Jerusalem, and *they interpreted that to mean* that he should not go there (see also below in vv. 10–13). In other words, the Spirit's message was not that Paul should stay away from Jerusalem, but that arrest awaited him; their understanding of the true message was that he should stay away.

At the end of the seven days (21:5–6) the team boards the ship, leaves Tyre, and continues on their way. They had all grown quite close to the Christians in Tyre in those few days, so everyone, including wives and children, accompanies them to the ship and kneels with them in prayer, undoubtedly for safekeeping in light of the prophecy. The prayer requests of Romans 15:30–32 would certainly also be high on the list.

Ptolemais was twenty-seven miles south of Tyre and less than a day's sailing, and all Luke tells us in verse 7 is that they spent a day there as well, probably also due to the ship unloading cargo. This would probably be similar to the time in Troas, where Paul, his team, and the believers there met, worshipped together, and shared news with one another. He would have spoken of the spread of the gospel in Asia Minor, Macedonia, and Achaia, and the Ptolemaic brothers and sisters of the state of the church in Palestine. It would have been a joyous time together, but still filled with worry about the prophecy at Tyre and its ramifications for Paul and the team.

Caesarea is another thirty miles or so further south, and there they disembark for good and stay at the home of Philip, the one who had evangelized Samaria and the Ethiopian eunuch (8:4–40). Luke identifies him as "one of the Seven" chosen by the apostles to deal with practical needs in Jerusalem, in particular the widows (6:3–6). They apparently had become a well-known group in the early church akin to the Twelve.

Luke in particular mentions his "four unmarried daughters who prophesied," highlighting the centrality of prophecy in this section. Philip apparently had ceased his itinerant early ministry and settled in Caesarea, where he served the church for the next twenty-plus years as an "evangelist" (called in Eph 4:11 an office in the church).[1] During those years he also raised four daughters who became well-known prophetesses. Women as well as men could be prophets (1 Cor 11:4–5), and at Pentecost Peter prophesies through

---

1. It apparently was often a local ministry rather than a traveling ministry like it tends to be today. Philip lived in Caesarea and probably reached out to the lost in Caesarea and the surrounding regions.

Joel 2:28-32 that the gift would come on both groups (Acts 2:17-18). The fact that they were virgins is not added as a requirement to be a prophet; rather, it shows their dedication to the Lord.

We saw Agabus last in 11:27-30, but clearly he had a major ministry of prophecy in the early church and seems to be chosen by the Spirit to deliver divine messages on many auspicious occasions. His central location was apparently Jerusalem, and from there he would have traveled to key spots as the Spirit led him. The Spirit leads him here to present an acted prophetic parable, a method often used (Isa 8:1-4; Jer 19:1-13; Ezek 4-5), and used by Jesus during passion week at the triumphal entry (Mark 11:1-11), cleansing of the temple (Mark 11:15-19), and cursing of the fig tree (Mark 11:12-14, 20-21).

Agabus came up to Paul (probably during a service) and, no doubt shocking everyone there, took off Paul's own belt and from a kneeling position (like a prisoner) tied his own hands and feet with that belt. Clearly he looked like someone under arrest, crouched on the ground and bound hands and feet. He then uttered his prophecy, which everyone would have understood because he was well known as a leading prophet in a community that contained prophets (Philip's daughters). It would have been an electric scene as he prophesied, "The Holy Spirit says, 'In this way the Jewish leaders in Jerusalem will bind the owner of this belt and will hand him over to the Gentiles.' "

This is exactly what happened to Jesus, and Paul was now to experience that "participation in his sufferings" (Phil 3:10) that God often wills for his followers. The next five years will be given over to the fulfillment of this prophecy and will take us through the rest of the book of Acts. The reason he would have to be handed over to the Gentiles is that the Jews would seek the death penalty, which only the Romans could inflict.

Agabus had drawn no conclusions, but Paul's companions are quick to leap to the conclusion that Paul should stay far away from Jerusalem. Agabus simply reinforced their understanding from

Tyre, and now they were absolutely certain this was God's will. For him to continue his journey would not just be dangerous but would be going against God's clear intention.

This is a great exercise in trying to discover God's will. All of Paul's friends are convinced God is saying one thing, while Paul himself is sure of exactly the opposite. They are interpreting the same data: God is saying that to go to Jerusalem will mean arrest and imprisonment. One says that means, "Don't go," the other that it means, "When you go, this will happen." That is often the case when trying to decide the implications of what God is showing us. It is not just accepting the message from the Spirit; it is understanding it and following it.

Paul is deeply distressed by their insistence, crying out, "Why are you weeping and breaking my heart?" No one supports his own understanding, and their heartbreak just increases his. He is all alone and begs for support. However, he is also certain that his position is the correct one and will stand by it even if no one will stand with him. He has been thinking about it throughout this journey and has faced it with the Ephesian elders (20:23, 37), his friends in Tyre (21:4, 5), and now in Caesarea. He knows what the Lord wants, and it hurts a great deal to see no one standing with him.

His response to their concern is to say, "I am ready not only to be bound, but also to die in Jerusalem for the name of the Lord Jesus." Protecting his life at all costs is not his priority, and he would return to what the apostles said in 5:41 when they rejoiced "because they had been counted worthy of suffering disgrace for the Name." Suffering for the name of Christ has been a theme throughout the book of Acts (see also 9:15-16) for there is great power in the name (3:6, 16; 4:10), and suffering unleashes that power.

Luke and the others continue to argue the point, but nothing they say will dissuade him, and they finally surrender, saying, "The Lord's will be done" (21:14). In accepting the Lord's will, it is clear Paul is correct in understanding what God wants, and all that follows is indeed "the Lord's will." The theme continues: everything in Acts is not "the Acts of the Apostles" but "the Acts of the Holy Spirit through the Apostles." If anyone had told Paul how God would answer his prayer of Romans 15:31 to "be kept safe from the unbelievers in Judea," he would have had a hard time accepting it. If they had told him what the next five years of his life would be like, he would have doubted nearly all of it. God truly works in mysterious ways, but only eternity will reveal the whole extent of how God will use this time and these most difficult events.

The walk to Jerusalem from Caesarea is about sixty miles. It would have been a good-sized group, with the seven delegates from 20:4, Paul and his mission team (including Luke), and a group from Caesarea. With that many people, they probably walked. When they arrived, the Caesarea church had set up a large home for them to stay in belonging to a wealthy believer from Cyprus, Mnason. He is described as "one of the early disciples," likely meaning that he was a believer from the early days of the church, perhaps one of those forced to flee in the persecution of 8:1–3 who took the gospel to Cyprus in 11:20 and now has returned. Paul's difficult time in Jerusalem at least has a good beginning.

PAUL EXPERIENCES CONFLICT
IN JERUSALEM (21:17–36)

In 21:17, there is a transition to the last major section of the book (21:17–28:31), encompassing the events of Paul's opposition and arrest in Jerusalem, his tumultuous series of mini-trials that led the Romans to transport Paul first to Caesarea and then Rome, and the deep irony of his entering Rome both as a conquering spiritual warrior for God and as a prisoner on trial before the Romans. This series of events will change to world forever, for it is the means God chose to initiate the worldwide evangelistic movement to the nations.

MEETING THE JERUSALEM ELDERS (21:17–26)

Paul has been hoping for a peaceful and history-changing time
in Jerusalem. With the significant collection he had gathered
from the Gentile churches and the delegates they had sent to the
Jerusalem churches, he was hoping that a new salvation-historical
unity could be forged between Jewish and Gentile factions and a
oneness resulting that would last until the Lord returns. In the
meeting between Paul and James the respective leaders of the
Jewish and Gentile church were coming together, and with the
representatives from the Gentile lands and the Jerusalem elders,
a Christian United Nations could be established.

To accomplish that, however, God had to deliver him and them
from their Jewish opponents and their nefarious plots. That was
not to be, for reasons only God knew. Still, for us this is a critical
message on the importance of unity in the church. We today are
barraged by a plethora of issues—racial, ethnic, economic, and
even denominational—that threaten the oneness that is so important to God and church. We must work as hard as Paul and James
did to overcome these tensions.

After a very complicated trip, Paul arrived in Jerusalem to a
warm reception. By now they were no longer afraid of him and
had long rejoiced at his conversion and remarkable ministry with
the Gentiles. All who had known him before would still be amazed
at his transformation and at the loving Christian leader he had
become. They were also aware of the salvation-historical importance of this moment, as in a sense the aftermath of the Jerusalem
Council (chapter 15) is taking place with the leaders from the
Gentile church meeting those of the Jewish church.

Some have said that the absence of any mention of the collection on the part of Luke here in Acts means that it was rejected
by the Jerusalem church, but that hardly makes sense. If it had
been, Luke would have mentioned it like he does other failures
in the church. Rather, he focuses on the meeting itself and the
impending explosion of Jewish opposition that was soon to take

place. Likely, the warm reception includes their thanks for the love offering as well.

The fact that "all the elders were present" is significant, for it demonstrates how thoroughly the Jewish Christians loved and accepted their Gentile counterparts. The sense of oneness is palpable, and as Paul gives his report (vv. 19-20), the meeting place erupts with praise and joy. They are overjoyed to hear "what God had done among the Gentiles through his ministry" (21:19). We don't know where the Judaizers (the opponents in Galatians and at the Jerusalem Council) are at this time, but they likely have left the regular churches and formed their own splinter movement. There is a united front now praising the Lord for the Gentile believers and churches.

The Jerusalem churches have certainly remained abreast of the success of the Gentile mission, but it had been seven years since the council and about four years since his visit after the Corinthian ministry (18:22). They would have been amazed at stories of the evangelization of the province of Asia (part of the "reported in detail"). No one would have ever guessed anything like that could happen. We don't know for certain, but Paul probably told his hopes for his future ministry to Spain as well.

Luke relates that it is the elders as a whole and not just James who make the report, probably because it is an official statement of the Jerusalem leadership and not just personal concerns from James. The initial report is very positive about "how many thousands of Jews have believed," a remarkable number we would not have guessed from the rest of Acts, where it seems that far more Gentiles than Jews have come to Christ.[2] So this is an exciting detail.

However, then they add a sticky point: "And all of them are zealous for the law." A certain tension enters with this and leads

---

2. For Jewish conversions, see 2:41; 4:4; 5:16, 42; 6:7; 9:31.Many of these "thousands" (*myriades*, literally, "tens of thousands") have probably been recently converted.

directly to the main point, their worry over reports they hear about Paul, especially since the believers in Jerusalem are bearing some of the brunt of the animosity these rumors are causing. Most of those who have recently come to faith have retained their zeal for the law. Paul needs to know that fact as well as certain difficulties that could arise for Paul as missionary to the Gentiles. The rumors in the next paragraph will not help this difficult situation.

Now comes the bad news (21:21). His enemies have spread rumors that "you teach all the Jews who live among the Gentiles to turn away from Moses, telling them not to circumcise their children or live according to our customs." It is easy to see how this could arise, and there is some small truth in it. When a Jewish person converts to Christ, circumcision and obedience to the law are no longer central, for their salvation is based on faith in Christ, not on the law. Of course, he has never said any such thing in any synagogue, only to those who have found Christ, and then outside synagogues in a Christian setting. Nor did he ever tell Jewish Christian parents they should not circumcise their children. So the only ones Paul has told this to are those Jews who have become believers, and he himself still keeps the law in many ways.

The source of these rumors could be Judaizers who have fought with him ever since his mission to Galatia in chapters 14–15, but even more likely are Jewish opponents who have given him trouble on every missionary journey. One such group (from Asia) will appear in 21:27–29. They come to Jerusalem on a fairly regular basis and would have brought their hatred of Paul with them.

Paul's arrival is probably known all over Jerusalem, so "they [his enemies as well as the new converts] will certainly hear that you have come" (21:22). In light of that, the question is, "What shall we do?" The elders have already decided the best action to take so as to stave off disaster, so this question is merely rhetorical, to get everyone focused on the solution they are proposing. The purpose of their suggestion is to show the Jews of Jerusalem that Paul is still faithful to his Jewish tradition and keeps the law.

Actually, it is more than a suggestion, for they virtually demand that he do it.

There are four Jewish Christians who have taken a Nazirite vow, which we know from the fact that they are going to shave their heads (like Paul in 18:18, from Num 6:1–21). It was a monthlong vow (Num 6:4),[3] and they apparently have a week to go. They were unable to pay the expenses, so Paul would join them with a week to go and pay for them, which would be quite a bit, lambs or rams without defect depending on the type of offering (Num 6:14–15). It is also possible the four had become unclean during that time and would have further sacrificial expenses. Paul is being asked to take part in their vow and in addition to be purified himself from defilement incurred by extensive travels in Gentile lands.

The desired result (21:24) would be twofold: the Jerusalem Jews and new converts in the church "will know" that the rumors of Paul's defection from his Judaism are false, and they will realize he still does live "in obedience to the law." This doesn't mean he has returned to his Jewish roots, for these elders are Christians as well and concur with the Jerusalem Council's decision. Rather, it means that he still respects the law and within these parameters is committed to it. Whether this was a wise decision has long been debated, for it certainly did backfire. However, this was their decision, and Paul decided to follow their desires.

Probably for the sake of the delegates, the elders want to make sure (21:25) that they are aware of the decree sent to the Gentile churches after the Jerusalem Council in 15:23–29. The purpose of the letter was to inform Gentile believers how to avoid offending their Jewish brothers and sisters by overutilizing their freedom in Christ. These were areas in which Gentiles should be sensitive and respect Jewish customs. They don't have to be circumcised or obey every detail of the Mosaic law but should "abstain from food sacrificed to idols" (see 1 Cor 8), avoid eating food still containing

---

3. Seen as thirty days in the Mishnah (m. Naz. 1:3).

blood or meat from strangled animals (again with blood still in them), and refrain from all types of immoral behavior. The goal is not to hamstring the Gentiles but to promote harmony between Jews and Gentiles in the church.

Paul acquiesces to the request of the elders and immediately the next day joins the four men, purifying himself along with them. They would have immersed themselves in one of the large pools on the way to the temple, probably one of the six in Jerusalem, for instance the pool of Siloam or the pool of Bethesda. They went and reported to the priest "to give notice" of the day they would make the ritual offerings (two doves or young pigeons, Num 6:10–11; see also 6:14–15). The four were nearing the end of their monthlong period, while Paul was joining them for the last week and performing the weeklong ritual of purification.

Arrest in the Temple (21:27–36)

Relative peace reigned until the seven days were nearly finished. Paul came to the temple, most likely to be with the four men as they offered the sacrifices to end their Nazirite vow. However, some Jews who had apparently opposed Paul in the province of Asia (Ephesus, chapter 19) raised their voices in protest and stirred up the crowd there. It was not a formal arrest at first, more of a mob "seizure," but it quickly became an arrest as the Romans stepped in. This all is occurring in the precincts of the temple itself, in particular the court of Israel, where Paul was fulfilling his duties for his purification ceremony.

Gentiles were not allowed in the inner courts on penalty of death. One of these **diaspora** Jews had seen Paul walking in Jerusalem with Trophimus, the delegate from Ephesus (20:4) and "assumed that Paul had brought him into the temple" (v. 29), though that was completely untrue. So there were two charges, the first the same one often leveled against him, that he was teaching "everyone everywhere against our people and our law and this place" (v. 28), and the second that he was desecrating the temple with Trophimus.

Their shouts bring Jews running from all around. The rumors
have been swirling about him for some time (v. 21), and now the
tumult increases manifold, as their former champion-turned-
enemy is apparently unmasked as one of the true blasphemers
of Torah. The first general charge actually has three segments, as
he supposedly defiled with his teaching first the Jewish people
(that they are no longer the covenant people but sinners like the
Gentiles), then the Mosaic law (saying it no longer governed the
people of God), and finally the temple itself (as no longer the dwelling place of God).

The specific charge, then, is that Paul has defiled the temple by
bringing a Gentile, Trophimus, into the inner sanctuary. We have
even found the plaque placed at the steps into the inner courts
warning non-Jews of the death penalty for entering that sacred
space. This is strange because they never try to catch the actual
person, Trophimus, implicated in the warning but address all their
animosity toward Paul, who supposedly did nothing more than
accompany the Gentile into the inner courts. Nor did they try to
prove that the Gentile had actually been in the inner courts. They
show no interest in the legal side of the issue at all. They only want
to get rid of Paul by any means possible.

The mob is so inflamed by these many charges that they "arouse"
the entire city. People run from every direction, seize Paul anew,
drag him out of the inner courts ("temple" = inner sanctuary), and
close the seven gates to the inner area of the temple. It is possible
that all temple activity was effectively canceled by the riot that
ensued. Paul is forcibly removed into the outer court of the Gentiles.

The desire of these Jews is to kill Paul. Stoning would be the
legal penalty for blasphemy (Lev 24:14), but they seem to be bent
on beating him to death (21:31). Before they can do this, the Romans
arrive. While only the Romans were technically allowed to carry
out capital punishment, they gave a certain amount of freedom,
as in the death of Stephen in 7:59–60, and the Jews come close to
getting away with it here.

Roman soldiers are garrisoned in the Antonia Fortress at the northwest corner of the Temple Mount, and their commander is a Roman tribune named Claudius Lysias (his name is given at 23:36). The Roman soldiers' primary responsibility is to maintain order in the city, so he and his men rush to intervene before the mob action gets totally out of hand. They would have got there quickly, for they merely had to descend the one set of steps from the fortress to the outer court itself. As soon as the rioters saw the Romans, they ceased beating Paul and handed him over. The "officers" would have been centurions, so there would have been two to three centuries of soldiers, enough to strike fear and stop any rioter immediately.

The commander felt the only way to gain control was to place Paul under arrest and then find out the cause of the chaos (21:33). He could release him if it came to naught. He had him manacled with two chains, probably in effect handcuffed between two soldiers. Once the situation was in hand, he then asked the Jews who this man was and what crime he had committed. He thought maybe the man was a hardened criminal who had committed some great offense, perhaps the Egyptian who led a revolt (v. 38). He is thinking like a Roman, for no Jew would riot against such a person as the Egyptian.

The mob mentality still prevails, so he gets no real answer, as everyone shouts something different at him (21:34). Most of them had no idea; they were attracted by all the action and excitement (as in the Ephesian riot of 19:22). All the commander heard was the tumultuous "uproar," so he remained completely confused. The Romans could never figure out these Jews anyway, and rioting just made it worse. He had to get out of the chaotic situation, so he ordered Paul into the barracks of the fortress so he could interrogate the man privately.

Just getting Paul up the stairs proved the correctness of his assessment, for he had to be carried by the soldiers due to "the violence of the mob," for everyone continued not only to shout but also to take swings at Paul, hoping to hurt him. You would think they would have been quelled by the Roman soldiers, but mob insanity is a very real thing on such occasions. With a unified voice, they all shout, "Get rid of him!" (*aire auton*). In other words, they want the Romans to finish what they had started, his execution. This is exactly what the crowds had shouted at the Barabbas incident in Luke 23:18, "Away with this man!" (*aire touton*).[4] How easily the sheep are led astray!

This is a key chapter, providing a transition from the missionary journeys and the fulfillment of the prophecy of Acts 1:8 "to the ends of the earth." From this point on to the end of the book, Luke's emphasis will be on persecution, trial, and the way the gospel triumphs over incredible adversity. In this section (vv. 1–16) Paul is not just traveling down to Jerusalem to share the gift of the Gentile churches with their Jewish brothers and sisters but also wrestling with the growing tension of being hated and pursued by people who want to rid the earth of them. How to discern the will of God and live by it becomes a critical issue.

It all comes to a head in Caesarea (vv. 8–14), when Agabus echoes the prophecy of Tyre (v. 4) that Paul will face arrest and imprisonment in Jerusalem. All of Paul's associates and the other believers there immediately tell Paul that the Spirit doesn't want him to go, but he is convinced that he must and that the Spirit is telling him what awaits, not that he shouldn't go. This of course contains an important message to all of us for discovering the will of God and what place our friends have in that decision. Their loving counsel is important but not binding. In the end we ourselves have to decide what the Spirit is saying to us.

------

4. See also Jesus' trial before Pilate in John 19:15.

The Jerusalem elders received Paul's report to them (vv. 17-19) with great joy (as was certainly the monetary gift from the Gentile churches), and a new unity between Jew and Gentile was quite apparent. However, there was a very serious concern (vv. 20-25), as Paul's enemies were spreading rumors that he was telling diaspora Jews (those living among the Gentiles) to turn away from Judaism. To disprove that and to show he was still a good Jew as well as Christian, they asked him to join four of their group who had made a Nazirite vow and pay for their expenses as well as purify himself after being in Gentile lands. Paul agreed (v. 26) and joined the four for the last part of their vow.

Very quickly it all descended into chaos. Toward the end of the seven days, some of Paul's enemies saw him with a Gentile, Trophimus, and assumed he had taken the man into the inner sanctuary, thus desecrating the temple. A riot ensues that the Romans have to quiet down (vv. 31-36), with the result that they end up having to put Paul under protective arrest. The difficult times and fulfillment of the Spirit's prophecy from 21:10-11 have begun, and nothing again will be the same.

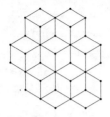

PAUL'S DEFENSE AT THE TEMPLE
(21:37–22:29)

This passage includes the first retelling of Paul's conversion story after chapter 9; chapter 26 is the other. Of these two latter versions, the one here is for Jewish ears, the next for the Gentiles. Paul is hoping that his retelling here will assuage the mob by assuring them that as a Christian he has not abandoned his Jewish roots. This too will backfire, for they don't want to listen to reason, and in their minds he is a blasphemer from the very fact that he is a Christian. He has been judged guilty before the proceedings have even begun. Luke's message to us is to not be surprised by the depth of hatred we will face from the world of unbelievers.

PAUL GETS PERMISSION TO
ADDRESS THE MOB (21:37-40)

When Paul asks for permission to speak, the commander is quite surprised that he can speak Greek. He would not expect Jewish rabble to be able to do so, let alone speak it so well. He wonders if Paul is the Egyptian insurrectionist who had recently "led four thousand terrorists out into the wilderness." The term for "terrorists," *sicarioi*, is the word for a short sword or dagger and came to be used for mercenaries and assassins who killed for a living.

The Sicarii thus became their title and was used for centuries. Josephus (*Jewish War* 2.261–63) tells the story of just such a person who led thirty thousand people in a rebellion and fled into the desert, prophesying that the walls of Jerusalem would collapse and allow him to enter, defeat the Romans, and set up a messianic rule. He was defeated, and four hundred of his men were killed, but he escaped. The tribune hoped Paul was this man and would enhance his career with this capture.

Paul's answer would have been very disappointing: "I am a Jew, from Tarsus in Cilicia, a citizen of no ordinary city." This explains his excellent Greek and provides a warning to the tribune that he is no mere peasant but a person of substance. Paul clearly felt that identifying himself as a citizen of Tarsus was enough to establish his stature. "No ordinary city" stresses the importance of Paul's hometown. He didn't need to say he was also a Roman citizen (on which see 16:37–38 and 22:25). So Paul's request carries clout: "Please let me speak to the people." He is also saying he poses no threat to Rome or to the tribune.

The tribune gives in, and Paul steps forward (21:40), standing on the steps that descend from the Antonia Fortress to the court of the Gentiles, with the Jewish crowd spread out before him. The tribune hopes Paul will explain and enable him to understand what is going on. He is doomed to disappointment, for Paul speaks in Aramaic and speaks entirely of Jewish matters. Paul's commanding presence is seen in the fact that he merely motions and the crowd, formerly enraged, becomes silent in expectation. Of course, having the Roman army behind you doesn't hurt.

PAUL DELIVERS HIS DEFENSE SPEECH (22:1–21)

Paul shows great respect for the people assembled below him, beginning as Stephen did (7:2) in deprecation to his Jewish "brothers and fathers," then asking them to "listen now to my defense." As he spoke to them in Aramaic, they didn't hear a false prophet or a rabble-rouser but one like themselves. As a result, they "became very quiet" and listened politely.[1]

PEDIGREE AND LIFE AS A JEW (22:1–5)

Since Paul has been charged with heresy, he wants his listeners to know how upstanding his background as a faithful Jew really was. He was a **diaspora** Jew, born and raised in his early years in Tarsus of Cilicia, where he also spent ten years in the time between 9:30 and 11:25. So he had a **Hellenistic** but mainly a fully Jewish upbringing. By the time he was thirteen, but also possibly earlier,[2] he was sent to Jerusalem to study under the grandson of Hillel and leading rabbi of his day, Gamaliel (see 5:34). To be given such a privilege means he was precocious and gifted, and he certainly distinguished himself over the next several years there. It is safe to say he was one of the leading young rabbinic minds of his day.

Paul's early life up to his conversion could be given the title from verse 3b, "zealous for God." Zeal defined his every waking moment. In Philippians 3:5 he calls himself "a Hebrew of Hebrews," and in Galatians 1:14 he says that he was "extremely zealous for the traditions of my fathers." No one exceeded him in his zeal for the law.

He elsewhere defines the extent of his zeal as "persecuting the church" (Phil 3:6), and he does so here as well (22:4), saying he "persecuted the followers of this Way to their death, arresting both men and women and throwing them into prison" (see 9:2). This is an important point, for he did to Christ's followers what they were doing to him. Stephen's was not the only martyrdom

---

1. Commentators commonly use Greek rhetorical devices when organizing this speech, but I don't think they apply here. That was correct for his Mars Hill address in chapter 17, addressed to a Greek audience. However, this is a Jewish speech and should be understood through the eyes of Paul the rabbi.

2. Several interpreters read "brought up" as meaning from infancy or early in childhood, perhaps to live in Jerusalem with his sister (23:16). We cannot know, but I prefer his early teens, for he understood Gentile ways very well later.

in which he participated. Here and in 26:10 he admits that he had participated in several deaths.

We don't know how this was accomplished. It is doubtful there were many other Sanhedrin trials resulting in Roman executions like with Jesus. How many would the Romans have allowed like Stephen, a trial leading to stoning? But there were some, for he adds, "as the high priest [Caiaphas] and all the Council [that is, the Sanhedrin] can testify" (22:5). There had to have been several, and Paul had been planning more, for he went to Damascus to bring believers back to face these same kinds of trials (9:1–2: these were literally "murderous threats"). He had been planning countless more in the next months and years.

Clearly Paul had become a very important official with access to the highest corridors of power among the Jews. They could all bear witness to his murderous intent to eradicate Christianity from the land. Finally, Paul tells them of the letters from the Sanhedrin for the Jewish leaders in Damascus affirming that he had full authority from the high priest and Sanhedrin to arrest Christians and take them "as prisoners to Jerusalem to be punished." Certainly the full gamut of punishments we have seen in Acts—from warning to flogging to stoning—was enacted from time to time. Luke hasn't said a lot about this terrible period, but it lasted at least a few years, and Paul was the focus of it. His point to his listeners is that he has been where they are and knows much better than they what a terrible price it exacts on the participants. He wants them to listen closely to what he has to say.

THE VISION OF JESUS ON THE ROAD (22:6–11)

In chapter 9 this was a third-person narration, but now it is a first-person testimony. Paul's emphasis for this Jewish audience is on the **Shekinah**, the light that depicts the glory of God dwelling with his people (from *shakan*, "dwelling"). Paul wants them to realize how authentic the vision was that God sent him. The incident took place when he was only a short distance from Damascus on his journey from Jerusalem. Since it was at noon the sun was already straight overhead, so the "bright light from heaven" must have been astounding. It could not have been a dream, for he was traveling at the height of the day. It had to have been a direct heavenly event.

Both the other accounts (9:4–5; 26:14–15 = 22:7–8) stress these details. When the Shekinah hit him full force, he "fell to the ground and heard a voice." Who knows how many time he had told his story? The message is the same in all three, and what Jesus said was imprinted on Paul's mind: "Saul! Saul! Why do you persecute me?" Needless to say, these words turned his world upside down, in one fell swoop telling him he had been totally wrong about what his severe persecution was doing. He thought he was destroying the enemies of God, when in reality he was battling against the Son of God himself.

Paul's response, "Who are you, Lord?" is the same in all three, but Jesus' response is slightly expanded here, being "Jesus of Nazareth" for these Jewish listeners to identify him more exactly. He wants them to realize Jesus (as well as he) was as Jewish as they are. His hometown of Nazareth shows his humble roots (John 1:46: "Can anything good come from there?") and the ignominy of who became Messiah. Jesus is truly the humble King.

The light returns to center stage in 22:9. In 9:7 his companions "heard the sound but did not see anyone." The emphasis is on the voice commanding Paul. Here they "saw the light, but they did not understand the voice." In chapter 9 the stress was on the authoritative command (the sound), but here the emphasis is on the Shekinah glory shining on Paul and surrounding the event (the light). As in the exodus, God (Jesus here) reveals himself by shining in ineffable light and taking residence among his people. In reality those with him saw a light and heard a voice but could not distinguish anything. In chapter 9 Luke stressed the voice of commission; in chapter 22 Paul stresses the light of glory. Paul wants the Jews in the temple court to realize who was truly behind the vision.

Paul's response (22:10) to the light and the voice is complete surrender: "What shall I do, Lord?" There is no arguing the fact that God is behind it all, and so he recognizes Jesus as "Lord" and wants to know what the Lord would have him do. It undoubtedly had not sunk in that this Jesus must have risen from the dead to be speaking to him. It will take those three days in his room, blind and meditating the whole time, to organize his thoughts and realize the significance of all that has happened. He is willing to do anything the Lord wants.

Jesus' response, as we know from 9:6, is to tell Paul to "go into Damascus," his destination all along. However, what will transpire there has now been completely reversed. Rather than hunting down the Christians, it will entail searching for the Christ. Only then will all be known, for the risen Lord will explain "all that you have been assigned to do." Let us note the two emphases: *all* will be made known, and everything will be "assigned" (*tetaktai*, a divine passive) by God. There is an aspect of divine election to this, as Paul's commission from God will take the form of divine commands. Free will and election always work together, but Paul is stressing the divine side here. Paul's only choice is to obey or not; Jesus the Christ has already assigned him his marching orders. This is also important for us. It does matter what we do with our lives, and God *does* have a wonderful plan for us. Our task is to align ourselves with his elect will for us.

Once more Paul stresses the blinding brightness of the light (22:11). Paul's sight is so thoroughly gone that his companions have to lead him "by the hand into Damascus." The "brilliance of the light" in Greek is actually "the glory [*tēs doxēs*] of the light," stressing once again the Shekinah glory as the source of his blindness. There is symbolic meaning here, as the light of God first reveals the darkness of sin and then removes it as Paul turns to the light and finds salvation. Paul states this well in 2 Corinthians 4:4–6, speaking of "the light of the gospel that displays the glory of Christ." In that passage it is blindness from "the god of this age" that is dispelled in Christ and his glory.

ANANIAS AND THE DAWN OF UNDERSTANDING (22:12–16)

For the sake of his Jewish accusers Paul stresses that Ananias was "a devout observer of the law and highly respected by all the Jews living there." Paul is implying that Ananias would still be in Damascus and could testify about all this. His piety in observing the law assiduously was well attested. When he comes to Paul directly and restores his sight (22:13), he testifies to the latter's faithfulness as well. When he addresses him as "Brother Saul," he highlights him as a pious Jew on his own. And when "Brother Saul" looks up and is "able to see him," it is clear that a divinely sent miracle has confirmed the entire scene.

Ananias then becomes the bearer of the divine commission (22:14–15) and together with the temple vision of verses 17–21 tells Paul "everything" he has been "assigned" by the Lord (v. 10). In 9:17 Ananias' opening words centered on Paul's receiving the Spirit. Here for a Jewish audience they center on Paul knowing God's will, hearing his voice, and witnessing for him before "all people," meaning Gentile as well as Jew. Paul is presented here as a commissioned prophet, bearing God's truths to the world.

The "God of our ancestors" stresses the continuity from the Old Testament spokespeople for God and Paul himself (22:14–15). The Christians are not hostile to truth and the enemies of God's people but are the bearers of truth and the new Israel, in complete continuity with the Israel of the old covenant. The key phrase is "to see the Righteous One." The Damascus road vision is a divine encounter with the righteous Messiah, and Paul has both seen and heard him. Thereby his "witness" is divinely authorized by the One who has died as the Suffering Servant and been raised as the Son of God.

So it is time to quit meditating and start working for God: "What are you waiting for? Get up, be baptized and wash your sins away, calling on his name" (22:16). Paul had certainly come to faith in the hours following the vision itself as he lay blind and meditating on the meaning of those events that changed his life forever. Now he needed to make public witness to his salvation by immersing himself in water baptism (2:38) and signifying thereby that his sins have been washed away by the blood of Jesus. From the start the symbolic act has been labeled "a baptism of repentance for the forgiveness of sins" (Luke 3:3), signifying that in placing one's self under the blood of Jesus, people are cleansed of sin. In undergoing baptism, one calls on the name of Jesus to be saved. As stated in the Great Commission, believers are baptized "in the name of the Father and of the Son and of the Holy Spirit" (Matt 28:19).

THE VISION AND COMMISSION TO THE GENTILES (22:17–21)

Paul now skips ahead greatly, past his three-year ministry in Arabia to his return to Jerusalem. The vision is not related in chapter 9 but had to take place during that time of meeting the apostles in 9:27–28. He relates the vision because it shows that the rumors that he was teaching against the temple and defiling it (21:28–29) are false. For Paul as well as them, the temple was a house of prayer; and as it was God's house, he spoke with his servant Saul there. This was the second vision after Damascus, and it further cemented the message of that earlier time. In 9:29 he left Jerusalem after learning the Hellenistic Jews wanted to kill him. Here we learn what precipitated it, a vision in the temple where the Lord (Jesus) told him to leave immediately because the Jews of Jerusalem "will not accept your testimony about me." The need to rush away in a hurry was due to the plot described in 9:29.

Paul's response to the Lord in the vision (22:19–20) most likely constitutes a plea to be allowed to remain in Jerusalem because he is well known there and still has a vital witness to give. He notes two special things that he believes will enhance his current ministry there. First, he was well known for leading the persecution against the Christians when he "went from one synagogue to another to imprison and beat those who believe in you." In 6:9 the opposition to Stephen began in the Hellenistic synagogues of Jerusalem, and in 8:3 we are told of Saul "going from house to house" dragging people to prison. These were house churches, equivalent to Christian synagogues. In 9:2 he received official letters from the high priest and Sanhedrin authorizing him to do the same in the synagogues of Damascus. Paul had now become famous for this anti-Christian activity. His point here is that that fame was still there and would make his current witness all the more effective.

Second, he also was present at Stephen's martyrdom in 7:58–8:1 and stood guarding the clothes of the executioners, thereby giving his approval to what they were doing. Moreover, Stephen was a "witness" in his death, with the Greek *martys* bridging from his role of "witness" to that of "martyr." So Paul in his present role is continuing that of Stephen, and he is implicitly begging the Lord to be allowed to continue it. He believes that he still has a valuable service to render to the Lord here and so hopes to be allowed to stay.

The Lord, however, has other plans and so reiterates the command of verse 18, "Go; I will send you far away to the Gentiles." This is the third time Paul has been told that God's will was for him to lead the Gentile mission and become the missionary to the Gentiles. The first was during the original Damascus vision (26:17–18; also in Gal 1:16), the second via Ananias (9:15), and the third here in the temple vision. The Lord knew this call was so revolutionary that Paul needed all three direct occasions to help him assimilate a commissioning that he would never in his wildest dreams have thought possible. The verb "will send" is actually a present tense, "I am sending you" to show that his call to the Gentiles will be the ongoing mission of his life. The term "Gentiles" is the same term for "nations" (*ethnē*), repeating the Great Commission of Matthew 28:19, "Go and make disciples of all nations," including Jews as well as Gentiles. Still, in Romans 11:13 he is "apostle to the Gentiles," and that is uppermost here.

THE CROWD REJECTS PAUL AND HE IS INTERROGATED BY THE ROMANS (22:22–29)

Paul's defense seemed to be going well and his strategy working, but as soon as he mentioned going to the Gentiles, chaos exploded. This reminded them of all they despised about Paul and these Christians, confirming their suspicion that he had turned from his Jewish roots, blasphemed the God of the Old Testament, and embraced both Christianity and the Gentiles. Their shout, "Rid the earth of him! He's not fit to live!" was a demand for the death penalty for blasphemy and will be the theme of Jewish opposition for the rest of Acts. Tearing off their clothes (14:14) and throwing dust in the air (22:23) were gestures of rejection in the face of blasphemy (like throwing dust off the feet, 13:51).

Things had quickly got out of hand, so the tribune ordered his men to take Paul back into the barracks for his safety while he tried to figure out what was happening. Since people by nature are pathological liars, he thinks the only way to get at the truth is "under the whip," extracting the truth from Paul by torture in order to find out "why the people were shouting at him like this" (22:24). He is as much in the dark after all the shouting and Paul's speech as he was at the start.

However, his assumption that Paul was merely another Jew from Tarsus was wrong. He hadn't reckoned with Paul's pedigree as a Roman citizen. As soon as they "stretched him out to flog him," it took Paul about 0.1 seconds to demand his rights, and he asked the centurion, "Is it legal for you to flog a Roman citizen who hasn't even been found guilty?" As with the Philippian magistrates in 16:37–39, that changed everything. Roman citizens were promised due process of law, and these Roman officers would have been in serious trouble had they proceeded. Roman citizens could not be scourged (or crucified) except on command from Caesar himself.

Paul could have disclosed this earlier when he was originally arrested (21:33), but then it would have backfired and convinced the Jews completely that he had become a Gentile and abandoned his Jewish roots. He only does so here because his life is at stake and they are inside the fortress, away from his Jewish opponents.

The centurion immediately goes to the tribune and asks, "What are you going to do?" Tribunes were generally appointed by the emperor, and this one would have been in charge of the army in Jerusalem and possibly in Judea as a whole. He knows that they clearly cannot scourge Paul and must change their tactics (22:26). They have to figure a way to get at the truth that is allowed with Roman citizens. All the tribune can do at this time is to interrogate Paul directly (22:27-28). He wonders how in the world Paul could have acquired citizenship, telling him, "I had to pay a lot of money for my citizenship." As a tribune, he probably came from an upper-crust background, so he could afford to bribe the right people.

Yet while he was a very important person with enormous power, at that moment Paul had the upper hand, for he was "born a citizen," which meant in this area he was above Claudius Lysias in stature. Most likely Paul's father passed the citizenship on to his son, though we have no idea how he originally procured it. With this information everything changes, and there is a bit of deference in how Paul is treated. They all "withdrew immediately" and released Paul from his restraints (22:29). Now the commander is afraid because at the original arrest he had put this Roman citizen in chains. He still cannot release him, for he doesn't even know the original charges. But the circumstances of his imprisonment are altered, and he will be treated as well as possible while the authorities decide what to do.

———

In chapter 9 we read a third-person eyewitness narration of Paul's conversion and its aftermath. Here in chapter 22 Paul gives his own personal account and tells it from a Jewish perspective for a Jewish audience. This is the first of many defense speeches by Paul, as Luke tries to provide an apologetic approach to Christianity. Paul begins (vv. 1–5) by establishing his pedigree. He had been a leading Jew of his day, known for his zeal for the law, and he was also a major leader of the opposition against the Christians, not only arresting followers of the Way but also sending some of them to their deaths.

In this Jewish retelling of Paul's conversion (vv. 6–11) Paul emphasizes the Shekinah, the light of the glory of God and of Christ shining on him. It struck him blind, and for three days he lay in his room meditating on this glorious light, finally realizing its significance and being converted to Christ and to his mission on behalf of Christ. Here Paul is the model for us, allowing the light of the Godhead to shine in us and lead us to all that God has for us.

Ananias (vv. 12–16) is sent as the divine messenger both to explain the significance of the vision to Paul and to commission him as the prophet of God sent to both Jew and Gentile with the good news of the Christ. So Paul is not only converted but also sent out to the world with the gospel. His life has been completely reversed on the Damascus road, and everything he does for the rest of his life will have its origins and draw its meaning from these three days.

Three years later after his return to Jerusalem, God sent him a second vision (vv. 17–21), in which Christ clarified further that his future ministry would be to the Gentiles. He wished to remain in Jerusalem and correct his earlier tragic zeal that led him to hunt down God's new people. But the Lord had greater plans and wanted him to leave immediately and instead begin his task of hunting down the lost, especially Gentiles, to bring them to Christ.

Once Paul mentions going to the despised Gentiles, everything explodes, and another Jewish riot against Paul and Christianity begins (vv. 22–29). The commander is nonplussed at this sudden and disastrous turn of events, and he decides that the only way to find out the truth is to beat it out of Paul with a scourge. This galvanizes Paul into going the second step of his revelation of his background, and he declares himself not just a citizen of Tarsus (21:39) but also a citizen of Rome. That changes everything, and the commander now dare not lay a hand on him. He still has to keep Paul in custody in order to keep the Jews mollified, but he has to figure what his next steps should be. These "next steps" could almost be said to take us through the rest of the book of Acts.

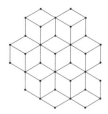

PAUL'S IMPRISONMENT
IN JERUSALEM
(22:30–23:35)

The tribune is still trying to find out what has instigated all the chaos over Paul. Now he turns to the Sanhedrin for information, but when he convenes them he again faces only chaos as factions within them debate arcane points of Jewish theology, especially rising from the dead. They divide over Paul along dogmatic lines, and the tribune is still in the dark. In the meantime, a plot to kill Paul comes to light, and he determines to get rid of the tricky issue by sending him to a higher court in Caesarea. The emphasis is on Paul's innocence and Jewish guilt, a point that will take us through the rest of Acts.

PAUL APPEARS BEFORE THE
SANHEDRIN (22:30-23:11)

In order to find out why and what the Jewish accusations were against Paul, the tribune releases him from jail and "orders" the Sanhedrin to assemble. This has occasioned a great deal of debate as to whether a Roman officer would have had the authority to do such a thing. First, Paul is released because he is a Roman citizen and cannot be arrested without good reason. The tribune knows of no such reason. Second, the "command" was probably couched as a request for the Sanhedrin to assemble and give him information about Paul's legal situation. They would certainly be happy to do so, for they want to get rid of him as well. They would have been advising Claudius Lysias as to how to handle the situation.

So the tribune, technically in charge throughout, brings Paul and stands him before the council to hear their input. The implications are clear: Paul is on trial before both the Sanhedrin and the Romans. The tribune has stepped back but is still very much a part of the proceedings. Moreover, he is immensely fair, honestly trying to ascertain what is actually going on. This is not a formal trial or even a pretrial hearing but a fact-finding expedition to enable the tribune to make a proper and judicious decision.

OPENING REMARKS (22:30–23:1)

Paul "looked straight" at them to make the opening comment. This is the second of five defense speeches (22:1–21; 23:1–9; 24:10–21; 25:8–11; 26:1–29) that show Paul's innocence and righteous behavior. This one is his counterclaim to the Jewish charges against him (21:28). He addresses the Sanhedrin as "my brothers," for before his conversion he served directly under their authority and probably knew most of them personally. He considers them peers.

He has three counterclaims: (1) "I have fulfilled my duty to God," meaning that he has been faithful to the law and lived his life as God would want him to do. (2) His conduct since following Christ is "in all good conscience," meaning he has maintained throughout an internal awareness that God is pleased with how he has conducted himself (on "conscience," see Acts 24:16; 1 Cor 4:4; 1 Tim 1:5, 19; 3:9; 2 Tim 1:3). (3) He has done so "to this day," meaning he is as faithful as a Christian as he was as a Jew. This is similar to Philippians 3:6, where he says, "As for righteousness based on the law, [I have been] faultless."

CONFLICT WITH THE HIGH PRIEST (23:2–5)

The high priest takes umbrage at what he views to be a false claim of innocence and commands those closer to Paul to "strike him on the mouth" for the falsehood. This particular high priest, Ananias, served from about AD 47 to 59 and was known for his bad temper.[1] He was also known for his pro-Roman stance and was killed by a Zealot in AD 66. Paul doesn't recognize who it is and counters with a strong verbal rejoinder, "God will strike you, you whitewashed wall!" We see here that Paul had a temper as well and lost it upon being struck by the high priest's assistant. His curse is virtually a judgment prophecy. Since the tribune called the meeting, the high priest is probably standing with other Sanhedrin members rather in front of the group as he normally did as its leader.

Paul is referring to final judgment, when God penalizes sins. Striking a defendant before they are judged guilty is against the laws of God and humankind. The language of God striking a sinner is fairly common (Deut 28:22; Ps 110:5; Job 34:26 KJV). The image behind "whitewashed wall" may stem from Ezekiel 13:10–16, in which the prophet Ezekiel accuses the false prophets of Israel who cry "peace" when there is no peace and build "flimsy walls" covered with whitewash, which collapse in time of crisis. The wall would be about to collapse from rot and would be whitewashed to look good. They would also whitewash tombs to make sure people saw them and didn't inadvertently touch them and become unclean (Matt 23:27). Both are images of a defiled person headed for judgment.

Paul is accusing Ananias of hypocrisy, judging Paul "according to the law" while violating the same Mosaic law by ordering him to be struck unfairly. Also, this is not supposed to be a trial, but several members of the Sanhedrin are trying to turn it into one. Paul sees them as far more guilty than he is.

---

1. Josephus, *Antiquities* 20.197–200.

With this several Sanhedrin members standing there admonished him, "How dare you insult God's high priest!" It didn't matter that he had been put in office by the Romans rather than God; he was still officially the high priest and deserved respect. Paul agreed, showing contrition, "Brothers, I did not realize that he was the high priest," and then cites Exodus 22:28, "Do not speak evil about the ruler of your people." However, several recent interpreters have seen this as an ironic condemnation, saying in effect, "a true ruler would not do such a thing," meaning he is not acting like God's high priest and does not deserve to be called such. On the other hand, Paul may never have seen the man, and the sudden convening of the assembly may have meant he had not had time to dress in his distinctive robes of office. When all is considered, it is best to take the language for what it is and see Paul apologizing for his behavior and submitting to the law. Paul did not recognize Ananias, spoke precipitously, and is genuinely sorry for not respecting the high priest's office. Luke may be intending a contrast, with Paul establishing a pattern of obedience to the law in contrast to the high priest.

THE DEBATE AND ITS AFTERMATH (23:6–10)

Paul realizes that there will not be a fair hearing before the Sanhedrin and that everything is stacked against him. So he decides to take action himself and disrupt the proceedings. At the same time, this was the primary truth he wished to get across to both the Jews and the Romans present, that he followed the risen Lord, Jesus the Christ. It was not merely a political ploy to divert attention from the so-called trial but the primary affirmation that determined Paul's purpose in life and ministry. Still, that was a side effect of Paul's cry and worked marvelously well. He deftly turned the Pharisees into supporters and created locked horns between them and the Sadducees in the Sanhedrin. It was a bold and effective move.

His statement that he is "a Pharisee, descended from [son of] Pharisees" is interesting, for it could mean his father was a Pharisee, highly unusual for a Pharisee living in a **diasporic** city like Tarsus. We have no record of Pharisees outside Palestine, but that is certainly possible. On the other hand, several commentators think that Paul is not speaking of family ties but of a tradition. In his training he became a Pharisee and joined a Pharisaic tradition. Either is possible, but I think it better to follow the more natural reading and see him as part of a family line of Pharisees.

As a Pharisee and at the same time a Christian, the central element that Paul had in common with the Pharisees was "the hope of the resurrection of the dead," and Paul states that that is why he is on trial. While Paul is stating his primary thesis, he is also enlisting supporters, and it works exceedingly well. Immediately the Pharisees and Sadducees begin fighting over this issue, which had long divided them (23:7-8). The Pharisees held doctrines on the afterlife that were similar to the Christians, but the Sadducees did not.

The Sadducees held that only the Pentateuch (first five books) is Scripture. All the passages that explicitly teach that there is an afterlife come later in the Old Testament (Job 19:25-27; Isa 26:19; Ezek 37:1-14; Dan 12:1-3, 13), so the Sadducees rejected them and believed this life was all there is, or at best in a half existence in Sheol like the Greek immortality of the soul. The major question is what Luke meant by "there are neither angels nor spirits" in the belief system of the Sadducees, for angels appear often in the Pentateuch (Gen 16:7-11; 19:1; Exod 3:2, 14:19; Num 22:22-35). It is generally agreed that they accepted the reality of angels but not of an intermediate state, with the spirits of God's people resembling angels (see Acts 12:15). So Luke is saying that the Sadducees refused to believe in either an afterlife or a conscious existence with bodies like angels.

Now the meeting descends completely into chaos, and a "great uproar" ensues as the two sides begin shouting at each other (23:9). The staid Sanhedrin becomes just another mob. After a while some scribes in the group gain the floor. Most scribes are Pharisees, but Luke tells the reader anyway in case some don't know that. These scribes "contended" or "argued vigorously" (NIV: *diemachonto*) for their position, meaning they defended the pro-afterlife position strongly, making a surprise statement about Paul: "We find nothing wrong with this man." Paul had chosen his argument well.

The Pharisees felt so strongly about their position vis-à-vis the Sadducees that they forgot all about the other areas where they opposed the Christians. They were thinking that perhaps when Paul spoke of Jesus addressing him in the vision it had been the case that "a spirit or an angel has spoken to him." In other words, it was Jesus' spirit speaking from Sheol. They simply were so focused on the debate that they for a time forgot about the other Christian beliefs in Jesus as Messiah and Son of God. Their point is that the idea of Jesus as alive beyond the grave does not contradict the Mosaic law and is in keeping with Jewish beliefs.

With this the debate became even more heated (23:10), so much so that the tribune felt he had lost control of the proceedings and that Paul's very life was endangered. The Sadducees were becoming more and more violent, and he was about to be "torn to pieces by them." The people in the chamber had become a lynch mob. The only thing he could do at this stage was to end the meeting and have his troops extract Paul and carry him back up to the barracks in the Antonia Fortress. Paul was indeed rescued, but the tribune was back to square one, with no real idea why all this was happening. The situation is in limbo, and Paul remains in custody until the tribune can figure out what to do.

An Encouraging Vision (23:11)

It seems as though Paul has a certain freedom in the fortress; he is not in chains or locked in a cell. But he is still in custody, not knowing what is taking place. He is that way for over twenty-four hours, when during the following night a vision comes. The Lord is standing next to him and assures him, "Take courage! As you have testified about me in Jerusalem, so you must also testify in Rome." In between the violent response of the Sanhedrin and another plot to kill him about to transpire, he is encouraged that God's greater purposes are being served. Paul had every reason to be scared, as every moment since he had been seized in the temple (21:27) people had been trying to kill him, and he had almost been scourged by the Romans. But all that has transpired, and all that is about to happen, is for the greater glory of God, so he need not worry.

The risen Lord refers to this entire time as testifying in Jerusalem and comforts him by saying that Paul will be protected through all that is going to happen (it will take over two years with a lengthy imprisonment in Caesarea in between) to ensure he extends this witness to Rome itself. His hopes to reach Rome will be realized, for it is God's will as well as his own desires. There are several visions at strategic points when Paul needs encouragement (also 18:9–10; 27:23–24), and so there is no longer any need to fear.

PAUL'S ENEMIES PLOT TO KILL HIM (23:12–22)

The very next morning after the vision a group of forty men "bound themselves with an oath not to eat or drink until they had killed Paul." They are clearly unhappy with the Sanhedrin and their wishy-washy lack of a decision regarding Paul and so decide to take matters into their own hands. Paul would have understood their plot, for it coincides with his own direct action against Christians after the death of Stephen (8:3; 9:1–2). Their seriousness is seen in the fact that they place themselves under a divine curse if they do not succeed. When they add their determination not to partake of any sustenance until the deed is done, they say in effect, "Either he dies or we die." They also are committed to kill Paul sooner rather than later. This is a very dangerous plot, for the Romans have committed to protect Paul, and anyone who tries to thwart their will is likely going to die in the attempt.

They make their plans an official conspiracy when they involve the chief priests and elders (23:14–15). This means that the entire leadership of the Jews is part of the conspiracy. They need the leaders and the Sanhedrin to create a situation where Paul is taken outside the fortress, where an armed force can get to him. So long as he is in the barracks under the eyes of the Romans he is completely safe. If the Sanhedrin asks them to bring Paul to a further meeting so they can provide "more accurate information about his case," the Romans will comply. They will send a small battalion with him, and an armed group of forty men will be able to overwhelm them and get to Paul (or perhaps a single assassin can get to him as the Romans bring him among the temple crowds).

On the surface this seems a foolproof plan. The leaders and the Sanhedrin will not be implicated since the attack will take place on the way to the council chambers, and the temple crowds should distract the Romans sufficiently for the conspirators to get at Paul. All is looking good for the plot.

Christ fulfills his promise to protect Paul. Paul's nephew learns of the plot (we never learn how) and comes to Paul with the dire news. Paul's sister lived in Jerusalem, and some think he may have been sent to live with her when he first came to study with Gamaliel as a teenager. He is now probably in his fifties, and the "young man" would have been in his teens or twenties. Apparently also Paul is allowed to have visitors in the barracks, for the young man is allowed to come to him and tell him of the plot. Most likely the tribune was (like Pilate with Jesus) convinced of Paul's innocence and so allowed certain privileges like visitors.

Paul must also have had friendly relations with both the centurion and the commander, for he asks the centurion to take his nephew to the commander, and he immediately complies with the request without even questioning it. The fact that he was a Roman citizen must have made a huge difference. The message was so explosive that he didn't even want to tell the centurion what it was. The fact that the centurion didn't demand to be told says a lot about Paul's status.

Paul's status and the respect in which he is apparently held is also seen in the commander's response to what seems to be a command to listen to his nephew. Instead of irritation at being bothered by a prisoner's request, he draws the young man aside (somehow understanding the need to keep it private) and asks, "What is it you want to tell me?" He might have thought it was further information that would help him make sense of all the chaos. At any rate, he trusts Paul enough to listen to the young man.

The young man's report (23:20-21) summarizes all we know about the plot—the pretext and false request to bring Paul to the Sanhedrin chambers, the forty men ready and waiting in ambush, the blood oath—and he begs the commander not to let the conspirators "persuade" him to carry it out when they arrive the next day. Needless to say, this startles the commander and galvanizes him into action. He sends him away with the command to tell no one the explosive news he has just reported (23:22). It must remain secret lest the conspirators find out that the tribune knows of their plot. God is working behind the scenes, orchestrating the actions of the centurion and tribune to fulfill his promise that Paul will indeed arrive safely in Rome. It is deeply ironic that he has to remain a Roman prisoner to guarantee his safety, and that it is the Romans who are God's instrument in protecting his servant from harm and even in providing transport to Caesarea and then Rome.

PAUL IS SENT TO CAESAREA (23:23-35)

To make sure Paul is kept safe, Claudius Lysias orders an enormous force to accompany him and gets them ready to leave in a single afternoon. Some think he is being treated as a king and that this has to be a fictional story, but Judea was a very volatile place, and the Romans had experienced several run-ins with mercenaries and revolutionaries. This was a very serious plot with virtually a death wish, so they had to expect anything. It was actually a wise

decision, for they didn't just want a battalion that could defeat
forty armed men; they wanted an overwhelming show of force that
would keep the Jews from even trying. That large a detachment
would not have been due to the importance of Paul but to the tribune's desire to show the Roman presence in Jerusalem and make
sure everyone knew the vast superiority of their military power.
The purpose was not to defeat the Jews when they attacked but to
keep the attack from even being attempted.

This many soldiers would certainly do that. Two centuries
of foot soldiers with all the armor, 70 horsemen, 200 spearmen
(many translate "bowmen")—that is 470 hardened soldiers from
the greatest army ever assembled. That was a large-enough force
to take down a medium-sized town. It was half of a Roman cohort,
therefore half of the soldiers stationed in Jerusalem. He probably
felt it would be a good exercise for his men and give them further
military experience.

Moreover, he has them deploy at nine that very evening, not
even giving the forty conspirators time to organize any opposition.
To make good time all the way to Caesarea, he also provides horses
for Paul to ride to Caesarea and Felix, the governor. It was a seventy-
mile journey and could be covered swiftly and with finality.

Luke cites the official letter the tribune sent to Felix. He somehow got a copy and cites it word for word, for it has all the legal
terms and style of a Roman letter explaining the transfer of a prisoner on appeal. The phrase "as follows" is literally "having this
set pattern" (*echousan ton typon touton*) and probably means it is
an official transcript. On a few other occasions (5:34–42; 25:13–22;
26:30–32) Luke includes official information, and it must be due to
diligent research on his part. Whenever an appeal forces a case to
be moved to the "higher court," in this case in Caesarea, adequate
reasons must be produced to justify taking the time of the governor
of the province. That is what the tribune Claudius Lysias is doing.

In ancient letters, the sender is named first, then the recipient followed by the greeting (*chairein*). The ruler of the province,

Felix, is called "Excellency" (*kratistos*), also used of Theophilus in Luke 1:3, and "governor" (*hēgemōn*), a general term for the "leader" or head of the government. Felix was a freedman whose brother was close to both Claudius and Nero, and he had been freed by the mother of Claudius. As a result he had been appointed the procurator of this region and ruled from about AD 52 to 60. He was a corrupt and cruel governor, and his mistakes were part of the reason for the revolt of AD 66–70. Still, he viewed himself as a good Roman ruler and sought the same kind of justice in cases like Paul that Pilate had shown with Jesus.

The letter is a two-part account of the volatile situations that led first to Lysias' arrest of Paul and then the subsequent transfer of the case to Felix. So he starts (23:27) with his "seizure" by the Jews in 21:27–30 and the necessity of his arrival with troops to quell the riot and arrest Paul in order to save his life (21:31–33). To cover himself, he moves his learning that Paul was a Roman citizen up to this early point and conveniently forgets that it actually was not until he was about to scourge him in 22:23–29. This of course was to cover himself and look good. He also plays down somewhat the series of riots that he never quite managed to control. Still, he is basically accurate, and a lot of the omissions are due to the necessity of making this a brief account of the events that led to his sending Paul to Caesarea.

He then proceeds (23:28–29) to the Sanhedrin incident and his discovery of the Jewish charges against Paul (from 22:30–23:10). Of course, we know he never did fully discover what had transpired, and it took him the entire time to do so, with the Sanhedrin actually providing only basic information. Still, overall he did learn enough to inform Felix and draw the most important conclusion, that everything was a Jewish rather than a Roman issue. He uses here the proper legal phrasing, literally "to know the cause of that which they were charging him."

His conclusions were crucial (23:29). The recognition that "the accusation had to do with questions about their law" actually guided Felix in all his deliberations. As with Pilate, the Romans only dealt with issues that affected Rome in their courts. All Jewish matters were to be handled by the Jewish legal system. If all the charges were Jewish, Rome would dismiss the case. Therefore, as far as Claudius Lysias and Felix were concerned, "there was no charge against him that deserved death or imprisonment." To the Roman judicial system, Paul was completely innocent.

The only reason Paul was being sent to Caesarea had nothing to do with the Jewish charges or the Sanhedrin. The tribune explains that in verse 30. Lysias learned "of a plot to be carried out against the man," and the man happened to be a Roman citizen. The tribune could not allow that citizen to be harmed and did not know who had instigated the plot. So he had to get Paul away from the extremely dangerous situation and felt that the only thing he could do to guarantee his safety was to send him to Caesarea, where he would get further protection. In order that Felix would be informed about the issues between Paul and the Jews, Claudius Lysias had "ordered his accusers to present to you their case against him." Paul would have to wait under the protection of Felix and be in effect under house arrest until the Jewish officials could get to Caesarea.

Paul, under an unbelievably huge armed guard, makes the first half of the journey at night in order to get away quickly before the conspirators can get organized to offer opposition (see on v. 23). They travel as far as Antipatris, about thirty-seven miles northwest on the way to Caesarea. That long a trip would take them into the next day, but there the tribune decides they are basically safe from their Jewish enemies, as the rest of the journey will be in Gentile territory. The infantrymen (and one or perhaps both centurions) return to Jerusalem, with the cavalry escorting Paul the rest of the way.

In Caesarea, their task is done. They hand Paul and the tribune's letter to Felix and depart for Jerusalem. The first thing Governor Felix does is ask Paul what province he is from and discovers he is from Tarsus in Cilicia. Many think he is hoping to avoid trying the case and to ship Paul there for the trial. Roman trials were often in the home province (in Paul's case Cilicia) rather than the province where the criminal offense took place (Judea). However, at this time Cilicia was a single province with Syria (they were separated in AD 72), and he undoubtedly felt he couldn't just hand the case off to the governor of Syria, leading the prefect of Syria to be annoyed with him for fobbing off a minor case on him.

So he tells Paul, "I will hear your case when your accusers get here" and places him in protective arrest in Herod's palace, his own domicile and headquarters, where many prisoners were kept. For the first part of his time he would have been treated as just another prisoner and apparently was not granted any freedom or privileges (including having visitors) until 24:23. The great irony is that his protective custody is actually a criminal imprisonment. In the Roman system he has been acknowledged by the tribune as totally innocent, but Felix doesn't care enough to do anything about it. Strangely, he even ignores the fact that Paul is a Roman citizen. It is more convenient with the vehemence of the Jewish demands to simply allow Paul to remain in custody.

———

The second stage of the legal series now takes place, the fact-finding confrontation between Paul and the Sanhedrin. The tribune still cannot make sense of the situation and so convenes the ruling body of the Jews to find out what is going on. He isn't ready for the explosive emotions (vv. 1–5), as right out of the blue the high priest orders Paul struck, and Paul angrily calls him a "whitewashed wall" headed for divine judgment.

Paul's strategy (vv. 6–10) is to derail what he sees as a set-up and divides the group by proclaiming one of the central truths, that the real issue is the resurrection from the dead. His purpose was to enlist supporters on his side, for immediately the scribes and Pharisees in the Sanhedrin leaped to Paul's defense and said they found "nothing wrong" with him.

God, knowing what is about to transpire, sends him a vision (v. 11) to encourage him that he will get to Rome to fulfill his immediate destiny. It is just at the right time, for a major plot begins the next day, as forty zealous Jews pledge to kill Paul or die trying (vv. 12-15). They enlist the Sanhedrin and chief priests themselves to get Paul transported to the judge's chamber, where they can get at him on the way. However, God is watching over him, and his nephew reveals the plot to him. They tell the tribune, who is immediately galvanized to action (vv. 16-22). In a single afternoon he readies his men and begins to take Paul to safety.

To ensure speed and safety, there were 470 soldiers, 70 of them cavalry and 200 of them spearmen. They left that evening and traveled halfway, to Antipatris, an overnight trip; then the soldiers went back, and the cavalry took Paul the rest of the way to Felix. The tribune sent a letter to Felix explaining the particulars (vv. 25-30) and making it clear that Paul was innocent but that the Jewish leaders were demanding he be killed. Technically, Felix should have held a trial and freed Paul, but he surrendered to the easier way and kept him in prison until he saw what the Jews were going to do (vv. 31-35). This is a great section on trusting God in dire circumstances and allowing him to bring good out of very bad situations.

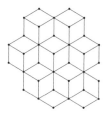

TRIAL BEFORE GOVERNOR FELIX
(24:1–27)

When the high priest arrived so quickly, Paul would have thought things had come to a head and that he would soon be free. However, that was not to be, and politics raised its ugly head once more. As with Jesus, the Jewish officials wanted a legal death sentence, and that required the involvement of the Roman courts, in this case at Caesarea. Their attempts to stone him had already been foiled, so all that was left was the Roman system.

The difficult thing was couching the Jewish charges in legal language and arguments that the Romans would accept and not dismiss as irrelevant. They had barely made it count with Pilate and wanted to do a better job this time. The only solution that could work was to hire the best Roman lawyer they could and get him to translate their charges of blasphemy into the language of sedition against Rome.

PAUL IS TRIED UNDER FELIX (24:1-23)

To show how important Paul's trial was to the Jerusalem officials, the high priest and his entourage arrive in only five days. That is so remarkable that many critics assume it cannot be historical, as trials then as today took months to organize, especially when key officials like the high priest are forced to travel to another province. The high priest is still Ananias, and he arrives with several "elders," leading Jews who may have been members of the Sanhedrin. This is unheard-of speed and shows the determination of the Jews to get rid of him as soon as possible. To get a good hearing they have hired a leading Gentile advocate named Tertullus in order to get the best possible hearing before Felix. Felix would have been pleased as well, for he could now be sure he would understand all that would be thrown at him by these Jews.

Their presentation of their legal charges to Felix is tricky, so they have hired Tertullus. The charges have to come from a Roman perspective, not Jewish, since Roman courts only deal with Roman issues. Even though Claudius Lysias told him the issues are Jewish and not Roman, Felix has to allow the trial to proceed because the charges are coming from a significant portion of the province, and the entire government of the Jews, both the Sanhedrin and the high priest, is demanding a guilty verdict. Paul would not have been present at this pretrial hearing, but it was virtually guaranteed that it would go to trial, and it does.

THE ACCUSATIONS (24:1–9)

At the trial proper, Tertullus is the first to take the stage. He opens with the ancient orator's usual flowery set of compliments, quite masterfully done. In truth, the "long period of peace" under Felix was accomplished by killing everyone who opposed him, but still he had done a few things that brought peace to the region, like suppressing the Egyptian revolutionary mentioned in 21:38 and ridding Judea of robbers (Josephus, *Jewish War* 2.252–53, 261–63). The *Pax Romana* (Roman peace) was always an emphasis, and the military presence guaranteed that any trouble would be dealt with severely and quickly.

Felix's "foresight" in introducing "reforms" refers to the quality of Felix as governor, and that is more difficult to ascertain. It seems more flattery than substance, for Felix's cruelty led to his recall in disgrace. Still, Tertullus' claim that "everywhere and in every way" the people feel "profound gratitude" (24:3) would have been very effective in pleasing Felix. So when he asks Felix to "be kind enough to hear us briefly," the governor is probably ready to look favorably on what he says.

There are four charges adduced by Tertullus, undoubtedly determined in consultation with the high priest and other officials but couched in Roman legalese.

1. He is a "troublemaker" or "public menace" (*loimos*), a word that means a "pestilence" or "plague," causing trouble everywhere he goes. This is undoubtedly a reference to the trouble that followed Paul into nearly every city he visited. This would have worked, for there were many of these that Rome had to deal with.

2. He is "stirring up riots among the Jews all over the world," a charge that could be easily proved. More than anything, Rome wished to keep the peace everywhere it existed. This was a very serious charge. Anything that disturbed the civil peace and quiet had to go. The Jews erupted wherever Paul's evangelistic enterprise operated, and often Gentiles joined in their demonstrations. His "sedition" is not against Rome, but it is a disturbance of the peace nevertheless. He didn't cause it—the Jews did—but Tertullus is hoping that won't matter to Felix.

3. He is "a ringleader of the Nazarene sect," a very interesting way to put it but also demonstrably true. The term for "sect" is *hairesis*, which in its negative sense is even transliterated into the English "heresy." Paul would agree in its positive sense, for the Jewish Christians called themselves "the Way" (see on 9:2), considering themselves a messianic sect in Judaism akin to the Pharisees or Sadducees. Paul indeed was a "ringleader," one who is "first" (*prōtostatēs*) among

the Christian leaders. Christians were called "Nazarenes" as followers of Jesus the Nazarene.

4. He "tried to desecrate the temple," a clear reference to the false witness of 21:28–29, when Paul was seen walking with one of the Gentile delegates, Trophimus from Ephesus, and some Jews from that province said he had taken this Gentile into the inner sanctuary of the temple, defiling it. Tertullus extends it even further, saying he "tried to desecrate the temple," in some way less severe (he then didn't actually succeed), but in other ways worse because it means that desecration was his intention all along. Moreover, these very Jewish opponents become the heroes, for they stopped him just in time by arresting him.

Of course, Tertullus conveniently omits the fact that at every stage of the narrative he just provided, it was the Jews who instigated the riots, not Paul. They are the guilty ones, not Paul. It was they who shut the gates of the temple and stopped all worship and sacrifices, and it was they who were stirring up trouble all over the Roman world.

Roman trials centered on direct interrogation of the defendant by the judge, in this case Governor Felix. So Tertullus, after seemingly answering everything Paul might say in his own defense, turns it over to the governor with a final glowing compliment (24:8), saying that he is certain he has given Felix more than enough to "learn the truth about all these charges." He is certain that Felix, when he hears what Paul has to say, is a brilliant-enough judge to ascertain guilt in these matters. The Jews who have brought Tertullus, namely the high priest and the elders, "joined in the accusation" (24:9), echoing and affirming what the lawyer has just said. They provide confirming testimony to the truth of the charges against Paul, and since they are not just anonymous witnesses but are actually Jewish leaders, that would be fairly convincing in a court of law. Paul has his work cut out for him.

DEFENSE BEFORE FELIX (24:10-21)

Paul takes on the charges one at a time and answers them in this, his third defense after 22:1-21 (to the crowd in the outer court) and 23:1-9 (to the Sanhedrin).

Paul gives his own flowery introduction, expressing appreciation that Felix "for a number of years" has "been a judge over this nation." Felix had been governor for five years (AD 52-57), and before that had ruled in Samaria for several years. The point is that he would be extremely knowledgeable of Jewish affairs and could be trusted to provide a fair hearing. As a result Paul can "gladly make my defense" (*apologoumai*) and know the verdict will exhibit that famous Roman justice.

Paul never had any intention of causing trouble. He first arrived in Jerusalem just twelve days previously, and his entire purpose was to worship God (24:11). The point behind the reference to "twelve days" was the ease by which Felix could discover and "verify" (*epignōnai*, "come to know") the facts for himself. He did not have to go back very far at all. It is difficult to ascertain how Paul calculated the twelve days. Some think he just adds the seven days of 21:27 to the five days of 24:1, but that leaves too many days unaccounted for. It is likely that Paul doesn't have in mind the five days he has been sitting in a cell since arriving in Caesarea, since he was in limbo that entire time.

So the twelve days would refer to the time he spent in Jerusalem, including the day with the Jerusalem elders, the seven days of purification, his arrest followed by his defense the next day in the temple court, his Sanhedrin hearing, the discovery of the plot, and his subsequent trip to Caesarea. The point is that Felix can ascertain that timeline for himself and see that there was no time to plot any terrorist-type disturbances. There was time sufficient only to worship God.

Moreover, Felix when he examines the actual evidence will find the Jews guilty of false witness (24:12), for there were no disturbances of any kind—no conflict or disputes in the temple, no agitation in the Jerusalem synagogues, no problems anywhere in the city. The only conflict occurred when the Jews exploded against him, and he was innocent in it all. This means Paul did not even teach or debate with anyone in the temple or synagogues—his usual activity in any city—but indeed did nothing but worship God whether in temple or synagogue.

This means, he concludes (24:13), that the Jews or Tertullus "cannot prove to you the charges they are now making against me." Tertullus can claim whatever he wishes, but he can prove none of it, because nothing he has asserted ever took place.

Paul now explains the third charge, that he is a "ringleader of the Nazarene sect," and explains that they call themselves "the Way," chosen from Isaiah 40:3, "prepare the way of the LORD." They were a messianic sect among Judaism, showing people the way to "worship the God of our ancestors" and to find God's salvation through his Messiah, Jesus (see on 9:2). So he admits to this charge but argues it is not criminal or dangerous for either Jewish or Roman interests. In fact, the beliefs of this new "sect" (used in a positive way) are completely in accordance with everything in "the Law and that is written in the Prophets." There is not only no criminal underground he is part of, but it is actually the case that Christianity is kosher vis-à-vis Judaism. The Old Testament is just as much the Scriptures of the Way as it is of the Jews, and he follows it as closely as possible. To the Romans such a "sect" would be a normal feature of any religion with different emphases highlighted in various groups.

Now he moves into the arena of the Christian belief system and is not only explaining the Way but also witness to Felix. He as both a Jew and a Christian centers his belief on "the same hope in God ... that there will be a resurrection of both the righteous and the wicked" (24:15). His is a future-oriented faith that believes in a final end—both the righteous and the wicked have an afterlife (see Dan 12:1-3). In other words, this sect is not completely new but is based on the same ancient truths as Judaism.

In light of these critical truths Paul has always striven "to keep my conscience clear before God and man" (24:16), reiterating his point of 23:1. Whether he will spend eternity with the righteous or the wicked depends on this task of maintaining a proper relationship with God, and his conscience is given by God to guide him in that righteous quest. Moreover, as a Christ follower it is essential that he maintain this relationship with God, but with people as well. His life's goal is to glorify God and bring people to him.

Paul had last visited Jerusalem and the temple six years earlier (AD 51–57), between his second and third missionary journeys (18:22). So he was not focused on the temple or on causing rebellion in Jerusalem. In fact, when he did come on this trip his purpose was to "bring my people gifts for the poor" and to worship God by presenting "offerings" to him. The literal translation is "to bring alms to my nation" and shows that Paul's heart was not centered on fomenting rebellion or profaning the temple but on worshipping God and serving the Jewish people by caring for the poor. This refers to the collection from the Gentile churches Paul was bringing with him, and his purpose in mentioning it here is to show that love rather than anger was driving him on this trip. He came to the temple not to desecrate it but to present offerings to it.

Now he comes to the problem of the false witnesses (24:18). When his enemies found him in the temple, there was nothing untoward going on at all. In fact, they actually found him "ceremonially clean" as he was giving these offerings. This means he had already gone through the rites of purification, offering sacrifices and immersing himself in the ritual pools of Jerusalem. That is hardly the picture of a man profaning God's house and fomenting riots. In fact, "there was no crowd with me, nor was I involved in any disturbance." These are simple facts that Felix can attest by looking into what actually transpired in those twelve days. The riots that did take place were later developments and caused by the Jews, not by Paul.

In verse 19 he goes on the offensive and tells what did cause the riots. These were Jewish pilgrims who had come from the province of Asia (see also 21:27–29). Paul argues that they were the instigators of the trouble, and they are the ones who should be standing before Felix making the charges. There are no eye-witnesses present in the entourage accompanying the high priest. None of them were present in the original events, so they should not be able to appear as witnesses in this "trial." In most Roman trials, they would all be dismissed as nonwitnesses. The **diaspora** Jews from Asia made the original charges (21:28), and only they should be allowed to do so now. So Paul is in effect asking for the case to be dismissed on the basis of the absence of true legal witnesses. The legal term is "abandonment," meaning the original plaintiffs have abandoned their case by failing to show up at the trial.

When Paul stood before the Sanhedrin, they found no evidence of any crime committed. So Paul now challenges the high priest and elders in the court chambers to produce some evidence from that trial that he had done anything wrong at all. The truth is that when he was accosted by the pilgrims from Asia he was engaging in worship, not creating a disturbance or profaning the temple. No one in the Sanhedrin could charge him with anything. The charges adduced by Tertullus were all generalities, because they could not find anything specific.

The only specific point came out at the Sanhedrin hearing (24:21), and it was a doctrinal point that half of the Sanhedrin agreed with—the resurrection of the dead. This echoes Claudius Lysias' point in 23:29 that all the issues had to do with "questions about their law," things that did not apply in a Roman court. Religious issues are not legal issues. Paul's point is that this is invalid and also grounds for dismissal. That question is important in a Jewish setting and central for Paul's Christian beliefs, but it has no place in the trial before Felix.

CASE ADJOURNED (24:22-23)

Felix is faced with a tricky case. He could have executed Paul but like the tribune knows that he is innocent. He could release Paul but also knows the Jews and their leaders will go crazy if he frees him. So he decides to adjourn the trial and call for Claudius Lysias to provide further information, hoping that he can find a way forward and serve Roman justice (with a Roman citizen) while at the same time satisfying the demands of the Jews. Luke never tells us if the tribune ever came to Caesarea, but if he did, it didn't make much difference. Paul remained in limbo for two years.

We are told that the governor, because he has been around a few years, "was well acquainted with the Way," probably with both the history and beliefs of the Christians. As the movement exploded in popularity, the Romans would have kept a close watch on it to make sure it was not going to cause trouble. Thus he knew well that the trouble was caused by Jewish overreactions, not by Christian politicking. He knows something is amiss but isn't certain exactly what and hopes Claudius Lysias can shed some light on it. It more and more looked like it would come down to truth versus political expediency. Plus, Paul was a Roman citizen, so pressure was on Felix to do the right thing.

So Felix set down the rules that likely governed the next two years of Paul's life (24:23). He remained under guard but was treated with the respect due him as a citizen of Rome and of Tarsus. In fact, a centurion was placed in charge, an unusual exception for prisoners of a certain status. He was not in chains and was allowed certain freedoms—for instance, allowing visitors and even friends to care for him, so that he had clean clothes, ate pretty well, and had some scrolls to read and papyrus for writing.

PAUL IS IMPRISONED IN CAESAREA (24:24-27)

Felix may have been "well acquainted with the Way" (v. 22), but his curiosity made him wish to know it better. His wife being Jewish made it a family affair. So they had Paul brought to them for a series of private conversations. The daughter of Herod Agrippa I and sister of the Agrippa II who speaks with Paul in chapter 26, she seems to have been both open to and interested in what Paul had to say. It is debated whether this interview was motivated by honest interest, the "bribe" that Felix was working for, or a desire to update his knowledge of Christianity. On the basis of the topics described in the next verse, there is likely some actual interest, certainly more honest on Drusilla's part than Felix's, but nevertheless a real desire to hear Paul.

Still, verse 25 shows Paul at his best. With his very life at stake, he takes every opportunity to share the gospel far more than to talk about his innocence. It is amazing how Paul reached every level of society with his witness to Christ. After the great evangelist Billy Graham died in 2018, his body lay in honor in the rotunda of the Capitol in Washington, DC. I have often thought of him as another Paul, not focused on honor but on the gospel, preaching to both "paupers and kings."

Luke mentions three major topics here: (1) "Righteousness," likely covering three levels itself: receiving forgiveness of sins by the blood of Christ and being declared righteous in God's sight; righteous conduct; and achieving "justice" in one's treatment of others. (2) "Self-control," expanding the aspect of righteous conduct above. They would have discussed Greek ethics versus Christian ethics, particularly that gaining control over one's desires and virtues needs more than personal discipline and rational thinking but demands a personal relationship and help from God. (3) "The judgment to come," not in this case the idea of Roman justice but undoubtedly the Christian doctrine that after we die we will have to give an account of our life to God and face his judgment. The gospel message of Jesus' death as atoning sacrifice and the need for repentance and belief in Christ would permeate all three areas.

Felix's response shows that Paul's witness penetrated deeply, as he did not just change the subject and exhibit disinterest but "was afraid" and terminated the discussion, asking Paul to leave and promising to send for him again when, as he says, "I find it convenient," or "find the time" (*kairos*). I think this reflects genuine conviction and not lack of interest. Certainly the next verse will show an absence of pure motives, but we do see here also a genuine realization that Paul seems to be speaking truth about Jesus, faith in him, and final judgment.

Still, Felix shows his true colors when his repeated conversations with Paul over the next two years betray not growing conviction but a desire for a bribe (24:26). He was known as a corrupt governor and one who frequently accepted bribes (see Josephus, *Antiquities* 20.163). The result is that for the next two years Felix "sent for him frequently and talked with him." We don't know the topics but several must have continued the topics from verse 25. This also means that at this time in his life Paul was not in poverty but quite the opposite—he had to have access to quite a bit of money for a Roman governor to want a bribe. He would not have been content with twenty bucks under the table.

Where did Paul get that kind of money? Most likely Felix knew of the gift for the Jerusalem poor Paul had brought with him. That money would have already been given, but Felix might assume more is available. There might also have been a considerable inheritance or some other financial means. It would have taken a great deal of funds for Paul to take the boat trip to Rome in chapter 27, and he was treated like royalty even though he was a prisoner. We will never know, but there is a good chance he was well off at this time in his life.

There are two reasons why Felix leaves Paul in prison for the entire two years in his tenure in Syria—the desire for a bribe, to which Paul never yields, and because he "wanted to grant a favor to the Jews." It is doubtful that they gave him bribe money to do so. More likely it was political: he wanted to gain political capital by doing so. Their hope was that some further evidence might arise that would enable them to get a capital sentence against Paul and finally get rid of him.

Felix was recalled to Rome for siding with the Gentiles in a dispute with the Jews over Caesarea. All of his excesses caught up with him, and he was removed from office and succeeded by Porcius Festus, a much more able administrator but who died of natural causes after just three years in office (AD 59-62).

———

Since Paul has been taken to Caesarea, the Jewish leaders have no choice but to force a trial under Felix (vv. 1-8), and they waste no time setting it up in just five days, undoubtedly a record. They hire a top Roman attorney named Tertullus who very effectively wins Felix over with flattery and then presents charges of sedition and causing riots, which would have guaranteed to make Rome look at Paul a second time. At the end of the presentation it sounds as if Paul will be judged guilty.

Paul's defense (vv. 9-21) responds to the charges one at a time. Paul did not cause riots or disturb the peace but in fact spent his entire time worshipping God and purifying himself. The only riot that took place was instigated by the Jews, not Paul. He did not profane the temple but in reality spent his entire time making offerings and serving God there. Moreover, as a member of the Christian sect, he had many of the same beliefs as the Jews and worshipped the same God. The Jewish charges were based on false witness. Paul showed that none of the charges were based on facts and called for dismissal. This is an excellent example of what to do when on trial for your Christian beliefs. Get your facts straight and use all the legal means available to prove your innocence, then trust the Lord like Paul did to drive the truth home.

Felix was faced with a difficulty. He knew Paul was innocent but did not want to enflame the Jewish leaders by dismissing the case. So he adjourned it on a fake demand for more information (vv. 22-23) but actually kept the case and Paul in limbo for two years. That is another side to the issue: What do you do when justice is not served? Then all one can do is be patient and again trust the Lord to work everything out for his glory. Felix frequently came and talked with Paul, certainly interested in hearing Paul's side of things but also hoping for a large bribe. He was succeeded after the two years and replaced by Festus, who will take us into the next chapter.

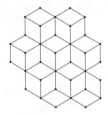

TRIAL BEFORE FESTUS
AND AGRIPPA
(25:1–27)

The final events leading up to Paul's trial in Rome now take place. The imprisonment under Felix was time in limbo. Paul wrote no letters and doesn't seem to have communicated with many of his churches (at least none are recorded). Probably Luke spent much of this time gathering material for his two-work masterpiece tracing the life of Jesus and the life of the church.

With the arrival of Festus, things are finally set in motion. Felix wanted only to line his pockets and please the Jews. His seeming interest in hearing Paul's gospel had apparently consisted of curiosity without a willingness to change. With Festus someone finally seems to care, and the Jews are galvanized into action. From all historians can gather, Festus did a good job correcting Felix's excesses and restoring order in the province. All Paul needed was a competent hand guiding the action, and he received it with Festus. He was so frustrated by Felix that almost the first thing he did was appeal to Caesar, forcing the action and the administration in Syria to send him on to Rome.

PAUL APPEALS TO CAESAR (25:1-12)

FESTUS IN JERUSALEM (25:1-5)

Festus didn't like to waste time. Just three days after arriving from
Rome, he traveled down to Jerusalem to consult the Jewish leaders. The fact that he went to them rather than requiring that they
come to him showed great respect and certainly surprised them,
going a long way to establish a degree of rapport. After Felix anything was a step upward. The trip there so soon into his reign was
a very wise move.

As soon as the chief priests and leaders (many of them members of the Sanhedrin) met with him, they brought up as their
first order of business the case against Paul. After two years they
were still incensed by it. They were up to the same old tricks as
before (25:3), trying to get Festus to have Paul brought to Jerusalem
so they (probably many of those who fomented the initial plot
of 23:12-15) could ambush and kill him on the way. Since Festus
was new to the scene, they assumed he would be unaware of the
past history and naively send Paul with just a small detachment to
guard him. It is surprising that this plot—quite dangerous in itself
for it would have invited Roman reprisals for ambushing some of
their soldiers—still existed this much later. It shows how deeply
these officials still hated Paul. They could see the handwriting on
the wall that they would never get the verdict they wanted and so
were willing to risk everything to see him gone.

Festus inadvertently thwarts their plot, undoubtedly led by
God's protective hand.[1] His plans made it more convenient to
have the pretrial meeting in Caesarea, where he was headed next
(25:4-5), so some of the Jewish leaders could travel with him and
present their charges there. Festus is a true Roman judge and

---

1. It is possible he had done his homework and knew of the previous plot.
However, he had just arrived, and I think it difficult to imagine he could have
studied the lengthy history of this case. It is impossible to know for sure.

speaks clearly of *alleged* charges, saying "if the man has done anything wrong." He makes no assumptions. In other words, they will have to *prove* their accusations in a court of law.

PAUL'S DEFENSE AND APPEAL (25:6-12)

An important sign of Luke's desire for accuracy is the fact that when he is not certain, he says so, as in the phrase "eight or ten days" here. Those who say he makes up timelines and stories and so on don't pay close enough attention to passages such as this one. Festus spent a little over a week in Jerusalem learning the ropes and the Jewish ways of doing things. He then went to Caesarea. Once he got there, he convened a trial for the next day. What a contrast to Felix, who dawdled for two years! It is wonderful to see a competent leader at work. The Jewish leaders who had come with him surrounded Paul and brought "many serious charges against him," but they turned out to be nothing but invented accusations that could not be proved. Luke does not detail the charges, but Paul's defense in the next verse tells us what they were.

As he defends himself (25:8), we see three categories of charges. The first two are Jewish in nature and so would have been discounted in a Roman court. First, they charge that he has acted "against the Jewish law," as in 18:13; 21:21, 28; 23:29. Paul responded in 24:14 that he believed "everything that is in accordance with the Law." Gallio in 18:14-15 had already declared that this accusation had nothing to do with Roman law. Second, they charged that he had desecrated the temple in 21:28-29 and 24:6. Paul had disproved that in 24:12 (no disturbances) and 24:18 that he was ritually pure when they found him in the temple. Third, and this was more substantial in Roman courts, he had committed sedition against Caesar (Nero was now on the throne, AD 54-68). They claimed that Paul was causing trouble and riots throughout the empire (see 16:20; 17:6-7; 24:5), and that this constituted sedition. Still, in the previous trials and situations, the charge had proved false, and no Roman court ever found him guilty of this, the most serious of the charges.

Festus' question to Paul about his desires in the situation (24:9) sounds very strange. However, two things tell us why he does so. First, he feels that all the resources available to him in Caesarea have been exhausted. If he wants to bring this case to a proper conclusion, it needs to be tried in Jerusalem, where all the offenses took place. Second, Paul is a Roman citizen and has some rights in this situation. If he tried to force Paul to return to Jerusalem for the trial, he could get in trouble for it (see the reactions of the magistrates in 16:38–40).

Still, Festus was under the same pressure as Felix had been and wanted to "do the Jews a favor" (also 24:27) in this. Moreover, he was not abandoning Paul and handing him over to the Jews. He would "stand trial before" Festus there. Festus would preside over the trial, but the Sanhedrin and other leaders would be present, and it would take place in their courtroom. The idea of a Roman judge presiding over a Jewish trial is quite difficult to contemplate, and some think he planned to have a formal trial before the Sanhedrin on the religious charges followed by a legal Roman trial on the charge of sedition. Either way, Paul certainly does not find it to his liking. It sounds like Festus had not thought it through very well, and perhaps it is best to think of a Roman trial but with access to the entire Jewish leadership.

Paul's response (25:10–11) betrays his awareness that to be taken to Jerusalem is to be taken to his death. Festus cannot conceive that the Jewish plot holds any real danger with Roman soldiers present, but Paul knows how serious the resolve of his enemies actually is. Moreover, he had seen enough of Roman corruption not to trust Festus' intentions in the matter. Political expediency too often wins out over individual rights. So he calls on all his rights as a Roman citizen and demands to be tried "before Caesar's court" and not surrendered to so-called Jewish justice. Moreover, both from Claudius Lysias' letter (23:25–30) and the proceedings of all the interactions with Felix, he knows that the fact that he has "not done any wrong to the Jews" is known "very well" to Festus.

He is relinquishing his life to Caesar, fully willing to face Roman justice in this instance (25:11). This means that if the court deems that he has done "anything deserving death," he is fully willing to die. However, by appealing to Caesar he announces his desire to be tried in Rome. He is certain of one thing: to be handed over to Jerusalem will mean his death. He is not certain that he can receive a fair hearing in Caesarea. So only one option remains viable: he cannot trust Festus, but he can trust Roman law. Like a clarion call, he cries out, "I appeal to Caesar!"

There is a difference of opinion on how binding such an appeal was on lower courts or on Festus as the judge. He could have rejected the appeal and released Paul anyway (25:25; 26:32), but to do so would turn the entire Jewish leadership against him. So this appeal to Caesar offers him an easy out with the pressure on him from the Jews. So he grants the appeal (25:12) with a summary verdict couched quite succinctly, "You have appealed to Caesar. To Caesar you will go!" The Caesarean trial is over, and all that remains is formulating a transfer letter similar to that written by Claudius Lysias in 23:25–30 explaining the reasons for sending Paul to Nero. Moreover, all the costs must be borne by the one appealing, so only the wealthy could afford to make such an appeal, another indication that Paul had access to funds at this time.

FESTUS PRESENTS PAUL'S CASE
TO AGRIPPA (25:13–21)

This passage begins a larger section that encompasses Paul's trial before Herod Agrippa II (25:13–26:32). It starts with a consultation in which Festus brings Herod Agrippa into the case in order to tap his knowledge of Jewish life and get his advice on what to do with Paul. He knows Paul is innocent, but he is strongly aware of the political complexities with the Jewish authorities demanding that he be found guilty. He doesn't know how to satisfy the Jews

and yet meet the standards of Roman justice. So he is desperately
looking for help from Agrippa.

The Jerusalem Trial Summarized (25:13–16)

The letter to the emperor was even more critical than the earlier
one by the tribune (23:25–30), for Nero would have demanded very
strong reasons for taking up his time on the issue. Festus knew
Paul was innocent and had broken no Roman laws, so that made
it all the more tricky, because for all these reasons it was indeed
a frivolous trial. So when King Agrippa (grandson of Herod the
Great and made king over the Palestine region by the Romans)
came for a state visit to pay his respects to the new governor,
Felix used the opportunity to get his advice on the "Paul issue."
Agrippa was the perfect liaison, for he had grown up both Roman
and Jewish, and hopefully could interpret the confusing issues in
the dispute between Paul and Jerusalem. He was considered an
expert on Judaism and arrived at just the right time for Festus. His
wife Bernice was the older sister of Felix's wife Drusilla and was
also deeply interested in Jewish things.

Festus and Agrippa became fast friends, and at some point
Festus asked his advice about Paul and his conflict with the
Sanhedrin (25:14–15). He explained Felix's failures,[2] especially in
leaving Paul "a prisoner" with an undecided case and a Jewish leadership unanimously bringing charges and demanding a guilty verdict. Agrippa would have been quite interested in the recent events
in Jerusalem and Caesarea, and must have listened avidly. While
Festus would have summarized all that transpired in his "eight to
ten days" in Jerusalem (25:6), the trial with Paul would have been

---

2. Several think there is no negative implication about Felix, but to me that
is hard to imagine in light of the man's desire for a bribe and the fact that his
corruption was well known. Two years in limbo, and all the complexity of the
case thrown at Festus when it should have been resolved long before—there
must be some frustration on Festus' part.

first on the agenda, for it was a critically important issue regarding a movement well known all over the Roman world—the growth of Christianity. Moreover, if Paul were to receive the same guilty verdict and face execution just like Jesus did, that would have critical repercussions for all involved.

Festus responded to the Sanhedrin (25:16) that he would not hand Paul over until he had faced his accusers and answered their charges. The "Roman custom" in all jurisprudence was based on a confrontation between a defendant and those making charges against them. No charge would be accepted by a court without such a "defense" (*apologia*). Guilt would not be determined by the persons making the accusations, and Roman fairness demanded that the plaintiff have the right to respond to every detail before a verdict could be reached.

THE CAESAREA TRIAL SUMMARIZED (25:17–21)

Festus emphasized his prompt action to show Agrippa how important he thought this case was, telling Agrippa that he had convened the trial the very next day after returning to Caesarea. He also stated how he had ordered some of the leaders to come with him in order to present the charges in an official Roman trial. So he ordered Paul brought before the judicial bench and had his accusers stand and present their charges (25:17–18).

Luke adds one new fact here. Festus is surprised when none of the charges detailed the crimes he had expected to hear about. This means that none of them touched on matters that concerned Roman law. As we see in verse 19, they were all "points of dispute with him about their own religion and about a dead man named Jesus who Paul claimed was alive." The first aspect concerned tensions between the two belief systems of Judaism and Christianity. They shared the same God but viewed him differently (with Christian trinitarianism), and they especially differed on matters of salvation (the works of the law versus faith in Christ). Second, and primarily, there is the dead man come alive, Jesus the

Christ. To the Sanhedrin, with Judeo-Christian beliefs regarding rising from the dead, Paul would label it "the hope of the resurrection of the dead" (23:6). To the Roman Festus, who found ideas of physical resurrection incomprehensible, it was "a dead man named Jesus who Paul claimed was alive."

Since Festus could not understand these matters of religious doctrine, he was "at a loss" as to how to proceed and thought the best way forward was for Paul to face his opponents in a Jewish setting rather than Roman (25:20). Thus, he tells Agrippa, he asked Paul "if he would be willing to go to Jerusalem and stand trial there." He thought he might hear enough in that setting to enable him to understand the issues and how to proceed.

Now came the second surprise. Instead of acquiescing to the request, Paul appealed "to be held over for the Emperor's decision," that is, to be sent to Rome and tried under Nero (25:21). The "decision" is a legal term (*diagnosis*, transliterated "diagnosis") for an investigation that produces a verdict. The term for "Emperor" is *Sebastos*, the Greek for the title given to Julius Caesar's nephew, Gaius Octavius, when he became emperor in 27 BC, "Augustus" or "Revered Majesty." Many of the following emperors, including Nero, took that as part of their name. At any rate, Festus tells Agrippa that in light of that appeal, he "ordered him held until I could send him to Caesar."

AGRIPPA HEARS PAUL (25:22–27)

Agrippa tried to keep abreast of current events and certainly had been hearing quite a bit about this Paul, former Christ-hater who is now the hated. He looked forward to the opportunity for firsthand knowledge and so meant it when he replied, "I would like to hear this man myself." In fact, the imperfect tense of the verb (*eboulomēn*) could be translated, "I have been wanting," indicating a longtime desire to interact with Paul. Festus has been hoping for this response and so promises, "Tomorrow you will hear him." After the incredibly long wait Paul has had to endure because of the indolence of Felix, things are now rapidly moving to a conclusion.

The following day, a state occasion takes place, as all the leaders come together "with great pomp," trumpets blaring, banners flying, and people lining the streets. The "audience room" was in the banquet hall of Herod's magnificent palace in Caesarea. Not only were the major players present (Festus, Agrippa, Bernice), but the five tribunes commanding all five cohorts of the Roman troops in Syria were also in attendance. This is the equivalent of the military chiefs of staff in Washington joining the president and the visiting royalty for a state dinner. Finally, the city council and important leaders and aristocracy were also present. It was quite the occasion. Paul is being treated almost as another visiting royal dignitary, hardly as just another lowly prisoner drug in manacled in chains. Luke tells it this way to show that these events were "not done in a corner" (26:26), and that Paul's innocence was recognized far and wide.

Paul is "brought in" with similar pomp and circumstance as the featured event of the occasion. Festus explains to everyone present (25:24) that this is the man the Jewish people not only "petitioned" him about both in Jerusalem and Caesarea, but did so "shouting that he ought not to live any longer." The raw emotions were surprising, especially for a new governor who had just arrived on the scene. Clearly Festus is looking for advice and information that will help him understand the intensity of the demands. This isn't just a request for a capital trial; this is a demand for an execution. Moreover, it is not just a small committee of leaders but "the whole Jewish community" insisting this, and they aren't simply asking but shouting their demands.

On the other hand, Festus admits that all his research into the case revealed that Paul had "done nothing deserving of death" (25:25). From the letter of the tribune Claudius Lysias on (23:29: "no charge against him that deserved death"), all the evidence supported his innocence. This complicates transferring the case to Nero greatly, since in reality Paul should be set free and Nero will be asking why he wasn't.

However, due to the political climate Festus decided to honor his appeal to the emperor and send him to Rome. On the surface that does not seem like a logical decision, and Festus is stating it baldly—sending an innocent man to take up Nero's valuable time with a lengthy trial—in order to get a reaction and hopefully some good advice from Agrippa.

The problem is obvious (25:26–27): "I have nothing definite to write to His Majesty about him," and yet at the same time "it is unreasonable [and illegal] to send a prisoner on to Rome without specifying the charges against him." He was in the same quandary that Lysias found himself in when sending Paul on to Caesarea: explaining why he was doing so when it was so clear that none of the charges were valid. This was a legal requirement, and Festus had to present the charges and tell what in the evidence made a trial in the higher court necessary. He had to explain why he failed to produce a verdict, and the difficulty in this instance was explaining Jewish charges to a Roman emperor/judge. He needed Agrippa for this, as neither Lysias nor he could figure it out. It will take all of the next chapter to provide that information for Festus.

———

This is a transition chapter, moving from a Jewish-centered to a Rome-centered situation as Paul gets closer to fulfilling God's will to bear witness in Rome while imprisoned there. The able administrator Festus takes over from the corrupt Felix and immediately goes to Jerusalem to become acquainted with that most difficult region in the Roman Empire, Judea (vv. 1–5). There the Jewish leaders waste no time accosting him about Paul, hoping to get him to bring Paul to Jerusalem so they can fulfill their plot to kill him. With God orchestrating the situation, Festus refuses and tells them to come to Caesarea, which they do just a few days later (vv. 6–12). They bring the same charges that had been made to Felix in the last chapter, and Paul, realizing there will be no chance in Caesarea, appeals to Caesar. Festus, wanting to get this case out of his hair, agrees to the appeal.

Agrippa arrives, and Festus summarizes for him the results of both the Jerusalem (vv. 13–16) and Caesarea (vv. 17–21) trials, explaining the failures of Felix in letting everything lie in limbo in the midst of Jewish demands for a guilty verdict. He also describes his surprise at the absence of relevant charges for a Roman trial, telling Agrippa how they were all Jewish religious issues such as Jesus rising from the dead. That should have made the trial very short-lived, but Jewish demands keep lengthening the proceedings and making everything very complex. When a single trial produces national outrage and an empire-wide crisis, you know something is very wrong.

Finally, he tells Agrippa how Paul has appealed to Caesar and the difficulty of penning the appeal letter to Nero explaining why he was sending Paul to him. The lesson for us in all this is the necessity of readiness to face very difficult and complex issues in cross-cultural situations. There are many times when we, like Paul, have to find answers when cultures and ideologies clash and when the repercussions are hard to understand. Then God must guide us as he did Paul in steering our way through these issues and using all the tools at our disposal to discover answers.

The final section (vv. 22–27) describes how Paul finally gets his opportunity to present his side of the case to the authorities in a fair trial. Again God has taken charge. Agrippa expresses his interest in hearing Paul's side, and Festus explains to him why the verdict has been so long in coming when the evidence is so clear that Paul is innocent. Everything is complicated not just by the adamant and very loud demands of the Jewish leaders but even more by Paul's appeal to Caesar, which Festus for political reasons is upholding. But the result is he must compose the letter to Nero explaining why Paul with all the evidence in his favor is being sent rather than freed. For that Festus needs help from Agrippa, and this will carry us over to the next chapter.

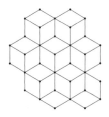

PAUL MAKES HIS DEFENSE
(26:1–32)

I n this chapter, Luke presents for the third time Paul's Damascus road conversion, and for the second time as a defense. Paul's narration of his conversion in chapter 22 was Jewish in essence, while here it is Gentile, Paul using it to defend himself before Agrippa and Festus. However, Paul never merely defends himself. The last half is an evangelistic proclamation of the gospel with the clear intention not to support Paul's innocence but to challenge Agrippa and the others to come to Christ. In the end Paul defends Christ and the Christian movement more than he defends himself.

PAUL BEGINS HIS DEFENSE WITH GRATITUDE (26:1-3)

Paul, like Tertullus in 24:2-4, begins with flattery. Agrippa gives him permission to speak, and like any good orator, Paul motions with his hand to get people's attention and then starts his speech. Festus steps into the background and gives Agrippa the floor, so that this chapter is mainly between the two of them. As before the Sanhedrin in chapter 22, Paul gives his defense speech in the form of a story. In one sense this was not a defense, for the purpose was to enable Agrippa to give advice for writing the letter to Nero. However, Paul considers it a "defense" (v. 1) and wants to help Agrippa and Festus understand him and his Christian faith more thoroughly. It is not a legal defense, but it is an "apology" (*apologia*)[1] for his Christian beliefs.

Since this is a **Hellenistic** setting, the opening remarks follow proper rhetorical techniques (26:2-3), with compliments for the judge, a humble presentation of himself, and a brief comment on the legal setting. Then the speech proper exhibits a rhetorical outline similar to the one on Mars Hill in 17:22-31. There is an introductory prologue (*exordium*, vv. 2-3), a narration (*narratio*, vv. 4-18), a confirmation of evidence (*confirmatio*, vv. 19-20), a refutation of the charges (*refutatio*, v. 21), and a concluding summation (*peroratio*, vv. 22-23). Paul was truly a gifted speaker and could use Jewish or Greek strategies depending on the audience.

Here he begins with a statement of gratitude to King Agrippa for being allowed to defend himself against "the accusations of the Jews." He is especially thankful that Agrippa is the one listening due to his deep knowledge of "all the Jewish customs and controversies." Paul considers him a Hellenist rather than a Hebrew, and an expert on Judaism, well able to discern the points and counterpoints in the debates. His hope is that the king will be able to see beyond the Sanhedrin's false claims and understand what is truly going on in the case. In all this he asks that they listen "patiently" as he explains the situation and provides his defense.

PAUL PROVIDES THE STORY
BEHIND THE CASE (26:4-18)

PAUL'S PHARISAIC BACKGROUND (26:4-8)

It is interesting that Paul skips his birth in Tarsus (he notes it in 22:3) and begins with his Torah education in "my own country" and in Jerusalem. His point is that even his opponents know ("the

---

1. The term for the discipline of "defending" Christianity is taken from this term, "apologetics."

Jewish people *all* know") his strict Pharisaic background from the time he was a small child. He had not been merely a Pharisee but a member of "the strictest sect" among them, possibly the Shammai school, strict literalists in interpreting the law, but more likely Hillel, since his mentor was Gamaliel (see below), thus more likely a very strict follower of Hillel. Even his enemies could "testify, if they are willing" to this fact. "Known me for a long time" refers to the fact that he had been trained under Rabbi Gamaliel, the grandson of Hillel and the leading Pharisee of his day. Before his Damascus road conversion, Paul was a very well-known Pharisaic leader and likely personally knew every member of the Sanhedrin. They could all testify to how devout he had been as a Jew.

Paul makes clear in verse 6 that the Christian belief in resurrection is not a new doctrine, for it is grounded in "what God has promised our ancestors," and yet it is also the reason he is now on trial. So it has taken on a new form and is the basis for the Christian hope, since it is now anchored in the resurrection of Jesus from the dead (13:30–37). The Pharisees have embraced the central truth of resurrection (23:6–9) but have rejected the resurrection claims regarding the risen Lord, Jesus the Christ. The Christians and Paul affirmed that all the hopes of the Jewish people have been fulfilled in Jesus. All the Old Testament promises (for example, Pss 16:8–10; 49:15; Job 19:25–27; Isa 25:6–12; 26:19; Ezek 37:1–14; Dan 12:1–3; Hos 6:2) have their true meaning in him.

Likely Paul mentions the "twelve tribes" (26:7) to stress the fact that every person in Israel has their hope finalized in the Christ and his resurrection. Christ chose twelve disciples to signify that the church constitutes a new and true Israel in him. Israel's restoration was to take place via this new Israel, and the promises have come true only via Jesus the risen Lord. His claim is that Israel's earnest worship/service (*latreuon* is a present-tense participle referring to both continuous worship and service to God) draws its true meaning from the work of their Messiah Jesus Christ on their behalf. However, since God's people the Jews have rejected "this hope" and their Savior, Paul has been accused and faces trial at this time.

Paul concludes that in light of the Pharisaic acceptance of resurrection from the dead, "Why should any of you consider it incredible that God raises the dead?" (26:8), by which he means raising Jesus from the dead. It is not beyond the bounds of belief (*apiston*) to accept the Christian doctrine of afterlife centered on the resurrection of Jesus from the dead. From this standpoint the accusations against Paul have also been disproved. The Hellenistic world of Festus and the Romans reject all ideas of physical resurrection and embrace only the idea of the immortality of the soul, that the body is destroyed but the life-spirit crosses the River Styx to walk the Elysian fields for all eternity. So Paul is addressing them as well in this.

PAUL THE PERSECUTOR (26:9-11)

He goes back to his background, showing he was not just a Pharisee but a major enemy of the Christian movement. He was absolutely "convinced," or certain (*edoxa*), that Christianity was a dangerous heretical sect that had to be completely eradicated. His zeal for persecution was connected to what has been called "building a fence around the law," a way of protecting the law from being broken. In this case the law would be destroyed by blasphemous claims regarding Jesus as the Christ. So long as blasphemy existed in the land, the Messiah would not come. So Paul had to remove this heresy from the sacred land of Israel. As we have seen elsewhere, the name "Jesus of Nazareth" (2:22; 3:6; 4:10; 6:14; 22:8) stresses his earthly origin. To claim he was the God-man was ultimate blasphemy to Saul the zealous Pharisee. He became a full-time opponent of everything Christian.

The most complete description of what this "all that was possible" in verse 9 entailed is found in verses 10-11. Paul did not only receive authority to arrest Christians when the letters authorizing him to do so were given him as he left for Damascus. Here we see that this authority had been his long before, as he "put many of the Lord's people in prison" and had "the authority of the chief priests" to do so in Jerusalem as well. The "letters" of 9:2 simply extended that authority to **diasporic** regions outside Palestine. We have no idea how many believers were martyred in Jerusalem in those dark days, but there must have been quite a few, and Paul was one of the ringleaders of those enemies of the Christian movement. As the disciples cast lots in the choice of Matthias as the twelfth apostle, likewise Paul, perhaps as a member of the Sanhedrin, "cast [his] vote" against many who were put to death.[2] This is a major difficulty, for as we have seen with the death of Jesus and Stephen, the Romans kept strict control of capital crimes and executions. It is hard to imagine the scenario Paul asserts here. Some think this is nothing more than an expanded reference to the death of Stephen or a purely rhetorical rather than factual claim. However, these were tumultuous times, and it is not difficult to see the Romans allowing the Jews a limited right to stone some Christian "blasphemers" as the lesser of two evils. The death of a few Christians is better than massive riots. What they allowed with Stephen they could have allowed several more times over the next few years.

Paul's goal (26:11) was to use punishment as a goad to force Christians to "blaspheme" Christ by renouncing their faith rather than blaspheming the Jewish God and the Torah. The punishment was likely the "forty lashes minus one" (2 Cor 11:24), which synagogues often used against lawbreakers. He went from synagogue to synagogue in Jerusalem and the surrounding area ferreting out the Jewish Christians and bringing them up on charges, then having them beaten to force them to reject their Christian beliefs. This

---

2. However, he was probably too young to be a member of that august body. He may be referring to votes in synagogues for stoning someone designated a blasphemer, with the Romans looking the other way like they did with Stephen. It is amazing that the chief priests and Sanhedrin could have been so open and public with such capital cases.

would reverse charges against Christians earlier. In other words, Paul would force these Christians to stop blaspheming Jewish dogma by getting them to blaspheme or repudiate Christ.

Moreover, as we know from 9:1-2, he took his "rescue" movement from Jerusalem and "hunted them down in foreign cities" like Damascus as well. In 9:1 Luke describes him as "breathing out murderous threats" against followers of the Way; here he uses very strong language, *perrisōs emmainomenos*, which is defined, "to be so filled with anger as to be obsessed by it." Paul wrestled for the proper language to show his former anger and determination against Christians. More than any other thing in his life, he strove to get rid of these blasphemous Christians.

The Damascus Road Vision (26:12-18)

For the third time we learn of Paul's vision on the Damascus road, one of the central events in the history of the church. Paul had been leading the persecution for some time and together with the leadership in Jerusalem decided it was time to cleanse Judaism outside of Palestine as well. So with official letters authorizing him, he headed for Damascus with a delegation, probably of Jewish officials, to start arresting Jewish Christians in Damascus and send them back to Jerusalem for trial.

He had almost arrived there when suddenly about noon on the last day he "saw a light from heaven, brighter than the sun, blazing around" the party of travelers. As I noted in my comments on 22:6, this was the **Shekinah** glory, which led Israel as it fled from the Egyptian army at the exodus and then dwelt among them in the tabernacle and temple. Here on the Damascus road it is to be a rescue of a different sort but just as significant a redemption. In each of the three accounts the description has got more spectacular, from "light from heaven" in 9:3 to "a great light" in 22:6 to "brighter than the sun, blazing around me" here in 26:13. The emphasis is on the heavenly, supernatural origins of the light. The glory of Christ is surrounding the group on the road in the same

way the Shekinah cloud surrounded the mount of transfiguration in Luke 9:34.

With the blinding light, they all fell to the ground, but only
Paul/Saul heard the voice, "Saul, Saul why do you persecute me?"
What Paul adds here to the other accounts is that they all saw the
light and fell to the ground (it was only Paul in the other accounts),
probably to stress that the experience was real and experienced
by all. The second half of the message is found only here: "It is
hard for you to kick against the goads." This is a Gentile rather
than Jewish metaphor and refers to a pointed stick used to prod
an ox to get it to turn right or left. The animal fights against the
goad and tries to kick it out of the way. It pictures Paul resisting
the prods of his conscience and of Jesus, which try to guide him on
his God-appointed destiny. God and Jesus were "goading" Paul to
cease resisting, find faith in Christ, and find his God-given destiny.

Paul's query (26:15) about the person behind the voice is much
the same in all three (22:8 adds, "of Nazareth"), and he stresses it
here for the sake of Agrippa and Festus, for Paul's primary purpose in this speech is not to defend himself but to proclaim Jesus
to these Gentiles. Jesus is not dead but alive, and this Risen One
is "Lord" of all.

In chapter 9 he is commissioned to go to the Gentiles by Ananias
(9:15); in chapter 22 it comes via the vision in the temple (22:21); here
he is commissioned in the Damascus road vision itself (26:16–18).
Certainly all three took place. Turning perhaps the most zealous
lover of Torah in the land into the missionary to the Gentiles was
incredibly traumatic for Paul and needed all three repetitions to
help him come to grips with it. Paul's call was initially given in
the Damascus road vision and confirmed both by Ananias and the
voice of the Lord in the temple vision. It took all three to enable
him to understand the incredible transformation Christ had in
mind for him.

The purpose in each account is theological. Ananias is the commissioning agent in 9:16 and provides an official confirmation of

the divine call. In the Jewish context of 22:21, it is critical to place the appointment in a temple vision to stress its sacred nature. Here it was critical for these two rulers to realize that Paul was initially commissioned by King Messiah himself. It is a royal appointment.

The risen Lord here in verse 16 tells Paul to stand up and ready himself to be appointed "as a servant and as a witness of what you have seen and will see of me." This is a prophetic commissioning, with Paul the servant of Yahweh like Isaiah (Isa 6:1–8) or Ezekiel (Ezek 2:1–4). The commissioning is couched in prophetic terms similar to Jeremiah 1:17 and Ezekiel 2:1–2, in language drawn from the Servant songs (Isa 42:6–9).[3] His task will be that of official Spirit-inspired "witness" of the risen Jesus to all the world (Acts 1:8). The content of his witness has both past ("what you have seen") and future ("will see") components. The past aspect is Jesus risen from the dead, revealed to him on the Damascus road. The future aspect refers to further revelations of his glory as the Spirit-empowered witness goes out into the world.

Paul could attest to how difficult the church's mission to both Jews and Gentiles had become, for he had been largely responsible for many of the arrests and martyrdoms that attended that witness in the early days. He was probably thinking that his would be a (literally) short-lived ministry, for Jesus immediately promises him, "I will rescue you from your own people and from the Gentiles" (26:17). To gain a feel for the reality behind this prediction of danger, we should read 2 Corinthians 11:23–29 and the unbelievable amount of suffering and persecution he endured for the sake of the Lord and his witness.

This promise was frequent in the Old Testament. Joshua was three times commanded to "be strong and courageous" in Joshua 1:6, 7, 9, undoubtedly because he was scared to death with all the pressure on him to replace Moses. The basis for that courage

---

3. The opening of blind eyes = Isa 42:7; turning from darkness to light = Isa 42:16. Colossians 1:12–14 echoes this and reflects the whole commissioning.

was in 1:9, "for the LORD your God will be with you wherever you go." God is ever vigilant over those he calls to serve him. Paul had a double danger, for he was called to Jew and Gentile and so faced opposition from both groups. At that initial stage in his Christian life he couldn't comprehend this calling, but very soon this promise of divine protection would be incredibly precious to him.

Next, Paul wants to describe for Agrippa (26:18) his threefold task as God's agent: (1) He is sent to both Jews and Gentiles to "open their eyes" to the reality of Christ as Savior and Lord. The lifting of Paul's blindness by Ananias was a prophetic action symbolizing this new sight (Isa 42:7). (2) His mission is to "turn" people from two things: "from darkness to light" (Isa 42:6, 16), namely, from the darkness of sin and evil to the light of God and the gospel; and "from the power of Satan to God," namely, from the prince of darkness to the Shekinah glory of God (see 22:6; 26:13) dwelling among us.

(3) He is sent "so that they may receive" two things: first, "forgiveness of sins," from the darkness of the world and a life without God. Everything Paul has said thus far relates to this forgiveness, and his main hope for this speech is to convince Agrippa and Festus to embrace this forgiveness. His message here is more evangelistic than apologetic, and he desires their conversion. Second, he wants them to receive "a place among those who are sanctified by faith in me." The word for "place" is *klēros*, a "lot" or share in the inheritance God has for his people. In John 14:2-4 Jesus told his disciples of going "to prepare a place for you." The "place" was to be a heavenly home with those "who are sanctified by faith in me," a reference to conversion. To be "sanctified" is to be cleansed from sin and made holy by saving faith and the Spirit. He is asking the two leaders to consider accepting a home in heaven with Christ.

PAUL CONCLUDES HIS DEFENSE (26:19-23)

As I said at the beginning of this chapter, these last five verses conclude the rhetorical outline, with the *confirmatio*, or proofs that Paul is indeed innocent and chosen of God. There are two pieces of evidence, one his faithful obedience (v. 19) and the other his successful witness and ministry (v. 20). In fact, Paul's obedience covered the rest of his life, as it has been well-known that everything he said and did from this moment forward reflected the impact of this vision on his life and perspective. In verse 20 he covers the years following, the three years in Damascus and Arabia (Gal 1), followed by his return to Jerusalem and Judea (Gal 2) and then the ensuing years as he reached out on mission to the Gentiles (Acts 11–28). He became the premiere pioneer missionary of the early church and took the gospel from one region to another in order to fulfill his call to "the ends of the earth" (Acts 1:8). All this was in answer to his commissioning at the Damascus vision.

Verse 21 is the *refutatio*, or proof that the charges made against him in the temple (Acts 21–22) were wrong. As Paul was obedient to God's call (v. 19), the Jews were not and tried both to arrest and kill God's chosen agent. He states, "That is why some Jews seized me … and tried to kill me." They are guilty from two directions—guilty before God for trying to kill his witness and stop the divinely ordained gospel proclamation, and guilty legally for breaking Roman law by trying to kill Paul. God had called Paul as a witness to the Jews and Gentiles, and the Jews had opposed not just Paul but God himself in their attempts to rid the earth of him.

The *peroratio*, beginning in verse 22, draws his message to a close with a summary of the gospel itself. When you are facing an entire nation that wants you dead, that is rather daunting. Paul needs an immense amount of help, but rather than ask Agrippa and Festus to provide it, Paul joyously admits that he is already receiving it from God, who has promised to protect and rescue him when he needs it (v. 17). Even though his problems have intensified and seem quite desperate, that divine vigilance is his "to this very day." On the surface there is hardly any hope since an entire nation has declared war on him personally. But Paul is not worried, for God is on his side.

So in spite of it all, he is able to "testify to small and great alike."
He is on trial for his life, but that has enabled him to witness to
Festus and Agrippa and their entourages. So Paul looks at capital
trials as just another kind of witnessing! The fact that all these
plots and legal charges have produced nothing but further witness is proof not only of Paul's innocence but also of the fact that
Christ is real and acting on Paul's behalf.

Further proof of the rightness of his cause is the fact that he is
"saying nothing beyond what the prophets and Moses said would
happen." In other words, these events are fulfilling Scripture and
are in keeping with biblical truth. The sufferings of Paul in particular and the people of God in general are a participation in Jesus'
sufferings (Phil 3:10) and in keeping with "the sufferings of the
Messiah and the glories that would follow" (1 Pet 1:11).

The final point of Paul's address is a summation of his gospel
message (26:23, echoing the summary of Luke 24:44-47). The core
of the gospel is the arrival of God's salvation for sinners, accomplished through the Suffering Servant of Isaiah 52-53, in particular his death and resurrection, with the result that the light of the
gospel (Isa 49:6) is poured out on all humankind. Forgiveness of
sins can come only through his suffering, in particular his atoning
sacrifice on the cross. The victory that is won through suffering
is encompassed in his resurrection as firstfruits (1 Cor 15:20, 23),
guaranteeing that we will live with him for eternity. The light of
God shines through the proclamation of the gospel, and it unites
Jew and Gentile into one new Israel.

FESTUS AND AGRIPPA AGREE (26:24-32)

Now we turn to the reactions of the two rulers to Paul's defense.
Festus, like Romans generally were (see Pilate at the trial of Jesus
in Luke 23), is completely befuddled by the incomprehensible logic
and beliefs of the Jews. He thinks Paul must have lost his mind
and interrupts his concluding statements, "Your great learning
is driving you insane." Many commentators think this a positive

statement, that Festus is greatly impressed by Paul's argumentation but finds these Jewish ideas of physical resurrection crazy. However, in the context he is hardly complimenting Paul. Gentiles are immersed in ideas of the immortality of the soul and cannot accept a physical afterlife, assuming that the body is destroyed at death. So since Paul has such far-fetched ideas, his brilliant mind has led him into insanity.

Paul denies the accusation (26:25) and counters that his claims of salvation and physical resurrection are actually "true and reasonable," literally, "words of truth and reason." In other words, he believes that the evidence and the facts support what he is saying, and that if Festus will just use his logic or reasoning better, it will bear up everything he has said. This is a brilliant strategy on Paul's part, for he is claiming that Greek logic is actually behind what he is arguing and, properly applied, will show the truth of everything he has claimed, including the idea of physical resurrection.

Paul's claims are all based on the life, death, and resurrection of Jesus the Christ, and so he argues further (26:26) that the king (Agrippa) is "familiar with," or "knows" (*epistatai*, "understands"), these very things and can testify to the reality of the Jesus story. Paul is not basing his assertions on mere speculation but on historical events that can be reasonably verified. Therefore, he "can speak freely to" Agrippa, who can then explain these things to Festus and show him they are not crazy ideas.

Paul is certain that none of this has "escaped [Agrippa's] notice, because it was not done in a corner." They were public and well known all over the Jewish world, so there is nothing crazy about them. In his Gospel, Luke often situated the events of Jesus' life in the context of world history (Luke 2:1-2; 3:1-2), and that is Paul's point here. The Jesus story is a part of world history, and Agrippa is quite aware of it and can be a witness to it with Festus.

So he now challenges the ruler, "King Agrippa, do you believe the prophets? I know you do" (26:27). This was strategic on Paul's part. The Herodian family always tried to keep the fiction that they were faithful Jews, even though they were more Gentile in outlook and lifestyle. So Agrippa would have to answer yes to this and to an extent probably did believe. But he was also aware that Paul was going to use this to support his Christian beliefs and did not want to get caught up in his argument. The Christ-idea, Paul is saying, originated with the prophetic witness of the Old Testament and so is not a new movement but one that is actually at the heart of ancient Jewish truth, a phenomena with which Agrippa is familiar.

So Agrippa decides to go on the offensive and stop Paul's developing point right now: "Do you think that in such a short time you can persuade me to be a Christian?" (26:28). Paul has made him quite uncomfortable, and he doesn't wish to look gullible to Festus. So he wants to stop any such discussion at that very moment and turn the attention away from him.[4]

Paul agrees with his understanding. Paul wants far more than to support his legal case; he wants to usher them into the kingdom of God. So he answers, "Short time or long—I pray to God that not only you but all who are listening to me today may become what I am" (26:29). Paul had subtly moved from apology to sermon, and his true purpose was to make his speech a presentation of the gospel. Whether this goal can take place in the short run or whether it takes a long time is inconsequential to Paul. All that matters is that everyone there experience forgiveness of sins and faith in Christ. As a last comment Paul adds an ironic twist, "except for these chains." He doesn't wish his chains on anyone there.

The state visit ends on a note of gospel proclamation, and with this those who entered in 25:23 arise and leave the banquet hall. The three dignitaries leave first, followed by the military tribunes and other leaders from Caesarea. The consultation is over, but we

---

4. Others have taken a positive approach, as the KJV, "Almost thou persuadest me to be a Christian," or "In a short time you might persuade me to be a Christian." However, the more negative interpretation fits the context better.

see them discussing the results of the conclave after they have left (we don't know where).

There are two main areas of agreement between Festus and Agrippa. First, "This man is not doing anything that deserves death or imprisonment." Claudius Lysias stated this at the start of all this, in his original letter to Felix in 23:29: "There was no charge against him that deserved death or imprisonment." Festus himself echoed this in 25:25 when he told Agrippa, "I found he had done nothing deserving of death." Note the present tense here: "is not doing anything," which indicates every part of Paul's life and beliefs. Throughout the entire process Paul has been exemplary and deserves nothing of what he is receiving. It is only the adamant Jewish demands and Roman cowardice that have kept the process going. One would think it would stop here, but this capitulation to the Jewish leadership will continue.

The second area of agreement is the fact that it is not going to end soon, but this is due also to Paul's own actions: "This man could have been set free if he had not appealed to Caesar." Yet we had learned earlier that this appeal did not require that Paul be sent. Festus could have released him (25:21, 25) but decided to get Paul out of his hair and the Jews off his back by sending him on anyway. Roman justice has once again been shown to be nothing but a facade. Everyone involved in the case on the Roman side—the military (Claudius Lysias), the political (Festus), and the religious (Agrippa)—agrees that Paul is innocent and should be released, but none are willing to stand up to the Jews and free him. Virtually everything Festus would be sending to Nero would support setting Paul free, but Nero would do the same thing as Felix and Festus, keep him in chains in Rome for another two years.

This is the final of Paul's five defense speeches (22:1-21; 23:1-9; 24:10-21; 25:8-11; 26:1-29) and shows that his purpose is never simply to prove his innocence or even to defend Christianity against its opponents. His main purpose is to present the gospel and win as many people as possible to Christ. He is a no-nonsense, totally focused evangelist, using every opportunity to proclaim God's salvation to rich or poor alike. Even when his very life is on the line, he still wishes to introduce every individual to Christ and the salvation he won on the cross for sinful humankind. Still, showing the truthfulness of Christianity is a part of that, and he wants his innocence proved in a court of law as a precedent for others who may be arrested and face trial in the name of Christ.

———

Paul shows himself to be the equal of Tertullus as a barrister here, crafting an excellent rhetorical address in his own defense in this chapter. In stating his appreciation that Agrippa is hearing his case (vv. 1-3), he not only compliments the king for his knowledge of Jewish issues but already begins to show the truth of the Christian cause.

He begins by telling his life story (vv. 4-18), beginning with his Jewish origins and strict Pharisaic background, especially his belief in the resurrection of the body (vv. 4-8), which he sees as the central issue, for Christian beliefs are anchored in that reality (see 1 Cor 15). He wants Festus and Agrippa to understand that formerly he was one of the greatest persecutors of Christians, perhaps the leading one (vv. 9-11). He not only arrested many but also was instrumental in their deaths in order to rid the land of everything Christian. So the irony in this trial is that he spent his early years on the other side of the aisle, masterminding the persecution and even the deaths of believers.

The primary emphasis in this account is the vision itself, for Paul wants these two rulers to understand that what lies behind his calling and beliefs is the commissioning of nothing less than the royal Messiah himself (vv. 12-18). The light that shone on the whole party and could be verified by all who were there was the Shekinah presence of the Lord, his very glory encompassing the whole scene. The call that came and commissioned him to go to the Gentiles was the voice of King Jesus, and Paul could do nothing but obey his royal orders. Here he turns to evangelistic outreach, inviting the two leaders to accept the same heavenly home that is promised to all who come to Christ. He has stopped defending himself and Christianity and started to invite them to find God's salvation themselves. Paul the evangelist has taken over from Paul the legal defender.

The final verses of his defense (vv. 19-23) are incredible, for Paul freely admits that he is more interested in presenting the gospel to Festus and Agrippa than he is in defending himself. He is actually defending the right to present the truths of Christ more than to argue his innocence, and he wants them to consider these truths carefully, for they are life to them as well.

The reactions of the two leaders (vv. 24-29) are quite interesting. Festus, who like all Greek thinkers cannot accept any idea of physical resurrection, thinks Paul has lost his mind. Agrippa with his background in Judaism recognizes Paul's true intentions to turn them into Christ followers but wants nothing of it. This chapter is an excellent example for a class on evangelism, showing how people react so differently to conviction by the gospel. Paul rarely lost an opportunity to call even kings to Christ. Nothing daunted him.

In the end nothing changes (vv. 30-32). Justice is fleeting, and these two upper-echelon leaders are no different, knowing Paul should be freed but afraid to incur the wrath of the Jews by doing so. Paul is the model for us all. Light will rarely find anything but opposition from darkness, and the people of light must be willing to endure injustice when proclaiming God's truth.

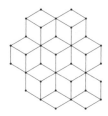

SEA JOURNEY TO ROME
(27:1–44)

Luke uses a form of writing here that had been very popular since Homer's *Odyssey*. The sea is a favorite setting in Scripture as well, as in the famous Jonah story, and is a symbol of suffering and evil in the book of Revelation. Paul is depicted as God's prophet, a righteous man who is protected by God and, as God decides, given power over the sea. Although a mere prisoner headed for trial, he has a certain status, due both to his Roman citizenship and extensive experience as a traveler (2 Cor 11:25, three times shipwrecked), and the Romans often turn to him for advice. It is the last of several sea journeys, which always in Acts signify the movement of the gospel to fulfill the universal mission and reach "the ends of the earth" (1:8). The supernatural aura depicts God's vigilant care as his agents go forth with the good news.

Many scholars have believed this to be a fictional creation built on both Old Testament miracle stories and Greco-Roman myths, with Paul's speeches (27:10, 21–26, 31, 33–34) inserted into the story. However, the literary details seem much more aligned with an eyewitness account (it is "we" material, meaning Luke was with Paul for the trip) than with a dramatic "sea voyage" fictional account. The details are carefully provided, every one of them accurate for an actual Mediterranean voyage of the first century.

Such things as the three ships that take the party to Rome (27:2-5, 6-44; 28:11-13—likely due to shipping schedules) would not have been accurately portrayed in a work of fiction but are here and fit a historical account. My outline in this chapter will follow the geographical movements of the journey motif.

THE SHIP TRAVELS FROM
CAESAREA TO MYRA (27:1-5)

Paul is first handed over with a group of prisoners to a centurion with a detachment of soldiers. Servants are apparently allowed, so some of Paul's assistants have permission to travel with him, for instance Luke (this is a "we" passage, resumed from 21:18) and Aristarchus (v. 2). We don't know whether Paul was manacled. That was common, but he seems to have been given some privileges, and one of them may have been limited freedom of movement on the ship. It is doubtful that the "other prisoners" were also going on appeal to the emperor, for that would have been a fairly rare thing due to restrictions on who was allowed to do so (no one but a Roman citizen) and then the necessity of it being a serious trial situation.

The centurion was named Julius likely because his family had been freed from slavery and given their citizenship under the reign of Julius Caesar (or perhaps Augustus), as was the case with Claudius Lysias (22:27-28), given citizenship under the emperor Claudius. That is one of the reasons why he treats Paul so well, as they shared Roman citizenship (plus he may have been aware that Festus considered Paul innocent). The "Imperial Regiment" or "Augustan Cohort" refers to the auxiliary troops of Syria, one of several under the authority of Agrippa II. Also joining Paul is Aristarchus, a colleague who was part of the delegation, being from Thessalonica in Macedonia (19:29; 20:4). He stayed with Paul through his imprisonment in Rome (Col 4:10; Phlm 24) and was a trusted associate.

The first ship they boarded carried trade goods to "ports along the coast of the province of Asia" (modern Turkey), its home port being Adramyttium, between Ephesus and Troas in the region of Mysia. They will take this ship as far as Myra in the region of Asia southeast of the province of Asia and there board a ship to cross the Mediterranean. Rome did not have a navy fleet that could transport soldiers and prisoners. Centurions who had to travel would requisition passage just like any other traveler. Luke and Aristarchus would have booked passage separately and on their own.

The first port of call is Sidon north of Tyre, and there the first act of kindness takes place when the centurion allows Paul to visit "friends" from the churches of Sidon who care for him and probably provide clothes and provisions for the trip. The centurion would have taken care of the passage on ships, but Paul would have paid for food and other supplies. Paul was evidently allowed to go off the ship accompanied by a guard, and the "kindness" probably meant the removal of the shackles at this time.

The next stop was a ways away and meant sailing "to the lee of Cyprus" (27:4) to the north of the island "because the winds were against us." This is another of the details that points to historical veracity and would have been exactly correct with an autumn voyage with strong northwesterly winds. It was a fifteen-day trip to sail the five hundred miles to Myra (added in several Western manuscripts like 614, 2147). This was a perfect stop, for they needed to transfer to an Alexandrian grain ship to begin the long sea voyage.

THE SHIP TRAVELS FROM MYRA TO CRETE (27:6–8)

Myra was a major shipping port where the huge grain ships could be found on the coast of Asia Minor. Egypt supplied a large percentage of Rome's grain (as much as a third), so they needed a huge number of ships to transport it all that way. There was hardly anything more important to Rome than its grain, so this shipping was priority number one for the empire. Grain ships would try to make the circuit twice in a year, and this was the second, always questionable because when winter hit, the winds made transport impossible. So at this time (late fall), things were always anxious and hurried to make it on time.

Due to the strong headwinds, they made very slow progress. They would have preferred to steer around south of Rhodes, but the northwest wind forced them to go north around Rhodes then sail past the town of Salmone on the northeastern tip of Crete and make an unscheduled stop there. Crete is 155 miles long, and they sailed along its southern coast, fighting the winds every step of the way. They were finally able to anchor at a place called *kaloi limenes*, or "Fair Havens," a harbor that was somewhat unsafe as it left boats partly unprotected from the winds. It was not a good place to spend the winter, and Phoenix, further along the coast to the west, would have been better situated for keeping their ship safe. However, with the heavy winds it was dangerous to try to get there.

PAUL AND THE CENTURION DEBATE
ABOUT GOING OR STAYING (27:9-12)

Paul's new status under the centurion is seen in the debate that takes place. How often is a prisoner allowed to give major advice on such an important decision? Two things made Paul advise them to stay where they were. First, much time had been lost due to the bad wind conditions, and they were approaching the exceedingly difficult winter season. Second, as a result sailing had become quite dangerous and could result in the loss of their ship and of their very lives. While Fair Havens was not a good place to winter, it was better than the destruction of everything.

Paul is acting almost as a prophet here with his severe warning. The Day of Atonement was early in October, and travel was considered very unsafe from mid-September on and impossible after early to mid-November. From November to mid-March no ships sailed, and it was getting very close. Plus the winds had already become very dangerous. So Paul does not mince words, telling them that the voyage will be "disastrous and bring great loss to ship and cargo, and to our own lives also." He feels the navigation hazards are already too great to travel even the short distance to Phoenix. Paul acts as the prophet, the owner and the captain as the profit-oriented businesspeople. It is the age-old dilemma of following God or money.

Paul is thinking practically and prophetically, but the owner of the ship and the captain are thinking profit margin and the greater safety of the harbor at Phoenix. Their advice prevails, and the centurion, who appears to have the final say because the ship has been requisitioned for grain for Rome, goes along with their decision. Phoenix was a much better harbor and only forty miles away, so they were convinced they could make it. It was on the very tip of the island, so its harbor faced both north and south. It would have been a very good place to winter.

THE STORM DRIVES THE SHIP
TO DISASTER (27:13-26)

Everything begins smoothly, with moderate south winds carrying them along the coast, and they make good time at the beginning. There was a good possibility of reaching Phoenix yet that very day. However, sudden typhoons are a feature of Mediterranean travel, and suddenly the worst possible kind, called "the Northeaster," struck and changed everything. Apparently they had just reached open water when it hit, sweeping out of the mountains of Crete with "hurricane force" (typhōnikos, transliterated "typhoon" today) winds. The "Northeaster," or eurakylōn, took immediate control of the ship, and they could no longer steer it in the direction they wanted.

Caught in the fierce typhoon, they were unable to "head into the wind" and control the ship by running counter to the waves. They "gave way to it" and were driven away from the coast and out to sea (27:15). As a result, they were driven southwest thirty miles to a small island called Cauda and sailed to the southeast side, or "lee" of it, providing some protection from the wind. But it was only four miles in diameter, so the protection is short-lived.

Still, it allowed them to do three things (27:16-17): First, they secured the lifeboat, emptying it of water and pulling it on board. Second, they undergirded the ship by passing huge rope cables under the hull, securing it and anchoring loose boards in the hull. There is some debate as to whether the cables ran the length of the ship or the width of the ship, but the latter makes more sense. It is hard to imagine sailors swimming these cables under the hull, hoping they can go deep enough and swiftly enough to get it done. When it was done, the boat was stabilized, and the leakage from loose boards stopped. Third, they lowered the rigging and sails, keeping only the minimal amount to keep the ship moving. There was a lot of danger around the "sandbars of Syrtis" near North Africa, where the ship could run aground, so they needed to be able to maneuver the ship easily and often to avoid running aground on the shoals. With the heavy wind driving the ship southward and possibly aground on the shores of Africa, they had to be ready for these dangers.

The storm was so fierce that the ship was in danger of capsizing, so the next day they had to jettison the cargo in order to make the ship lighter (27:18-19). Otherwise, they could sink. They threw all the cargo overboard but kept the wheat, since it was the most precious commodity they carried (it will be jettisoned in v. 38). Then on the following day they cast off the extra rigging and tackle, anything they didn't need for staying alive. They were now past Cauda and on the open sea at the mercy of the elements.

As night turned to day and back to night for several days and the storm remained at its zenith, everyone on board "gave up all hope of being saved" (27:20). Despair overwhelmed them. They didn't know where they were, for they could not navigate by either sun or stars, nor could they see any hazards that might suddenly come on them. The ship could only take so much battering, and there was no sign the storm would let up any time soon.

In the depths of their grief and agony, every person on board lost their appetite (most likely seasickness contributed as well), and they were getting weaker and weaker. The lethargy of imminent death was taking over. After several days had passed, Paul stood among them as a prophet and proclaimed a message of hope. He begins by reminding them that none of this would have happened if they had followed his original advice not to sail from Crete in the first place.

He does this to get their attention as a knowledgeable and regular traveler who knows what he is talking about. And he certainly was. This was the *fourth* shipwreck Paul had experienced, and on one of them he had "spent a night and a day in the open sea" (2 Cor 11:25). He is the expert on what they are going through. It seems remarkable that a prisoner rather than the captain or centurion would be the speaker at such a crisis meeting of crew and passengers, but they may have spoken as well, and Luke is only recording Paul's speech. His message came from God and so had instant credibility and command behind it.

Although all the signs would say they were soon going to die, Paul urges them to maintain their courage (27:22) and gives them startling news that they no doubt could hardly have believed: "Not one of you will be lost; only the ship will be destroyed." This will indeed be the case (vv. 43–44), but at this time it did not seem possible. It was a miracle that no one had yet been lost at sea and everyone was okay. Still, everyone there expected that to change any minute. Who could believe such an impossible prediction?

Paul becomes immediately credible when he shares the source of this announcement (27:23): "Last night an angel of the God to whom I belong and whom I serve stood beside me." Jesus had often spoken to him directly (9:4-6; 18:9-10; 23:11), but here he speaks through his messenger, an angel. Those on board would have accepted this even though they were all Greco-Roman. The God of Paul would have been one of many gods in the pantheon to them, but they would have accepted such a revelation as this. Besides, they would have wanted to believe such a thing. Their gods had proved helpless against these forces, and they would have been overjoyed that Paul's God was willing to intervene. Paul shows they can trust what he says when he declares he is God's "special possession" (1 Pet 2:9; see also Exod 19:5) and his servant. As the special messenger of God, he speaks for the angel, who speaks for God.

The promise was for Paul, but it included everyone aboard the ship. There was no need for fear, for God was fulfilling his promises. First, God had told him he would testify for him in Rome (23:11), and his appeal to Caesar (25:12, 21) constituted an appeal to God as well. Therefore, he would survive the shipwreck and get to Rome so he could "stand trial before Caesar." Second, along with this, "God has graciously given you the lives of all who sail with you." So no lives would be lost. Out of his grace and mercy God has included all the crew and passengers in his promise to Paul. Implied here is that Paul had been praying for all his companions aboard the ship, and God was granting his request.

Paul concludes with a promise and a prediction (27:25–26). He calls for courage and confidence in the God who made these promises and would fulfill his word: "I have faith in God that it will happen just as he told me." Prophetic encouragement is a hallmark of God's servants in the Old Testament, and it continues here. When God speaks, everything happens exactly as he has promised. This is followed by a prophecy centering on the divine "must" (*dei*) — "We must run aground on some island." As many interpreters have pointed out, when the storm forced them to miss Sicily, the large island just south of Italy, they lost hope and thought they would crash on North Africa. Their only hope is the small island of Malta south of Sicily, but that was highly unlikely. It would take a miracle, and that is what God is promising them.

THE SHIP IS WRECKED ON MALTA (27:27–44)

With this promise they continue to be driven by the storm for fourteen more days. By this time they are beyond exhaustion. They have traveled 476 miles from Cauda to Malta in the Adriatic Sea, which divides Greece from Italy and flows between Crete and Sicily.

On the fourteenth night the experienced sailors feel land is near, perhaps from the distant sound of breakers crashing on the rocks of the shore. They "took soundings," obviously not modern radar but a weighted line to the bottom of the sea, and found it 120 feet deep (twenty fathoms[1]), which has been estimated to be at what is called Koura Point at the tip of the island. Then a short time later it registered 90 feet deep (fifteen fathoms) as they were entering St. Paul's Bay. Needless to say, everyone is overjoyed, as God's answer to Paul's prayers was coming to pass.

Needless to say, they didn't wish to run aground on the rocks, which would kill them all, so "they dropped four anchors from the stern and prayed for daylight," definitely prayers to Paul's God rather than their own powerless gods (27:29). In the dark, they would not see danger approaching, so they wanted to anchor while they were still safe. They needed four anchors rather than one lest the ship swing around and still hit the rocks.

A group of sailors is about to try to escape from the ship in the lifeboat (27:30), a very foolish thing to do, but they have been frightened for the last two weeks and are desperate to get off ship, so they pretend they are going to drop anchors and are about to steal the dinghy. They were planning to abandon all the passengers while they saved themselves. In the middle of the night, they thought the ship could not keep from being dashed against the rocks and that their only chance to live was to escape in the lifeboat. They could not save everyone, so they tried to sneak away so they could live, concocting a lie that they were going to lower further anchors.

Paul intervenes (27:31) in order to save both passengers and crew, as the latter's attempt to steal the lifeboat would certainly fail and they too would perish. God had promised to save all on board, but if the crew ignores that promise and leaves the ship,

---

1. A fathom is the distance from fingertip to fingertip when the arms are stretched out from the body, about six feet in length.

the promise will be voided, and everyone will die. He doesn't tell the crew, as their minds are made up, but instead tells the centurion and soldiers. While the crew doesn't care about the passengers, Paul cares about every person aboard the ship. He wants every single one to live through the night and escape. The centurion has seen enough on the perilous journey to convince him that Paul is indeed God's prophet, and so he has the soldiers cut the ropes securing the lifeboat to the ship, and it drifts away, forcing everyone to stay on the ship (27:32).

Paul repeats his promise that everyone will be saved and tells them to get some needed food. The imperfect tense "was urging" (NIV: "urged") has Paul repeatedly encourage them to eat throughout the long night. He reminds them that during the fourteen-day storm that had driven them across the Mediterranean and the constant seasickness that resulted, none of them had eaten and they were all quite weak. Without gaining some strength for the difficult escape, it will be hard to get off the ship to dry land. Note that Paul has taken over the ship and is giving the commands that we would expect the owner and captain to be providing. It is clear to all that they are alive only due to the direct intervention of God and his servant Paul. They now trust him alone as God's mouthpiece. For the third time (after vv. 24, 31) Paul reiterates the promise that "not one of you will lose a single hair from his head" (27:34). This was a divine promise and would definitely come to pass, but they all needed to follow the directions for getting themselves to safety, and getting nourishment was a good place to begin.

Paul took the initiative himself (27:35), taking bread and giving "thanks to God in front of them all." It was his God who had saved everyone on board, and all would have understood this focus not on the gods they had grown up with but on the actual God who had rescued them from death. There is even an evangelistic aspect, as Paul is introducing them formally with prayer to his great God. Some read too much into this scene, seeing a eucharistic celebration taking place. That is highly unlikely, but it is a Judeo-Christian celebration of God's provision of food and undoubtedly included thanksgiving for his provision of salvation from death, with this salvation shading over from physical rescue to the promise of spiritual rescue. So when the entire assembly followed Paul's lead and "ate some food themselves" (27:36), they also participated in giving thanks to God for rescuing them as well as for his provision of food.

It was a very large company on board (27:37), although 276 was in keeping with a large grain ship and a company of soldiers with their prisoners. Josephus tells of a similar shipwreck he experienced where there were 600 people on board (*Life* 3 par. 15). The point is that every single one was saved and now had accepted God's promises by taking nourishment and gaining strength to make it to shore. All the passengers apparently ate their full amount, for afterward they had sufficient strength to lighten "the ship by throwing the grain into the sea." Such an endeavor would have taken everyone, passengers and crew, for there would have been an immense amount of grain. They need the boat lighter so it will ride higher in the water and enable them to pass over the sandbars and rocks as they approach the shore and to ride as far onto the beach as possible when they ground the ship that day.

One more disaster remains, but again God proves faithful and saves everyone, though the ship is completely lost. After an incredibly busy night with no sleep but with needed nourishment, they finally see where they are in the inlet. They can tell they are in "a bay with a sandy beach," perfect for running the ship up onto the beach, but they don't recognize where this is on the island of Malta. The difficult part is avoiding the shoals on the way in, and the problem is that they have never been in this bay, so they don't know where the shoals are. They want to go as slowly as they can so they can watch for sandbars and rocks, but at the same time they need some speed to get the ship grounded as high on the beach as possible. It will be very difficult.

The sailors do three things to enable them to get to the beach (27:40). First, they cut the ropes holding the four anchors that had been lowered from the stern (v. 29), allowing them to fall into the sea so the ship can drift in the current. Second, they untied the ropes holding the rudders, large paddles or oars for steering the ship, allowing them to fall into the water so they could steer the ship to land. Third, they "hoisted the foresail to the wind" to guide and drive the ship swiftly toward shore. This was the small sail attached to the foremast, for the foresail had been cast off earlier (v. 19). Luke has developed a real knowledge of ships, for every word is a technical nautical term describing what the actual sequence of steps would have been. With this they would be headed to the beach to ground the ship.

On the way to the shore they "struck a sandbar and ran aground" some distance away from shore (27:41). The bow is firmly stuck in the rocks, jammed solid and unable to shift at all, while the stern of the ship is at the mercy of the storm-tossed waves and begins to be "broken to pieces" by the pounding surf. Scholars have shown that the seabed there is made of a very hard clay or mud, which would hold the ship at the mercy of the tidal forces.

The soldiers decide they have to kill the prisoners, including Paul, "to prevent any of them from swimming away and escaping." This was not cruel but wise from their perspective. If a prisoner escaped, the guard who failed to stop them would himself receive the sentence the prisoner had, nearly always the death penalty. (See also 16:27, where the Philippian jailer was going to commit suicide for the same reason.) Better to kill than to be killed.

The centurion had become quite close to Paul during the trip and didn't want him to die, so he ordered his men not to kill them and to trust Paul's promise that all would be saved. They could round up any who might try to escape. In one sense all the prisoners were saved because of the centurion's friendship with Paul. In actuality it all was part of God's providential plan, and he orchestrated every detail. The centurion ordered everyone who could to swim to shore and had the others hold on to pieces of debris from the ship and float to shore. As the Lord had promised through Paul, "everyone reached land safely," and no prisoners escaped. The prophetic promise of Paul (vv. 24, 31, 34) is realized.

———

The dramatic sea journey in this chapter echoes the story of Jonah, and as in that prophetic book it is God who is in charge of the sea winds and orchestrates every detail. This is highly unusual because Paul is at one and the same time both a prisoner on trial for his life and one of the most respected travelers on board the ship. He and the very centurion who has him in chains become fast friends. Paul also is a prophet, consistently giving messages from God and predicting the events to come.

The early part of the voyage finds them taking two ships to find a grain ship that will carry them to Rome (vv. 1–5), heading first to Myra, where they transfer to a ship that will take them to where they will winter on Crete. They are in Fair Havens and want to get to a safe harbor at Phoenix on the west of the island (vv. 6–12), but it is too late into the fall season, and the winds are dangerous. Paul advises against doing so, but the owner and the captain prevail and they decide to make the attempt.

The gale-force winds (vv. 13–20) did not abate and drove them inevitably southward toward disaster on the shores of Africa. They had no hope and no way to regain control except to lighten their ship by throwing as much as they could overboard—cargo, rigging, everything they had except the valuable wheat—in the hopes of somehow being able to wrestle the ship away from the deadly winds. Nothing worked.

This is when God took over (vv. 21–26). Their situation was beyond hope and no earthly power could save them. Paul is now no longer a mere prisoner or even a passenger but a divine spokesman. We are at the heart of the message of Acts as God once more rescues his chosen agent, as he did the apostles in 5:19 and Peter in 12:6–11 from prison. This time he includes all Paul's companions and the people aboard the ship, and Paul gives the good news to everyone as the prophet speaking for God.

God as always is as good as his word, and the miracle takes place (vv. 27-32). Unbeknownst to them, their ship stops veering south to the African shores, and after two more weeks of being driven by the wind they are suddenly at the island of Malta. As they anchor in the bay there, there is still great danger from the rocks, and a group of sailors is about to steal the lifeboat to save themselves when Paul tells the centurion, and he has his men cut the lines, freeing the dinghy so no one can leave the ship. God had told them that everyone would be saved only if everyone stayed on board, so Paul once more saved everyone, ironically by cutting the lifeboat free. The necessity of doing things God's way continues to be the focus.

Paul has now become the true captain of the ship, and he commands everyone to eat and gain strength to rescue themselves (vv. 33-38). They all partake of the standard meal, and Paul's giving thanks becomes also thanksgiving for God's rescuing them from danger and death. The spiritual dimension comes more and more to the fore.

In the final scene (vv. 39-44) God continues to fulfill his promises in spite of serious danger. They face two obstacles. First, they run aground on a shoal far from shore, and all 276 either have to swim to shore or hold on to debris and float there. Second, to save themselves from punishment if any escape, the soldiers plan to kill the prisoners, even Paul, but the centurion out of friendship for Paul commands them not to do so but to trust God's promise to save them all. In the end God proves Paul right and does indeed save everyone aboard.

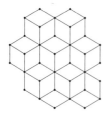

PAUL REACHES ROME
(28:1–31)

For all who lived in the Roman Empire, Rome was the center of the world, and symbolically Paul reaching Rome means that the universal mission launched in Acts 1:8 (and all the "great commissions" of Matt 28:18–20; Luke 24:47; and John 20:21–23) is now fulfilled and fully engaged. Rome had been evangelized long before, possibly by those who returned home from Pentecost and definitely by Christian merchants and others who brought the gospel there and established churches. However, with Paul the universal commission reached Rome, from which the spokes of the Roman wheel reached out in every direction. The universal mission is now given new impetus.

This chapter draws everything to a close and finalizes the themes that began in chapter 1, in particular the universal mission "to the ends of the earth" (1:8). The Jew-Gentile tension is at the heart of that mission, and while reaching the Jews was central in the early chapters, reaching the Gentiles has come to the fore in the later chapters. The Jewish people have been proved an obdurate, obstreperous group, and this chapter closes with Isaiah 6:9–10: "This people's heart has become calloused," and "God's salvation has been sent to the Gentiles" (28:27–28). Still, Luke highlights especially Paul's ministry among the Jews (fulfilling Rom 1:16, "first to the Jew"). The Jews are still the object of evangelistic effort, but the fruit comes more from the Gentiles.

PAUL SHAKES OFF A VIPER (28:1–6)

Since none of the sailors had recognized the bay where they landed, they didn't know where they were until the next day when they encountered the island's inhabitants. Then they discovered it was Malta (Greek: *Melitē*), a fairly small island eighteen by eight miles in size. Luke chooses the term "natives" (*barbaroi*; NIV: "islanders") or "barbarians," the term they used for anyone who did not speak Greek as their native language or failed to follow Greek customs. They were actually of Phoenician background and spoke Punic. Many, perhaps most, would have spoken Greek as a second language.

The survivors expected a certain measure of hostility for invading the island but were pleasantly surprised when they were shown "unusual kindness." The term is transliterated "philanthropy" (*philanthrōpia*) and pictures people who are quite friendly in welcoming strangers and caring for them. It was a rainy, cold day at the start of winter, so the islanders showed them hospitality by building a fire so they could rest and warm themselves after their arduous task of swimming to shore as their ship was breaking up on the rocks.

Paul was helping to gather brushwood for the fire when suddenly disaster struck (28:3). A snake was ensconced in the pile of wood, and the fire caused it to leap out and fasten itself to Paul's hand. Malta does not contain poisonous snakes today, so some believe it was either a different island or that the snake was not poisonous but resembled a viper. However, the simpler answer is that two thousand years ago there were poisonous snakes on the island. The natives would certainly not be fooled by a mere resemblance if the island had no such snakes.

At any rate, the shock to everyone would have been great indeed. Paul had survived a terrible storm for over two weeks and a horrendous shipwreck only to be killed by a viper. Their assumption would seem logical: "This man must be a murderer; for though he escaped from the sea, the goddess Justice has not allowed him to live" (28:4). Greek *Dikē* was the name of "the goddess Justice," daughter of Zeus and Themis. She made certain that the law of reciprocity functioned properly and wrongdoers paid for their sins.

As people said this, they were watching in anticipation for Paul to swell up and fall over dead. They experience further shock when he "shook the snake off into the fire and suffered no ill effects" (28:5–6). They obviously waited several minutes, expecting it to take place any moment. It didn't, and Paul simply went about his business with no aftereffects or even any concern for his wellbeing. Clearly Paul knew that nothing would happen because God had promised him he would reach Rome. As Jesus said in Luke 10:19, "I have given you authority to trample on snakes and scorpions and to overcome all the power of the enemy; nothing will harm you." Luke uses present- and imperfect-tense verbs to stress the drama of their continual watch and expectation—"were expecting," "were waiting," "were seeing," "was happening." All eyes were on Paul and his imminent demise.

When nothing happened and Paul kept on acting as if he hadn't even been bitten by the viper, shock changed to awe—they "changed their minds and said he was a god," echoing Acts 14:11–13, when the Lycaonians of Lystra thought the same thing of him and Barnabas. Paul was a prophet on board the ship; now he is an agent of God under his protection. It is interesting that he does not react to this surmise of his divinity like he did in Lystra. Probably it is due to the actual situation here. They weren't worshipping him as deity like before, and this was not a scene of witness and proclamation. That would come later. He probably did respond somewhat, and Luke simply doesn't record it.

PAUL MINISTERS IN MALTA (28:7-10)

The "first man [NIV: "chief official"] of the island" (*tō prōtō tēs nēsou*) was named Publius and owned a large estate, welcoming the group there and showing them "generous hospitality" for three days. We don't know if that meant all 276 people or just Paul's group (including the centurion). Most likely it would have included the owner and the captain of the ship along with the ship's officers. Malta was a part of the Roman Empire, so Publius was likely a Roman citizen and the governor of the island. At the end of the three days the survivors were undoubtedly divided up and cared for by the islands inhabitants until they could head for Rome, which we know from verse 11 was three months later, when winter was over and the shipping lanes reopened.

Publius' father was seriously ill from fever and dysentery (28:8). The combination of the two was life-threatening, and the man may have been ill for some time. Paul, the prophet and miracle worker, went in to him, prayed, and laid hands on him (Matt 9:18; Mark 5:23; Acts 9:12, 17), and he was healed. While not stated directly, the "power of the Name" of Jesus (see 3:6, 16; 4:10, 12) is certainly implied.

The result is that the entire island brings their sick to Paul (28:9), and as in Jerusalem, every single one is cured. Luke uses imperfect-tense verbs, meaning that many healings took place over the three months they spent on the island. It is very interesting that, unlike the rest of Acts, Luke makes no mention of the proclamation of the gospel or the call to repentance. Everywhere else miracles lead to evangelism. Likely this does not mean that nothing occurred but that Luke is centered on Paul's reaching Rome rather than on him planting churches. The people would certainly be quite interested in Paul's God in light of his miraculous ministry. The Romans didn't have gods who cared much for their followers, and they would have found the Judeo-Christian covenant God fascinating. So I personally think he did this, but Luke's interest was elsewhere.

The result (v. 10) was that great honor was accorded them and many gifts showered on them when they left. Some think that "honored" (*timais etimēsan*) refers to fees paid for medical services rendered. That is possible, as the Greek *timē* can refer to payment given, but that is unlikely here. It just doesn't fit the context. These are miracles, not medicine dispensed to heal diseases. Also, the provisions given for the journey are gifts from a grateful populace rather than fees for medical services.

PAUL JOURNEYS FROM MALTA TO ROME (28:11-15)

There was no leaving Malta for the three months of winter due to the terrible winds that drove them there in the first place. During that time Paul was even more the main figure lauded from the ship, not the centurion or ship's captain, as he was considered almost a divine figure and had healed countless sick in the name of Christ. When that time had ended and the shipping lanes finally opened up (possibly early February), they left as soon as they could in order to get to Rome. The island's occupants heaped gifts on them and provisions for the journey, and they left.

The Alexandrian ship was almost certainly a grain ship and would be desperate to unload its wheat for Rome as early as possible and get back to Egypt for another supply of grain. Luke makes a strange comment that the figurehead of the ship was "the twin gods Castor and Pollux," who were sons of Zeus, symbols of divine help especially for seamen and at the apex of a very popular Greco-Roman cult. Luke may mention it to contrast the actual powerless nature of such gods in comparison with the true divine help God gave the ship Paul brought through the storm safely to Malta.

Their first stop after setting sail was 80 nautical miles, about a full day's sailing, to the capital city of the island of Sicily, Syracuse, a large harbor on the east side of the island (28:12-13). Probably due to a spate of bad weather, they had to remain there for three days before they could leave. Another day away, 70 nautical miles, was the town of Rhegium, at the tip of the boot of Italy and only 6 or 7 miles from the island of Sicily, in what is called the Strait of Messina. Leaving there the next day, due to a favorable south wind they made the 175 nautical miles to Puteoli by the second day. It was the regular practice to disembark from Puteoli and travel by land up to Rome. The grain ship would then sail up to the port of Ostia and leave the wheat there.

There was a significant Christian presence in Puteoli, which was a major port on Italy's west coast and a large town (28:14). They seemingly offer to put up Paul and his companions (we should also include the two soldiers who were guarding Paul) for seven days. Julius, still friends with Paul, apparently agrees to this, and he and his soldiers may have stayed with them. Paul has at every step shown himself trustworthy, so the centurion is not worried about any attempt to escape. They would have used the seven days to rest for the lengthy walk to Rome and to get the provisions they needed for the trip.

After the week of fellowship, they leave for Rome, a journey of 150 miles, about eight to ten days. A title for a sermon on Paul reaching Rome could be "The Triumphal Entry." As they got closer, the Christians in Rome heard they were on the way (28:15). Word of Paul reaching Puteoli probably went all over Italy in the seven days they were there. They would have come up the famous Appian Way along the coast, and the church of Rome apparently sent out two groups to welcome them, the first going south about forty miles to the Forum of Appius, a market town forty miles south, while another group met them at the Three Taverns, a rest station and shopping area about twenty-five miles south. Both were well-known stops for travelers. Paul had written his famous letter to Rome three years earlier, and the Christians there had no doubt been eager to see him ever since. So as these believers walked with Paul, it was almost as if they spread palm branches and Paul were riding a donkey into Rome.

PAUL STAYS IN ROME (28:16–31)

God's promises are now fulfilled. From the day they left Caesarea to their arrival in Rome, it had been a four- to five-month journey with, needless to say, a great deal of adventure. But Paul "thanked God and was encouraged" by the joyous greeting of his Christian brothers and sisters and their obviously positive reception of both his letter three years earlier and himself now. As he had written in that letter (Rom 1:11–12), he was certain that through his time in Rome God would "impart to you some spiritual gift to make you strong," and that he and the Romans would be "mutually encouraged by each other's faith."

He and his party arrived through the southern gates of Rome on the major thoroughfare, the Appian Way. Due to his excellent rapport with the centurion, he was considered an exemplary prisoner and allowed to live in a home by himself, with only a single guard, probably near both the prison house and the barracks of the famous Praetorian Guard, the elite guards of Rome. Still, he would have been bound by a light chain to this guard (v. 20) to ensure he didn't try to escape. This was also near that section of Rome where the Jewish people dwelt. It has been estimated that as many as fifty thousand Jews lived in Rome. All the costs—the large home,[1] food, and all other provisions—would be borne by Paul himself. He is being treated as an elite (partly due to his Roman citizenship), wealthy prisoner.

ENCOUNTER WITH JEWISH LEADERS (28:16–22)

In his own rented place of residence, Paul is allowed to entertain visitors and twice has a contingent of Jews in for discussion of his

---

1. While Paul had likely stayed in an apartment in Caesarea, this would almost certainly have needed to be a large home, because it had to have space for large numbers of visitors, as in verse 23. Some think it was a room in a tenement building because of the cost, but he would not have been able to entertain the number of visitors he had in a small tenement apartment.

legal situation and a presentation of the gospel (vv. 17–22, 23–28). In the two years he would be on trial, there would certainly have been many such occasions, as can be seen by perusing the Prison Letters (Colossians, Philemon, Ephesians, Philippians) for details regarding Paul's imprisonment. This first encounter takes place only three days after he arrives. He is anxious to ascertain where he stands with the "local Jewish leaders," the heads of the synagogues in Rome. He wants them to know he is not guilty of the charges made against him. The understood subject of the passive-voice verb "was arrested" is the Jewish people of Jerusalem, who seized him and "handed [him] over to the Romans." However, he had "done nothing against our people or against the customs of our ancestors." He is hoping they won't stand up against him in the Roman courts like the Jerusalem Jews did in Caesarea.

Verse 17 probably serves as a legal introduction to Paul in Rome, explaining the charges that will be leveled against him by his Jewish opponents from Jerusalem. At every stage, with the tribune, with Felix, and with Festus and Agrippa, Paul has been judged "not guilty" of all charges. The only thing he is guilty of is inciting the Jewish leaders against himself, echoing what Jesus also went through. Their hatred of Paul constitutes rejection of Christ and of the gospel, so Christianity itself is on trial in Rome.

Notice how Paul calls them "my brothers," trying to get across that they are not enemies but members together of God's family, though estranged at the moment. He still thinks of himself as a Jewish Christian and of Christianity as "the Way" (see on 9:2), a messianic sect of Judaism. He is hoping that the Jews of Rome will take this perspective and refuse to join the Jerusalem leaders against Paul. Luke records that they apparently never turned against Paul, but at the same time most of them rejected the gospel. Thus as elsewhere Paul turned from them to reach out to the Gentiles, who were far more receptive to God's truths.

In the rest of his initial dialogue with the Jews of Rome (28:18–20), he stresses the contrast between Rome, who at all times found him innocent, and Jewish obduracy. The Roman authorities wanted to release him, finding no evidence of any crime committed. Here in verse 18 he is summarizing the findings of all three Roman officials—Claudius Lysias, Felix, and Festus—and the hearings and trials they represented in chapters 22, 23, 24, 25–26. Of course, the Gentiles too will later turn against Paul and the Christian movement, but at this early stage they are quite tolerant.

Paul wants them to know why he had appealed to the emperor in spite of the fact that Roman judges had found him innocent. The objections of the Jewish leaders were so severe that the Romans capitulated, and he had no choice except to make appeal (28:19). However, he wants these Jewish leaders to know that this appeal did not in any way constitute "any charge against my own people." He has not turned against his Jewish roots or rejected his Jewish background. He is telling them that in the trial here in Rome he does not plan to bring any countercharges against the Jewish people. Here he reveals something of his legal strategy. As he did in Caesarea, he will be stressing that these are religious rather than political problems and have no connection to Rome at all. Judaism will not be getting into trouble with Rome over this.

Still, there could be significant misunderstandings over this, so Paul wants to clear the air with the Jews of Rome at the outset. He is not here in Rome out of enmity for Judaism. In reality he is here and bound by a chain to a Roman guard "because of the hope of Israel" (28:20). These prominent Jews could clearly see the chain and the member of the Praetorian Guard standing there, so this was a poignant point. In the Sanhedrin trial this was expressed as "the hope of the resurrection of the dead" (23:6). Clearly the "hope of Israel" is Jesus the Messiah and the new salvation he is offering God's people the Jews, namely, the eternal life made available in him. He is on trial not just for his Christian beliefs but for his love for his fellow countrymen as he seeks to introduce them to the resurrection "hope" that can be realized only in Jesus.

The response of these synagogue heads (28:21–22) is quite surprising and seems impossible. They have neither received any letters nor heard any negative reports about Paul, even from Jewish merchants and others who have come from Jerusalem to Rome. With all the hostility experienced in Caesarea and the concerted efforts to see Paul executed, how could nothing untoward have reached Rome? All they had heard were rumors "against this sect" coming to them from "people everywhere."

The shocking thing about this is that it is now eleven years since Claudius had to expel Jews and Jewish Christians from Rome (AD 49) because of the riots erupting among the Jews against the Christians. However, there are a couple explanations that make sense. The absence of letters could simply be due to the fact that Paul was sent fairly directly from Caesarea, and the news from the Sanhedrin had not arrived yet. The time lost due to the shipwreck would have been lost anyway, for they would have had to winter in Crete. There was no way for letters or word to have arrived in Rome sooner. Moreover, the Jewish leaders could have decided not to pursue the case further, for anti-Jewish sentiment in Rome had been high ever since the incident with Claudius in AD 49. There was no way they could appeal to Rome without repercussions. The Jerusalem Jewish leaders likely just hoped (and expected) that the Jews of Rome would echo their animosity toward the followers of the Way.

While they had heard nothing negative about Paul, they had heard a great deal against this "sect" (hairesis, see 5:17; 15:5; 24:5, 14; 26:5). In every part of the Roman world, Jews have opposed and reacted with hostility toward everything Christian. So the "people everywhere" is not an exaggeration. These leaders now have an opportunity to hear from one of the primary leaders, and so they look forward to hearing "what your views are." They have heard a lot secondhand and thirdhand, and now they have a chance for firsthand knowledge.

FURTHER ENCOUNTER WITH MANY JEWS (28:23–28)

On the basis of their expressed interest in further interaction with him, Paul schedules a meeting where a large number of representatives can come for an interview with him. That day arrived, and he "witnessed to them from morning till evening." This was a truly God-sent opportunity, and Paul was not one to pass it up. The fact that "even larger numbers" were there may point to this being a Sabbath when they would not be working and would have a tradition of religious and Bible-centered dialogue.

Luke stresses two items in particular here in verse 23: the kingdom of God, and Jesus. The Jewish people had long expected God's special reign over this world to be finalized with the arrival of the Messiah (Isa 9:7; 24:23; Dan 2:44; Zech 14:9), and this age arrived with Jesus (Mark 1:15; Matt 3:2; 10:7). In Acts the kingdom was at the heart of messianic proclamation (1:3; 8:12; 14:22; 19:8), and Paul would be stressing how the concept of Jesus and the kingdom fulfilled Old Testament expectations. With "Jesus" he would have explained why the early church called itself "the Way," since Jesus fulfilled Isaiah 40:3, with his followers the voices in the wilderness proclaiming him the way to Yahweh and his salvation. With Jesus as suffering Messiah, his death on the cross as atoning sacrifice provided the way to salvation and eternal life.

The result of the intense evangelistic campaign of this sixteen-hour day of messianic proclamation closely resembled the missionary journeys—"Some were convinced by what he said, but others would not believe"—fulfilling Simeon's prophecy in Luke 2:34 that "this child is destined to cause the falling and rising of many in Israel." The people of God will be divide into believers and unbelievers.

This division of Israel is caused by disagreement (28:25) over Jesus, and it leads to the conclusion of the book of Acts as a whole. There is an absolute contrast between these Jews who find only division over Jesus, and the Jewish Christians who find complete togetherness or accord in Jesus (1:14; 2:46; 4:24; 5:12). Those who agree with Paul are converted and join believing Gentiles to form the new Israel, while those who disagree are rejected by God and cease to be his people. These former branches on God's olive tree have been broken off and replaced by Gentile "wild olive shoots" who have been grafted onto his tree to replace them (Rom 11:17-21).

It seems that the number of Jews who reject Jesus far outweighs those who become followers, for Paul sums it all up with what in a sense is the concluding major point of the book, called by Luke the "final statement" not just of this episode but of the Jewish mission as a whole, beginning with "the Holy Spirit spoke," which makes it not Paul's concluding thought but the Spirit's final message. The "ancestors" or "fathers" (*pateres*), the Jewish people of Isaiah's day, were harbingers of the Jews of Paul's day, who resemble them in every way. So what the Spirit spoke to them is now his message to these Jews. These earlier Jews rejected God and paid the consequences. The Jews of Paul's time have turned against Jesus and likewise will pay for their folly.

The citation of 28:26-27 is taken from Isaiah 6:9-10, the commission of Isaiah to his prophetic calling. Paul clearly sees himself in Isaiah. Like the eighth-century-BC prophet, Paul was proclaiming repentance to a people who were obdurate in their response and refused to get right with God. Isaiah was commanded to preach a message that would not be heeded, as Paul is also doing. There are three parts to the message:

1. God's former people will continue to both hear and see God's call to repent, but they will never understand it (v. 26), and their hardness of heart renders them incapable of proper response. In other words, they are physically able to receive God's truths but spiritually closed to them.
2. The reason for their closed minds (v. 27a) is that their "heart has become calloused" or "dull" (*epachynthē*), literally, "fat" or "obtuse," so weighed down with the things of this world that it cannot respond to the gospel. So even though they hear God speaking and see what he is doing in their lives,

they have closed their ears and shut their eyes so that they cannot perceive the true meaning of the divine message.

3. The result (v. 27b) is that God has rejected them. This has been played out often, as Paul has shaken the dust off his feet and turned to the Gentiles (13:46-47; 18:6-7; 19:9). The message is this: when people refuse to listen, God sends a hardening process that anchors them in their sins. Human rejection of God produces God's rejection of them (see the use of Isa 29:10 in Rom 11:8). The guilt falls on those who have hardened their hearts. There is a twofold purpose here—expansion to the Gentiles is paralleled by the rejection of the Jews. The effect of both Isaiah's and Paul's ministries is to make the deaf more deaf and the blind more blind. The Jews in Rome are following a national pattern of sin established in Isaiah's day (though those people were following a pattern established in the wilderness wandering). Guilt for hardened hearts is a national disgrace.

The Isaiah quotation explains why the reality of verse 28 has once more taken place—God's salvation has left the Jews and turned to the Gentiles. God's former people have ears to hear but can't hear, while the Gentiles "will listen" and respond. Messianic salvation is for those who will hear and respond with repentance and belief. This does not mean that the Jews will never again be offered salvation. God's offer of salvation "first to the Jew, then to the Gentile" in Romans 1:16 still continues, but the Gentiles are now the focus of the universal mission and will join believing Israel in the new and true Israel of the messianic community (Rom 11:17-21).

PAUL'S MINISTRY OVER THE NEXT TWO YEARS (28:30-31)

Luke summarizes two years of ministry in a couple sentences.[2]

---

2. A few manuscripts (Byzantine readings) include verse 29, "After he said this, the Jews left, arguing vigorously among themselves," but it is missing in major manuscripts like 𝔓74 ℵ A B E Ψ and is unlikely to have been included by Luke.

Paul's mission continues unabated except for one trivial complication—he is chained to a guard, and his large, rented home is his prison. So instead of going to the people, they have to come to him. We have no direct evidence that Paul was released at the end of the two years. Some have thought he was executed, but the Prison and Pastoral Letters have him released, saying that problems in the province of Asia with false teachers led him to send Timothy (Phil 2:19–24) and then to come himself after he was released (Phil 2:25–26).

It is also possible that his case was dismissed because the Jewish officials never came from Jerusalem with charges against him. There was a later rule that a case would be dismissed if the accuser failed to come within eighteen months, but we don't know whether this rule existed in the first century. Still, this is indeed possible, especially after two years. However, an actual trial before Nero was possible, and the emperor was not interested in wasting time on a case that had so little evidence against a Roman citizen and dismissed it (in AD 62). We will never know. I think the latter is a little more likely.

The added comment that Paul "welcomed all who came to see him" hints that Paul had a lot of company during this time, probably from both Jewish and Christian visitors. The Prison Letters would support a Paul who stayed in touch with the churches he had founded and regularly saw people like Philemon (see the letter) come to him and assistants like Tychicus and Onesimus (Col 4:7, 9) whom he would send to the churches from Rome fairly often. Paul was not locked up in a dark cell far from the light of day like he would be in his second imprisonment (2 Tim 1:15–17; 4:16).

Luke closes his account by showing that Paul preached the same gospel in Rome that characterized his ministry everywhere he went in his ministry for Christ: he "proclaimed the kingdom of God and taught about the Lord Jesus Christ," which repeats what Luke already said in verse 23. There has never been a truer statement about Paul than to describe his preaching as "with all boldness" (see on 4:13, 29, 31). Few in history have exhibited a more fearless verve in proclaiming God's truths even if it should lead to their death. This could almost be the moral of the story of Acts as a whole.

The surprising thing here is that the Romans allowed him to minister "without hindrance." From the start (from Claudius Lysias in 23:29 to Festus in 25:25 to Festus and Agrippa in 26:31-32) they realized he was innocent of all charges and was no danger to Rome, so they gave him free rein until they could decide his case. Of course, this does not mean total freedom, for there is no evidence he was able to leave his rented house and roam freely to speak in synagogues. He was probably connected by a chain at all times to the wrist of a guard. It means anyone could come to him who wished, and he could meet with them freely, but he could never go to them.

Luke wants us to know that nothing can stop the gospel from being proclaimed to fallen humanity, not all the power of Rome or the animosity of the Jewish people. The gospel of the kingdom of God and of Jesus goes forth with incredible power, even when Paul is undergoing a capital trial and when an entire nation is seeking his death. All the hindrances that Satan or a sin-drenched world can throw at the gospel can in no way deter it. In fact, this entire book makes absolutely clear that opposition and crisis serve to fill situations with energy and power, and God's word goes forth with even greater might and effectiveness as a result. The message of Acts 28 is that, if Paul could achieve all this while on trial for his life, how much more should we be doing for the glory of God and of Christ?

———

This final chapter forms a perfect conclusion, consummating the themes of the book. The first section (vv. 1-10) traces Paul's three months with the crew and passengers on Malta, showing him as a wonder-working prophet who survives an attack by a poisonous viper and then spends the winter healing and receiving honors from the people of the island. He will enter Rome almost as a conqueror, as he, not the captain or owner or centurion, appears to be the one truly in charge.

The trip to Rome was likely quite tiring but marvelously triumphant (vv. 11–15), and Paul is lauded the entire way and enters Rome almost as a conqueror, though we know in fact that he is "more than a conqueror" (Rom 8:37) and is the vanguard of an army that will be encased in the armor of God and conquer the Roman world for Christ. He is feted by Christians in Puteoli; and as he nears Rome he will be met and accompanied by two groups of Christians into Rome. There he will be treated as an elite prisoner and allowed to rent a large home and greet groups of visitors whenever he wishes. His "prison house" will become the headquarters of the Christian movement in Rome.

His first visitors are the heads of the synagogues in Rome (vv. 16–22), and they surprisingly are fairly open, wanting to hear Paul's views and judge for themselves. Paul assures them that he is in no way planning to turn against Judaism and accuse them of anything in his trial, and that encourages them. His strategy is to stress that all the issues are religious in nature and not antagonistic to Roman law, an approach that has been working in Caesarea. So these Jews are waiting to hear more from him and at this stage are not opposed to him.

The second meeting likely took place just a few days later (vv. 23–28) and involved a fairly large contingent who met with Paul literally from dawn to dusk, discussing what the Christian Way actually believed, especially regarding the coming of God's final kingdom with Jesus and who that Jesus actually was. The result was the same as before, a division of the people, with most of the Jews rejecting Paul's gospel but a significant minority becoming followers of the Way. However, the extreme animosity and virulent opposition did not seem to result.

Still, Paul concluded with a citation from Isaiah 6:9-10
(28:26-27), accusing them of continuing the rejection of God and
his truths from the days of Isaiah. They are reenacting the Jews
of Isaiah's time by closing their hearts and minds to God, with
the result that he has turned from them as well and found them
wanting. They have hardened their hearts, so he has sent a further hardening and turned to the Gentiles.

The final two years of Paul's time in Rome (vv. 30-31) show
him imprisoned and on trial for his life but with virtually the
same powerful evangelistic presence in Rome that he had in cities
when he was free. He is a man so filled with the Spirit that nothing can dampen his impact on an entire region, even Rome itself,
for Christ. No one has ever shown more strongly the difference the
Spirit makes in a person totally surrendered to him and empowered by him. Rome was changed forever during these two years
that introduced the gospel of Christ and the Holy Spirit into the
Roman world.

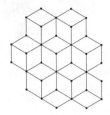

GLOSSARY

apocalyptic Refers to truths about God's plans for history that he has hidden in past generations but has revealed (the Greek *apokalypsis* means "unveiling") to his people. The name also describes a genre of ancient literature (including Revelation and parts of Daniel) that communicates these truths using vivid symbolism.

christological (adj.), Christology (n.) Refers to the New Testament's presentation of the person and work of Christ, especially his identity as Messiah.

diaspora (n.), diasporic (adj.) Refers to the (often Greek-speaking) communities of Jews living outside Israel. The term comes from the Greek word for "scattering."

eschatological (adj.), eschatology (n.) Refers to the last things or the end times. Within this broad category, biblical scholars and theologians have identified more specific concepts. For instance, "realized eschatology" emphasizes the present work of Christ in the world as he prepares for the end of history. In "inaugurated eschatology," the last days have already begun but have not yet been consummated at the return of Christ.

eschaton Greek for "end" or "last," referring to the return of Christ and the end of history.

Gnosticism Refers to special knowledge (Greek: *gnōsis*) as the basis of salvation. As a result of this heretical teaching, which developed in several forms in the early centuries AD, many gnostics held a negative view of the physical world.

Hellenist (n.), Hellenistic (adj.) Relates to the spread of Greek culture in the Mediterranean world after the conquests of Alexander the Great (356–323 BC). "Hellenist" can refer to people, both Jewish and Gentile, whose primary culture and language is Greek.

Mishnah An ancient Jewish source, compiled around AD 200, that contains the sayings of the rabbis. While it was not written down until later, it tells us about oral traditions that were in existence in Jesus' time.

parousia The event of Christ's second coming. The Greek word *parousia* means "arrival" or "presence."

Qumran A site near the northwest corner of the Dead Sea where a collection of scrolls (called the Dead Sea Scrolls) was found beginning in the 1940s. The community that lived at this site and wrote these scrolls separated themselves from the rest of Jewish society. Many scholars believe they were a branch of the Essenes, one of the three major Jewish sects mentioned by Josephus (*Antiquities* 13.171–72). The Dead Sea Scrolls include manuscripts of Old Testament books as well as other writings that are not part of Scripture. They do not refer to Christianity, but do shed light on aspects of Judaism around the time of Jesus.

Septuagint An ancient Greek translation of the Old Testament that was used extensively in the early church.

Shekinah A word derived from the Hebrew *shakan* (to dwell), used to describe God's personal presence taking the form of a cloud, often in the context of the tabernacle or temple (e.g., Exod 40:38; Num 9:15; 1 Kgs 8:10–11).

typological (adj.), typology (n.) A literary device in which Old Testament persons or events are the types that correspond to and are fulfilled in New Testament realities (antitypes).

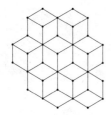

BIBLIOGRAPHY

Arnold, Clinton E. *Acts.* Zondervan Illustrated Bible Background Commentary. Grand Rapids: Zondervan, 2002.

Barrett, C. K. *A Critical and Exegetical Commentary on the Acts of the Apostles.* 2 vols. International Critical Commentary. London: T&T Clark, 2004.

Bock, Darrell L. *Acts.* Baker Exegetical Commentary on the New Testament. Grand Rapids: Baker Academic, 2007.

Bruce, F. F. *The Book of the Acts.* New International Commentary on the New Testament. Grand Rapids: Eerdmans, 1988.

Fernando, Ajith. *Acts.* NIV Application Commentary. Grand Rapids: Zondervan, 1998.

Fitzmyer, Joseph A. *The Acts of the Apostles.* Anchor Bible. New York: Doubleday, 1998.

Hughes, R. Kent. *Acts: The Church Afire.* Preaching the Word. Wheaton, IL: Crossway, 1996.

Johnson, Luke Timothy. *The Acts of the Apostles.* Sacra Pagina. Collegeville, MN: Liturgical Press, 1992.

Keener, Craig S. *Acts: An Exegetical Commentary.* 4 vols. Grand Rapids: Baker Academic, 2012–2015.

Krodel, Gerhard A. *Acts.* Augsburg Commentary. Minneapolis: Augsburg, 1986.

Larkin, William J. *Acts*. IVP New Testament Commentary. Downers
Grove, IL: InterVarsity Press, 1995.

Longenecker, Richard. "Acts." In *The Expositor's Bible Commentary*,
ed. Frank E. Gaebelein, 205–573. Grand Rapids: Zondervan,
1981.

Marshall, I. Howard. *Acts*. Tyndale New Testament Commentary.
Downers Grove, IL: InterVarsity Press, 1981.

Peterson, David. *The Acts of the Apostles*. Pillar New Testament
Commentary. Grand Rapids: Eerdmans, 2009.

Polhill, John B. *Acts*. New American Commentary. Nashville:
Broadman, 1992.

Schnabel, Eckhard. *Acts*. Zondervan Exegetical Commentary on
the New Testament. Grand Rapids: Zondervan, 2012.

Stott, John R. W. *The Message of Acts: The Spirit, the Church and
the World*. The Bible Speaks Today. Downers Grove, IL:
InterVarsity Press, 1994.

Witherington, Ben III. *The Acts of the Apostles: A Socio-Rhetorical
Commentary*. Grand Rapids: Eerdmans, 1998.

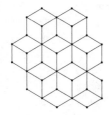

SUBJECT AND AUTHOR INDEX

Paul turning to, 328–29,
    479–80, 484
Paul's mission to, 180, 399,
    448–51, 456–57
as proselytes, 45
and revelation, 261, 267
and the temple, 387
geography
    and the mission, 187, 216–17
    of Pentecost, 44–45
Gerizim, vs. Sinai, 157
ghost, of Peter, 227–28
gift, of tongues, 43–44
glory
    of God, 147, 153, 225–26
    of Jesus, 27–28, 55, 175, 394–95,
        402, 447–50, 456
glossolalia. See tongues,
    speaking in
Gnosticism, and Simon Magus,
    164
goads, symbolism of, 448
God
    and the church, 116, 217–18, 255
    and Cornelius, 201
    as Creator, 319–22, 326
    and the Gentile mission,
        274, 277
    and hardships, 264–65
    and Herod Agrippa I, 230–32
    impartiality of, 202
    and Jesus, 50–52, 56, 73, 204–5
    as living, 261–62, 267
    and Moses, 139–42
    and Paul's trials, 441
    protection and care by, 371,
        449–51, 458, 464–71, 474
    and salvation, 113–14
    testing of, 275
god(s)
    foreign, 317, 322

Paul and Barnabas as,
    258–63, 474
Roman, 237, 332, 350–52,
    464–66, 474–75
unknown, 318–19, 326
God-fearer(s)
    Cornelius as, 194, 199–200
    Lydia as, 297
    in Pisidian Antioch, 241
    in Thessalonica, 310
    Titius Justus as, 329
godliness, of Peter and John, 71
golden calf, 141–42
gospel, the
    in Acts, 5–6, 16
    in Asia Minor, 350–51
    and the Gentiles, 274
    Paul's proclamation of,
        451–57, 475
    at Pentecost, 59
    preaching of, 249–50
    rejection of, 262
    and Simon Magus, 163
    wonder of, 45–46
governor
    Felix as, 413–16, 419–22, 428–29
    Publius as, 475
grace, of God, 96–97, 248–49
Graham, Billy, 427
Great Commission, 147–48, 170
    and the Gentile mission, 278
greed, of Ananias and Sapphira,
    98–99
Greek
    vs. Aramaic, 176
    Luke's use of, 3
    Paul as speaking, 391–92
Greeks, Gentiles as, 257
greeting(s)
    from the Jerusalem
        church, 285

faith in, 73, 206, 247–48, 342
family of, 30
as a foreign god, 317
and Gentiles, 92–94
as giving the Spirit, 55, 38–39
glory of, 27–28, 55, 175, 394–95, 402, 447–50, 456
and God, 50–52, 56, 73, 204–5
in Isaiah, 167–68, 171
and Jerusalem, 88–89
and John the Baptist, 243–44
as judge, 205–6, 210, 323
as King, 54–56
last days of, 20–28
as Lord, 50, 55–56, 203, 347, 395–96, 409–10, 448
miracles of, 50
and Moses, 76–78
name of, 58, 69, 73, 82–84, 87–89, 117, 345–47, 380
of Nazareth, 82–83, 219, 395
and Paul, 16, 175–77, 389, 409–10
and peace, 202–3
and Peter, 189, 192
in Peter's sermon, 50–57
power of, 72–73
as Prince, 113–14
revelation of, 176
and salvation, 28, 36, 84–85, 89, 113–14, 205–6, 210
and the Samaritans, 156–59
and the Sanhedrin, 80, 244
and Satan, 203
and the Spirit, 20, 203
and Stephen, 146–48
and teaching, 21–24, 238–39
and the temple, 127–28
See also Messiah; resurrection, of Jesus; Servant of Yahweh
Jew(s)
in Egypt, 135–36

in Ephesus, 335
and Felix, 428–29, 434
and Festus, 432–36, 455–57
and Gentiles, 219, 310–11, 383–86, 390
vs. Gentiles, 6, 15, 199–202, 209–15, 249–51, 472–73, 482–83
in Iconium, 256–57
and Jesus' death, 204, 244–45, 254
and Paul, 332–33, 343, 405
at Pentecost, 42
and Peter, 227
in Philippi, 296–97, 300
from Pisidian Antioch and Iconium, 263
and the prophets, 76–77
and revelation, 261, 267
in Rome, 478–84
vs. Samaritans, 156
from Thessalonica, 313
Jezebel (false teacher), 370
Joanna (Chuza's wife), 235
Joel, prophecy of, 47–50, 64–65
John (disciple)
and the Sanhedrin, 79–89
in Samaria, 160–61, 164–65, 171
in the temple, 68–69
John (Jonathan), 81
John Mark, 231–32, 239, 253, 290–91, 307
John the Baptist, 338–43, 356
and baptism, 57
and James (disciple), 224
and Jesus, 243–44
Joppa, Peter in, 188–90, 196–98
Joseph (patriarch), 133–35, 152
Joseph Barsabbas, 34, 282n4
Joseph of Arimathea, 115
Josephus, and Herod's death, 230
Joshua, 143, 330, 449

and the centurion, 426, 459-64,
464, 469-71, 476-78, 487
childhood of, 92-94, 443-44
and chronology, 183-86, 270,
289n1, 327-28, 331, 383
citizenship of, 300, 305-8, 354,
400-404, 411, 414-16, 426,
434, 458-49
commissioning of, 180, 234-36,
399, 448-51, 456-57
companions of, 176-77
conscience of, 405, 424
conspiracy against 183-84
conversion of, 172-83, 180-83,
394-98, 401-2, 447-50, 456
and the council letter, 282-87
and the crowds, 300
defense of, 391-405, 422-25,
429, 433-35, 442-52
and election, 396
and encouragement, 330-31,
409-10, 417, 465-67
farewell of, 373-75
fear of, 346-47
and Felix, 413-30, 433-38,
441, 479-80
and Festus, 429-57, 479-80, 486
freedom of, 305-6
and Gamaliel, 115, 174, 218, 393,
411, 443-44
and Gentiles, 180, 328-29,
399, 448-51, 456-57,
479-80, 484
as a god, 258-63, 474
and the gospel, 451-57, 475
greeting of, 477-78
healing by, 263-64, 267
and Hellenists, 185, 393
and Herod Agrippa II,
479-80, 486
honor of, 306, 476, 487
humility of, 364-65

innocence of, 367, 416, 426, 429,
435, 439, 450-52, 455-57,
479-80, 486
and James (Jesus' brother), 185,
191, 382-83
and the Jerusalem Council,
269-73, 276-79, 286
and Jesus, 16, 175-77,
389, 409-10
as a Jew, 405
and Jews, 332-33, 343
and John Mark, 231-32
and Justice (goddess), 474
and the law of Moses, 405-7,
414-15, 425, 433, 445-47
letters of, 349, 356, 360, 374,
479, 485
and Luke, 2-3, 380-81, 458-60
ministry of, 343-48
miracles of, 257-59, 267,
276-77, 344-45
and mission, 288-89
and money, 371-73, 428
name of, 175-76
nephew of, 411-12
and Nero, 433-35, 438-42,
455, 485
obedience of, 451, 457
opposition against, 252, 257-58,
330-31, 343, 352, 370-71
and the Passover, 361
and Pentecost, 361-62
persecution of, 252-55,
330-31, 389
as a persecutor, 150-51, 172-76,
179, 183-84, 190-91,
393-94, 399, 445-49, 456
and Peter, 185, 191, 201
as a Pharisee, 408-9,
443-45, 456
plots against, 258, 365, 374-75,
382, 410-17, 422, 432

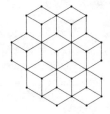

INDEX OF SCRIPTURE AND OTHER ANCIENT LITERATURE

Old Testament

New Testament

Greek Manuscripts of Acts